D1608155

METAPHOR, ALLEGORY, AND THE CLASSICAL TRADITION

Metaphor, Allegory, and the Classical Tradition

Ancient Thought and Modern Revisions

Edited by
G. R. BOYS-STONES

OXFORD
UNIVERSITY PRESS

Great Clarendon Street, Oxford OX2 6DP

Oxford University Press is a department of the University of Oxford.
It furthers the University's objective of excellence in research, scholarship,
and education by publishing worldwide in

Oxford New York

Auckland Bangkok Buenos Aires Cape Town Chennai
Dar es Salaam Delhi Hong Kong Istanbul Karachi Kolkata
Kuala Lumpur Madrid Melbourne Mexico City Mumbai Nairobi
São Paulo Shanghai Taipei Tokyo Toronto

Oxford is a registered trade mark of Oxford University Press
in the UK and in certain other countries

Published in the United States
by Oxford University Press Inc., New York

First published 2003

British Library Cataloguing in Publication Data
Data available

Library of Congress Cataloging in Publication Data
Data applied for

ISBN 0-19-924005-1

1 3 5 7 9 10 8 6 4 2

Typeset by Regent Typesetting, London
Printed in Great Britain
on acid-free paper by
T. J. International,
Padstow, Cornwall

PREFACE

In Hilary Term of 1997, baffled as I had become by ancient definitions of allegory in the course of my own research into the philosophical *use* of the term, I organized a seminar on metaphor and allegory at Corpus Christi College Oxford, under the aegis of the Centre for the Study of Greek and Roman Antiquity. The idea was that, since ancient rhetoricians defined allegory in terms of metaphor, the study of each might contribute to our understanding of the other. Joining me in the attempt were Paul Crowther, Andrew Laird, Christoph Leidl, Geoffrey Lloyd, Glenn Most, Donald Russell, Anne Sheppard, and Michael Silk. I would like to thank all of them for making a successful and enjoyable series in the first place; also Stephen Harrison, who was Director of the Centre when the seminar was held. That I was able to down pen and organize a seminar like this for the frivolous (and not entirely unusual) circumstance that I found something baffling, I owe to the British Academy and Corpus Christi College itself, for a Junior Research Fellowship each. The present volume is, of course, based on the seminar. It has been helped and hindered on its course in various ways: among our benefactors have been, from its earliest days, Hilary O'Shea, and the anonymous readers at Oxford University Press. During the latest stage of its production, it was materially benefited by Tony Woodman's advice and help. Most regrettable of the hindrances was the death of Don Fowler, who was part of the original proposal submitted to OUP in the Summer of 1997. We take this opportunity once again to regret his passing.

G.B.-S.

April 2002

CONTENTS

List of Contributors ix

Abbreviations x

1. Introduction — G. R. Boys-Stones 1
2. Metaphor, Simile, and Allegory as Ornaments of Style — Doreen Innes 7

Part I: Metaphor

3. The Harlot's Art: Metaphor and Literary Criticism — Christoph G. Leidl 31
4. Plato on Metaphors and Models — E. E. Pender 55
5. Literary Metaphor and Philosophical Insight: The Significance of Archilochus — Paul Crowther 83
6. The Problem of Metaphor: Chinese Reflections — G. E. R. Lloyd 101
7. Metaphor and Metonymy: Aristotle, Jakobson, Ricoeur, and Others — Michael Silk 115

Part II: Allegory

8. Figures of Allegory from Homer to Latin Epic — Andrew Laird 151
9. Allegory and Exegesis in the Derveni Papyrus: The Origin of Greek Scholarship — Dirk Obbink 177
10. The Stoics' Two Types of Allegory — G. R. Boys-Stones 189
11. The Rhetoric of the *Homeric Problems* — Donald Russell 217

12. Origen on Christ, Tropology, and Exegesis 235
MARK EDWARDS

Bibliography 257

Index of Passages Cited 279

General Index 299

LIST OF CONTRIBUTORS

G. R. Boys-Stones is Lecturer in Classics at the University of Durham.

Paul Crowther is Professor of Art and Philosophy at the International University of Bremen.

Mark Edwards is Lecturer in Patristics at the University of Oxford, and Tutor in Theology at Christ Church Oxford.

Doreen Innes is Emeritus Fellow of St Hilda's College Oxford.

Andrew Laird is Reader in Classics at the University of Warwick.

Christoph G. Leidl is Lecturer in Classics at the University of Heidelberg.

G. E. R. Lloyd is Emeritus Professor of Ancient Philosophy and Science at the University of Cambridge.

Dirk Obbink is Lecturer in Papyrology and Greek Literature at the University of Oxford, and Tutor in Greek and MacArthur Fellow of Christ Church Oxford.

E. E. Pender is Lecturer in Classics at the University of Leeds.

Donald Russell is Emeritus Professor of Classical Literature, and Emeritus Fellow of St John's College Oxford.

Michael Silk is Professor of Greek Language and Literature at King's College London.

ABBREVIATIONS

ANRW	H. Temporini and W. Haase (edd.), *Aufstieg und Niedergang der römischen Welt: Geschichte und Kultur Roms im Spiegel der neueren Forschung* (Berlin: de Gruyter, 1972–)
CEG	P. A. Hansen (ed.), *Carmina Epigraphica Graeca*, 2 vols. (Berlin/New York: de Gruyter, 1983–9)
CPF	*Corpus dei papiri filosofici greci e latini. Testi e lessico nei papiri di cultura greca e latina* (Florence: Olschki, 1989–)
CPG	C. Austin and R. Kassel (edd.), *Poetae Comici Graeci* (Berlin: de Gruyter, 1983–)
DK	H. Diels and W. Kranz, *Die Fragmente der Vorsokratiker*, 3 vols., 6th edn. (Dublin/Zurich: Weidmann, 1954)
FGrH	F. Jacoby, *Die Fragmente der griechischen Historiker*, 3 vols. (Berlin, Weidmann: 1926–30)
FHSG	W. W. Fortenbaugh, P. H. Huby, R. W. Sharples, and D. Gutas (edd.), *Theophrastus of Eresus. Sources for his Life, Writings, Thought and Influence*, 2 vols. (Leiden/New York/Cologne: Brill, 1993)
LSJ	*Greek–English Lexicon*, compiled by H. G. Liddell and R. Scott, revised by H. S. Jones, 9th edn. (Oxford: Oxford University Press, 1940)
OCD^{3}	S . Hornblower and A. Spawforth (edd.), *The Oxford Classical Dictionary*, 3rd edn. (Oxford: Oxford University Press, 1996)
SE, *M*	Sextus Empiricus, *Adversus mathematicos*
SVF	J. von Arnim (ed.), *Stoicorum Veterum Fragmenta*, 3 vols. (Stuttgart: Teubner, 1903–24); vol. iv (indexes) by M. Adler

1
Introduction
G. R. BOYS-STONES

> A *trope* is an expression transferred from its natural and principal signification to another, for the sake of embellishing speech (*ornandae orationis gratia*).
>
> (Quintilian 9.1.4)

> So let us begin from that trope which is the most common and much the most beautiful—I mean *transfer* (*tralatio*), which is called *metaphor* (*μεταφορά*) in Greek . . .
>
> (Quintilian 8.6.4)

In the last forty years, the 'classical' definition of metaphor inherited from the ancient rhetoricians has lost its canonical status. While argument still rages over the kind of model needed to replace it, there is now general agreement at least that an account of metaphor which makes it merely an ornament to language, verbal wrapping-paper brought in only after the serious business of meaning has taken place, simply does not hold up to the realities of metaphorical usage. Metaphor (or whatever should stand in its place) belongs, we now believe, at the heart of thinking about language use in all its aspects—not sidelined as a form of 'deviant' usage of primary interest only to students of literature.[1] But if the 'classical' account of metaphor as traditionally understood strikes us now as limited and implausible, it is worth considering whether this is because the

[1] See e.g. Steen (1994), 3–4 for a brief survey of landmarks in contemporary discussions of metaphor (and further references at Innes in this volume, n. 2). It is worth noting a tendency among those willing to engage with classical theory to skip the rhetoricians, who are the proximate source for the later Western tradition, in favour of Aristotle, the remoter source from whose works they in turn took their rise. Cf. e.g. Ricoeur (1996).

ancients' view was, as a matter of fact, limited; or whether it is more to do with the way in which their position was represented in the later tradition. It is certainly true that claims for the 'classical' account of metaphor, based as they are primarily on ancient rhetorical handbooks, are based, thereby, on a surprisingly limited range of texts: perhaps, then, this goes some way towards explaining the limitations of the theory reconstructed? If we look again at what the rhetoricians say, it quickly becomes clear that they did not have and did not claim to have a monopoly on theories of language use—indeed, they themselves encourage us to locate their contribution to the subject within a rather wider context of thought.[2] And one of their most significant pointers towards the possible existence of a rather fuller account of metaphor, an account which they adapted and restricted to their own particular interests, comes in the definition of allegory they offer: for allegory, they claim, is itself a form of metaphor.

When there have been more metaphors in a continuous stream, another kind of speech clearly arises: and the Greeks call this kind 'allegory' (ἀλληγορία). (Cicero, *Orator* 94)[3]

The word 'allegory' is not attested before the first century BC,[4] and it seems fair to assume that it was coined then by rhetoricians who wished to assimilate the concept into their growing taxonomies of language. The concept itself, however, does not

[2] In addition to the link between rhetorical and philosophical theory suggested in the definition of allegory that follows, one might point to cases where rhetoricians explicitly indicate the parameters which define the scope of their theoretical concerns. Consider for example Quintilian 8.6.1–3, where he says that he will 'omit all arguments [conducted among grammarians and philosophers] which are *irrelevant to the instruction of the orator*'. Cf. conversely 9.1.4, where Quintilian appends a grammarians' definition of a 'trope' which omits not only the reference to oratory present in his own, but also (significantly) the reference to *ornament*.

[3] Cf. also *De Oratore* 3.166; [Cicero], *Rhetoric to Herennius* 4.46; Quintilian 8.6.14.

[4] Cicero (*Orator* 94) and even Plutarch (*How to Listen to Poetry* 19 EF) are able to talk as if 'allegory' is a rather new-fangled word. One of our earliest attestations of the word is at Philodemus, *On Rhetoric* i. 164 Sudhaus—and it might not be coincidence that it comes in the work of a *philosopher* writing here about *rhetoric* (cf. also the Stoic Cornutus, who likewise uses the word only in a rhetorical context: see *Art of Rhetoric* 85, 17.13–16 Graeven with Hahn 1967: 29 and n. 31). See generally for an illuminating and comprehensive history of the term Whitman (1987), 263–8.

appear to have originated with the rhetoricians: arguably, it derived from the ancient practice of poets; certainly it referred to an exegetical principle which had been employed for centuries by philosophers who saw deeper meanings in texts which appeared to be 'saying something else'.[5] And if theoretical reflection on allegory began with the philosophers, it always remained, not exclusively, but characteristically a philosopher's tool.[6] If we are to understand ancient thinking about allegory, then, the obvious place to go is to philosophical texts. When we do this, however, we find that there is much more to be said about the subject than we might have been led to expect from the rhetoricians' account, which makes allegory an 'ornamental' trope just like metaphor, of which it is listed as a species.[7] For the philosophers might agree that allegory has an aesthetic appeal of its own; but they rarely argue that allegory is employed solely, or even mainly, for the sake of adornment. It was not for the sake of adornment that Orpheus wrote in allegory if one believes the writer of the Derveni papyrus; nor for the sake of adornment that Moses wrote the Torah as allegory according to Philo of Alexandria;[8] and the Platonist commentators on the ancient poets appear to have believed that allegory, far from adorning their meaning, was often the *only* means available for expressing what needed to be said.

A study of philosophical allegory, therefore, very quickly serves to put the rhetoricians in context, and to show us what we

[5] A Porphyrian scholion to Homer (8 fr. 2 DK) sees Theagnes of Rhegium (6th cent. BC) as the first practitioner of allegorical exegesis, but some scholars have traced the practice back even earlier: see Pépin (1958), 95–8, Détienne (1962), 65–7, and Lamberton (1986), 32 (Pythagoreans); Most (1993) (Homer himself). The terms which were employed (and later subsumed under the more general term 'allegory') include σύμβολον ('symbol', of an image within a text: e.g. *SVF* ii. 908, 909, 911) and ὑπόνοια (of the 'underlying intention' of a text: e.g. Plato, *Republic* 2, 378d; Xenophon, *Symposium* 3.6; cf. again Plutarch, *How to Listen* 19 EF).

[6] Indeed, the rhetoricians seem interested in allegory primarily to warn orators against its use: cf. Quintilian 8.6.14, and further, n. 9 below.

[7] 'Grandeur' is the ornamental contribution normally associated with allegory: see Hermogenes, *On Types* 246; Demetrius, *On Style* 99–102 (also 150–1 for piquancy).

[8] Often in Philo it is precisely violations of good rhetorical style which indicate the presence of allegory: e.g. *Who is the Heir?* 81; *On the Preliminary Studies* 73.

might have expected all along: that, when the rhetoricians talk of allegory (and *a fortiori* the same will be true of metaphor), they talk about it *only insofar as* it is of relevance to the needs of the orator—and only then within a certain view of the nature, not of language as such, but of oratory in particular. The gap between what the rhetoricians and the philosophers say about allegory is no ill reflection on the former: what it indicates rather is the rhetoricians' view that the orator's art is precisely a matter of being able to say the same thing in a variety of styles as appropriate, of being able to make it *attractive* to any given audience. But if the skill of the orator is to be able to adapt the appearance of his argument to the particular circumstances of its delivery without altering its substance, then, as far as oratory at least is concerned, it becomes quite reasonable to think of the tropes as the verbal cosmetics he needs. No one ever claimed that this is the *only* function that the 'tropes' perform in language; but by and large it was simply not thought to be the job of the orator, as it might be the job of the poet or philosopher, to be saying things that can only be expressed in allegorical or (more generally) in metaphorical terms.[9] If we read the rhetoricians without appreciating this vital limitation to the scope of their discussion, then it is no wonder if we come away with the idea that the classical theory of metaphor is inadequate to the realities of language use.

It is naive from the start to talk as if there was *a* 'classical theory of metaphor'; it is proportionally more misleading to suppose that the rhetorical texts of antiquity could on their own provide us with an account of that theory. If we are to understand anything of the breadth of ancient thought about metaphor, we need to contextualize our sources more carefully—and the bridge between rhetoric and philosophy furnished by the definition of allegory in terms of metaphor provides a particularly fruitful way of doing this. By considering philosophical

[9] Quintilian points to allegory as a limiting case in the effective rhetorical use of metaphor (8.6.14): when metaphor turns into allegory, he thinks, the orator has become too obscure, and obscurity is something the orator needs to avoid (cf. also Aristotle, *Poetics* 22, 1458^{a}25–6; Demetrius, *On Style* 102; Cicero, *Orator* 30; ps.-Longinus, *On the Sublime* 32.7). The orator, that is, in particular: he does not apply the same stricture to poets and philosophers (see Quintilian 8.6.52; cf. Philodemus, *On Poems* 5, col. 28.18–32; also for the general point Cicero, *Orator* 30: Cicero praises obscurity in Thucydides where he condemns it in oratory).

approaches to allegory next to rhetorical discussions of metaphor, and by placing studies of classical theory alongside analyses of literary practice that draw on the terms of contemporary theory, the chapters that follow aim to contribute to a fairer picture of classical approaches to language. Such a picture is not destined to reverse the 'turn' in contemporary thought about metaphor; but by challenging the rather narrow interpretation of ancient theory against which it turned, it might at least allow a more positive dialogue between modern theory and its historical roots.

2

Metaphor, Simile, and Allegory as Ornaments of Style

DOREEN INNES

The two notions basic to the classical theory of metaphor are similarity and substitution.[1] The word μεταφορά, found first in this meaning in Aristotle and his contemporaries, is itself a metaphor: it means 'carrying across' or transference (cf. Latin *transferre*, *translatio*), and vocabulary of movement, change/exchange, and place/domain is frequent, reflecting the basic idea that a term is transferred from its original context to another. It is, in Aristotle's words, 'the introduction of an alien term' (ὀνόματος ἀλλοτρίου ἐπιφορά: *Poetics* 1457^{b}7), and it is a successful metaphor if in its new place it seems to belong: 'you would say it had not invaded into an alien place but had migrated into its own' (Cicero, *Brutus* 274: 'non irruisse in alienum locum sed migrasse in suum').

Such vocabulary at least in part reflects the fundamental distinction which almost all ancient critics drew between content and style: style is something external to the thought, an ornamentation (Latin *ornatus*, cf. Greek κόσμος), in the same way as dress adorns the body, a common comparison, as in Cicero, *Brutus* 262, where Caesar's writings are stripped of all ornamental clothing of style, *tamquam veste detracta*. It is true that

[1] Principal texts: Aristotle, *Rhetoric* 3.2, 4 and 10–11; *Poetics* 1457^{b}6 ff.; Theophrastus F689–90 FHSG; *Papyrus Hamburg* 128; Demetrius 78–90, 99–102; Philodemus, *Rhetoric* i. 164–81 Sudhaus; *Rhetoric to Herennius* 4.45–6 and 59–61; Cicero, *De Oratore* 3.155–66, *Orator* 80–2, 92–4; Quintilian 8.3.72–81, 8.6.4–18 and 44–58; Longinus 31–2; ps.-Plutarch, *Life and Poetry of Homer* 2.19–20, 70 and 84–90; Trypho, *On Tropes* iii. 191–3 and 200–1 Spengel; Anon., *On Tropes* iii. 228–9 Spengel; Porphyry, *Homeric Questions* 6 and 17 Sodano. Cf. Lausberg (1998), §§ 552–64 (trope and metaphor), 843–7 (simile), and 895–901 (allegory).

more sensitive critics like Longinus and Horace saw content and style as a closely interlocking partnership, and that the Epicureans explore an organic approach to speech, but, in terms of extant classical theory, metaphor is a mode of expression. Its use does not change the essential meaning of a passage, but substitutes one term for another to set up a comparison of two things which are perceived as alike. This approach to metaphor is in contrast to more modern theory where language and thought are regarded as indissoluble, and the use of metaphor creates an interaction and change of significance in the terms used.[2]

Discussion of simile and allegory is similarly influenced by the style/content dichotomy. Comparison appears under two heads, as a type of proof under content (Lausberg 1998: §§ 422–5), and as the simile, a feature of style always closely linked with metaphor. Thus Aristotle has separate discussions of comparison as proof, παραβολή, and simile, εἰκών (*Rhetoric* 2.20 and 3.4), as does Quintilian (5.11.5): 'Comparison is also sometimes used for the ornamentation of speech (*et ad orationis ornatum*); but I will deal with that at the right time [i.e. 8.6.8]. For the moment I deal with those relevant to proof.' Broadly speaking, allegory can be similarly divided into an ornament of style, the continuous metaphor, and the more extended allegorical interpretations found in texts such as 'Heraclitus', *Homeric Problems*; Plutarch, *On How to Listen to Poetry*; ps.-Plutarch, *On the Life and Poetry of Homer*; or Porphyry, *Homer's Cave of the Nymphs*. This type of exegesis has a long history, but though there may be discussion of linguistic details, the aim is to discover and explain the hidden underlying thought—or ὑπόνοια, Plato's term, as in *Republic* 378d (see Lamberton and Keaney 1992; Buffière 1956; Gale 1994: 19 ff.; also Obbink and Russell in this volume).

Criticism of metaphor, simile, and allegory is also almost entirely concentrated on the single word and the single continuous piece of text. This means that much of the best criticism

[2] See esp. Black (1954); for an introductory survey of theories of metaphor, e.g. Hawkes (1972). On classical theory, Innes (1988), 314 ff.; Jürgensen (1968); McCall (1969); Schenkeveld (1964), 88 ff.; Barker (1999); Eggs (2001). On Aristotle, Kirby (1997); Laks (1994); Lloyd (1996*b*); Ricoeur (1996); Tamba-Mecz and Veyne (1979); with application to literary texts, Silk (1974); Asper (1997).

is strongly text-based, and there are some fine instances of practical criticism, such as some of the Homeric scholia on Homer's use of similes.[3] The scholia praise, for example, vivid visual impact and selection of detail (e.g. on *Iliad* 17.674–8, the sharp sight of the eagle is emphasized by the detail that it is flying high, yet sees a hare the colour of earth, small in size and crouched hidden under a bush).[4] They analyse the extent to which a simile fits its context, and approve sustained multi-correspondence similes (e.g. on *Iliad* 11.558–62, the slowly retreating stubborn Ajax, compared to a donkey which boys repeatedly beat with their sticks) and similes which are symbolic representations of inner psychological states (e.g. on *Iliad* 13.754, Hector like a snow-capped mountain, suggesting immovable steadfastness and a fearsome savagery remote from civilization). As part of a wider interest in foreshadowing (προαναφώνησις),[5] on occasion they note a detail in a simile which predicts later events of the narrative (e.g. on *Iliad* 16.752–3, the foreshadowing of Patroclus' death in the simile of the wounded lion 'whose own courage destroyed him'), and Porphyry (*Homeric Questions* 6 and 17 Sodano)[6] even recognizes transfer of vocabulary from simile into narrative and vice versa, in modern terminology interaction, transfusion, or trespass between vehicle and tenor or source domain and target domain. For example, in a simile comparing a wave to an army at *Iliad* 4.422–6, the wave 'crests' (κορύσσεται); and expansion by simile supports the bold metaphors at *Iliad* 4.273 ff., where a metaphorical 'cloud of infantry' in the narrative anticipates a storm-cloud simile, and *Odyssey* 20.13–15 where the metaphor of the heart 'growling' is followed by a simile of dogs growling.

There is also interest beyond the single isolated simile. The scholia note particularly the accumulation of two or more similes in close succession (e.g. on *Iliad* 15.624 ff., 'the passage is

[3] Examples mostly from Richardson (1980), 279–81. Add Schlunk (1974), 25–48, 78–9, 95 ff., and Lyne (1989), 63 ff. for influence on Virgil.

[4] For the vividness of similes cf. Quintilian 8.3.72–81 and Demetrius 209, where precision (ἀκρίβεια) and full accompanying detail are illustrated from 'the whole simile' of the man drawing off water in an irrigation channel (*Iliad* 21.257 ff.).

[5] Richardson (1980), 267 ff.; Duckworth (1933).

[6] Text and translation at Schlunk (1993), 18–21 and 86–9.

densely packed, *πεπύκνωται*, with similes to emphasize the subject'; or on *Iliad* 12.293, that after this first brief simile Homer elaborates on a second lion simile, at 299 ff.). Less often they note their distribution over an episode (e.g. on *Iliad* 16.298, that Homer refers to Zeus 'stirring up' a cloud, reserving the 'arrival' of a cloud for the simile at 364 where it suits the narrative of an attack causing headlong rout). A particularly sensitive detailed analysis elucidates *Iliad* 12.278–86, with comparison of an earlier snowstorm simile (12.156–8): the former depicts the onset of snow (to parallel the vigorous beginning of the fighting), while the second snowstorm (to fit the continuing battle) is said to be worked up more grandly, as Homer rivals himself: now the snowstorms are frequent, so they are set in winter; their impact is emphasized by the fact that Zeus himself wished to show his power; the lack of wind suits the steady downfall; and there is good ordering of details in the way the snow covers the high mountain-tops before it moves down to cover the plains below.

There are hints here of theory to match the more complex patterns of imagery and foreshadowing in authors such as Virgil, though the Homeric scholia are essentially concerned with the appropriateness of each simile to its specific context or character, the appropriateness, for example, of each snowstorm simile in its place. Suitability is the criterion in cross-references, as in the case of the repeated simile comparing Paris and Hector to a suddenly released prancing horse (*Iliad* 6.506–11 and 15.263–8): the second was particularly controversial (Aristarchus obelized), and the scholia record criticism that the details of the horse are more appropriate (*οἰκειότερον*) to the character and situation of Paris, together with a defence that the emphasis in the first is on Paris' exuberance, in the second on Hector's speed. On either view, what matters is the match of style and content. Yet despite their limitations and much that is jejune and mistaken, these scholia on poetic texts have deservedly excited modern interest, both for their insights and as representative of views which influenced poets such as Virgil. They suggest a level of sophistication absent from much of classical theory, which is mostly on prose, primarily oratory, and after Aristotle often consists of simple schoolroom systems of classifications. It is particularly unfortunate that we have only part of the discussion of metaphor and simile by the most sensitive critic of antiquity, Longinus (*On the Sublime* 31–2), all the more tantalizingly given his own complex patterns of imagery, and self-referential habit of illustrating points off his own practice.[7]

Classical theory is further restricted by the assumption that a term has a single primal meaning, so that all other uses are in some sense metaphorical. Aristotle draws no such lexical distinctions,[8] but most later critics develop a more precise terminology: κύριος refers to the primary, literal, or 'proper' meaning of a word. All other meanings are tropes, and metaphor is distinguished from catachresis (κατάχρησις/*abusio*, the use or literally the ill-use or improper use of a term), where there never was a 'proper' term, as in a standard Greek example, 'eye of the vine'. These may even be seen as the original form of metaphor: 'necessity generated metaphor, forced by lack and limitations, but later the pleasure and delight it gives widened its appeal' (Cicero, *De Oratore* 3.155). Related to the 'necessary' metaphor, sometimes rather confusedly, is 'dead' metaphor, an extension of a word's meaning which becomes part of customary speech. So, for example, Demetrius 86: 'Almost every expression in common use involves a metaphor but we do not notice because they are safe metaphors, such as "clear voice", "keen man", "rough character", "lengthy speaker", and all the other instances where the metaphor is applied so aptly that it seems the proper term.' All this reflects a natural wrestling with the fact that metaphor is part of ordinary speech (Aristotle, *Rhetoric* $1404^{b}34$–5: 'we all use them'; Cicero, *De Oratore* 3.155; Quintilian 8.6.5), and that extended meanings of a word are frequent and often part of normal usage. This is in modern terminology semantic stretch, an idea which Varro approaches when he speaks of the roots of a word extending beyond its boundaries like the roots of a tree into a neighbouring field (*Latin Language* 5.13). But he too retains the usual notion of metaphor moving to a different place, an image clearly brought out in Cicero's comment on an extended meaning of *fideliter*, faithfully (*Letters to Friends* 16.17.1): 'the word's proper home is in duty, but it has many

[7] Blume (1963); Innes (1994), 48–53, and (1995).

[8] Nor do *P.Hamburg* 128 (*c*.200 BC) and Demetrius (probably early 1st cent. BC or earlier), though the latter shows knowledge of ideas associated with catachresis and necessary or dead metaphors (Innes 1988: 314–15, 324–5).

migrations elsewhere' ('cui verbo domicilium est proprium in officio, migrationes in alienum multae').[9]

The necessary metaphor is an important source of technical vocabulary, including that of metaphor itself, as we have seen, and of literary criticism in general.[10] Aristotle had already recognized that metaphor might fill a lexical gap (*Poetics* 1457ᵇ25; *Rhetoric* 1405ᵃ36–7), and in his more scientific works he exploits metaphor to provide new technical terms (Lloyd 1996*b*). Among later writers, Philodemus explicitly associates technical vocabulary with metaphor (*Rhetoric* i. 175 Sudhaus: 'Every art is speechless, if deprived of metaphors'), and Cicero includes the use of metaphor (*aut ex aliis transferenda*) as well as new words to provide vocabulary for new concepts throughout the arts (*Academica* 1.25); he defends neologism but metaphor seems taken for granted, and in practice, like Lucretius (D. West 1969), he prefers to extend the use of existing words.

Classical theory, however, regards metaphor as primarily or exclusively a form of ornamentation, a poetic device, and it is significant that Aristotle refers us in the *Rhetoric* (1405ᵃ5–6) to his fuller account in the *Poetics*. In both texts metaphor is one in a list of types of word. For poetry he lists the normal word (*κύριον*), gloss, metaphor, epithets,[11] neologism, and various poetic forms where the word is lengthened, abbreviated, or changed in some way (*Poetics* 1457ᵇ1–3). For prose the list is shorter: ordinary words, metaphor, and the occasional use of glosses, compounds, and neologisms (*Rhetoric* 1404ᵇ27 ff.). There are similar, though not identical lists among his contemporaries: so *Rhetoric to Alexander* 23 ('there are three types of word, simple, compound, or metaphorical'), and especially Isocrates 9.9: 'decorative ornamentations (*κόσμοι*) are found not only in ordinary words (*τεταγμένα*) but also in those which are unusual (*ξένα*), new, and metaphorical'. For Aristotle, poetry can make use of all these types, but metaphor is especially suited to prose. For precise philosophical definition, 'all metaphorical expression is obscure' (*Topics* 139ᵇ34: *πᾶν γὰρ ἀσαφὲς τὸ κατὰ μεταφορὰν λεγόμενον*), and Plato's vocabulary for his theory of

[9] I return to this passage in n. 18.

[10] There is a useful range of examples in Assfahl (1932).

[11] For this unusual meaning of *κόσμος*, cf. *Rhetoric* 1408ᵃ14 and Schenkeveld (1993*b*).

Forms is condemned as poetic metaphor (*Metaphysics* 991ᵃ22 with Lloyd 1996*b*: 208–10), but unlike geometry (*Rhetoric* 1404ᵃ12), oratory does more than instruct. Since it aims to persuade and win over an audience, good prose style (ἀρετὴ λέξεως) will combine clarity from the use of ordinary words with some pleasing degree of ornamentation from the unusual (1404ᵇ6 ff.). Metaphor is especially recommended because it is in effect a mean between the ordinary and the over-exotic: it has clarity, charm, and the unusual (1405ᵃ8).

Later critics neglect this justification and are less interested in the clarity of metaphor (though note Demetrius 82, Quintilian 5.14.34–5). More influential (see further below) is Aristotle's recognition of metaphor's aesthetic appeal (1405ᵇ18–19), especially the vivid visual impact of analogical metaphors where there is personification (1411ᵇ24 ff.). This is because expressions which signify human activity (ἐνέργεια) are vivid, and Homer is particularly successful when he uses metaphor to animate the inanimate (1411ᵇ32: τὰ ἄψυχα ἔμψυχα ποιεῖν), for example: 'Again the pitiless boulder rolled down to the plain' and 'The spear rushed through his chest, quiveringly eager' (*Odyssey* 11.598 and *Iliad* 15.542). The inanimate is in movement and alive (1412ᵃ9: κινούμενα καὶ ζῶντα).

Metaphors must also be suitable (1405ᵃ10 ff., 1406ᵇ5 ff.), and not far-fetched (this produces a lack of clarity: 1406ᵇ8). Far-fetched metaphors are those which do not involve a shared *genus* or *species* (1405ᵃ35–6: ἐκ τῶν συγγενῶν καὶ τῶν ὁμοειδῶν), and good metaphors are based on transference between *species* and *genus* (*Poetics* 1457ᵇ7 ff.). These are (i) from *genus* to *species* (e.g. 'My ship is stationary', since being at anchor is a type of being stationary); (ii) from *species* to *genus* (e.g. use of a specific number, ten thousand, instead of countless); (iii) from *species* to *species* (e.g. drawing off life and cutting off water, since both are types of removing); and (iv) especially from *genus* to *genus*, the analogical metaphor (e.g. old age is the evening of life, since old age is to life what evening is to day). This last type dominates his examples and is particularly recommended and praised (*Rhetoric* 1405ᵃ11 ff., 1411ᵃ1 ff.).

Metaphor depends on an innate ability to see likenesses (*Poetics* 1459ᵃ7–8, cf. *Rhetoric* 1405ᵃ9–10). These are from what fits but it is not immediately obvious (1412ᵃ10–11), and as the audience recognizes the likeness, there is pleasure from learning, μάθησις (1410^{b}14). The audience perceives a likeness between *a* and *b* which stirs a sudden new understanding (or recognition) of a relationship between *species* and *genus*. This ability to draw likenesses is compared to the same ability in philosophy (1412^{a}11), and skill in metaphor thus necessitates an understanding of abstract relationships, a cognitive element. Though Aristotle does not explicitly say so, it can be compared to his wider concept of poetic *mimesis* in the *Poetics*:[12] to construct a good plot the poet must know abstract generalities (1451^{b}7: τὰ καθόλου), and in recognizing likenesses the audience enjoys the pleasure of learning something and using its powers of reasoning (1448^{b}15–16). There has been considerable modern interest in this cognitive aspect of Aristotle's theory.[13]

In later critics, metaphor loses the special cognitive status deriving from the understanding by writer and audience of *species/genus* resemblances. There is some sign of interest in the cognitive skills of the poet in Philodemus: 'It is necessary for a poet who has studied philosophy to have considered the nature and origins of figurative (τροπική) as well as philosophical language, or else he will choose and avoid metaphors at random' (*Rhetoric* i. 180 Sudhaus). We may also compare Cicero, who had promised a more philosophical approach in his *De Oratore* (*Letters to Friends* 1.9.23) and presents the classifications of metaphor as hackneyed and familiar (*De Oratore* 3.156). Cicero recognizes the special nature of metaphor as a mark of innate ability, *ingenii specimen*, able to extend the listener's thought in a different but purposeful direction (*De Oratore* 3.160: 'alio ducitur cogitatione neque tamen aberrat'). But Cicero does not link such insight to an understanding of *genus* and *species*. It is significant and more typical of later concerns that Quintilian, though strongly influenced by Cicero, neglects precisely these wider aspects.

Aristotle's account is both the earliest and the most stimulating, and though his influence is strong, what later critics

[12] The two do not of course necessarily coincide in the same author: Empedocles fails to qualify as poet because he lacks mimetic form (*Poetics* 1447^{b}18), though he is skilled in metaphor (μεταφορικός) and the other poetic accomplishments of style (fr.70 Rose).

[13] See Ricoeur (1996); also Kirby (1997), and Laks (1994).

select, expand, and modify from Aristotle are points restricted to style. Metaphor dwindles to become one in a list of ornaments or tropes, though as such it is particularly important (e.g. Quintilian 8.6.4: 'Let us begin with the one which is the most frequent and also by far the most splendid'). But theoretical insights are rare, and most of the later texts seem obsessed with lists and classifications which map out the relation between the term transferred and the 'proper' term. Thus, if *a* replaces *b*, can *b* similarly replace *a*? was there ever a *b*? are there specific types of *a* and *b*? on what criteria and for what purposes should *a* replace *b*?

We sometimes find the full Aristotelian scheme of *genus*/*species* (e.g. Philodemus, *Rhetoric* i. 171 Sudhaus), but metaphor is often narrowed to Aristotle's fourth type, the analogical metaphor (e.g. ps.-Plutarch, *Life and Poetry of Homer* 2.19: 'according to the analogical likeness which links both terms', *κατὰ τὴν ἀμφοῖν ἀνάλογον ὁμοιότητα*).[14] The same is true of Demetrius, who seems particularly influenced by the Peripatetics:[15] 'Metaphors should not be far-fetched but from the same area and based on a true likeness, for example general, pilot, and charioteer share the resemblance that they are all leaders. So a safe expression will be a general as "pilot of the city" and conversely a pilot as "charioteer of the ship".'[16] He then corrects Aristotle's advice

[14] Aristotle includes under metaphor what the later theory of tropes isolates as catachresis (discussed above), metonymy, metalepsis, and synecdoche (Lausberg 1998: §§ 565–77; see also Silk in this volume: Ch. 7), simile, enigma, and proverb (see below), and hyperbole (1413^b21 ff.). Already in *P.Hamburg* 128, metaphor is distinguished from *metousia*, a rare term used there to cover metaphors from *species* to *genus* and vice versa (= Theophrastus Appendix 9 at 612–7 FHSG; against authorship by Theophrastus, see Schenkeveld 1993*a*).

[15] For example in 85, where he is the only later critic to mention Aristotle's subdivision of the analogical metaphor, the use of a negative epithet invoking a metaphor, e.g. a bow described as 'the lyre with tuneless strings' (*Rhetoric* 1413^a1), or a shield as 'the wineless cup' (*Poetics* 1457^b31 ff.). He adds that the epithet makes the metaphor safer (presumably by drawing attention to the fact that it is a metaphor).

[16] *On Style* 78. For the manuscript reading 'leader of the ship', I accept Finckh's conjecture, 'charioteer of the ship'. This gives reciprocity and is a traditional example (= [Homer] fr. 20 Davies): see ps.-Plutarch, *Life and Poetry of Homer* 2.20 and Anon., *On Tropes* iii. 228 Spengel; also the Latin equivalent *auriga carinae* in Charisius, i. 272 Keil.

(*Rhetoric* 1407^{a}14 ff.) that analogical metaphors should be reciprocal. This, he says, fits the examples so far but is not always the case: 'Homer can call the lower slope of Mount Ida its foot but not a man's foot his lower slope' (Demetrius 79).

More popular is another fourfold classification. It was already known to Philodemus (*Rhetoric* i. 171 Sudhaus; cf. e.g. ps.-Plutarch, *Life and Poetry of Homer* 2.20), and it defines relationships according to the animate and inanimate, *ἔμψυχα/ἄψυχα*. Thus animate may be compared to animate, inanimate to inanimate, inanimate to animate, and animate to inanimate (personification). Further subdivisions are known (e.g. Quintilian, who dismisses all of this as lessons for schoolboys: 8.6.13; cf. Cicero, *De Oratore* 3.156). The classification expands upon Aristotle, who knows only the fourth type, personification. This remains the most important: it is the only type mentioned by Demetrius, who says Aristotle termed it the best kind of metaphor (81), a natural deduction from its possession of the two prized qualities of analogy and personification (Schenkeveld 1964: 90). For Quintilian, personification is bold and risky, but produces a marvellous sublimity (8.6.11: *mira sublimitas*). Longinus presumably discussed personification in the lacuna at 31.1 or 37.1, but we may note his approval of the personification of nature rather than man-made buildings at 15.6, where he contrasts Aeschylus' excessive boldness ('The palace is in ecstasy, the roof is in bacchant madness': fr. 58 Radt) with Euripides' milder version: 'The whole mountain shared their bacchant madness' (*Bacchae* 726).

Metaphor is used because it is in some way 'more effective than the term it ejected' (Quintilian 8.6.18: 'plus valere eo quod expellit'), and this effectiveness is variously subdivided. For Demetrius, metaphor gives grandeur, forcefulness, and charm, but is unsuitable for a plain style (78, 142, 190, 272); for Cicero it gives vividness, emphasis, or brevity, it provides euphemisms, and it can magnify or denigrate (*De Oratore* 3.155–64); and in the very similar list in *Rhetoric to Herennius* 4.45 it gives vividness, brevity, euphemism, magnifying or denigrating, and ornamentation. Details vary in different lists, but vividness, emphasis, and ornamentation are particularly prominent.

There is considerable attention to what is appropriate, with various restrictions on the use of metaphor. Metaphor should not be obscene or too low,[17] too frequent, or too far-fetched. For Theophrastus, metaphor should be apologetic, αἰσχυνομένην,[18] 'making its entry just as if into someone else's house'. This is itself an apologetic metaphor. Compare Longinus, who cites Aristotle and Theophrastus for the clearly related advice to soften bold metaphors by modifiers such as 'just as if' (32.3 = F690 FHSG), and Demetrius, who advises the conversion of bold metaphors into similes by adding 'just as if' (80). Boldness in imagery is thus risky.

Metaphors should not be packed too closely together (μὴ πυκνοῖς: Demetrius 78), and too many produce obscurity and tediousness (Quintilian 8.6.1). But Longinus scorns Caecilius' restriction to two or three metaphors in succession (32.1–2): Demosthenes' own strength of emotion justifies the torrent of metaphors in his fierce attack on traitors (*On the Crown* 296). But he condemns mixed metaphors: compare Quintilian 8.6.50: 'Most especially make sure that you continue with the same type of image; many start with a storm and end with fire or collapsing ruin, which is a most hideous mixture.' Longinus similarly criticizes Aeschylus' use of imagery which is not worked through properly and seems woolly and tangled (15.5), and attacks (3.1) the inappropriate and confused imagery used to describe the wind Boreas (probably by Aeschylus, fr. 281 Radt): 'The images make for confusion rather than forcefulness.' Boreas is presented as vomiting to heaven and as a flute-player, both inappropriately undignified; and, in a further confusing medley of images, as producing the glowing fire of a furnace, an octopus' tentacle, and a torrent of flame, which reduces the roof to cinders. What is admired is a consistent, single, sustained image, like the beginning of Pindar, *Isthmian* 6, where the scholia praise the way the image of his song as a libation from a mixing-bowl is preserved

[17] e.g. Cicero, *De Oratore* 3.165. But Longinus approves the impact of vivid colloquial metaphor, such as the mad king Cleomenes killing himself by slicing his skin to shreds and 'chopping himself into mince' (31.2, quoting Herodotus 6.75).

[18] F689A FHSG = Philodemus, *Rhetoric* i. 173 Sudhaus. The new reading αἰσχυνομένην has given us the Greek behind Cicero's *pudens* (*De Oratore* 3.165) and *verecunda* (*To Friends* 16.17.1 = F689B FHSG). The rest of my translation assumes as text τὴν εἰς ἀλλοτρίαν ὥσπερ οἰκίαν εἰσίουσαν. This is less certain, but the image of the house (οἰκίαν) seems confirmed by Cicero's use of *domicilium* in the second passage (quoted above, pp. 11–12).

throughout (διόλου). We may compare the parallel praise of vividly detailed similes illustrated earlier from the Homeric scholia (cf. n. 4 above).

Simile and allegory can be treated more briefly. Simile is distinguished from metaphor by its form. For Aristotle metaphor becomes simile if it is modified with some expression to mark likeness, such as the change of 'he was a lion in his attack' to 'he was like a lion in his attack' (*Rhetoric* 1406^{b}21–2), and good metaphors (the kind from analogy: 1412^{b}32 ff.) produce good similes. Similes are 'metaphors lacking the explanation provided by the simile' (1407^{a}13–14: μεταφοραὶ λόγου δεόμεναι); and this explanation is the added preliminary signal of comparison, πρόθεσις (1410^{b}18), the first part of some longer unit, a part which signals that something else will follow correspondingly before the unit is complete (cf. 1392^{a}3).[19] Similes are therefore longer because metaphors just identify *a* as *b* (1410^{b}18), and Aristotle draws no distinction between long and short similes. He probably recognized only the long Homeric type of simile. Simile is poetic and to be used rarely in prose (1406^{b}24–5), and the apparent short simile illustrated by his lion simile (1406^{b}21) is illusory: an inaccurate echo of various Homeric lion similes, it is intended to refer to a whole long simile (cf. Schenkeveld 1964: 99; McCall 1969: 37).

Simile as a type of metaphor fits Aristotle's perception of metaphor as his primary generic term (cf. n. 14 above), but in later critics metaphor is usually an abbreviated simile, as in Cicero, *De Oratore* 3.157 (text suspected) and Quintilian 8.6.8. Peripatetic influence (probably from Theophrastus)[20] can be detected when Demetrius agrees with Aristotle in defining simile as 'expanded metaphor', μεταφορὰ πλεονάζουσα (80), but Aristotle's notion of πρόθεσις is replaced by a blunt lexical point: simile is metaphor with the addition of a word like 'just as if', ὥσπερ (80, 89). Demetrius also distinguishes between the longer developed simile, παραβολή, which is poetic and to be used in prose only rarely and with great caution, and the short, virtually single-word simile, εἰκασία (89–90, 272–4). But the short simile

[19] See Tamba-Mecz and Veyne (1979) on the relationship between these two difficult terms.

[20] Note the context of adding apologetic phrases to make metaphors safer: see above on Theophrastus and the 'bashful' metaphor (n. 18).

attracted little interest: Quintilian appends a brief reference, linking it to ordinary speech (8.3.81), and is more concerned whether a simile has antapodosis or not, i.e. the patterning 'as *a* . . ., so *b* . . .', where the simile is explicitly resumed with correspondence of detail (8.3.77 ff.). We also find a third type, the personal likeness or *εἰκών*, when a person is the object of the comparison (e.g. ps.-Plutarch, *Life and Poetry of Homer* 2.84). This type is often used for mockery and is listed among the sources of wit and humour (*imago*: Cicero, *De Oratore* 2.265–6, Quintilian 6.3.57–9; *εἰκασία*: Demetrius 160, 172). Further subdivisions proliferate, but the typical simile is, as in Aristotle, the longer poetic type familiar from Homer.

Allegory is the term given to sustained metaphor, as in Cicero, *De Oratore* 3.166–7, and Quintilian 8.6.44. With an interest we have already seen in the case of similes, Quintilian distinguishes three types according to the extent to which the details of the image match what is being compared, whether all of them, a mix, or none (*tota*, *apertis permixta*, *sine translatione*). In prose the first is rare, the second normal. An example is Cicero, *Pro Milone* 5, where the allegory is broken by the reference to the public assemblies: 'I have myself always thought Milo had to meet all other storms and gales, at any rate those in the buffeting waves of public assemblies.' The ship of state is also the subject of his first example of allegory, Horace, *Odes* 1.14, chosen in conscious debt to the parallel use in Greek texts of Horace's model, Alcaeus Z2 Lobel–Page (Cocondrius, *On Tropes* iii. 234–5 Spengel, 'Heraclitus', *Homeric Problems* 5.3–9, where it is one of a series of allegories of the ship of state). Allegory has a hidden meaning and, in a particularly fine passage (100–1), Demetrius calls it a sort of veil or shroud (*συγκάλυμμα*); this is why, he says, 'The mysteries[21] are expressed in allegories, to inspire the terror and awe of darkness and night; in fact it is itself like darkness and night.' But allegory can, of course, like metaphor, be colloquial (Quintilian 8.6.51), and provide comic humour and invective, like the image of Athens as an old hag in her slippers gulping soup (Demetrius 286; cf. 151, 282–6; Cicero, *De Oratore* 2.261; Quintilian 6.3.69).

[21] Cf. Proclus (I owe this reference to Donald Russell): 'The parallel between understanding allegory and understanding mystery rites runs right through Proclus' theoretical justification of allegory' (Sheppard 1980: 146).

In keeping with its etymological meaning of 'other-speech' (cf. Cicero, *Orator* 94: *alia oratio*), allegory has various subtypes, such as the brief riddling story, a compressed comparison presented without explanation of its application. Quintilian 8.6.52 cites 'Dionysius in Corinth', a warning that tyrants may be forced into exile (it is an example which 'all the Greeks use', and it duly appears in e.g. Demetrius 102). There is influence from Aristotle in the inclusion of proverbs and the enigma or riddle (allegory taken to excess and made obscure: Quintilian 8.6.52). Though he does not know the term allegory,[22] proverb and enigma come under 'saying what is not said' (ἐκ τοῦ μὴ ὅ φησι λέγειν: *Rhetoric* 1412ᵃ22 ff.), and are linked to metaphor: proverbs are metaphor from species to species (1413ᵃ14–15), an excess of metaphor produces enigma (*Poetics* 1458ᵃ25), and successful enigma is a source of metaphor since 'metaphors pose riddles' (*Rhetoric* 1405ᵃ37 ff.).

I end with a riddle: the puzzling absence of metaphor in Horace. In two passages, *Epistles* 2.2.109–25 and *Ars Poetica* 46–72, Horace discusses style, yet in both he omits metaphor and simile. Even once can hardly be an accident since he is omitting what was normally the most important ornament of style. Twice must be deliberate, all the more so since the two passages are obviously complementary. Both give advice on neologism and archaism, but in *Epistles* 2.2 the emphasis is on archaism (111–18), with a brief mention of neologism (119), and conversely in the *Ars Poetica* the emphasis is on neologism (48 ff.), with a brief mention of archaism (70–2). One begins, the other ends with the metaphor of the 'laws' of poetry (*Epistles* 2.2.109 and *Ars Poetica* 72), both employ imagery of life and decay and the 'enriching' of the Latin language (*Epistles* 2.2.118 and 121, *Ars Poetica* 60 ff. and 57), and both refer to the Cethegi[23] of old (*Epistles* 2.2.117 and *Ars Poetica* 50). The crucial importance of *Epistles* 2.2.109 ff. is also clearly signalled: it holds central position in the middle of the whole poem, and is marked by a

[22] The word occurs first in Demetrius, Philodemus, and Cicero, and is almost certainly the Greek term behind *permutatio* in *Rhetoric to Herennius* 4.46. Enigma, proverb, and irony are standard subdivisions (e.g. Philodemus, *Rhetoric* i. 181 Sudhaus; Quintilian 8.6.44); irony qualifies because it is the expression of a meaning opposite to what is said.

[23] An echo of Ennius' praise of Cethegus' oratory (*Annals* 303–4); cf. Cicero, *Brutus* 57–60.

sudden shift of tone as Horace moves from ironically negative reasons against writing poetry to a positive and prescriptive delineation in serious style of the *legitimum poema*, poetry which observes the rules (109). Why then might Horace omit metaphor? Editors of Horace give little help, and Brink offers no explanation: metaphor is 'surprisingly' omitted, and Horace 'jettisons' metaphor.[24]

Horace evidently aims to surprise us. Misdirection and elusive trains of thought are after all characteristic of Horace. But elsewhere his surprises and apparent digressions or omissions serve to highlight key concerns (cf. Innes 1989). Horace will have positive reasons for selectivity: he will include neologism and archaism to fit what he wishes us to see as central issues, and he will omit metaphor[25] not because he thought it unimportant or made little use of it (see below) but because (i) it may obscure or conflict with more important points (the omission of an item which should be prominent will in itself throw emphasis on what is included) and/or (ii) it is covered in some other way or in some other place.[26]

One factor is that even in the *Ars Poetica* Horace is concerned to avoid the rigid structure of a textbook and prefers gliding transitions and an impression of the informality of conversation, *sermo*. Archaism, neologism, and metaphor are the three standard categories of ornamentation in vocabulary (e.g. Cicero, *De Oratore* 3.152: 'aut inusitatum aut novatum aut translatum'). If Horace had included metaphor he might have seemed to be following too closely the traditional headings of the textbook. Instead in both passages he reshapes the traditional categories of diction to create an analysis of style which by its selectivity will focus on key themes and have its own internal unity, *simplex et unum* (*Ars Poetica* 23).

[24] Commentary on *Ars Poetica* 46/45–72 at Brink (1971), 133; on *Epistles* 2.2.111–19 at Brink (1982), 332.

[25] In the case of the *Ars Poetica* it is in theory possible that he follows an omission in his source, Neoptolemus of Parium (so tentatively Asper 1997: 13 n. 15), but this is intrinsically unlikely. It would also fail to explain the parallel omission in *Epistles* 2.2, and why Horace would have chosen to accept such an idiosyncratic position.

[26] But though other omissions appear elsewhere in the *Ars Poetica* (note compounds at 97, and ornament, clarity, and ambiguity at 447–8), metaphor is nowhere treated (Brink 1963: 95).

Most obviously, he emphasizes originality by exploiting a contrast of the old and the new. Archaism revives the old, neologism invents the new. Within an analysis of vocabulary, archaism and neologism neatly serve also as symbols of old and new, tradition and originality, encapsulating in microcosm and thereby validating an issue of wider importance: change and growth in the development of Roman poetry. This is an important theme in Horace, especially dominant in *Epistles* 2.1, where he pleads the case for new modern Roman poetry (such as his own) against those content with the familiar favourites of older Roman poetry, and demands a Roman poetry which will be new, yet also draw on the traditions of classical Greece. Archaism and neologism provide dynamic and diachronic examples of change and renewal, signals which would be weakened by the inclusion of metaphor, a form of synchronic/horizontal change, the transference or substitution of term *a* for term *b*.

In the case of the *Ars Poetica* change, growth, and decay are also powerful unifying themes, seen for example in the Four Ages of Man (156 ff.), music (202 ff.), and, most relevantly, the selective treatment of metrical skill (251 ff.), where the iamb has a symbolic role similar to that of neologism and archaism. Horace selects one particular metre, the iambic trimeter, and gives rules governing the adoption of spondees. The choice fits the immediate context of drama but is framed to illustrate the development of Roman metre from the crude past of an Ennius to the refined skill of his own day. Metre thus illustrates the development of standards of excellence in technique, *ars*, and from metre Horace moves to approval of change and development more generally in Roman literary technique. It is striking that only here and on neologism does Horace in the *Ars Poetica* turn explicitly to Roman poets; it is no accident that both passages involve the importance of technique, *ars*, in the development of Roman poetry from old poets like Ennius to what Horace demands for himself.[27]

Horace's advice on style in *Ars Poetica* 46 ff. is marked by

[27] Note the insistent first persons in 55 (*ego cur* . . .: 'Am *I* . . .?', this immediately following a reference to Virgil and Varius; cf. *Epistles* 2.1.247), and in 265 (*idcircone vager scribamque licenter?* 'Am I for that reason to wander around and write without restraint?'). Selectivity in the *Ars Poetica* is shaped by Horace's own poetic practice, despite his ingenuous disclaimer at 306: *nil scribens ipse*.

originality from the beginning, with a new polemical direction to the traditional first heading of diction, the use of ordinary words, *propria*. What is needed is discriminating and careful placing of words (46: 'in verbis etiam tenuis cautusque serendis'): *tenuis* immediately sets the standards of Callimachean polish,[28] and that polish is linked to combinations of words, not single words. This focus on the ordering of words picks up the preceding section on the ordering of content (43–5: *ordo*), and its own word-order illustrates the immediately following advice (47–8) that shrewd combination, *callida iunctura*,[29] makes a familiar word new. Thus *notum* ('the familiar') becomes *novum* ('the new'), and Horace again illustrates his own advice with intricate interlacing of adjective and noun, so that *notum* and *novum* encircle the clause, and *novum* is in emphatic final position. *Novum* also neatly looks ahead to the following account of neologism (cf. 52: *nova fictaque nuper*, 'new and recently invented words'). These gliding transitions, however, also mask antithesis and polarity. Neologism and archaism offer a sharp contrast to the manipulation of familiar words: as overtly unusual and decorative, they are to be used only in need and rarely (48: *si forte necesse est*; 51: *pudenter*; 53: *parce*). Horace thus organizes his advice on style round a polar antithesis which emphasizes newness: (i) use mostly ordinary words, but do so with care (*tenuis cautusque*), but (ii) since poets are granted the power to dare anything at all (*Ars Poetica* 10: 'quidlibet audendi semper fuit aequa potestas', the traditional ποιητικὴ ἐξουσία, 'poetic licence'), use neologism and archaism, but do so rarely and (again) with care. Metaphor would spoil this patterning: it too may need care, but it is not rare, and though richly poetic, it is also, as we have seen, a familiar and regular feature of ordinary prose.

Metaphor may be implicitly included as a form of juxtaposition. After all, metaphor requires a context, as Quintilian notes with the same weaving image we have detected in Horace, 'translata probari nisi in contextu sermonis non possunt' (8.3.38: 'metaphor cannot be accepted without reference to the whole fabric of what is being said').[30] Brink (on *Ars Poetica* 47–8) notes

[28] e.g. Virgil, *Eclogue* 6.8 in echo of Callimachus, *Aitia* fr. 1.24 Pfeiffer.

[29] On *callida iunctura* as characteristic of Horace's style, see Nisbet (1999).

[30] Note also *P.Hamburg* 128: 'words in combination' (συνθέτων): see Schenkeveld (1993*a*) for attractive arguments to support the following definition: 'They

that semantic collocation may indeed include metaphor, 'but this is not to the fore'. He is right to the extent that *callida iunctura* is conspicuously instantiated not by metaphor but by the intricate word-order of *notum . . . novum*. But Horace also provides less obtrusive examples of metaphor: there is an apparently new meaning of the term *iunctura* (Oberhelman and Armstrong 1995: 252), with added personification from *callida*; and the phrase *in verbis . . . serendis* is an analogical metaphor, whether *serere* refers to 'joining' words or 'planting in place'. The former meaning seems unique but is surely correct (cf. 242: *series iuncturaque*),[31] and it then activates the latent weaving metaphor of *tenuis*, finely woven. New juxtapositions may thus evoke new imagery or revive dead or latent metaphors.

Horace accepts the standard view that a word has its own 'place' or 'home', an original meaning from which other uses are deviations or tropes. In *Epistles* 2.2.111–14, the discriminating poet will remove stale words from their place, *locus*, even if they move reluctantly and still lurk within the *penetralia Vestae* ('the shrine of Vesta'). This last phrase has puzzled commentators, but there is no need to attempt to explain the reference to Vesta by flight *to* her temple in an otherwise unattested claim of asylum. The words which are being moved from their *locus* (114) are words lingering in their *original* house or home.[32] They are *propria*, and that is why they are so unwilling to leave home. Their house or home, however, is a temple or the inmost shrine

call metaphor after the transfer of the same nouns and/or verbs, in a new combination, from one similar thing to another.' We may also wonder if there was influence from Philodemus in emphasizing the importance of ordering. Though this is not stated in what survives (see *Rhetoric* i. 164 and 170 ff. Sudhaus), it would seem logical that he linked metaphor with word-order as part of a wider theory that thought and style are indivisible and any new ordering will change the sense. On an atomist theory, single words are combinations of elements (the letters of the alphabet, cf. Lucretius, e.g. 2.1004 ff.) and, since in the case of metaphor the same elements of the alphabet appear in both the original and transferred context, it will be the new context, the new combination of words, which will provoke an interaction which may be labelled metaphorical. On Lucretius, Philodemus, and Horace see Armstrong (1995), and Oberhelman and Armstrong (1995).

[31] See Brink (1971) on *Ars Poetica* 46. Cf. also the compounds *conserere* and *inserere*.

[32] Note Cicero, *On the Nature of the Gods* 2.92 for *mota loco* of stars moved from their *original* position.

of the house (both are possible explanations of *penetralia*), and this temple or household shrine is suitably that of Vesta since she is the goddess of the hearth at the centre of a home. Words in the *penetralia Vestae* are words at home in a shrine, in other words they are venerable and old. In standard terminology they are both *prisca* and *propria* (cf. Cicero, *Orator* 80 for archaisms among *propria*). But some old words have become stale and obsolete, and are to be removed, losing their citizenship.[33] Other old words (115 ff.) have been long lost but may be unearthed to renewed life, an echo of Varro: 'Things which buried by age . . . I shall try to unearth' (*Latin Language* 6.2: 'quae obruta vetustate . . . eruere conabor'). Later in that same book Varro refers to a set day when Vesta's temple was swept clean of rubbish (*Latin Language* 6.32: 'ex aede Vestae stercus everritur'): Horace asks us to visualize a similar cleansing of rubbish, this time the rubbish of old words.

The use of imagery here is strikingly complex and multi-layered. It suggests the most attractive answer to Horace's neglect of imagery as a type of diction. Theory is replaced by practice.

There is conspicuous use of metaphor/allegory as Horace develops a sustained image of the poet as censor in *Epistles* 2.2.109 ff. In a series of vivid personifications, 'the poet will take the role of the upright censor with his tablets' (110)[34] and remove vocabulary which does not deserve its place; some words withdraw reluctantly and try to linger in Vesta's temple, others are brought to light, unearthed after long decay (110–18). With a change of semantic range, Horace then develops a cluster of images, and two similes enclose metaphors as the poet in full flow like a river enriches Latin (120–1), prunes back what is too lush, *luxuriantia*, and employs the care which encourages healthy growth, *sano cultu* (122–3),[35] and yet for all this careful effort he

[33] Note the similar combination of citizenship and hearth in Porphyry's interpretation of Homeric ἐφέστιος, 'at the hearth' (*Homeric Questions* 2 Sodano): πάντες πολῖται καὶ ἐφέστιον πῦρ ἔχοντες ('all *citizens* at the *hearth's* fire').

[34] See Brink's commentary for terms suggesting a continuation of the image (111, *splendoris*; 112, *honore*; 113, *movere loco*; 116, *in lucem*; 119, *asciscet*).

[35] Brink rightly extends the pruning image over the whole of 122–3. Such pruning is of central importance to Horace: note the similar extended image of a strict editor of a text in *Ars Poetica* 440 ff.: the critic will mark faults for deletion,

will seem like an untrained dancing satyr or Cyclops (124–5). Further careful patterning of imagery unites the whole passage within an antithesis of nature and (unobtrusive) skill: technical skill, *ars*, controls nature, just as human skill in the censor's law and the dancing Cyclops frames and encloses imagery from the world of nature.

The section on style in the *Ars Poetica* begins with less obtrusive use of metaphor, mostly the quickening of what had become dead metaphors in Greek technical vocabulary: so 46, the weaving of words; 49, *indiciis* in the new Latin sense of Greek signs or symbols (σημεῖα or σύμβολα); 53, *Graeco fonte*, the image of a stream supporting the 'influence' of Greece; and 59, newly minted coinages. The last is the most elaborate, and Horace seems to have completed his section on neologism and archaism. But he abruptly introduces a very striking example of a lengthy simile (60–9). He evokes one of Homer's most famous similes, on the generations of men rising and falling like leaves (*Iliad* 6.146–9), a simile much imitated but here rejuvenated by a new and original application to style, a proof that in imagery too the *notum* can become *novum*. The original context is further echoed by a further inset simile, that words grow like men, *iuvenum ritu* (62), and the image of the cycle of birth, growth, decay, and renewed life continues through a series of metaphors (or allegory). These then form part of a cluster of different but related images from the natural world, but the concluding image is, as in *Epistles* 2.2, one of *ars*, the controlling laws and rules of usage (72: 'arbitrium . . . et ius et norma loquendi'). It acts as a concluding symbol of Horace's own carefully controlled use of imagery.

Both passages thus embody the basic points of the classical theory of metaphor, illustrating metaphor and simile (short and long), analogical metaphor, 'catachresis' or dead metaphor, vivid personification of the inanimate as animate, continuous metaphor or allegory, and densely packed series of metaphor and simile. In both, imagery is used with sophisticated and complex artistry, and if in Horace the theory of metaphor is replaced by practice, it may be significant that theory is usually *reinforced* by practice, as we have seen in the exemplification of *callida*

and he will prune back over-ambitious ornamentation, *ambitiosa ornamenta* (447–8).

iunctura. This may suggest one last reason for the lack of explicit reference to metaphor: unless the papyri of Herculaneum give new evidence to the contrary, the theory of metaphor seems moribund, and Horace may omit reference to that theory as one which is both too stale and hackneyed for innovative poetic treatment, and which, as a poet himself, he knew to be inadequate in its focus on metaphor as the transference of a single word and its preoccupation with systems of classification. Linguistic theory, for example, may value the distinction between ornamental metaphor and 'catachresis', but for the poet this distinction is at best fluid: dead metaphor remains latent metaphor and may be revived. I suspect that Horace has chosen, like Homer, to omit what he thinks cannot be made to shine: 'quae desperat tractata nitescere posse' (*Ars Poetica* 149–50).

PART I
Metaphor

3

The Harlot's Art: Metaphor and Literary Criticism*

CHRISTOPH G. LEIDL

* *To Hans-Jürgen Horn sexaginta quinque annos nato*

How smart a lash that speech doth give my conscience.
The harlot's cheek, beautied with plast'ring art,
Is not more ugly to the thing that helps it
Than is my deed to my most painted word.[1]

This is most brave,
That I, the son of a dear father murder'd,
Prompted to my revenge by heaven and hell,
Must like a whore unpack my heart with words
And fall a-cursing like a very drab,
A scullion![2]

Although opponents, King Claudius and Hamlet share at least the same imagery for expressing their attitude to artfully embellished speech and attribute the same socially degraded

This article is part of a larger project, now almost completed, on metaphor in ancient literary criticism. In this form, theoretical issues will be given further discussion and other metaphorical fields investigated. Earlier versions were read as papers at a conference in Warsaw, at Durham, and in the seminar at Oxford. I should like to offer my thanks to all participants, especially Prof. D. A. Russell, for their suggestions, and to the editor for his perceptive reading of the draft and his helpful comments.

[1] King Claudius in Shakespeare, *Hamlet* III. 1.50–3.

[2] Hamlet at *Hamlet* II. 2.578–83; cf. also II. 2.208: 'how pregnant sometimes his replies are' (Polonius about Hamlet), and Polonius I. 3.126–31: 'In few, Ophelia, | Do not believe his vows; for they are brokers | Not of that dye which their investments show, | But mere implorators of unholy suits, | Breathing like sanctified and pious bawds [Theobald; printed texts: *bonds*] | The better to beguile.'

position to the art to which they nevertheless are forced to have recourse. The personification of rhetoric as a woman, and, in general, the category of 'male vs. female', has a long-standing tradition in rhetorical theory.[3] The ancient part of this tradition, together with the complex connotations attached to it, provides a good example for studying how metaphor functions in ancient literary criticism.

Metaphors are everywhere. They come naturally and no higher education is required to be able to use them. In fact many people apply them without even noticing.[4] On the other hand, to use metaphors to some effect, to hit the right note, to impress the audience, is a matter of natural talent and cannot, at least not entirely, be acquired from another.[5] If, then, modern thinking tends to assign to metaphor (and its fellow master-tropes) the status of a (or rather the) principle of all language, or puts the explanation of creative, novel metaphor, the product of poetic imagination as opposed to mere everyday usage, into the centre of investigation, it can avail itself of Quintilian and Aristotle as authorities. Highly elaborate and generalized linguistic and philosophical theories as well as most intricate studies of poetical language can spring from this source.[6] In practice, however, two

[3] On 'male–female' in Renaissance rhetorical theory (esp. in 16th- and 17th-cent. French and Italian writers) and its relation to the Atticism–Asianism debate, cf. Kapp (1991). An English example is Smith (1657: 7 f.), who uses this category without the essentially negative evaluation to characterize the distinction between two types of rhetorical figures: 'Garnishing of the frame of speech in a sentence, called Figura Sententie, is a figure, which for the forcible moving of affections, doth after a sort beautifie the sense and very meaning of a sentence: because it carries with it a certain manly majesty, which far surpasses the soft delicacy of the former Figures [i.e. Figurae dictionis], they being as it were effeminate and musical, these virile and majestical.'

[4] Quintilian 8.6.4: 'quae (scil. translatio) quidem cum ita est ab ipsa nobis concessa natura, ut indocti quoque ac non sentientes ea frequenter utantur, tum ita iucunda atque nitida, ut in oratione quamlibet clara proprio tamen lumine eluceat.'

[5] Aristotle, *Poetics* 22, 1459[a]5 ff. (*εὐφυΐας τε σημεῖόν ἐστιν*). But cf. *Rhetoric* 3. 10, 1410[b]7 ff. on *ἀστεῖα* and *εὐδοκιμοῦντα* (urbanities and well-liked expressions, among which metaphor is prominent): *ποιεῖν . . . ἐστὶν τοῦ εὐφυοῦς ἢ τοῦ γεγυμνασμένου, δεῖξαι δὲ τῆς μεθόδου ταύτης* ('it is possible to create them by natural talent or by practice, but to show what they are belongs to this study': translation from Kennedy 1991: 244).

[6] Good surveys of the current theoretical discussion are given by Haverkamp (1996); Eggs (2001). Cf. also the collection of articles in Ortony (1993*a*).

types of book or article are found to prevail: first, the detailed theoretical analysis, aimed at defining once and for all what metaphor is, and reaching very divergent and often incompatible results largely depending on whether the approach is based on analytical, structuralist, or hermeneutic traditions;[7] and, on the other hand, the collection and interpretation of individual passages from literature containing metaphors, with the subspecies of author-based studies (the metaphors in author *x*) or content-based studies (metaphor *x* in a selection of authors, a literary genre, a period of literary history).[8] But whereas the former all too often reach their aims with a minimum involvement with real metaphors (using either constructed examples or highly simplified ones or no examples at all), thus leaving to the reader the task of finding an application for the analytical tool provided in the theory, the latter frequently offer very useful catalogues mainly arranged according to the domain from which the metaphors were taken, but stop short of a detailed analysis of the material collected.[9]

A student starting his research in metaphor may be tempted to follow what in modern epistemological parlance is called a 'top-down' strategy: trying to establish a firm theoretical equipment for deciding what metaphors are, to what uses they may be put, and whether they can contribute to knowledge beyond the function of being an ornament of speech and so forth. Thus he will form strong opinions on many of these subjects. But these will not withstand for long the test to which they are subjected by the 'bottom-up' strategy—which is, plainly speaking, the reading of ancient texts. Many a well-designed terminological building soon begins to crumble under the assault of accumulated material. Without entering into a prolonged theoretical discussion,[10] I shall limit myself here to only two introductory remarks. After consulting a number of texts, it might be possible

[7] Cf. e.g. Ricoeur (1978); White (1996) (attempting to rehabilitate Quintilian's theory of *translatio*); Müller-Richter and Larcati (1996); and the whole discussion triggered by Davidson (1978).

[8] Still of great value is Assfahl (1932); recently e.g. Asper (1997); Nünlist (1998); for Shakespeare: Spurgeon (1935); Clemen (1977) (106 ff. on Hamlet).

[9] An example is the first attempt to treat comprehensively metaphors in literary criticism by van Hook (1905); cf. also the previous note.

[10] But cf. the chapters by Doreen Innes and Michael Silk in this volume.

to suggest answers to some questions not only regarding literary criticism, but metaphor in general.

1. The application of the term 'literary criticism' to a special kind of ancient literature has been queried.[11] It is certainly true that nothing exactly like the modern literary history and theory are to be found in antiquity and that there is also no clearly defined literary genre of 'literary criticism'. Besides, the question is complicated by the fact that in modern languages the term is used differently: 'literary criticism' as a term in English is much wider than the German *Literaturkritik*, which puts a strong emphasis on the non-academic occupation of writing reviews about works of literature.[12] There are no reviews in ancient literature, but individual passages of certain authors are frequently reviewed and general judgements are passed on their value. This usually serves special purposes in teaching rhetoric, such as demonstrating faults and virtues and providing examples (or authors) for imitation and, though literary critique here is not its own purpose, one may somehow loosely apply the term to all literature which contains such judgements, or which discusses the terms in which these judgements are expressed.[13] From these remarks it might already be apparent that special interest will be paid to the way in which metaphors may not only entail an element of evaluation, but can also, indeed, be critical.

2. Looking at the inflationary use of the term 'metaphor' in all fields of intellectual and artistic activity, one might be reminded of Augustine's introduction to his study of time: 'What, then, is metaphor? If nobody asks me I know. But if I were desirous to explain it to one that should ask me, plainly I know not.'[14] A first general definition of the term metaphor is to state that metaphor may be regarded as any way of talking about one kind of thing in the terms of another. (Please note that for present purposes, I concentrate on metaphors as expressed in linguistic forms,

[11] Classen (1994), 308–12.

[12] Jaumann (1995) sketches the different models of literary criticism from antiquity to the 18th cent.

[13] Many poetological and self-referential utterances in poetry are naturally enough couched in metaphors and that is why they could be included in the investigation. But given the limited space here I shall concentrate on examples from prose. Cf. on Latin poetry Deremetz (1995), esp. 45–71.

[14] Cf. Augustine, *Confessions* 11.14: 'quid est ergo tempus? si nemo ex me quaerat, scio; si quaerenti explicare velim, nescio.'

leaving aside, for example, the application of metaphor to the arts or to music.) The underlying cognitive process involved in its formation is, in most cases, that of constructing an analogy between what can be called the source, on the one hand, and the target, on the other (or 'vehicle' and 'tenor' in the perhaps more familiar terms introduced by I. A. Richards).[15] The underlying analogy is formed in accordance with three basic constraints: that of similarity (that is, there has to be a point of initial resemblance between the two domains), that of structure (the single elements in the source domain and the target domain are paired together thus creating a network of relations), and that of purpose (affecting both the way in which the potentially innumerable similarities and relations are chosen).[16] These terms will become clearer once we have started looking at the texts.

This certainly does not suffice as a definition but, astoundingly, even though the schools of theorists are never unanimous about how to define metaphors, most of them agree on whether an actual passage from a text contains a metaphor (though they might not agree about where exactly it occurs).[17] So it is fairly safe to start with what have always been regarded as examples of metaphor.

Nos autem, Brute, quoniam post Hortensi clarissumi oratoris mortem orbae eloquentiae quasi tutores relicti sumus, domi teneamus eam saeptam liberali custodia et hos ignotos atque impudentis procos repudiemus tueamurque ut adultam virginem caste et ab amatorum [MSS: armatorum] impetu, quantum possumus, prohibeamus. (Cicero, *Brutus* 330)

As for us, Brutus, since with the death of Hortensius, the brilliant orator, we are left to be the guardians of orphaned eloquence, let us keep her within our own walls, protected by a custody worthy of her liberal

[15] Richards (1965), esp. 89 ff.; or *Bildspender—Bildempfänger* according to Weinrich (1967). The terminology of metaphorology is only surpassed by that of psychology in diversity and richness.

[16] I am not using 'analogy' in the sense Aristotle refers to it in his discussion of metaphor (as proportional metaphor $a:b::c:d$), but in the wider sense developed in the cognitive theory of Holyoak and Thagard (1995). The vast recent scholarship on Aristotle's concept of metaphor is surveyed by Kirby (1997), to which can now be added Lloyd (1996*b*).

[17] It is as though there existed an unspoken consensus as to what may be called a metaphor, especially amongst those whose interest is mainly focused on the 'source domain'.

lineage. Let us repel the pretensions of these upstart and impudent suitors, and guard her purity, like that of a virgin grown to womanhood, and, so far as we can, shield her from the advances of rash admirers.[18]

The text quoted above appears near the end of Cicero's dialogue *Brutus*, which is set in 46 BC. Cicero has given a description of his rival Hortensius' career closely interwoven with his own (*Brutus* 300–29), ending with the former's death (in 50 BC), just in time before the outbreak of the civil war. He praises Hortensius for being happier than both himself and Brutus, who had to live through the war, and whose experience pervades the whole atmosphere of the dialogue.[19]

When the reader comes to the words *orbae eloquentiae*, he will first notice that a tropical expression is involved: we are talking about oratory as an orphaned person. Since the death of Hortensius has just been mentioned, there is no difficulty in interpretation: the achievements of Hortensius gave him a special position towards *eloquentia*, that of a father. Once this basic social relationship is established, there are numerous ways of expanding it by creating a structure of connections around it, thus implying that similar relations exist for *eloquentia*. (Here the role of structure in analogy, mentioned earlier, comes into play.) However, only some of them are actually made explicit in the following words (*quasi tutores* . . .): that an orphan needs protection, both legal and moral, from those who want to corrupt her and that there are persons to fulfil that task. There would have been other possible implications (grief and consolation, the dowry of the virgin, the mother, to name but a few), but the choice of them is regulated by the purpose (the third constraint) of the analogy. Orphanage as an image is quite common in Cicero but, interestingly enough, he usually applies it to the situation of the state, or rather the republic, in danger, deprived of help in periods of civil unrest.[20] If here then we find it applied to

[18] Translation taken from Hendrickson in Hendrickson and Hubbell (1962).

[19] Cf. already *Brutus* 6 f. on the *forum*, the *theatrum* of Hortensius' *ingenium* now being *orbatum*.

[20] Cf. e.g. Cicero's speech *Post Reditum in Senatu* 4: '(res publica) neque solum parentibus perpetuis verum etiam tutoribus annuis orbata' ('(the republic) not only bereft of its parents who would be there for life, but even of annually changing guardians'); and its counterpart *Ad Quirites* 11: 'orba res publica consulis fidem tamquam legitimi tutoris imploravit' ('the orphaned

eloquence, and in a context in which the critical situation of the state has just been mentioned, the purpose of the analogy is not only to present eloquence as being endangered by men who have different views on stylistics from Cicero and Brutus (who certainly did not agree completely in that respect), but also to argue that eloquence in turn stands for the *res publica* in which it is practised, thus merging the literary and the political judgement into one through the use of metaphor.[21]

On the formal side, the question 'Where is the metaphor in this passage?' can be answered in several ways. Some would (and do: cf. note 20) maintain that since we have a *quasi* and an *ut* in the passage it is transformed into a simile. But on reading or hearing it, we meet first, as I pointed out, the expression *orbae eloquentiae*, which up to this point in the sentence would have to be interpreted as a metaphor, and it seems to make the words *quasi*, *ut* carry much too heavy a burden. Instead it might be argued that every word from *orbae* to *prohibeamus*, except *eloquentiae*, is to be taken metaphorically. That metaphor cannot be tied up to a single word or phrase, but is a product of the interaction of words and their context, is one of the few results of modern metaphorology on which most scholars would agree (and of which Quintilian might have already had a

republic implored the consul as its lawful guardian for tutelage'). We also find in *De Oratore* 3.3: . . . 'orbitatem senatus, cuius ordinis a consule qui quasi parens bonus aut tutor fidelis esse deberet, tamquam ab aliquo nefario praedone diriperetur patrimonium dignitatis' ('the bereavement that had befallen the senatorial order, whose hereditary dignities a consul, whose duty it was to be its fostering parent or faithful guardian, was plundering like some unprincipled brigand': quoting Crassus in the Senate, shortly before his death in 91 BC). Fantham (1974: 122) regards the passage in *Ad Quirites* 'as a mere simile': 'the same metaphor is diluted to a simile in de orat. III 3,3 [sc. III 1,3] . . . and Brut. 330'; cf. also *Letters to Friends* 3.11.3 ('tanta penuria est in omni vel honoris vel aetatis gradu ut tam orba civitas tales tutores complecti debeat': 'such is the lack of suitable persons of whatever rank and age that the orphaned republic has to embrace guardians of such a character'); *On the Laws* 3.3.9; *Pro Flacco* 23.54; etc.

21 A scribe might have been induced to *armatorum* not only because of similarity in spelling, but also because of the associations provided by the context of the passage. On *adultam*: it would be part of the imagery of the growth of eloquence, perceived both on a historical level (development of rhetoric) and in an individual (cf. *maturitas* in Tacitus, *Dialogus* 26 below): she is grown up in the age of Cicero.

presentiment).[22] There is, however, the possibility of doing justice also to our *quasi* and *ut*, if we envisage the possibility of an interaction between metaphor and other tropes in a given context. It is, in fact, a very common feature in ancient literature that even in elaborate comparisons or similes terms belonging to one domain are carried over to those belonging to the other. So what starts off as metaphor can be continued with similes or comparisons. This is well recognized in Porphyry's *Homeric Questions* (6, 22.25–23.25 Sodano; cf. also chapter 17):[23]

θαυμαστὸν δὲ αὐτῷ κἀκεῖνο· ἐκ μεταφορᾶς γάρ τι τολμηρότερον φθεγξάμενος οἰκείαν ἐπάγει παραβολήν, κρατύνων αὐτὴν ὡς εὔλογον ἔσχε τὴν τόλμαν. εἰπὼν οὖν "κραδίη δέ οἱ ἔνδον ὑλάκτει" [υ 13] *ἐπάγει·*

> *ὡς δὲ κύων ἀμαλῇσι περὶ σκυλάκεσσι βεβῶσα*
> *ἄνδρ' ἀγνοιήσασ' ὑλάει μέμονέν τε μάχεσθαι* [υ 14–15] . . .

ἐπί τε τῶν Τρώων ἔτι ποικιλώτερον κέχρηται· ἀρξάμενος γὰρ ἀπὸ μεταφορᾶς ὁμοίωσίν τε αὐτῇ τὴν ἀκόλουθον ἐπάγει καὶ ἐπ' ἀμφοῖν τὴν παραβολήν· "Τρῶες μὲν κλαγγῇ" [Γ 2]*· τοῦτο μὲν δὴ ἡ μεταφορά· τὸ δ' "ὄρνιθες ὥς" ἡ ὁμοίωσις· εἶθ' ἡ παραβολή.*

> *ἠύτε περ κλαγγὴ γεράνων πέλει οὐρανόθι πρό* [Γ 3]. . .

This, too, is striking in Homer: after he has coined a rather bold metaphor, he adds a simile which is consistent with it, confirming it, as though he considered its boldness well-taken. Saying, then: 'and his heart "growled" within him' [*Odyssey* 20.13], he adds:

> and as a bitch, facing an unknown man, protects her tender pups
> and growls, eager to fight [*Odyssey* 20.14–15] . . .

He has, moreover, made a still more intricate use (of this) for the Trojans by beginning with a metaphor and adding not only a comparison consistent with it but also a simile consistent with both. This is the metaphor: 'The Trojans came on with a scream (*κλαγγή*)' [*Iliad* 3.2], the comparison, 'like birds', and then the simile:

> as when the clamouring (*κλαγγή*) of cranes goes heavenward
> [*Iliad* 3.3]. . .[24]

[22] Black (1962); Quintilian 8.3.38: 'translata probari nisi in contextu sermonis non possunt'.

[23] Richardson (1980) has drawn attention to it, without prolonged discussion. Further possible candidates for views 'diverging' from the standard substitutionist theory of metaphor, which most ancient theorists—except Aristotle!—followed, are (ps.-)Hermogenes, *On Invention* 4.10 (199.4–9 Rabe); cf. Barker (1999), 1–3 (against Stanford 1936: 18); and Aristides Quintilianus, *On Music* 2.9, 68.14–69.8 Winnington-Ingram (analysed by Barker 1999: 8–14 against the backdrop of the Stoic tradition).

[24] Translation at Schlunk (1993), 19.

Since actual usage of metaphors, and not ancient theory of metaphor, is the issue here, the passage cannot be discussed further, but its approach seems to me to be much more relaxed than that of many moderns. It is not merely theoretical exigencies which force Porphyry to be more liberal in this respect, but the empirical findings. Similar though not identical analogical images are found to be expressed in metaphor and in simile, and ancient theory, to which the formal distinction between these is often referred (Aristotle and ps.-Longinus)[25] does in fact not state that in this case metaphors cease to be metaphors.[26]

Since the application of a qualifying expression does not, I think, change the ontological status of the proposition, at least not in the usual context of literary criticism, I shall use texts with similes and metaphors to illustrate my points, not wanting to completely blur the distinction (which certainly depends to a large extent on considerations of literary genre and context of delivery, and has to be taken into account on another level of analysis).

Now that the role of context for the interpretation of metaphors and their interaction with other tropes (metonymy is a further important companion to metaphor, and is not only an alternative) should have become somewhat clearer, we move on to our next example.

Cicero is distinguishing the style of philosophical writing (Theophrastus, Aristotle, Xenophon, Plato are mentioned) from that of oratory proper (Cicero, *Orator* 63–4):

ergo ab hoc genere non difficile est hanc eloquentiam, de qua nunc agitur, secernere. mollis est enim oratio philosophorum et umbratilis nec sententiis nec verbis instructa popularibus nec vincta numeris, sed soluta liberius; nihil iratum habet, nihil invidum, nihil atrox, nihil miserabile, nihil astutum; casta, verecunda, virgo incorrupta quodam modo. itaque sermo potius quam oratio dicitur; quamquam enim omnis

[25] Aristotle's remark on the difference between *εἰκών* and metaphor as being only slight, *Rhetoric* 3.4, 1406b20, and Longinus' remark about softening bold metaphors with *μειλίγματα* (32.3 with reference to Aristotle and Theophrastus): cf. the same recommendation in Cicero, *De Oratore* 3.165: cf. McCall (1969), 29 ff. On *προθέσει* (not *προσθέσει*) defining the difference between them in 3. 10, 1410b18: McCall (1969), 39 n. 43; Tamba-Mecz and Veyne (1979), 85 f.

[26] An exception is Demetrius, *On Style* 80, who recommends changing the metaphor to a simile, but at the same time regards the simile as an extended metaphor.

locutio oratio est, tamen unius oratoris locutio hoc proprio signata nomine est.

It is therefore easy to distinguish the eloquence which we are treating from the style of the philosophers. The latter is gentle and suits the shade of the schools; it has no equipment of words or phrases that catch the popular fancy, it is not arranged in rhythmical periods, but is loose in structure; there is no anger in it, no hatred, no ferocity, no pathos, no shrewdness; it might be called a chaste, pure, and modest virgin. Consequently it is called conversation rather than oratory. While all speaking is oratory, yet it is the speech of the orator alone which is marked by this special name.[27]

At first glance, the metaphor of virginity is applied in a very similar way to that in the previous text. (The commentaries consequently put the passages, together with that by Dionysius of Halicarnassus, to which we shall turn presently, side by side, suggesting that the same image is being used in all cases.) In the *Orator* passage we slide slowly from the context into the metaphor: *mollis* has connotations of gentleness and softness, which are generally associated with the female (although it is left open yet whether this is to be associated with philosophy), and hence can be said in a way to foreshadow the *casta virgo*. With the attributes *iratum* and *astutum* we get a stronger hint that the speech of philosophers is described as a person, which becomes evident with *casta virgo*, and only after it has been uttered is the statement softened by *quodam modo* (on this problem of qualifying particles see above). However, a closer examination reveals important differences between the two virgins; and a look at the most conspicuous other metaphor, *umbratilis*, may help to elucidate this. Since Plato's *Phaedrus*, with its setting in the shade of a plane-tree, it had become commonplace to set the schools (both philosophical and rhetorical) and their shady retreats (*umbracula*)[28] in opposition to the sun, the contests, and the

[27] Translation adapted from Hubbell in Hendrickson and Hubbell (1962).

[28] For the contrast shade–sun, also in gendered contexts (shade: women and effeminacy; sun: men and strength) cf. Plato, *Phaedrus* 239c; Euripides, *Bacchae* 457–9; Cicero, *De Oratore* 1.157; *Brutus* 32 (Isocrates), 37; *On the Laws* 3.6.14; Dionysius of Halicarnassus, *On the Eloquence of Demosthenes* 32 (comparison of Plato's *Menexenus* and Demosthenes' *On the Crown*). In rhetorical contexts it is often directed at school declamations: Seneca, *Controversiae* 9, *preface* 4; Petronius, *Satyricon* 2 (*umbraticus doctor*); Quintilian 1.2.18; 10.5.17; Tacitus, *Annals* 14.53.4 (Seneca defending his *studia* against Suillius' attacks); Pliny,

challenges of the dusty forum. The metaphor evokes an opposition between an 'in' (the quiet of the schools) and an 'out' (real life, which here is also brought out by *popularibus*), and assigns the roles accordingly to philosophical *eloquentia* and oratory. In combination with this metaphor, a similar pattern can be made out for the virginal philosophy. Knowing that the place of chaste virgins in antiquity is nowhere but in the house (thus making use of knowledge about the social context, which is indispensable to the explanation of metaphor), which in the text quoted first had been expressly stated, we get the same pattern, but used to a quite different effect. Whereas in the *Orator* the opposition is that between the study and the assembly or lawcourt, and the virgin is not true oratory—which in turn is supposed to be 'out', and certainly not to be described as an unchaste woman but rather somebody active in the sun (a man no doubt)—in the *Brutus* the virgin is the whole of oratory. She is 'in'; outside is the threat of corruption: not the field for her activity but, as I suggested, a clique of corrupt politicians aiming at the destruction of the state, with which she is to be associated. In a non-rhetorical context, but with the same evaluative consequences this contrast of 'in' and 'out' is used in Numenius when he describes his dream-vision of the Eleusinian goddesses drawn out of their inner sanctuary and transformed into prostitutes by his profanation of the mysteries.[29] Structures of opposition like

Epistles 9.2.3–4 (in contrast to *arma, castra, cornua, tubas, sudorem, pulverem, soles*); Juvenal 7.8 (*Pieria umbra*), 105, 173 (*pugna—rhetorica umbra*) with Mayor (1872–8), notes ad loc.; Statius, *Silvae* 5.2.103–9. The imagery has of course a real background, the Roman courts being at times exposed to the weather: cf. Quintilian 11.3.27.

[29] Numenius, fr. 55 des Places (Macrobius, *Commentary on the Dream of Scipio* 1.2.19, 7.23–8.3 Willis): 'Numenio denique inter philosophos occultorum curiosiori offensam numinum, quod Eleusinia sacra interpretando vulgaverit, somnia prodiderunt, viso sibi ipsas Eleusinias deas habitu meretricio ante apertum lupanar videre prostantes, admirantique et causas non convenientis numinibus turpitudinis consulenti respondisse iratas ab ipso se de adyto pudicitiae suae vi abstractas et passim adeuntibus prostitutas' ('Indeed, Numenius, a philosopher with a curiosity for occult things, had revealed to him in a dream the outrage he had committed against the gods by proclaiming his interpretation of the Eleusinian mysteries. The Eleusinian goddesses themselves, dressed in the garments of courtesans, appeared to him standing before an open brothel, and when in his astonishment he asked the reason for this shocking conduct, they angrily replied that he had driven them from their

the one presented here function as regulative principles in the employment of metaphors,[30] although perhaps it would be too wide an extension of the term to call these principles themselves 'metaphors'.[31]

What I meant by the constraints of 'structure' and 'purpose' in the design of metaphorical similarities should by now have gained more profile. The same association between the quiet virgin and the secluded, 'cloistral' atmosphere is created, the same opposition of an interior and an exterior area, but to a different effect. The single elements of the two domains in the analogical complex are placed in relation to each other (or 'mapped') in different ways, so that different aspects are activated according to the purpose, which in turn has to be deduced from the context. So what in one context is formed into an image of rhetoric in its civic function, in another is an exact representation of what true rhetoric is not.

Therefore we may ask: is there a conceptual framework in which these metaphors can be grouped together, are comparable, or even the same? Even the love for the *virgo* at home does not always qualify the caring father for unrestricted approval.[32] It is not enough to tie the metaphor to a single word

sanctuary of modesty and had prostituted them to every passer-by'; translation by Stahl 1952: 87). (My attention was drawn to this text by George Boys-Stones; and cf. below, Ch. 10.)

[30] The role of 'quantifying antitheses' in Callimachus' *Aitia* prologue is investigated by Asper (1997), 135–207.

[31] Lakoff (Lakoff and Johnson 1980: 14–21) speaks of 'spatialization metaphors'.

[32] In Cicero, *De Oratore* 1.234 f., Antonius portrays jurisprudence as a girl (*virgo*, though the word is not used) without a dowry (*indotata*): the oratorical embellishment is to be her dowry, provided by the suitor Crassus (we think of the *proci* in *Brutus* 330), but the idea is rejected because it would be an inappropriate change of dress (*spolies atque denudes*). In striking contrast to this passage and to *Brutus* 330 (quoted above), Cicero in *Pro Murena* 23 ridicules Sulpicius Rufus and jurisprudence: 'et quoniam mihi videris istam scientiam iuris tamquam filiolam osculari [on this habit cf. *On Divination* 1.103] tuam, non patiar te in tanto errore versari ut istud nescio quid quod tanto opere didicisti praeclarum aliquid esse arbitrere.' (There follows a comparison with other *artes*, esp. eloquence, at 29 f., opposed to military prowess—*orator*—*imperator*—in 30: *cedat . . . forum castris, otium militiae, stilus gladio, umbra soli* . . . Cf. above, n. 28.) 'Since you seem to me to be hugging your knowledge of jurisprudence as if it were a darling daughter, I shall not allow you to be so mistaken as to think that this whatever-it-is that you have taken such pains to

or phrase and say, in both cases, *virgo* (or a woman etc.) is used as a metaphor because, as we have seen, detecting a metaphor involves the whole context, and that can cause quite diverging interpretations. Nevertheless, this is the manner in which studies in the application of metaphors are traditionally arranged[33] and I do not wish to denounce the effort put into them and their immense usefulness. But there still remains something to be done besides cataloguing metaphors.

Having sharpened our perceptivity for the way metaphors work let us now turn to the most elaborate version of the Shakespearean motif 'rhetoric—virgin or harlot?': in Dionysius of Halicarnassus' introduction to his essays on individual orators. Written in Augustan Rome, it leads us into a vivid literary controversy, which is labelled nowadays as the debate between 'Asianism' and 'Atticism' (and one which was even more prominent in Cicero). To assess it fully is well outside the scope of this chapter, and particularly difficult, because the main points of controversy are not always clear.[34] If one hoped for a clarification from Dionysius' introduction, however, one would be somewhat disappointed. It pleads its case in a style especially rich in imagery—as befits a preface and as is generally the case with Dionysius. What we have here is an extended personification (similar to, but not fully identical with 'prosopopoeia' in its terminological sense),[35] thus producing a text that verges on the allegorical (Dionysius of Halicarnassus, *On the Ancient Orators* 1.2–7 Aujac):

ἐν γὰρ δὴ τοῖς πρὸ ἡμῶν χρόνοις ἡ μὲν ἀρχαία καὶ φιλόσοφος ῥητορικὴ προπηλακιζομένη καὶ δεινὰς ὕβρεις ὑπομένουσα κατελύετο, ἀρξαμένη μὲν ἀπὸ τῆς Ἀλεξάνδρου τοῦ Μακεδόνος τελευτῆς ἐκπνεῖν καὶ μαραίνεσθαι κατ' ὀλίγον, ἐπὶ δὲ τῆς καθ' ἡμᾶς ἡλικίας μικροῦ δεήσασα εἰς τέλος ἠφανίσθαι·

learn is in any way remarkable.' English translation from MacDonald (1976), 213.

[33] Like Assfahl (1932), van Hook (1905), or Demandt (1978).

[34] Important contributions to the discussion are Dihle (1977); Gelzer (1979); Wisse (1995); Hose (1999).

[35] On metaphors as basis for personifications: cf. Newiger (1957), 8, 181. On metaphor—allegory cf. Kurz (1993), esp. 58 on personification: 'daß Personifikationen auf der Reifikation metaphorischer Bedeutung beruhen' ('personifications are based on the reification of metaphorical meaning'); cf. also nn. 48 and 50 below.

ἑτέρα δέ τις ἐπὶ τὴν ἐκείνης παρελθοῦσα τάξιν, ἀφόρητος ἀναιδείᾳ θεατρικῇ καὶ ἀνάγωγος καὶ οὔτε φιλοσοφίας οὔτε ἄλλου παιδεύματος οὐδενὸς μετειληφυῖα ἐλευθερίου, λαθοῦσα καὶ παρακρουσαμένη τὴν τῶν ὄχλων ἄγνοιαν, οὐ μόνον ἐν εὐπορίᾳ καὶ τρυφῇ καὶ μορφῇ πλείονι τῆς ἑτέρας διῆγεν, ἀλλὰ καὶ τὰς τιμὰς καὶ τὰς προστασίας τῶν πόλεων, ἃς ἔδει τὴν φιλόσοφον ἔχειν, εἰς ἑαυτὴν ἀνηρτήσατο καὶ ἦν φορτική τις πάνυ καὶ ὀχληρὰ καὶ τελευτῶσα παραπλησίαν ἐποίησε γενέσθαι τὴν Ἑλλάδα ταῖς τῶν ἀσώτων καὶ κακοδαιμόνων οἰκίαις. ὥσπερ γὰρ ἐν ἐκείναις ἡ μὲν ἐλευθέρα καὶ σώφρων γαμετὴ κάθηται μηδενὸς οὖσα τῶν αὑτῆς κυρία, ἑταίρα δέ τις ἄφρων ἐπ' ὀλέθρῳ τοῦ βίου παροῦσα πάσης ἀξιοῖ τῆς οὐσίας ἄρχειν, σκυβαλίζουσα καὶ δεδιττομένη τὴν ἑτέραν· τὸν αὐτὸν τρόπον ἐν πάσῃ πόλει καὶ οὐδεμιᾶς ἧττον ἐν ταῖς εὐπαιδεύτοις (τουτὶ γὰρ ἁπάντων τῶν κακῶν ἔσχατον) ἡ μὲν Ἀττικὴ μοῦσα καὶ ἀρχαία καὶ αὐτόχθων ἄτιμον εἰλήφει σχῆμα, τῶν ἑαυτῆς ἐκπεσοῦσα ἀγαθῶν, ἡ δὲ ἔκ τινων βαράθρων τῆς Ἀσίας ἐχθὲς καὶ πρῴην ἀφικομένη, Μυσὴ ἢ Φρυγία τις ἢ Καρικόν τι κακόν, [ἢ βάρβαρον] Ἑλληνίδας ἠξίου διοικεῖν πόλεις ἀπελάσασα τῶν κοινῶν τὴν ἑτέραν, ἡ ἀμαθὴς τὴν φιλόσοφον καὶ ἡ μαινομένη τὴν σώφρονα.

In the period preceding our own, the old, philosophical Rhetoric was trampled in the mire and collapsed under the grievous injuries it was forced to endure. Its slow wasting and expiration may be said to have begun with the death of Alexander of Macedon; by our own age it had almost completely disappeared. In its place arose another kind of rhetoric, intolerable in its melodramatic shamelessness, tasteless, innocent of philosophy or any other liberal study. Unnoticed and undetected by the ignorant vulgar, this rhetoric not only enjoyed an abundance, luxury, and elegance unknown to its predecessor, but attached to itself the honours and political supremacies which belonged by right to its philosophical sister. With its crudeness and vulgarity, it ended by making Greece like the household of some desperate roué, where the decent, respectable wife sits powerless in her own home, while some nitwit of a harlot, there only to ruin the property, thinks she has the right to rule the roost, and bullies the wife and treats her like dirt. Just so, in every city, even—worst of all—in the highly cultivated, the old, native Attic Muse was in disgrace, cast out of her inheritance, while another, sprung from some Asian sewer the other day—some Mysian or Phrygian or, God help us, Carian plague, claimed the right to govern the cities of Hellas, and, in her ignorance and madness, to drive out her sane, philosophical rival.[36]

The decay in Greek rhetoric is here for the first time identified with the beginning of the Hellenistic age according to our

[36] Translation adapted from Russell in Russell and Winterbottom (1972), 305 f.

modern construction of historical epochs.[37] To depict this decay, Dionysius first uses the analogy of the exhaustion, decomposition, and withering away of a human body in several stages of illness (adopting usual ancient theories of decline). Although the reference to the injuries suffered give the impression that the decay had been brought about more speedily by an external action, just who it was who abused the woman is not yet made clear. This philosophical rhetoric—philosophical in the sense in which Isocrates would have defined it—is pushed into the background by an uneducated upstart full of theatrical insolence (which probably refers to the style of delivery in her practitioners)[38] who also takes away her political influence. She is depicted in colours strongly suggestive of an oriental background (*τρυφή*). Although nothing is explicitly stated about when this pretender arrived or from where, the opinion we get from reading the passage is in fact that here we have two parallel processes: the illness of philosophical rhetoric is matched by the rising of its ignorant rival. But before we get time to unravel this complex situation we meet our virgin, who is married now (we shall see to whom) in an imbedded simile.

The same pattern as in the preceding examples is recognizable. Again we have the opposition between 'in' and 'out', this time on a much larger scale. The whole of Hellas is 'in', the 'out' is thus outside the most civilized part of the world. But only in the second part of the simile is it made clear that the threat from without comes in fact from Asia. The situation is more dramatic since the enemy has managed to get in, resulting in a kind of very unhappy *ménage à trois*. A link with the preceding personification is provided by *σκυβαλίζουσα* ('treating like dirt': 1.5) which

[37] The best discussions of Dionysius are by Goudriaan (1989), 566–78, and Hidber (1996), 100–12.

[38] *Brutus* 303 ('Hortensius: motus et gestus etiam plus artis habebat quam erat oratori satis': 'in his delivery and gesture was even a little too much study than fit for the orator'), and Quintilian 11.3.8 (*actio* in Hortensius especially good); Gellius 1.5. 2 (Hortensius as actor: 'multaque in eum quasi histrionem in ipsis causis atque iudiciis dicta sunt': 'and many criticisms were levelled against him, even while he was pleading in the courts, for appearing like an actor'); Valerius Maximus 8.10.2; on the male–female imagery in discussions of delivery cf. Enders (1997) *passim*, although the alleged systematic link between theatricality, effeminacy, and delivery is not always borne out by the texts quoted.

picks up *προπηλακιζομένη* (literally, 'being spattered with mud': 1.2; another instance of the phenomenon of interaction between the simile and its context), and so an answer as to who is responsible for the maltreatment of rhetoric is suggested. Finally, names are given to the agents.

Asia's reputation (exemplified by Phrygia, Mysia, or Caria) as the home of *τρυφή* ('luxury') since the Persian wars is put to use in order to denounce the rival rhetoric as the enemy of the Attic Muse. But something has changed while we have been moving through the simile. Now the rival, which all the parallels (see also the act of dispossessing, the lack of education, and the depriving of political and civic status) suggested to be the same person throughout, appears to have arrived only recently, a fact which cannot be reconciled easily with the idea that the decline had been going on since the death of Alexander. This shift in thought was concealed by a shift in the imagery: the analogy of illness and age is superseded by, or rather merges into, the analogy of the wife deprived of her status. In this process of blending several analogues with similar, though not identical structures, it has become possible to combine the opposition of old (the autochthonous rhetoric) versus new (the insolent rival) with the local opposition (Attica versus Asia as the concrete representation of an abstract in—out structure), with the latter implying an additional strong judgement as to the moral value of the two rivals. The shift in imagery is in fact a sign of the intrinsic problem of Dionysius' case. In so far as the literary movement heralded by Dionysius and others is a reaction against the decline of eloquence, whenever that occurred, it should be seen as coming later than its cause. By identifying the pure, unadulterated eloquence with the rightful wife and additionally depicting it/her as no longer being ill (although she had been pushed into the background, she had nevertheless been around all the time), a continuity is created which allows a polemical reversal of the situation. Dionysius is on the side of the old (*ἀρχαία*) rhetoric and can claim precedence. The typical three steps which determine the self-consciousness of classicistic movements—the golden past, the dark age, and the return of the old glory[39]—are at the same time stated and revoked, since the past is in fact identical

[39] Cf. Gelzer (1979), 10f.

with the present. The simile even already suggests from where the solution is to come. Since it is the head of the household who is corrupted (1.4: ἀσώτων καὶ κακοδαιμόνων), a change here might help to get rid of the harlot and reinstate the wife in her rights. And since the house is Hellas, the new masters of the house, the Romans (or rather the cultural and political elite with its refined taste) turn out to be the rescuers of rhetoric ('whether some god set it in train, or the revolution of nature itself recalled the old order, or human impulse guided multitudes to the same goal . . .').[40]

Here metaphor and simile have proved to be weapons in a polemical argument, and even tools for creating a special version of history, the version most favourable to the author. At the same time, the term 'critical' should by now assume an additional connotation. Besides being an instrument of criticism, metaphor entails a certain risk in its application. Since the structural relations between the source- and the target-domain associated can never be entirely determined, a certain ambiguity can arise which may give opportunity for creative development as well as polemical distortion.

More limited is the use of the virginal association in two passages in Tacitus' *Dialogus* and Dionysius of Halicarnassus' *On Literary Composition*, which shall stand here in place of the numerous further examples from rhetorical literature using gendered metaphors:

[MESSALA:] Quod ad Servium Galbam et C. Laelium attinet et si quos alios antiquorum agitare non destitit (scil. Aper), non exigit defensorem, cum fatear quaedam eloquentiae eorum ut nascenti adhuc nec satis adultae defuisse. Ceterum si omisso optimo illo et perfectissimo genere eloquentiae eligenda sit forma dicendi, malim hercule C. Gracchi impetum aut L. Crassi maturitatem quam calamistros Maecenatis aut tinnitus Gallionis; adeo melius est oratorem vel hirta toga induere quam fucatis et meretriciis vestibus insignire. neque enim oratorius iste, immo hercule ne virilis quidem cultus est, quo plerique temporum nostrorum actores ita utuntur, ut lascivia verborum et levitate sententiarum et licentia compositionis histrionales modos exprimant. quodque vix auditu fas esse debeat, laudis et gloriae et ingenii loco plerique iactant cantari saltarique commentarios suos. unde oritur illa foeda et praepostera, sed tamen frequens, sicut his

[40] Dionysius of Halicarnassus, *On the Ancient Orators* 2.

clausula est, exclamatio, ut oratores nostri tenere dicere, histriones diserte saltare dicantur. (Tacitus, *Dialogus* 25–6.)

[MESSALA:] As for Servius Galba and Gaius Laelius and other ancients that Aper couldn't stop chasing, the defence can be waived; I agree that their eloquence, still growing and adolescent, lacked much. But if we leave out of account supreme and perfect oratory, and look round for a style to choose, I should distinctly prefer Gaius Gracchus' impetuosity or Lucius Crassus' ripeness to Maecenas' curling-tongs or Gallio's jingles: better clothe oratory in a hairy toga than prink it out in gaudy and meretricious costumes. That sort of refinement doesn't suit oratory—or even a real man: I mean the sort many pleaders of our day so abuse that they come to reproduce the rhythms of the stage: language obscene, thoughts frivolous, rhythms licentious. Many people actually boast, as if it were a step towards fame and a sign of their genius, that their model speeches are sung or danced: it ought to be almost out of the question even to listen to talk like this. Hence the common remark—shameful and perverse though it is—that modern orators speak lasciviously, modern actors dance eloquently.[41]

ἡ δὲ γλαφυρὰ σύνθεσις . . . συνηλεῖφθαί τε ἀλλήλοις ἀξιοῖ καὶ συνυφάνθαι τὰ μόρια ὡς μιᾶς λέξεως ὄψιν ἀποτελοῦντα εἰς δύναμιν. τοῦτο δὲ ποιοῦσιν αἱ τῶν ἁρμονιῶν ἀκρίβειαι χρόνον αἰσθητὸν οὐδένα τὸν μεταξὺ τῶν ὀνομάτων περιλαμβάνουσαι· ἔοικέ τε κατὰ μέρος εὐητρίοις ὕφεσιν ἢ γραφαῖς συνεφθαρμένα τὰ φωτεινὰ τοῖς σκιεροῖς ἐχούσαις. εὔφωνά τε εἶναι βούλεται πάντα τὰ ὀνόματα καὶ λεῖα καὶ μαλακὰ καὶ παρθενωπά, τραχείαις δὲ συλλαβαῖς καὶ ἀντιτύποις ἀπέχθεταί που· τὸ δὲ θρασὺ πᾶν καὶ παρακεκινδυνευμένον δι' εὐλαβείας ἔχει. (Dionysius of Halicarnassus, *On Literary Composition* 23.2–4 Aujac)

The smooth type of arrangement . . . likes the individual parts to merge into one another, to be woven together so as to appear as far as possible like one continuous utterance. This is achieved by exactly fitting joints which leave the intervals between the words imperceptible. It is like cloth finely woven together or pictures in which the light merges into the shade. All the words are expected to be euphonious, smooth, soft, virginal; it hates rough, recalcitrant syllables, and has a cautious attitude towards anything at all bold or risky.[42]

In Tacitus, we are dealing with a (partial) defence of older orators whom Aper had attacked quite fiercely, and in which one-word characterizations and judgements are given.[43] If we

[41] Translation by Winterbottom in Russell and Winterbottom (1972), 448.

[42] Translation by Russell in Russell and Winterbottom (1972), 339.

[43] Well based in tradition. On Maecenas' style, cf. Suetonius, *Augustus* 86.2

turn to the question where the basic opposition in this case might be, we find that oratory is in fact male (*virilis cultus*). Although it is a disreputable woman whose clothing is rejected and associated with an actor-like delivery, it is in fact all that is female which is to be shunned by the orator. I think there may be a social and historical reason as to why there could be no image of a reputable *matrona* (or her guise)—as opposed to the enclosed virgin—standing for concrete, practical public oratory. Women were not to appear in public (to be 'out') on any of the occasions fitting the oratorical tasks. What we are left with on the positive side is shown by the passage of Dionysius. In a chain of metaphors so typical for his rhetorical treatises we have the softness, the cautiousness, the shying away from anything risky (*mollis*—μαλακός) that again recalls in the extremely rare word παρθενωπός ('virginal') the world of seclusion known to us from our first example but which is now without any political associations.

The gendered model in the evaluation of speech and literature has a long tradition: it can possibly be found at work already in Sophocles,[44] and is fully in action for example in the *Rhetoric to Herennius*, Valerius Maximus, the Elder Seneca, Persius, Quintilian, or Fronto, to name but a few authors.[45] How the more stereotyped of these applications of the male–female model are rooted in the ancient one-sex gender model, which regards

(*cincinni*, μυροβρεχεῖς); Seneca, *Epistles* 114.4 ff. (cf. Richlin 1997: 94 ff.); the imagery in Cicero, *Orator* 78, *Brutus* 262, and *De Oratore* 3.100 (*cincinni*); Dionysius of Halicarnassus, *On Literary Composition* 25: Plato 'combing and curling' (κτενίζων καὶ βοστρυχίζων) his dialogues; the same combination of toga and hairstyle also in Quintilian 12.10.47. Cf. Austin (1953), ad loc.

[44] Sophocles, fr. 963 Radt (Trypho, *On Tropes* 8; Polybius Sardianus, *On Figures* iii. 106.9 Spengel): οἱ γὰρ γύνανδροι καὶ λέγειν ἠσκηκότες ('woman-men and those who have studied oratory': translation by Lloyd-Jones 1996: 417); cf. also Euripides (n. 28); plenty of material on the concept of effeminacy in Herter (1959), esp. 625–8, 636. *Androgyne* appears in Valerius Maximus 8.3.1 as nickname for the female orator (?)Maesia Sentina.

[45] *Rhetoric to Herennius* 3.22 (on the orator's voice); Valerius Maximus 8.5.3 (on women in lawcourts; only Hortensia, Hortensius' daughter, is less severely condemned); Seneca, *Controversiae* 1, *preface* 8–10 (on the moral decline of youth in his age); 1.22 (on Alfius Flavus); *Suasoriae* 7.12 (Cestius to Surdinus during a declamation); Persius, *Satires* 1.103–5; Quintilian 5.12.17–20; 8, *preface* 19–26; 11.3.32; Fronto 119.10–11; 156.3–4 (attacking Seneca's style, cf. 153–5). Only a few examples are given, cf. also n. 47 below.

women as deviant men,[46] and how they are linked with particular social spaces, has been brought out well by recent studies using the methods of modern gender studies.[47] Less successful seems the attempt, following deconstructivist lines (Paul de Man) to see the rhetorical figure of personification itself as feminine, thus making women themselves the 'figures of figuration',[48] which in turn should explain why concrete personifications (and, by implication, also personifications like that in Dionysius of Halicarnassus) are female. There is one basic problem in this theory: it starts from the wrong assumption, that 'classical and early medieval allegorical personifications were exclusively female'.[49] The grammatical explanation (the personifications take the gender of the grammatical genus of the abstract noun) is still preferable.[50] Nevertheless, there is a very conscious play with the metaphorical and allegorical possibilities involved in the female character of Rhetoric (and the male of Philosophy) in Lucian, when he describes the woman before her transformation into the harlot standing for the seduction of rhetoric as *ἐσχηματισμένην* (literally 'figured', 'decked out'), and after it as *κοσμουμένην* ('made up'), thus playing with the Greek terms for rhetorical figure (*σχῆμα*) and oratorical *ornatus* (*κόσμος*: 'orna-

[46] Laqueur (1990), 25–62. An excellent introduction into gender-based studies of literature is offered by Heydebrand and Winko (1995).

[47] Richlin (1997), 92–9 (esp. on the Senecas and Quintilian); Gleason (1995) (for the Second Sophistic). For terminology, cf. Santoro L'Hoir (1992).

[48] Paxson (1998), 165. Demetrius, *On Style* 265 cannot be used to support this position, because the words *λαβοῦσαν γυναικὸς σχῆμα* ('taking on the form of a woman') are not part of a definition of *προσοποποιία*, but belong to the examples given by Demetrius (*Ἑλλάδα, πατρίδα*). So this passage is far from being 'the very first published definition of personification' and making 'the embodying of an abstraction as a female body a formal requisite of the device' (Paxson 1998: 152; cf. also Innes in Halliwell, Fyfe, and Innes 1995, note ad loc.).

[49] Paxson (1998), 149; but cf. Deubner (1902–9).

[50] Paxson's main thesis (1998: 157) against grammatical theories of personification will also not stand because the grammatical genus of the word *prosopopoeia* could only have been influential after the term was coined, but female and male personifications are of course much older than the term. To give the relatively marginal figure termed 'anthimeria', based in English rhetorical theory since the Renaissance as a subspecies of grammatical 'enallage' (cf. Lanham 1991: 62) the status of an ontological counterpart to prosopopoeia by expanding its application beyond any traditional usage (Paxson 1998: 163 f.), seems of equally little help.

mentation'). By assigning the first stage to Demosthenes, he may also be hinting at a literary and historical judgement.[51] And again, the same basic metaphorical construction can also convey an entirely positive evaluation, when Martianus Capella uses the same pun to describe the figure of the supreme ruling art of rhetoric (practical public oratory is not an issue here).[52] The metaphorical implications are very consciously used by Lucian and Martianus Capella, which should warn every student not to pass over any of these rhetorical virgins as mere traditional embellishment.

A few concluding remarks are now possible on the tasks involved and the unsolved problems still remaining in the interpretation of metaphors both in literary criticism and in general. If more questions arise than answers, it means that I must undertake a programme for further research, the outlines of which, however, should have become clearer.

[51] The passage escaped Paxson's notice. Lucian, *Double Indictment* 31: a Syrian rhetor (Lucian) accuses Rhetoric of having changed from an honest woman to a disreputable hetaira: ἐγὼ γὰρ ὁρῶν ταύτην οὐκέτι σωφρονοῦσαν οὐδὲ μένουσαν ἐπὶ τοῦ κοσμίου σχήματος οἷόν ποτε ἐσχηματισμένην αὐτὴν ὁ Παιανιεὺς ἐκεῖνος ἠγάγετο, κοσμουμένην δὲ καὶ τὰς τρίχας εὐθετίζουσαν εἰς τὸ ἑταιρικὸν καὶ φύκιον ἐντριβομένην καὶ τὠφθαλμὼ ὑπογραφομένην, ὑπώπτευον εὐθὺς καὶ παρεφύλαττον ὅποι τὸν ὀφθαλμὸν φέρει. ('Seeing that she was no longer modest and did not continue to make the respectable figure she made once when Demosthenes took her to wife, but made herself up, arranged her hair like a courtesan, put on rouge, and darkened her eyes underneath, I became suspicious at once and secretly took note where she directed her glances'; translation adapted from Harmon 1921). The counterpart is a male personification: Διάλογος. On the female figures in Lucian cf. Braun (1994), 285–91. Lucian is possibly further developing Dionysius' motif: Braun (1994), 287 n. 1; Gera Levine (1995); Laplace (1996); cf. Lucian, *Teacher of Rhetoric* 6.8, 10, 24; *The Hall* 7; *Fisherman* 12. On the motive of *fucus eloquentiae* in ancient theory cf. Blümer (1991), 9–22. (I am grateful to Dr Peter von Möllendorff, Munich, for discussing this topic with me.)

[52] Martianus Capella 5.426: 'ecce quaedam . . . vultus etiam decore luculenta femina insignis ingreditur, cui galeatus vertex ac regali caput maiestate sertatum . . . [peplo . . . tegebatur], quod omnium figurarum lumine variatum cunctorum schemata praeferebat; pectus autem exquisitissimis gemmarum coloribus balteatum' ('In strode a woman of outstanding beauty; she wore a helmet, and her head was wreathed with royal grandeur . . . [covered by a robe:] this robe was adorned with the light of all kinds of devices and showed the figures of them all, while she had a belt under her breast adorned with the rarest colors of jewels'—punning on *lumen*, *figurae*, *schemata*, *colores*, *gemmae*; translation by Stahl and Johnson 1977).

Is the detailed analysis of individual passages the only way to deal with metaphor in literary criticism? I think some alternative, or complementary, approaches which lend the interpretation a more solid background might seem to emerge, if only vaguely, from what we have looked at so far. Under the formal aspect, metaphors have to be regarded not only in terms of similarity of constituent parts, but also in the way in which the similarity is expanded (or even created) in accordance with a structuring process that brings out certain features that are relevant to the purpose of the passage. We saw how that works in the variations on the *virgo*-theme, and some of the possibilities of variation I hinted at are indeed realized by Cicero.[53] There is, then, a necessity to look at the metaphors in a way that allows for variance but which nevertheless preserves a kind of unity. The different metaphors could be ordered semantically into 'fields of metaphors or images' (*Bildfelder* to use the term of Harald Weinrich).[54] These would comprise combinations of both source and target and be organized in a hierarchical way: e.g. 'speech is a body' containing e.g. 'speech is a woman', 'words are the clothes of speech', or 'the structure of the arm is the structure of a sentence'. This metaphorical field, combined with another one, 'the physical appearance of a man corresponds to his interior qualities', gives the underlying structure for the moral criticism so pervasive in ancient popular thinking which strongly influences literary criticism. In this approach quite different tendencies in scholarship seem to overlap, namely the semantic theory of Weinrich and the cognitive science of Lakoff and his colleagues.[55] Because this may seem a rather far-reaching prospect, on a more modest level I propose to look at metaphors as interactive combinations of two concepts containing variables (or slots to be filled in). In actual usage not all possible structural relations are established, not the whole connotative background is activated (as this is impossible). Bearing this in mind may help to avoid a very common over-interpretation of individual metaphors: Max Black had presented metaphors as the visible tips of submerged models (that is, generally speaking, behind meta-

[53] Cicero, *De Oratore* 1.234 f. See above, n. 32.

[54] Weinrich (1967). On the importance of his contribution cf. Jäkel (1999), 17 ff.

[55] Lakoff and Johnson (1980); Lakoff and Turner (1989), 57–139.

phors there is a whole structure which guides understanding of a particular concept).[56] The attention paid to the discovery of submerged icebergs could lead to the assumption, based on an extensive collection of 'parallels', that a metaphor can be tied down to a specific origin and, whenever it occurs, will carry with it all the connotations documented in the comparative material. This, as we have seen, does not always work, because what decides the scope of the metaphor is the context. This respect for the context also involves allowing for interaction of metaphor with other tropes, among which metonymy, although not discussed by me now, seems particularly prominent.[57]

As for the function of the metaphors, I have concentrated on the way in which they entail judgements, but there are of course further functions, of which in the case of literary criticism the 'descriptive' somehow overlaps with the use of metaphor out of necessity (a further aspect would be the didactic purpose of metaphor). I just want to make two points here. First, metaphor is necessary when a new field of knowledge is to be organized, when new concepts have to be designed for something which had not been talked about before. In the development of rhetoric and poetics, which form the basis of literary criticism, metaphors seem to have been used from the very beginning because a new way of observing language had emerged. So looking at the metaphors, we may get a glimpse of how language in general, and literature in particular, were not only perceived but made to be recognizable in the first place. This in part explains why metaphors in literary criticism may be singled out as rewarding objects for investigation. Secondly, in a new field of activity, such as rhetoric or literary criticism, one might expect a terminology to be developed out of metaphorical beginnings, which then will shed (as far as possible) its metaphorical connections, and become fixed. This is what has, at least to a great extent, not happened in ancient literary criticism. It may indeed be tantalizing for a modern theorist of stylistics to read descriptions of different types of styles and to discover that the best way to describe them seems to have been an accumulation of metaphors.[58] I should assume that the reason lies, at least partially, in

[56] Black (1977), 445; (1993), 30.

[57] Lakoff and Johnson (1980), 35–40; Lakoff and Turner (1989), 102–110.

[58] The wide range of terms, to a large extent metaphorical in origin, employed

the literary character of literary criticism. Though it is hard to decide to which genre it should be assigned, I would suggest that using a still, so to speak, liquid critical equipment at least aims at upholding the fiction that what the critic has to say continues to be accessible to a wider educated public of non-professionals.

This leaves us with a number of questions, with which, as I consider to be appropriate for a paper on such a subject, I shall end. How do the metaphors in literary criticism relate to the general way of talking about language? This takes us back to the Greek beginnings of critical metaphors. How far is there a continuity between poetical metaphors, the everyday language, and the emerging sophistic rhetoric in, for example, Aristophanes' criticism? What about the possibility of transferring metaphorical concepts from poetry to prose, or from one language to another? How strong is the power of tradition? When and how do innovations occur: within a known metaphorical field or by creating a new one? Has metaphor become an inhibition to the development of the discipline of literary criticism? No single comprehensive theory of metaphor will be able to solve all these questions by assigning to them definite positions within a fixed system, but following various lines of modern thinking about metaphor—as has been tried in this chapter—may help to elucidate some of the problems, and to have begun the investigation, even without hope to arrive at a final conclusion, is perhaps the only choice available in such a vast field as metaphor.

terminologically by Hermogenes in *On Types* (περὶ ἰδεῶν), and by other ancient writers treating *idea*-theory may give an impression of the problem. Cf. now Rutherford (1998), 6 ff.

4
Plato on Metaphors and Models

E. E. PENDER

1. Introduction

The role of metaphors and models in developing ideas and creating new theories has in recent times been the subject of much attention in various disciplines, particularly science and the social sciences.[1] Debate, once centred on the poetic or rhetorical potential of metaphor, has now shifted to metaphor's key role in developing understanding and shaping experience. In this chapter I should like to set out Plato's account of the role of *eikones* and *paradeigmata*—'images' and 'models'—in argument and inquiry, showing that in considering both the capacities and limitations of these devices Plato developed a consistent position and achieved valuable insights which anticipate various contemporary ideas on the cognitive significance of metaphors and models.

2. Plato on the cognitive role of metaphor

a. How does Plato refer to metaphor?

Plato does not use the rhetorical term μεταφορά[2] and there is no separate term in the dialogues for metaphor as distinct from other types of image and comparison. Rather, Plato uses *eikon*

[1] e.g. Black (1962); Hesse (1966); Kuhn (1970); Ricoeur (1978); Lakoff and Johnson (1980); Johnson (1981); van Noppen (1983); Soskice (1985); Kittay (1987); McFague (1987); Kearns (1987); Leary (1990); Sternberg (1990); Ortony (1993*a*); Gibbs (1994); Barnes (1996).

[2] The noun μεταφορά does not occur either as a rhetorical or non-rhetorical term, but the related verb μεταφέρω is used in the non-rhetorical sense of 'carry across, transfer' (*Timaeus* 58b and 73e).

('figure, image, likeness') as a general term for images, comparisons, and likenesses, along with other more specific terms, such as ὁμοίωσις ('likeness', 'comparison') and εἴδωλον ('image', 'likeness'). The noun *eikon* and the related verb ἀπεικάζω ('express by a comparison; liken, compare with') are general terms for comparisons and illustrations in Plato, but they also refer explicitly to metaphors. In his examination of the use of *eikon* in ancient texts, Marsh H. McCall has shown how *eikon* refers to simile as well as to other rhetorical comparisons. His conclusion, that the most common rhetorical usage of *eikon* in Plato is in the general sense of 'illustration', 'image', 'comparison', would seem correct,[3] but his view that the term *eikon* is never a synonym for metaphor[4] requires qualification. For *eikon* is used to refer to metaphor at *Meno* 72a and *Republic* 531b,[5] and there are other terms in Plato which point to this figure. The defining feature of metaphor is that of a semantic clash which forces the reader to resolve the incompatibility between tenor and vehicle and their different domains of reference.[6] Such a 'clash' between a particular word and its context can be seen in both the *Meno* and *Republic* passages.

At *Meno* 72a Socrates has asked Meno to explain his idea of virtue and Meno replies that there are different virtues for men, women, children, old men, free men, and slaves. Socrates then comments, rather wryly (72a6): 'I seem to be enjoying a great piece of good luck, Meno, if, when I was looking for a single excellence, I have found a swarm of excellences in your posses-

[3] McCall (1969), 17: 'The total impression of Plato's concept of εἰκών is hardly in doubt. Of the four instances in which the term refers at least in part to simile, all but one [*Symposium* 215a] allow in fact considerable latitude of meaning. More than a dozen other instances show εἰκών in an unambiguous sense of "illustration", "image", "comparison". This is certainly Plato's understanding of the term.' For the use of *eikon* in these senses, see McCall (1969), 15–17.

[4] Commenting on *Phaedrus* 267c, McCall (1969: 5) observes: 'Nothing in the context narrows εἰκονολογία to any specific form of likeness, let alone equates it with metaphor (μεταφορά) for which the simple term εἰκών is never a synonym.' Kirby (1997: 530 n. 46) accepts McCall's point that whereas *eikon* does refer to simile, it does not refer to metaphor.

[5] McCall cites *Meno* 72a in a footnote (1969: 14), and discusses *Republic* 531b at (1969), 16.

[6] In seeing semantic clash as the defining feature of metaphor, I follow the tradition of Richards (1936) and Ricoeur (1978) amongst others, as explained in Pender (2000), 3–6.

sion' (*Πολλῇ γέ τινι εὐτυχίᾳ ἔοικα κεχρῆσθαι, ὦ Μένων, εἰ μίαν ζητῶν ἀρετὴν σμῆνός τι ἀνηύρηκα ἀρετῶν παρὰ σοὶ κείμενον*).[7] The phrase *σμῆνος ἀρετῶν* ('swarm of excellences') offers the semantic clash that is distinctive of metaphor, with a tenor (excellence, virtue) and vehicle (swarm of bees) juxtaposed with no explicit term of comparison.

At *Republic* 531b, *eikon* again refers to metaphor. In this section, Glaucon comments on students of musical harmony who engage in fruitless empirical experiments and Socrates replies (531b2–7):

> *Σὺ μέν, ἦν δ' ἐγώ, τοὺς χρηστοὺς λέγεις τοὺς ταῖς χορδαῖς πράγματα παρέχοντας καὶ βασανίζοντας, ἐπὶ τῶν κολλόπων στρεβλοῦντας· ἵνα δὲ μὴ μακροτέρα ἡ εἰκὼν γίγνηται πλήκτρῳ τε πληγῶν γιγνομένων καὶ κατηγορίας πέρι καὶ ἐξαρνήσεως καὶ ἀλαζονείας χορδῶν, παύομαι τῆς εἰκόνος καὶ οὔ φημι τούτους λέγειν.*
>
> You, said I, are speaking of the worthies who vex and torture the strings and rack them on the pegs. But—not to draw out the comparison with strokes of the plectrum and the musician's complaints of too responsive and too reluctant strings—I drop the figure, and tell you that I do not mean these people. (Trans. McCall 1969: 16)

The phrase *ταῖς χορδαῖς πράγματα παρέχοντας* ('causing trouble to the strings') is a metaphor, as it offers the novel presentation of musical strings as people, an idea further developed by *βασανίζοντας* and *στρεβλοῦντας* ('torturing' and 'racking'). It is possible to take these words literally in this context as they can mean 'testing' and 'tightening', both of which are appropriate to musical strings. But both terms carry very strong secondary senses of 'torturing' and 'stretching on the rack', and these senses are clearly activated, since the introductory phrase *πράγματα παρέχοντας* has already established the relationship of persecutor and victim. As there is a semantic incompatibility in the phrase *τοὺς ταῖς χορδαῖς πράγματα παρέχοντας* and as there is no explicit term of comparison between strings and people, *eikon* here refers to a metaphor rather than to a general type of illustration or comparison.

Apart from the noun *eikon*, Plato also uses verbs to indicate the presence of metaphor. First, as Stanford has shown,[8] a passage in the *Theaetetus* (180a) speaks of the verbal distortions

[7] Translation from Sharples (1985).

[8] Stanford (1936), 4.

(*μετωνομασμένῳ*) of the Heracliteans, where the use of the verb *μετονομάζειν* sounds very much like a reference to metaphor.[9] Second, the verb *ἀπεικάζω* is used to refer both to general types of comparison and illustration,[10] and to metaphor in particular.[11] In *Laws* book 2, the Athenian is discussing music and comments on the correct terms of musical appreciation (655a4–8):

> *ἀλλ' ἐν γὰρ μουσικῇ καὶ σχήματα μὲν καὶ μέλη ἔνεστιν, περὶ ῥυθμὸν καὶ ἁρμονίαν οὔσης τῆς μουσικῆς, ὥστε εὔρυθμον μὲν καὶ εὐάρμοστον, εὔχρων δὲ μέλος ἢ σχῆμα οὐκ ἔστιν ἀπεικάσαντα, ὥσπερ οἱ χοροδιδάσκαλοι ἀπεικάζουσιν, ὀρθῶς φθέγγεσθαι.*

> But music is a matter of rhythm and harmony, and involves tunes and movements of the body; this means that, while it is legitimate to speak of a 'rhythmical' or a 'harmonious' movement or tune, we cannot properly apply to either of them the chorus-masters' metaphor 'brilliantly coloured'. (Trans. Saunders 1970)

Here *ἀπεικάσαντα* and *ἀπεικάζουσιν* refer to the use of the description 'brilliantly coloured' when applied to movement or music, and thus the verb denotes the forming of an expression which is readily identified as a metaphor. The Athenian even makes explicit the point that this particular usage is not 'proper' (*ὀρθῶς*), a comment which anticipates Aristotle's discussion of metaphor among forms of speech which are not 'current' or 'standard'.[12]

Thus although he does not use the noun *μεταφορά*,[13] Plato does have various other means to refer to metaphor.

[9] A similar passage in the *Phaedrus* (267b) also refers to the creation of new ways of speaking, this time by the sophists.

[10] For examples of this general use of *ἀπεικάζω* and the related verb *εἰκάζω*, see *Phaedo* 76e2, 92b9, 99e6; *Cratylus* 431c4; *Theaetetus* 198d1; *Politicus* 297e9; *Parmenides* 137a3; *Symposium* 221d1, 4; *Phaedrus* 265b6; *Meno* 80c4, 98b1; *Republic* 404e1, 464b2, 488a2, 489c4; and *Laws* 905e6, 906d8, 964d8, 967c8.

[11] Outside rhetorical contexts *ἀπεικάζω*, along with its root verb *εἰκάζω*, is used for forming and expressing likenesses (*Cratylus* 414a9, 426e4; *Republic* 488a5; *Critias* 107d2, 107e3) and in the sense of 'serving as an image for' (*Cratylus* 432b3; *Philebus* 61c5). In the middle voice, *ἀπεικάζομαι* means 'make oneself like, copy' (*Republic* 369d4, 563a6) and in the passive 'to be made like, be made as a copy' (*Timaeus* 39e4).

[12] Aristotle's interpretation of metaphor (in *Poetics* and *Rhetoric*) is closely analysed by Ricoeur (1978), 10–43.

[13] Although his contemporary Isocrates does (*Euagoras* 9), as Stanford (1936: 3) notes.

b. The limitations and possibilities of eikones

As well as using *eikon* as a rhetorical term, Plato also uses it outside the rhetorical sphere for works of art,[14] reflections, shadows,[15] copies, and imitations.[16] In order to understand Plato's attitude towards verbal images, it is useful to try to clarify what the different types of images have in common. Each of these types of image is based on some sort of comparison or likeness between the two entities, *a* and *b*. In verbal images and illustrations object *a* is likened to *b* for the sake of comparison, as, for example, the soul is likened to the state throughout the *Republic*.[17] Both simile and metaphor establish a comparison between tenor and vehicle. Sculptors and artists aim to create likenesses of the originals when they create statues and representational paintings. The shape of visible reflections and shadows are like the objects which cast them, and copies and imitations are designed to be as alike as possible to their originals. Each image, then, is like the original in some way. But in each case there is both a primary (*a*) and secondary entity (*b*), and these are distinct from each other: in illustrations, comparisons, similes, and metaphors there is the original subject under discussion and the extraneous subject introduced for the sake of comparison (e.g. soul as state); in works of (representational) art the original entity is the artist's model of which a likeness is created; in reflections and shadows there is an original entity which casts a reflection in water or a shadow when illuminated in

[14] The term *eikon* is used of statues (*Phaedrus* 235d9 and *Critias* 116e5), and of paintings, the figures in paintings, the likenesses captured by paintings (*Cratylus* 424e3, 431c11–12; *Sophist* 236a8; *Philebus* 39b7), and artistic representations in general (*Protagoras* 312d3; *Laws* 669a7–b8 and 931a1). The term also denotes representation in music (*Laws* 668c7), and the likenesses created by actors on stage (*Laws* 935e5, *Philebus* 49c3). Finally, *eikon* is also used for the representations of good and bad characters in poetry (*Republic* 401b2).

[15] *Eikon* is used in the senses of visible reflection and shadow at *Phaedo* 99e1; *Republic* 402b5, 509e1, and 510e3.

[16] *Eikon* is an established term for copies or imitations in works of art but Plato also uses the term for the relationship between the phenomenal world and ultimate reality, as he depicts God the craftsman fashioning the universe (*Timaeus* 29b2–c2, 37d5–7, and 92c7). But *eikon* is also used in the sense of 'imitation' or 'copy' at *Republic* 402c6 where there is no such artistic or artisanal context.

[17] See e.g. 440ab, 559e–560e, and 590c8–591a3.

a particular way; and finally, in the case of copies and imitations, there is an original which the imitator attempts to reproduce as closely as possible and which serves as the standard against which the copy is to be measured, as can be seen in the example of an original and counterfeit coin. So, while there is some sort of likeness between original and image, there is clearly also a great and necessary difference, a point that is made at *Cratylus* 432d1–4:

ἢ οὐκ αἰσθάνῃ ὅσου ἐνδέουσιν αἱ εἰκόνες τὰ αὐτὰ ἔχειν ἐκείνοις ὧν εἰκόνες εἰσίν;
Ἔγωγε.[18]

Do you not perceive that images are very far from having qualities which are the exact counterparts of the realities which they represent?
Yes, I see. (Trans. Jowett 1892)

For Plato, 'image' and reality are different in important respects, and the reality or truth (that which is primary) is always and in all cases superior to the image (that which is secondary or derived).[19] The extended allegory of the cave in the *Republic* (514a–521c) shows that Plato was concerned with the gulf between image and reality and, moreover, considered images very much the inferiors of the realities they reflect or represent. As Richard Robinson[20] observes, 'Plato's whole theoretical philosophy is largely a condemnation of images and a struggle to get away from them'. In various passages throughout the dialogues, Plato stresses the deceptive nature of likenesses and the dangers of relying on them in argument.[21] For example, *Sophist* 231a6–8: 'But a cautious man should above all be on his

[18] See also *Cratylus* 432b.

[19] See e.g. comments at *Cratylus* 439a7–b3, *Republic* 533a1–4.

[20] Robinson (1953), 220.

[21] Some of these passages are discussed by Lloyd (1966: 394–400). Lloyd shows how Plato makes a firm distinction between an image or probable argument, on the one hand, and a proof or demonstration, on the other (394 ff. on *Phaedo* 92cd and *Theaetetus* 162e), and at times stresses that the conclusions suggested by certain analogies cannot be accepted without verification (400). Lane (1998: 19) also draws attention to Plato's concerns about likeness or resemblance: 'Resemblance is called into question in the *Protagoras*' doubts about similarity (331d1–e4), in the *Parmenides*' regress of likeness (132d1–133a7; cf. 147–8), in the *Philebus*' debate over whether all pleasures, and all forms of knowledge, must be like one another (12c–14a), in the *Sophist*'s warning about the slipperiness of resemblance (231a4–b1).'

guard against likenesses: they are a very slippery sort of thing' (τὸν δὲ ἀσφαλῆ δεῖ πάντων μάλιστα περὶ τὰς ὁμοιότητας ἀεὶ ποιεῖσθαι τὴν φυλακήν· ὀλισθηρότατον γὰρ τὸ γένος).[22] In such passages Plato is candid that 'likenesses' and 'images', εἰκόνες and ὁμοιότηται, can be deceptive.[23] But in other passages he offers a more positive view about their contribution to argument and thought.

Plato at times introduces the use of images and likenesses as a preliminary or second-best method of undertaking an inquiry. In the *Republic* at 506de Glaucon says that he and Adeimantus would be happy to hear an account of the Good presented in the same way as those on the other virtues. Socrates says that he cannot oblige and that instead he will present something that is 'most like it' (ὁμοιότατος ἐκείνῳ), namely the image of the sun. Similarly, when discussing the nature of reason in the *Laws* (897d ff.), the Athenian advises switching[24] from an examination of the object itself to an 'image' (*eikona*) of it (897d8–e2). Plato is critical of images and likenesses on the grounds that they are inferior to truth and reality but when he is unable to give a direct account of various objects or concepts, he uses images to tell what the objects or concepts are like, clearly believing this to be a worthwhile exercise.

Plato also explicitly acknowledges the didactic and illustrative power of images. In the *Laws* the Athenian presents an image of human beings as puppets in order to illustrate the nature of virtue, vice, and self-control, and introduces the image in the following way (644b9–c2, trans. Saunders 1970): 'Let's take up this point again and consider even more closely just what we mean. Perhaps you'll let me try to clarify the issue by means of an illustration' (σαφέστερον ἔτι τοίνυν ἀναλάβωμεν τοῦτ᾽ αὐτὸ ὅτι ποτὲ

[22] See Lloyd (1966), 395. Translation adapted from Cornford (1935).

[23] Kirby (1997: 531) observes that Plato does not 'provide a theory of metaphor as such', and perceives this as curious in the light of Plato's concern with *mimesis*: 'This is perhaps the more curious in view of the representational nature of metaphor. It would not overstate the case to say that Plato's whole ontology, at least . . . in the *Republic*, is rooted in semiotics . . . This fact problematizes for us not only Plato's deep absorption in the topic of mimesis but also the fact that he does not really address the relationship between mimesis and metaphor.' But the fact that Plato includes metaphor within the class of *eikones* and spends time exploring the relationship between images and mimesis shows that he did address this relationship. See Verdenius (1949).

[24] See also *Phaedrus* 246a.

λέγομεν. καί μοι δι' εἰκόνος ἀποδέξασθε ἐάν πως δυνατὸς ὑμῖν γένωμαι δηλῶσαι τὸ τοιοῦτον). Here the didactic usefulness of the image (*eikonos*) is highlighted, as it is again at *Critias* 107b. In the *Critias* the image of paintings of human and divine subjects is given to illustrate a point about discourses on these themes, and Critias says that he employs the image 'to make my meaning still clearer' (ἵνα δὲ σαφέστερον ὃ λέγω δηλώσω: 107b4–5). On numerous other occasions in the dialogues, images and illustrations not only clarify points but are also explicitly referred to as being used for this very purpose.[25] Plato is, however, careful not to suggest that images and likenesses offer a short-cut to understanding. In all cases the ideas and suggestions provided by imagery have to be supported by the conclusions of dialectic before they can be accepted as knowledge.

The evidence reviewed in this section comes in the form of scattered statements from different dialogues. These comments on the nature and capacities of verbal images present a consistent view of the role of likenesses in argument and inquiry but there is no single discussion devoted specifically to the cognitive role of *eikones*. However, Plato has provided such a discussion on the role of likenesses and similarities, a discussion which takes up and develops some of the themes of these scattered remarks. This is the discussion in the *Politicus* on the nature and significance of *paradeigmata*. This more sustained analysis offers further views on what can be achieved in argument and thought through the use of images and comparisons, and in this account Plato breaks new ground.[26] Under scrutiny in the *Politicus* is the whole question of discerning likeness and difference, and in this context Plato arrives at some valuable insights on models and metaphors.

[25] See e.g. *Gorgias* 517d; *Republic* 487e, 509a, 514a, 517ab; *Theaetetus* 198d; *Critias* 107b; *Laws* 644c, 720a–c, and 969b; and *Phaedo* 87b. On these passages, see Lloyd (1966), 394 and 400.

[26] Lane (preferring to translate *paradeigma* as 'example', as will be discussed below) notes the significance of the discussion (1997: 61): '[The Stranger's] analysis (277d–279a) is the longest and most detailed discussion of example as such, or any of its sisters—analogy, image, comparison—in Plato.'

3. Plato on the cognitive role of models

In the *Politicus* the Stranger and Young Socrates search for a definition of the statesman. The method of the search is that of singling out the statesman by identifying the differences between him and the other professionals engaged in similar civic activities.[27] To facilitate their search the Stranger turns to *paradeigmata* and explains their nature and powers, a discussion designed to illuminate the process of identifying likeness and difference.[28] As the arts of combination and division are closely examined, combination or 'collection' is categorized as bringing together those things that are alike, and separation or 'division' as breaking apart those that are different from one another. Dialectic becomes a method of collection and division, in which recognizing likeness is what allows concepts to be collected together and recognizing difference is what allows them to be divided—tasks that demand a high level of expertise (285ab). Weaving is also presented as an art of combining and dividing (281a, 282b, and 283a),[29] and following this model statesmanship becomes a process of collecting and dividing where appropriate (306a ff.). After distinguishing 'moderate' from 'courageous' men and, later, good from bad men, the Stranger says that every kind of expert knowledge will first separate out and discard the bad elements as far as possible (308c), and then from the good—both 'like' and 'unlike' (*ὁμοίων καὶ ἀνομοίων*)—will bring them 'all together into one'. Thus good government lies in distinguishing bad men from good, discarding the bad (by death, exile, or punishment, 309a) and then combining the two different types of good men (moderate and courageous) to form

[27] Rowe (1996: 159) observes: 'the statesman is progressively distinguished from all the other experts who look after the needs of the citizens'.

[28] Lane has rightly observed that this dialogue's contribution to the debate on the role of likeness in argument has been overlooked (1997: 18–19): 'The Stranger's use of division has been all too often, and all too quickly, assimilated to mentions of "division" elsewhere in Plato. Yet the bearing of his use of example on the images, analogies, similarities, comparisons of all kinds so prevalent throughout the dialogues has gone relatively unexplored.' The standard study of *paradeigma*, as set out in the *Politicus* and elsewhere, is Goldschmidt (1947).

[29] See Lane (1997), 54–6 on combining and separating in the Stranger's account of weaving.

the 'fabric' (ὕφασμα)[30] of society. Thus the ability to recognize likenesses and differences between groups is crucial. Finally, the art of using models (*paradeigmata*) in argument is itself revealed as the art of recognizing and pointing up the likenesses and differences between concepts.[31]

Although the traditional translation of *paradeigma* in the *Politicus* has been 'example',[32] more recently Rowe (1995) and Rosen (1995) have opted for 'model' since, they argue, it captures more accurately what Plato envisaged by the term.[33] In his commentary on 277d1–2 Rowe explains why 'example' is an unsuitable translation (1995: 201):

> 'Models' are *paradeigmata* . . . a term which may have its primary use in the creative sphere (the artist's original or the architect's blueprint); it is also regularly used of precedents, exemplars or examples. Jowett and Skemp (e.g.) prefer 'example' in this context, but this seems less than wholly appropriate: what E[leatic] S[tranger] is leading up to is the use of an analysis of weaving to illustrate the structure of 'the kingly art', which—he will claim—is analogous to that of weaving; and weaving is scarcely an 'example' of ruling. (Something will then be a 'paradigm' or 'model' of or for something else in this context if it offers an illuminating *analogy* . . .)

Rowe's interpretation of Plato's use of the term *paradeigma* seems to me correct, since what is analysed in the dialogue is indeed the use of weaving as an 'illuminating analogy' for politics.

In his chapter entitled 'Paradigms'[34] Rosen discusses the question of how best to translate *paradeigma* and notes how 'model' and 'example' are related (1995: 79): 'The two translations can be combined by noting that a model is an example

[30] *Politicus* 306a3, 311a1, 311b7, and 311c2.

[31] Rosen observes the similarity between these different arts (1995: 102): 'In general, we see the underlying similarity of diaeresis, spelling, weaving and politics', and later, including models (111): 'Analysis depends on the intuition of analogies . . . both the perception of analogies and the employment of diaeresis depend on the perception of like and unlike.'

[32] 'Example' is the preferred translation of Campbell (1867), Jowett (1892), Fowler (in Fowler and Lamb 1925), Skemp (1952), and Taylor (1961).

[33] But other critics in recent times have used alternatives: Lane explains how she prefers 'the deceptively ordinary connotations of "example"' (1997: 46); and Waterfield (in Annas and Waterfield 1995) avoids both model and example in favour of 'illustration'.

[34] Rosen (1995), 81–97.

selected or constructed because it seems to illuminate all members of a single class.' In this way Rosen, like Rowe, observes that the role of a paradigm or model is to illuminate, a point which is central to Plato's use of the term. Rosen examines the ordinary usage of the two English terms 'model' and 'example' (81), concluding that there is a difference in how the words are ordinarily understood and that the differentiated use of 'model' depends upon an understanding of it as 'some kind of abstract entity or conceptual construction that allows us to understand' (82). It is this illustrative function of *paradeigmata* that determines his translation (83):

> The Stranger has just introduced the general case of paradigms, such as the use of the figures of the shepherd in the diaeresis and the divine helmsman in the immediately preceding mythical presentation. These were not merely examples of the nature of the king but were intended to illustrate the essential nature of the royal art.

Thus Rosen prefers to translate the term as 'model', a term which we use 'to refer to a standard, rule, or some other conceptual entity' (1995: 83). I accept these arguments and thus take the discussion on *paradeigmata* in the *Politicus* as evidence for a Platonic view of models.

The discussion begins at 277d, as the interlocutors consider the shortcomings of their previous account of the statesman. At this point the Stranger rather abruptly switches the subject to *paradeigmata*, declaring (277d1–4):

> *Χαλεπόν, ὦ δαιμόνιε, μὴ παραδείγμασι χρώμενον ἱκανῶς ἐνδείκνυσθαί τι τῶν μειζόνων. κινδυνεύει γὰρ ἡμῶν ἕκαστος οἷον ὄναρ εἰδὼς ἅπαντα πάντ' αὖ πάλιν ὥσπερ ὕπαρ ἀγνοεῖν.*
>
> It's a hard thing, my fine friend, to demonstrate [sufficiently] any of the greater subjects without using models. It looks as if each of us knows everything in a kind of dreamlike way, and then again is ignorant of everything as it were when awake.[35]

When this rather cryptic statement draws a puzzled response from Young Socrates, the Stranger asserts that 'the idea of a "model" itself in its turn also has need of a model to demonstrate it' (277d9–10). Before considering this 'model of a model', it is worth establishing the precise nature of the claim at 277d as to

[35] Translations of the *Politicus* are from Rowe (1995).

the cognitive role of a *paradeigma*. The Stranger says, then, that it is 'difficult' to demonstrate sufficiently any of the 'greater' subjects (*τῶν μειζόνων*) without using models. This is the claim that models play an important role in presenting adequate demonstrations of certain subjects. It is not the claim that without models this process is impossible, but merely that without models it is more difficult. Although it is left unclear what exactly a sufficient demonstration consists of, there is a relevant point here about the acquisition of knowledge. After making the statement about models the Stranger moves to a new idea: it seems that each of us (presumably the 'us' refers to human beings) knows everything but again is ignorant of everything. We know everything 'as a dream' (*οἷον ὄναρ*) but are ignorant of everything 'as a waking vision/as reality' (*ὥσπερ ὕπαρ*). This image of dream and waking states for ignorance and knowledge is common in Plato and earlier thought.[36] Although there is no explicit link between the first and second sentences, the train of the Stranger's thought seems to be: (i) certain subjects are difficult to demonstrate without models; (ii) these things are difficult to demonstrate because we do not have adequate knowledge of them; (iii) our knowledge of everything is in fact deficient. The move from the statement about models to that of our general poor state of knowledge suggests that models can form part of our attempts to gain knowledge, and this point is made explicit later in the dialogue where again the Stranger uses the dream/waking image (278e), a passage which will be discussed below.

The text at 277d1, then, indicates that models can help to give demonstrations in the wider attempt to gain knowledge. The particular subjects that are difficult to demonstrate without models are the 'greater' ones. The nature of these is not explained here, but in the course of the dialogue a coherent distinction emerges between those subjects which are concrete, corporeal, visible, tangible, and less important and those which are abstract, incorporeal, invisible, intangible, and more important.[37] In

[36] References in Plato include: *Symposium* 175e3; *Republic* 476c8, 476d3–4, 520c6–7, 533b8–c1, and 534cd; and *Phaedrus* 277d10. The contrast occurs again in *Politicus* at 278e10–11 and 290b7. For discussion of the motif, see Gallop (1971). For earlier uses of the contrast, see *Odyssey* 19.547 and 20.90; Pindar, *Olympian* 13.67; Heraclitus 22 B1, 73, and 89 DK.

[37] See Lane (1997), 61–75, and my discussion (Pender 2000: 52–6).

terms of the scheme established in the *Politicus*, there is a clear dichotomy between everyday, familiar, concrete objects and difficult, abstract concepts, and this dichotomy provides the framework for various statements on language and art/crafts. For, on the one hand, those who are less intelligent are concerned about everyday objects which can be demonstrated to the senses, while the more intelligent are concerned with abstract, conceptual matters that rely on language (285d10–286b1). There are two types of demonstration fit for two levels of ability: demonstration in speech and discourse for the intelligent, and demonstration in painting and handicrafts for the less intelligent.[38] Once in the realm of speech and discourse, however, there is still a new distinction to be made, for while ordinary speech and discourse is adequate for explaining many subjects, there are still those which require something more: namely, the use of a verbal model. There are, then, three levels of demonstration: through painting/handicrafts; through discourse; and through models in speech. It is thus perhaps a typical Platonic irony that models in speech, just like verbal *eikones*, themselves come to be spoken of as paintings and artistic objects.[39]

The model that the Stranger uses to illustrate how models work is that of children learning their letters (277e). This way of learning is shown to depend on the successful recognition of similar elements in different combinations: the children first become familiar with individual letters and then learn to recognize them in longer and more difficult combinations. At 278ab the Stranger explains the process of learning to read and—simultaneously—how models work in cognition:

Ἆρ᾽ οὖν οὐχ ὧδε ῥᾷστον καὶ κάλλιστον ἐπάγειν αὐτοὺς ἐπὶ τὰ μήπω γιγνωσκόμενα;

Πῶς;

Ἀνάγειν πρῶτον ἐπ᾽ ἐκεῖνα ἐν οἷς ταὐτὰ ταῦτα ὀρθῶς ἐδόξαζον, ἀναγαγόντας δὲ τιθέναι παρὰ τὰ μήπω γιγνωσκόμενα, καὶ παραβάλλοντας ἐνδεικνύναι τὴν αὐτὴν ὁμοιότητα καὶ φύσιν ἐν ἀμφοτέραις οὖσαν ταῖς συμπλοκαῖς, μέχριπερ ἂν πᾶσι τοῖς ἀγνοουμένοις τὰ δοξαζόμενα ἀληθῶς

38 See Lane (1997), 70–5; Owen (1973).

39 *Politicus* 277a–c. Cf. *Politicus* 297e12–13; *Republic* 377e1–3, 488a, 588b–d; *Laws* 898b; *Critias* 107a7–b4 and 107c6–d2 (discussed at Pender 2000: 64–8). On the use of the art image in *Politicus*, see Rosen (1995), 78; Scodel (1987), 99–100.

παρατιθέμενα δειχθῇ, δειχθέντα δέ, παραδείγματα οὕτω γιγνόμενα, ποιήσῃ τῶν στοιχείων ἕκαστον πάντων ἐν πάσαις ταῖς συλλαβαῖς τὸ μὲν ἕτερον ὡς τῶν ἄλλων ἕτερον ὄν, τὸ δὲ ταὐτὸν ὡς ταὐτὸν ἀεὶ κατὰ ταὐτὰ ἑαυτῷ προσαγορεύεσθαι.

Well then, isn't this the easiest and best way of leading them on to the things they're not yet recognizing?

What way?

To take them first back to those cases in which they were getting these same things right, and having done that, to put these beside what they're not yet recognizing, and by comparing them demonstrate that *there is the same kind of thing with similar features in both combinations*, until the things that they are getting right have been shown set beside all the ones that they don't know, and once they have been shown like this, and so become models, they bring it about that each of all the individual letters is called both different, on the basis that it is different from the others, and the same, on the basis that it is always the same as and identical to itself, in all syllables.

The act of learning a new word thus becomes the recognition of the same letters when presented in different formations—both when presented individually and in the longer unfamiliar syllables. As they learn to read and spell the children are led to discern that *there is the same kind of thing with similar features in both combinations* (τὴν αὐτὴν ὁμοιότητα καὶ φύσιν ἐν ἀμφοτέραις οὖσαν ταῖς συμπλοκαῖς). Learning to read and to spell requires the ability to distinguish like and unlike, as indeed does using models—a point made explicitly by the Stranger at 278c2–7:

> Οὐκοῦν τοῦτο μὲν ἱκανῶς συνειλήφαμεν, ὅτι παραδείγματός γ' ἐστὶ τότε γένεσις, ὁπόταν ὂν ταὐτὸν ἐν ἑτέρῳ διεσπασμένῳ δοξαζόμενον ὀρθῶς καὶ συναχθὲν περὶ ἑκάτερον καὶ συνάμφω μίαν ἀληθῆ δόξαν ἀποτελῇ;
>
> Φαίνεται.

Well then, have we grasped this point adequately, that we come to be using a model *when, being the same thing in something different and distinct*, it is correctly identified, and having been brought together with the original thing, it brings about a single true judgement about each separately and both together?

It seems so.

This passage, although difficult,[40] establishes that a model arises

[40] Scodel identifies this whole section (277e2–278e12) as one of the most difficult in Plato's work (1987: 104): 'This passage must be regarded as among the most difficult to interpret and to understand in the entire Platonic corpus.'

when a correct identification and judgement is made about the presence of 'the same thing in something different and distinct'. Indeed for Plato the model *is* the same element that is present in the two different entities. The likeness is not just one perceived but one that is objectively present, otherwise the model could not work, a point which Rosen stresses (1995: 93): 'a model is the conception of the sameness of two distinct instances'; and later (95): 'To see the same form, property or element in another is to see the same in the other, or sameness in otherness. This is the essential nature of the paradigm.'

So for Plato a model works through recognition of a common element present in two different entities, *x* and *y*, where *x* is an easier and more familiar entity and *y* is a more difficult, unfamiliar entity. In using *x* as a model for *y* the thinker is making a comparison (τιθέναι παρά, παραβάλλοντας: 278a9–b1) between *x* and *y*, so that the familiar features of *x* become discernible in the unfamiliar context of *y*. Thus, when weaving comes to be used as a model for statesmanship, this process can only work if there are common elements present—not just hypothesized but objectively there—in both weaving and statesmanship. If the common element is not objectively present, then recognition cannot take place. To use Plato's own example, if the same letter were not present in an unfamiliar, longer combination, then the child would not be able to recognize something familiar, and so would not be able to learn the new, difficult word.[41]

The third main passage relevant to Plato's views on the nature and role of models is 278e, where the Stranger draws the excursus on models to a close and returns to the theme of how to isolate the statesman for the purpose of definition. In this

Scodel's own translation of 278c runs: 'An example comes into being whenever the same entity, existing in a pair of media which are separated and dispersed from one another, can be correctly judged (in the case of one of them) and, through comparison (and combination with the other), makes it possible for one (and the same) true judgement to be entertained of either of them, since both are the same? Apparently.'

[41] The same point about common elements is made at 278c8–d6 where the Stranger applies the model of learning letters to learning about the world, using the metaphor of the 'letters and syllables of everything'. Here again recognition depends upon 'the same things' (ταὐτά) being present in the smaller constituents and the longer combinations.

passage the Stranger justifies their digression on models on the grounds that it helped to further their inquiry into statesmanship. Their intention, the Stranger maintains, was to find a 'small' model to apply to the greater case of the statesman/king, a strategy which would serve a particular purpose, as he explains (278e9–11):

διὰ παραδείγματος ἐπιχειρεῖν αὖ τὴν τῶν κατὰ πόλιν θεραπείαν τέχνῃ γνωρίζειν, ἵνα ὕπαρ ἀντ' ὀνείρατος ἡμῖν γίγνηται.

In an attempt once more through the use of a model to recognize in an expert, systematic way what looking after those in the city is, so that it may be present to us in our waking state instead of in a dream.

Thus the model (which will be that of weaving: 279b2) will be used in the attempt to make kingship present to the interlocutors in a waking rather than a dream state. This is entirely consistent with the idea that models play an important role in helping to demonstrate difficult subjects. For by examining the model and the points of contact it highlights between the objects or domains compared, the thinker is able to transform his hazy ideas (a dream state) on difficult subjects into more secure and more rigorous understanding (a waking state). The transformation is effected through the systematic testing of the model, a point conveyed by the phrase *τέχνῃ γνωρίζειν*. Rowe[42] has observed the significance of this detail, which seems to mark out for Plato one of the differences between model and metaphor:

The careful explanation of the use of 'models' in 277e–278e is fascinating for a number of reasons; but not least for its implications for the understanding of metaphor. The controlled use of *παραδείγματα* is what the philosopher substitutes for metaphor (NB 278e10 *τέχνῃ γνωρίζειν*—'recognize/understand in an expert, systematic way'): by separating out the comparanda, and looking at them apart, he can then see exactly what they have in common and use that to illuminate what he is looking for (see esp. 278a–c).

Plato's insight that the use of a model can provide a way of analysing a subject in a controlled and systematic way goes beyond any of his claims for the use of images. Although *paradeigmata* and *eikones* are clearly related for Plato, it does seem that he is striving to convey that a model can offer a more secure basis for understanding than an image or metaphor.

[42] Rowe (1996), 163 n. 25.

In terms of the relationship between *paradeigmata* and *eikones* as used within inquiry, Plato recognizes that both bring together two different domains for the purposes of gaining understanding. In the dominant model (*paradeigma*) of the dialogue, the physical activities of weaving are compared with the business of governing a city and the language of weaving is transposed into the political realm. This is just one of many comparisons that can be made between government and other arts, comparisons that can take different forms. At 297e8–12 the Stranger speaks of two other comparisons for the art of statesmanship and in this case refers to them as *eikones*:

> *Εἰς δὴ τὰς εἰκόνας ἐπανίωμεν πάλιν, αἷς ἀναγκαῖον ἀπεικάζειν ἀεὶ τοὺς βασιλικοὺς ἄρχοντας.*
> *Ποίας;*
> *Τὸν γενναῖον κυβερνήτην καὶ τὸν ἑτέρων πολλῶν ἀντάξιον ἰατρόν.*
>
> Well then, let's go back to the likenesses to which we must always compare our kingly rulers.
> Which likenesses?
> The noble steersman and the doctor who is 'worth many others'.

They must always compare the king/statesman to the likenesses of steersman and doctor because, presumably, they help to clarify the nature of kingship.[43] In this reference to the arts of steering and of medicine as images for ruling, Plato acknowledges that applying different frameworks (weaving, steering, healing) to a concept at issue (statesmanship) can be undertaken through the form both of a *paradeigma* and an *eikon*. Indeed it seems fair to conclude that on Plato's own terms use of an *eikon* can come very close to use of a *paradeigma*, since both can point up similarities as part of an attempt to achieve knowledge. So where for Plato does the difference between *paradeigma* and *eikon* (as used in inquiry) lie? The answer seems to be in the extent to which the comparison suggested can be tested and found to be useful in discovering a structural similarity between *x* and *y*. An image/metaphor can suggest a likeness or resemblance between the two subjects but if upon analysis this likeness leads to the discovery of a significant structural framework of

[43] Rowe (1995: 227 ad loc.) leaves the implication as a question: 'i.e. because they so clearly help to illustrate the structure of kingship—the role in it of expert knowledge, and its purpose of caring for those ruled?'

resemblances and analogies, along with common elements, then the image/metaphor can be said to have become a 'model'. The working out of such an extended structural framework requires sustained comparison, a cognitive process very different from that of interpreting an individual image or metaphor, which is typically a brief statement. Thus while Plato names the extended comparison between weaving and politics in the *Politicus* a *paradeigma* (e.g. at 305e8), the other comparisons which here remain undeveloped and untested he refers to simply as *eikones*.

4. Plato's conclusions, contemporary debate, and the question of knowledge

Now that the main evidence has been considered, it is time to draw together Plato's conclusions on the nature and role of models and assess how his account in the *Politicus* anticipates various aspects of the contemporary debate.

For Plato, a model (*paradeigma*) is like an image (*eikon*) in that it involves comparing two different domains. Plato identifies models as a developed form of language use, which is needed to illustrate difficult subjects. He recognizes that the same sort of analogies can be prompted by the use of images but where an *eikon* is typically brief and undeveloped, a *paradeigma* is an extended comparison developed specifically to explore structural similarities and differences.[44] Further, models (unlike images which depend merely upon likeness) can work only when a common element is present between the familiar x and the unfamiliar y which it is used to illustrate or explain (for example, where the same letter is present in a shorter and longer combination). Working out how many and what exactly the common elements are between weaving and governing becomes a means of discovering the nature of statesmanship. In Lane's

[44] Similarly, in recent discussions which consider the relationship between model and metaphor, critics reserve the term 'metaphor' for an individual phrase which brings together terms active in two different domains and use 'model' for an extended conceptual structure developed through the process of analogical thinking. See Black (1962), 238; Soskice (1985), 101; Kearns (1987), 40–1; Pribram (1990), 79, 97–8. Also McReynolds (1990), 137: 'The term "model", it seems to me, should be (and typically is) restricted to the more complex, deliberative attempts to construct predictive replicas (physical, conceptual, or mathematical) of given natural domains.'

words, 'Example reveals what is common, a matter of self-same identity, and what is different and so achieves a clarification of each entity being compared' (1997: 69). It is by this clarification of likeness and difference that the interlocutors are able to differentiate statesmanship from the other arts that lay claim to the title. Thus there is the emphatic statement at 279a1–6:

> Then we must take up once again what we were saying before, to the effect that since tens of thousands of people dispute the role of caring for cities with the kingly class, what we have to do is to separate all these off and leave the king on his own (*δεῖ δὴ πάντας ἀποχωρίζειν τούτους καὶ μόνον ἐκεῖνον λείπειν*); and it was just for this purpose that we said we needed a model (*καὶ πρὸς τοῦτο δὴ παραδείγματος ἔφαμεν δεῖν τινος ἡμῖν*).
>
> Very much so (*καὶ μάλα*).

Therefore the model is regarded as a device which is able to 'separate off' the king from all other claimants to the art of caring for cities, and is thus defined principally as a means of establishing similarities and distinctions.

Although it has been argued that models in the *Politicus* are identified as performing simply a didactic role,[45] this view is not supported by the text and has been challenged by various critics. Lloyd, for example, remarks (1966: 399) that the use of paradigms in the search for the statesman is undoubtedly heuristic, since 'in the problem in hand they are not being taught the definition of the kingly art by someone who already knows it—they are attempting to discover it for themselves'. And, more recently, Lane has argued that the sharp differentiation of teaching and learning is out of place in an assessment of Plato's work and that the use of 'example' is shown to offer 'a genuine epistemic advance' (1997: 68–9). Since the debate on *paradeigmata* does point to a role for models that goes beyond the narrowly didactic, Plato can be seen as a forerunner of contemporary critics who recognize the important contribution that models and metaphors can make in exploring ideas and achieving new insights. Recent scholarship has analysed the cognitive roles of metaphors and models in disciplines as diverse as neuropsychology, geography, and theology. A dizzying array of competing views has emerged but there is at least consensus on the point that metaphors and models are cognitively

[45] Robinson (1953), 213.

significant in that they stimulate new ways of understanding. Critics have described the way this works in various terms but one of the standard accounts is that of Max Black (1962). Black, developing his 'interactionist' view of metaphor, observes (1962: 236–7):

A memorable metaphor has the power to bring two separate domains into cognitive and emotional relation by using language directly appropriate to the one as a lens for seeing the other; the implications, suggestions, and supporting values entwined with the literal use of the metaphorical expression enable us to see a new subject matter in a new way . . . Much the same can be said about the role of models in scientific research . . . Use of a particular model may amount to nothing more than a strained and artificial description of a domain sufficiently known otherwise. But it may also help us to notice what otherwise would be overlooked, to shift the relative emphasis attached to details—in short, to *see new connections*.

Black's discussion (along with its language of *seeing*) is an important influence on Eva Kittay's analysis of metaphor, which she names 'perspectival'. She explains (1987: 13–14):

To call our theory perspectival is to name it for the function metaphor serves: to provide a perspective from which to gain an understanding of that which is metaphorically portrayed. This is a distinctively cognitive role. Since *perspectival* implies a subject who observes from a stance, we can say that metaphor provides the linguistic realization for the cognitive activity by which a language speaker makes use of one linguistically articulated domain to gain an understanding of another experiential or conceptual domain, and similarly, by which a hearer grasps such an understanding.

The re-structuring process offers a new perspective on the given concept, and the adjustment to the new view is termed a 'perspectival shift' (1987: 301) or 'reconceptualization' (302). The view that metaphors work cognitively by providing new ways of seeing and understanding also pervades the multidisciplinary study, *Metaphor and Thought*.[46] Plato's discussion of models and images reveals that he had grasped the essential point that new understanding can be achieved through viewing a less familiar concept through the 'lens' of a more familiar concept. Thus the model of weaving will allow the interlocutors

[46] Ortony (1993*a*); see the introductory essay, Ortony (1993*b*).

to gain understanding of the more complex art of statesmanship through the sort of 'reconceptualization' described by Kittay.

So far so good: Plato anticipates the contemporary consensus that metaphors and models prompt new insights that can be extremely useful in developing ideas and gaining understanding. But when one probes the question further, to try to establish the actual status of such insights, the consensus of contemporary criticism dissolves and Plato's position becomes harder to discern. The question of what exactly is achieved by looking at *y* through the lens of *x* raises perplexing issues of knowledge, reality, truth, and verification. In the nineteenth century, as is well documented, thinkers maintaining the positivist approach were apt to see metaphorical or analogical accounts as provisional versions of theories which would later be set out in more direct and literal terms.[47] The twentieth century has produced a wide and varied range of challenges to the positivist view and discussion of metaphor has often taken place within analysis of wider issues of knowledge and reality. Ortony (1993*b*: 1–2) comments on the shift:

> A basic notion of positivism was that reality could be precisely described through the medium of language in a manner that was clear, unambiguous, and, in principle, testable—reality could, and should, be literally describable . . . A different approach is possible, however, an approach in which any truly veridical epistemological access to reality is denied. The central idea of this approach is that cognition is the result of mental *construction* . . . This general orientation is the hallmark of the relativist view . . . that the objective world is not directly accessible but is constructed on the basis of constraining influences of human knowledge and language. In this kind of view . . . language, perception, and knowledge are inextricably intertwined.

If one accepts that reality is constructed through one's perception of it, then the new perspectives occasioned by metaphor take on a very different status and importance than on the positivist view, which presupposes a reality that is independent of human perception. Such a 'constructivist' or 'relativist' view of reality underlies the assessments of metaphor offered by, amongst

[47] See e.g. Gibbs (1994), 169–72; Johnson (1981), 16–18. Johnson explains how the positivist view of metaphor (17) 'is actually a version of the traditional centuries-old empiricist critique of metaphor'. On the empiricist view, see Lakoff and Johnson (1980), 190–2.

many others, Black, and Lakoff and Johnson, and it is clear that new approaches to the nature of reality and how we refer to it have opened up the subject of metaphor in very fruitful ways. The disputes about metaphor's relation to reality and its role in producing knowledge are complex indeed, and my purpose in raising these matters is simply to establish that the way a thinker judges the cognitive role of metaphor is (understandably) affected by his or her position on the question of how we gain and what actually constitutes knowledge.

So where does Plato stand on the question of metaphor's role in producing knowledge? Plato holds that reality exists independently of our perception of it, that knowledge of the truths of reality can be achieved, and, as shown above, that the gulf between image and reality remains firmly fixed. In line with these views his position on *eikones* is that they are a second-best method, unable on their own to provide direct access to the truth. But is this also the case with *paradeigmata*? Do conceptual models always remain a second-best method in Plato's view? Or does his account of models in the *Politicus* suggest that likenesses and images can produce knowledge? The key issue here is whether the model is expected to *prove* anything about the nature of statesmanship or expected merely to suggest propositions which would have to be verified by other means before being accepted as actual knowledge. Whereas one might expect Plato to draw a firm distinction between the insights prompted by models, on the one hand, and knowledge, on the other, Lane has argued that *paradeigmata* in the *Politicus* are presented as actually producing knowledge, a position which she herself admits is 'radical' (1997: 63) and even 'startling' (64).

Beginning with the children's situation in regard to their shaky grasp of words (62), Lane establishes that example (63): 'is the remedy prescribed to stabilize this precarious position and allow intellectual progress to be made'. This remedy, which she rightly sees as a 'dynamic method of comparison' (63), is indeed a means to allow intellectual progress, but does this intellectual progress constitute knowledge? On Lane's interpretation it does (63–4):

> In the description of the faltering children, their grasp of the letters in the shorter syllables is twice referred to in words deriving from 'belief' (278a9, b3). And in the explicit introduction to the topic of example we

were told that example is intimately and universally connected to the instability in 'the human experience of knowledge' (277d7). The implication, and it is a radical one, is that example constitutes a path from true belief to knowledge . . . This comprehensive framing of example as an explanation of the movement from dream- to waking- (i.e. genuine) knowledge holds despite the fact that the analytical summary of example will describe its yield as the formation of a 'single true *doxa*' (278c6) or judgment/belief. Despite the use of *doxa* here, the framing issue of knowledge decisively casts example in the role of successful path from true belief to knowledge.

I accept that the 'framing issue' of this section of the *Politicus* is knowledge (τὸ περὶ τῆς ἐπιστήμης πάθος: 277d7), but cannot accept (despite a certain equivocation in Plato's language)[48] that the *paradeigma* '*constitutes* a path from true belief to knowledge' or that it is identified as an 'explanation' of the movement from dream to waking knowledge. My judgement is based on the fact that in the debate on *paradeigmata*, after the initial 'framing remark' at 277d7, Plato studiously avoids the term ἐπιστήμη ('knowledge') and, despite some tantalizing suggestions, ultimately stops short of defining the insights stimulated by models as actual knowledge.

Lane herself acknowledges the crucial use of δόξα ('judgement', 'opinion') at 278c6 but other passages also reveal the same caution. The discussion of models in the *Politicus* uses the language of opinion, judgement, and discovery rather than that of knowledge and proof. There is talk of 'showing' which seems promising—at 277d1–2 it is 'difficult to *demonstrate* sufficiently' (χαλεπόν . . . ἱκανῶς ἐνδείκνυσθαι) any of the greater subjects without models, and at 278ab in the model of letters, the teacher leads the children on to understanding by *showing* (ἐνδεικνύναι) the common elements between words—but this verb does not necessarily denote proof. More telling is the passage at 278c, where the language is firmly that of opinion rather than knowledge, as the use of a model is defined as correctly *judging* (δοξαζόμενον ὀρθῶς) the same thing to be present in something different and distinct, so that it 'brings about a single true *judgement*' (μίαν ἀληθῆ δόξαν ἀποτελῇ). While ἀληθῆ ('true') is a strong term,[49] Plato is careful

[48] Scodel e.g. notes the 'grammatical and syntactic ambiguity' of 277e–278e (1987: 104).

[49] The vocabulary of 'truth' is also used at 277e8 (ἀληθῆ) and at 278d2 (ἀληθείας).

to use it alongside δόξα, which is reinforced by δοξαζόμενον in the preceding line and recalls the phrase τὰ δοξαζόμενα ἀληθῶς at 278b3. By this means he clarifies that the model produces true opinion not knowledge. Equally at 278e in the reference to dream and waking states, although the model is being used in an attempt to reach knowledge and truth, it is not stated that the model can achieve this on its own. Rather, use of the model seems to be conceived as part of an ongoing process, since the Stranger speaks only of the 'attempt' (ἐπιχειρεῖν) to recognize the nature of political tendance and since the statement about gaining knowledge comes in a final (ἵνα) rather than a consecutive clause. Plato is similarly circumspect in his language at 279ab. First at 279a7–b1 the Stranger speaks of the model as a means of discovering not the 'truth' but 'what is sought':

> *Τί δῆτα παράδειγμά τις ἄν, ἔχον τὴν αὐτὴν πολιτικῇ πραγματείαν, σμικρότατον παραθέμενος ἱκανῶς ἂν εὕροι τὸ ζητούμενον;*
>
> So what model, occupied in the same activities as statesmanship, on a very small scale, could one compare with it, and so discover in a satisfactory way what we are looking for?

And second, at 279b4–6 the model of weaving is described in a legal metaphor not as offering proof but as 'bearing witness':

> By Zeus, Socrates, if we don't have anything else to hand, well, there is weaving—do you want us to choose that? Not all of it, if you agree, since perhaps the weaving of cloth from wool will suffice; maybe it is this part of it, if we choose it, which would provide the testimony we want (τάχα γὰρ ἂν ἡμῖν καὶ τοῦτο τὸ μέρος αὐτῆς μαρτυρήσειε προαιρεθὲν ὃ βουλόμεθα).

Note also the hesitation in τάχα: *perhaps* the model will provide the witness they want. Since the legal image presents the interlocutors as bringing in the model of weaving as a witness, the model need not be seen as giving proof, but simply as lending a supporting voice to the Stranger's case.

In the light of these passages it seems to me that Plato's assessment of the power of models is ultimately careful and measured, claiming only that models can contribute to the effort to gain knowledge. Scodel has observed the cautiousness of this account, commenting (1987: 106): 'The predominant note struck in this passage (278c3–e10) is that of true opinion. This is a salient feature of the passage that has not been given sufficient emphasis.' On the issue of whether models are presented as able to turn opinion into knowledge, Scodel concludes that Plato does not give an answer (108):

> The method of paradigms described by the Stranger seems to give an adequate description of learning in the classroom but does little to distinguish between true opinion and knowledge, or to describe how, or even whether, the former is transformed into the latter. The Stranger elusively skirts questions of how first principles or ἀρχαί are known while managing to suggest that he has dealt with such questions.

I accept Scodel's point that Plato does not explain how the true opinion stimulated by the paradigm can be transformed into knowledge. The silence of the text on this central issue, alongside key passages that are at best ambiguous, prevents me from accepting Lane's claim that the *paradeigma* is presented as constituting a path from belief to knowledge. For although the goal of any inquiry is to reach knowledge, and although models are recognized as able to make a great contribution to this, it is not claimed that a model on its own can produce knowledge of statesmanship or any other of the 'greater' subjects.

However, I would not rule out the other conclusion reached by Lane on this issue, that true belief is transformed into knowledge for Plato through the dual method of *paradeigma* and *diaeresis* ('division') (1997: 65):

> Example also interacts with division, which effects revisions of common sense and expectations in the service of gaining a genuine understanding of the character or activity being investigated. Together the two constitute a method which retains true beliefs but achieves knowledge by drastically revising them.

A little later she again stresses that the achievement of knowledge requires the concerted action of *paradeigma* and division (66): 'Together and only together, for important topics, do these methods contribute to definitions relevant to and adequate for particular inquiries.' Scodel also sees a close relation between *paradeigma* and division (108): 'It seems inevitable . . . that the purpose of paradigms as envisaged by the Stranger here (278b5–c1) is precisely the same as that of diaeresis in the *Sophist* (253b8–e2), the recognition of εἴδη, of their possible combinations, and of the factors which make combination possible or impossible.' And it is worth noting that Rosen too holds that *diaeresis* is presented in the *Politicus* as leading to radical revisions of ideas, and new knowledge. He speaks of the Stranger 'reconceptualizing' (1995: 78) the nature of political activity, and maintains (at 115): '*diaeresis* is the method of perceptual and noetic vision and not simply a mechanical method for constructing concepts out of previously known elements'. Although the large and difficult topic of *diaeresis* is beyond the scope of this paper, I would like at least to register my general support for the approach taken by Lane in her second point on *paradeigmata*. For, since Plato evidently did regard knowledge as attainable, and since he did recognize that models could play a serious cognitive role, then it makes sense that he should recommend the use of models *alongside* other dialectical strategies as an effective means of gaining knowledge. While it seems to me that Plato stopped short of the claim that models could directly produce knowledge, he clearly did formulate the view that models could be an important supplement to other forms of reasoning and analysis.

To return to the question set earlier: it seems that in the end models, like images, do remain for Plato a second-best method. For although the *Politicus* reveals that Plato saw models as extremely useful cognitive tools, it does not claim that the use of models on their own can produce knowledge. Rather the discussion implies that while models can be extremely useful in gaining insights, once a conclusion can be reached and the truth attained (by a variety of means), the model can be dispensed with. Although this point is not made explicitly in the text, it follows from the comparison with children learning their letters. For while the children require a model when they do not know the difficult, complex word, once they do know it they no longer have recourse to the model. Similarly, the goal of the inquiry into statesmanship would seem to be the formulation of a definition of the statesman which no longer depended on the model and language of weaving.

To conclude: throughout his work Plato is careful to distinguish direct accounts of reality from versions relying on images or likenesses of it. *Eikones* and *paradeigmata* were for him at best heuristic devices, able to help the thinker to gain knowledge if used in the correct way—namely, in conjunction with other forms of argument and dialectical testing. Metaphor, imagery, and models are invaluable to Plato as a creative thinker and writer, but he seems ultimately to view both *eikones* and *paradeigmata* as supplements to and not substitutes for other types of reasoning. However, while accessing reality and gaining knowledge directly through dialectic may have remained his ideal, in his own writings metaphors, imagery, and models not only support but actually constitute various theories. But that is another story.[50]

[50] In Pender (2000), I have argued that while some metaphors and models can be replaced with alternative forms of discourse, others become integral and irreducible elements in Platonic theory.

5
Literary Metaphor and Philosophical Insight: The Significance of Archilochus

PAUL CROWTHER

To 'experience', in the most minimal sense, is to follow rules in relation to language, perception, and action. It is difficult to see how such a capacity could be formed and exercised in the absence of constants in the human condition. Such constants can be most easily identified at the level of perception and embodiment. They are, however, deeply entwined with our existence as rational and self-conscious beings. As Merleau-Ponty (1976: 170) observes: 'it is no mere coincidence that the rational being is also the one that holds himself upright or has a thumb which can be brought opposite to the fingers: the same manner of existing is evident in both aspects'.

This discussion will focus on the role of metaphor as a kind of junction between rational articulation and perception. Its general argument will be twofold. First, that the tensional structure of metaphor embodies a constant in human experience, which is capable of being expressed in different ways under different historical conditions; and, secondly, that literary metaphor (in this analysis I shall focus primarily on metaphor in poetry) is the clearest exemplar of this.

To establish these general points I shall, in Section I, analyse the logical characteristics of metaphor and the way in which they link predication and perception. I will further suggest that, whilst this linkage is not an overt focus of attention in the ordinary usage of metaphor, it is so in the literary context. In

I am indebted to J. O. Urmson, C. C. W. Taylor, and G. R. Boys-Stones for their critical comments on the original draft of this chapter.

Section II, I shall explore this possibility through its exemplification in Archilochus' use of metaphor.

I

Ricoeur (1978: 65) offers a useful 'nominal' definition of metaphor as follows: metaphor consists in 'giving an unaccustomed name to some other thing, which thereby is not being given its proper name'. However, even if metaphor hinges on a transposition of terms, it has further logical characteristics which, in conjunction with this, give it its peculiar linguistic potency.

Foremost amongst these is the fact that, since metaphor involves a kind of deliberate error, this can only be significant insofar as it occurs in a broader context of linguistic regularity—of conventional ordered usages. This is why Ricoeur, Emile Benveniste, and Max Black (among others) emphasize metaphor's discursive or sentential character. As Black (1962: 27) puts it, metaphor involves 'a sentence or another expression in which some words are used metaphorically while the remainder are used non-metaphorically'. (In the rest of this chapter I shall follow Black's practice in designating the metaphorical term as the 'secondary subject' and the non-metaphorical referent as the 'principal subject'.)

Now there are a number of reasons why the linking of metaphor and sentence are important. The first pertains to language itself. Following Strawson (1959) we can characterize the basic structural feature of language as that which permits singular identification. There is a fundamental polarity involved, which, as Ricoeur (1978: 71) puts it, 'on the one hand is rooted in named individuals, and on the other hand predicates qualities, classes, relations, and actions that in principle are universal. Language works on the basis of this dissymmetry between two functions.' The significance of this *vis-à-vis* metaphor is that, whilst having the character of a deliberate error, the secondary subject functions in the most formal terms as a feature predicated of the principal subject.

This predicative role, however, is an exceptional one. Starting from a metaphor that is not deadened by its frequent repetition, Nelson Goodman (1976: 69) claims that:

a metaphor is an affair between a predicate with a past and an object that yields while protesting. In routine projection, habit applies a label to a case not already decided. Arbitrary application of a newly coined label is equally unobstructed by prior decision. But metaphorical application of a label to an object defies an explicit or tacit prior denial of that label to that object. Where there is metaphor, there is conflict . . .

The point is, then, that in metaphor the predicated label gravitates around a formal element of incongruity. The predicative 'is' characterizes the primary subject in terms of a label which is, in the most literal terms, not applicable to it. The basic predicative structure of language is simultaneously and manifestly affirmed by form and denied by content. Metaphor is, in ontological terms, inherently tensional.

This carries a further implication. Since metaphor transgresses conventional literal usage, it is thereby conceptually tied to the notion of novelty in both an objective and subjective sense. The objective sense consists in the fact that at its point of emergence a metaphor defines itself as innovatory in relation to standard predicative practices surrounding its principal subject; the subjective (but more interesting) sense is that innovation of this sort presupposes wit or inventiveness in the one who formulates the metaphor for the first time. (I shall return to this issue.)

In logical terms, then, metaphor is a fundamentally predicative structure wherein a literally inappropriate term is applied to an item in a novel way. Kant judiciously notes the possibility of 'original nonsense';[1] so, mindful of this, one might ask what our criterion of a metaphor as opposed to merely nonsensical predication is. The answer is that a metaphor occurs when the act of untoward predication *works* in relation to the principal subject. But then, of course, we must ask what our criterion of 'works' in such a context is: what is the concrete function of metaphor?

In this respect, Black's theory proves instructive. He observes that (1962: 44–5):

the metaphor selects, emphasizes, suppresses and organizes features of the principal subject by implying statements about it that normally apply to the subsidiary subject.

Indeed, the metaphorical term draws, as Black (1962: 40) puts it, on a 'system of associated common-places' which pertain to

[1] Kant, *Critique of Judgement*, at Meredith (1978), 168.

opinions, values, beliefs, and institutions into which a member of a linguistic community is initiated through the very act of learning to speak. Black is, I think, right about the basic function of metaphor—which is the cognitive elucidation of a principal subject—but he is somewhat misleading about how this is achieved and the significance of the achievement. Ricoeur has suggested that what is lacking in Black's account is a sense of that key feature of metaphor which Aristotle noted, namely its capacity 'to set before the eyes'.[2] What this means, in effect, is that Black does not have an adequate theory of imagination. It could also be argued that Ricoeur's approach suffers from a similar failing.[3] However, rather than show the complex problems which beset Ricoeur's account, I shall instead address the central issue, namely how it is possible for a metaphorical term to offer cognitive elucidation of that to which it is applied.

In this respect, let us consider first how ordinary predication works. In order to articulate a proposition it is presupposed that such an articulation is consistent with the grammatical rules which govern the language of which it is a part. These rules constitute a kind of logical field in relation to which the sense of the proposition can be recognized. If the proposition is used to achieve singular identification in relation to the user's present perceptual field (and this ostensive function does seem to be the logically basic one), matters get rather more complex. For when propositions articulate perception, this perceptual discursiveness involves a latent field in addition to the rules of language.

To show this let us consider a simple example. I judge that the woman outside is wearing a red dress. This act of perceptual predication has what can be described as a perceptual sense as well as a linguistic one. The complex factors involved in perceptual sense have been powerfully illuminated by Merleau-Ponty. In relation to the example of perceiving a red dress, he describes how it is positioned as (1968: 132):

> a punctuation in the field of red things, which includes the tiles of roof tops, the flags of gatekeepers and of the revolution, certain terrains near Aix or in Madagascar, it is also a punctuation in the field of red garments

[2] Aristotle, *Rhetoric* 1405^b12, quoted in Ricoeur (1978), 207.

[3] Ricoeur makes much of Kant's notion of 'schematism' and its relation to the productive imagination. But whilst imagination plays a key role in metaphor it must be clearly linked to the structure of perception.

which includes, along with the dresses of women, robes of professors, bishops, and advocates general.

Any judgement concerning the red dress, therefore, is not *simply* an act of recognition. It is situated and defined in a broader perceptual and associational field. Hence, as Merleau-Ponty concludes (ibid.):

> If we took all these participations into account, we would recognize that a naked colour, and in general a visible, is not a chunk of absolutely hard, indivisible being, offered all naked to a vision which could be only total or null, but is rather a sort of straits between exterior horizons and interior horizons ever gaping open, something that comes to touch lightly and makes diverse regions of the coloured or visible world resound at the distances . . .

The point is, then, that predication in its most logically basic function—the articulation of perception—engages with the dimension of perceptual sense. Given a specific perceptual object, it is in principle possible to apply an infinite number of predicates to it. But in concrete perception this infinite stock is not in practical terms available to us. What we predicate of the object—the perceptual sense which we assign to it—is dependent upon both its position and our own position within an organized field of items and relations whose presence is not immediately manifest in the act of perception itself. This latent field is composed of hidden or peripheral items in perception, the body's actual and possible positionings, the percipient's objective knowledge of the world, and, equally importantly, the percipient's personal history, values, and social experience. It must be emphasized that this personal dimension is by no means a wholly private matter. This is why Merleau-Ponty's foregoing characterization of perception as 'a sort of straits between exterior horizons and interior horizons' is so appropriate. The common perceptual and physical basis of human embodiment means that the personal experiences of individual subjects will gravitate around shared or shareable patterns of interpretation and response. Hence, whilst my latent perceptual field and yours can never be exactly congruent, they will, nevertheless, have a deep structural continuity by virtue of our shared embodied condition, and our immersion in a world of mind-independent items.

Now, of course, the point about a latent field of this sort is that it *is* latent. Our acts of perceptual predication are defined by their position in such a field, but only exceptionally will we have an explicit understanding of the structure of such positioning. If this were not the case, our cognitive activity would be overwhelmed by an excess of sensory and imaginative data. Given this point, however, we must ask if there is any linguistic form (as opposed to linguistic strategy such as the present discussion) wherein the relation between perceptual predication and its latent field, is exemplified. The answer is Yes: metaphor. Metaphor hinges on a literally inappropriate predicate being applied to a principal subject. If, however, such a linkage makes sense, there must be some logical connection between the secondary and principal subject. This connection is provided by what I have called the 'latent field'. One of the key structural elements in the latent perceptual field is a space of imaginative association and projection. I would suggest that when language is used metaphorically it engages this imaginative space. The secondary term is able to achieve a cognitive elucidation of the principal subject because it posits some relation or quality, or whatever, which is a feature of the latent imaginative field surrounding that subject. In recognizing the relation between secondary and principal subject as metaphorical we discern an analogy. If the metaphor is living and forceful, we can imaginatively traverse elements in the latent field which connects the principal subject and its analogical predicate. In this way the principal subject is elucidated by virtue of our deepened experience of the field of relations in which that subject is positioned, and given its full definition. Of course, many metaphors—like many acts of predication *per se*—are applied without the referents of the terms involved being immediately present. This, however, is the power of metaphor. For, by virtue of its linguistic form—and the imaginative traversal which this invites—it involves a key feature of that latent field which is also implicated in language's most basic function, namely the articulation of perception. Metaphor is at least an echo of this function; and if the principal and secondary terms themselves refer to perceptible items (as is most often the case in metaphorical relations) then the effect of the metaphor will be to exemplify language's articulation of the perceptual world and the embodied subject's mode of inhering in it.

To illustrate my position further, let us consider an example. 'Falling in love' is one of the most common of all metaphors. It has, indeed, become deadened by repetition. However, the deadening of a metaphor is, ironically enough, a sign of its power. It is so effective as to be taken up by all sides and in all locations, thus becoming, in time, a commonplace. Let us ask then, what it is about the metaphor of 'falling' which makes it so effective as an elucidation of love.

Love, of course, is an emotional state rather than a position in space, hence one cannot literally 'fall into' it. However, falling as opposed to jumping into or taking possession of something is fundamentally a non-volitional act. And this is one of the most basic and poignant facts about love. One might wish to enter into such a state, but one cannot achieve it by choice alone. This is because of the latent field which situates all our emotional engagements. One can give a reason why, in emotional terms, one feels as one does. But the relation, event, or quality (or chain of such factors) which constitutes the reason does not simply 'register' in an individual's experience. It engages—in terms of harmony, tension, and conflict—with the totality of a life. The 'reason' which one invokes here is merely the salient feature which emerges from a multitude of latent factors and relations. This is the existential context for the metaphor 'falling' in love. 'Falling' signifies both the complexity of the field from which the emotion of love emerges, and the fact that we cannot control it in a volitional sense. The terms involved play off against our actual experiences and description of falling, and our own experiences of, and knowledge by description of, love as an emotion. In the most immediate terms, 'falling' is literally incongruous. However, the very incongruity of the juxtaposition provokes us to project avenues of imaginative association which, in ranging across publicly accessible and private experience, allow love and 'falling in' to be logically connected. The secondary term elevates a specific 'player' in the latent field surrounding the principal subject into an explicit role. If the metaphor is a living one, the unexpectedness of this elevation stimulates the imagination into filling out the space between the two terms. It is in the actual or potential traversal of this space that the principal subject achieves its cognitive elucidation.

Again it is important to reiterate that such imaginative

traversal involves a reciprocity of objective and subjective factors. For whilst, to return to our specific example, 'falling in' and 'love' are objective phenomena, and are informed by a common cultural stock of knowledge, our particular experiences of them also have a specific private character. Hence, how one imaginatively traverses the space between them will vary from individual to individual. This is why a metaphor cannot be paraphrased in literal terms. To be a metaphor is to posit an objectively significant connection, but in a way which provokes the connection to be made via avenues of imaginative, and thence, in part, personal association, rather than immediate logical relation.

On these terms, then, the phenomenon of metaphor is of the most profound philosophical significance. It is the form of language wherein the dependence of the recognition of presence upon items and relations which are not immediately present is the active basis of signification. More specifically, it affirms predication's primary function as an articulation of the perceptible. Metaphor thus exemplifies key structural features in cognition. However, as Goodman (1976: 52) has noted, exemplification involves not only possession, but also reference. Now the tensional character of metaphor—the predication of a literally inappropriate term—is, by virtue of its immediately incongruous nature, something which can provoke some awareness, however vague, of the relational complexity which situates all our cognitive acts. There are, nevertheless, two restrictions on the achievement of such awareness. First, a metaphor (for example 'falling in love') may be a dead one. This means that an awareness of its broader significance itself requires a philosophical analysis of the sort offered in this discussion. Secondly, since the function of metaphor is to achieve cognitive elucidation of the principal subject, the achievement of such elucidation may amount to no more than that. We comprehend the principal subject in a deeper way, but do not sense the more general significance of such elucidation *vis-à-vis* the structure of human experience.

To overcome these restrictions, metaphor needs a framing device. This would allow the metaphor to illumine its principal subject whilst, at the same time, being distanced from this function. The literary artwork and aesthetic object embodies such a framing device. It demands that, as well as attending to what a given linguistic structure is communicating, we are equally attentive to how this communication is achieved. Personal style in the articulation of literary form offers a context wherein the philosophical significance of metaphor is strikingly manifest.

Now it might be asked why the literary artwork should be singled out in this context: do not visual works of art, or even musical ones, have the capacity to disclose the philosophical significance of metaphor? The answer to this question is somewhat complex. Pictorial and sculptural representation, and (more debatably) music, have the character of twofoldness—i.e. we are able to see them both 'as' that which they represent and as physical objects or events. In order to recognize that something is, say, a picture of an X, we must know that it is not in fact an X; that it is only a configuration of material which shares certain visual qualities with the X. This gently tensional relation between the two elements of twofoldness gives pictorial representation a general structural affinity with metaphor.

There are also other connections. For something to be a picture of an X, that X must be represented in relation to a surrounding field. This might be constituted by background elements, or even, in the most minimal sense, the picture plane as such. We have, in other words, a basic exemplar of the relation between a perceived form and what I have earlier described as a latent field.

More significant still is the fact that, because the representation is not identical with that which is represented, points of sameness and difference in the relation enable us to see the kind of thing which is represented in a new light. The artist's style illuminates and projects avenues of significant association around the subject-matter. It gives it a kind of cognitive elucidation.

Now if these points are correct, pictorial representation is itself a visual mode of metaphor. However, there are a number of surprising factors involved. First, the metaphorical status is well concealed. In order to make a picture of an X one simply follows certain rules governing the appropriate implements and media. One 'intends' to make a picture rather than construct a metaphor. The metaphorical character of pictorial reference is absorbed into the broader conventions which govern such representation. Even more surprising is that it is not possible (within the framework of normal pictorial representation) to construct a *particular* metaphor. Caspar David Friedrich, for example, seems to have intended pictorial devices such as crescent moons as metaphors for the Resurrection and other aspects of Christian doctrine. However, particular visual metaphors of this kind cannot be recognized within the internal resources of the work itself. To determine whether a specific pictorial motif or relation is being used metaphorically requires collateral iconographic evidence drawn from the cultural context in which the work is produced and received.

The only possible exceptions to this are in idioms in which the normal conventions of pictorial representation are disrupted: Surrealist works are an example. In this context, however, whether a juxtaposition of items is intended as a metaphorical link is extremely difficult to determine in purely visual terms. It may be, for example, that the juxtaposition has been brought about purely to baffle or disturb the viewer.

Literary works relate to metaphor in a very different way. There is a twofold aspect to such works to the extent that we can distinguish the literal sense of the descriptions or narratives, or whatever, which constitute the work, and the stylized articulations of language in terms of which these are expressed. However, this twofoldness is much less clearly defined than in pictorial art, and it is not founded on physical or associational analogy between the referent(s) and the referring term(s). Meaning in literary language—indeed language itself—does not have an intrinsically metaphorical structure. Rather, metaphorical expression is one use to which language can be put—in a literary context or otherwise. It is this narrower scope of application which allows particular metaphors—rather than the globally metaphorical structures of pictorial art—to be constructed. In language and literature, indeed, a particular connection can be recognized as metaphorical purely on the basis of the internal recourse of the text or utterance itself in the broader context of general language use.

If, therefore, the philosophical significance of metaphor is to be disclosed in the most direct terms, it is to literary idioms that we must look. For present purposes, the case of the seventh-century Greek poet Archilochus is especially useful. His choice and deployment of metaphor is massively shaped by the specific societal and historical circumstances of his time and, of course, his own existence as a mercenary. However, it is precisely these historically specific factors, and their personalized expression in poetic form, which disclose the philosophical significance of metaphor in a heightened way. In Archilochus we can clearly recognize universal structure embodied in the particular.

II

Archilochus addresses recurrent themes of war, love, sex, friendship, revenge (both human and divinely sanctioned), civic propriety and impropriety, and political happenstances. His metaphors draw on all these themes, sometimes in a closely interwoven way. A useful starting point for analysis is fr. 196a West, a narrative description of an amorous episode which constitutes one of the longest of our fragments of Archilochus.[4]

In the epode from which this fragment comes, Archilochus recounts a conversation he has had with a certain woman. The fragment picks up with the woman's response to—and deflection of—an initial overture made by the poet. There is, she says, a 'lovely slender girl' within the house who might better appreciate Archilochus' advances. Archilochus appears to ignore this suggestion, but replies to the woman as follows (fr. 196a.13–15 West):

τ]έρψιές εἰσι θεῆς
πολλαὶ νέοισιν ἀνδ[ράσιν
παρὲξ τὸ θεῖον χρῆμα· τῶν τις ἀρκέσε[ι

The love-goddess offers young men
a range of joys besides
the sacrament, and one of them will serve.

This is his key move: by characterizing sexual intercourse metaphorically as 'the sacred matter' ('sacrament' in West's translation), Archilochus launches a twofold strategy of persuasion. On the one hand, he makes it clear that he reveres the act of

[4] In what follows, the text of Archilochus given is (with minimal editorial detail) West's. The translations are from M. L. West (1994): see esp. 3–4 (fr. 196a West), 5 (fr. 23 West); 11 (fr. 128 West); 13 (frr. 1 and 2 West).

physical love (and, thence, by implication, the woman who is the object of that act); on the other hand, he is able to indicate a space of possibilities which do not demand such a serious step. Indeed, Archilochus is able to reassure the woman further by allowing *her* to define where in this space of possibilities their assignation will rest ('I'll do it all just as you say': fr. 196a.19 West). But Archilochus continues his seduction with the following ambiguous passage (fr. 196a.21–4 West):

> θρ]ιγκοῦ δ' ἔνερθε καὶ πυλέων ὑποφ[θάνειν
> μ]ή τι μέγαιρε φίλη·
> σχήσω γὰρ ἐς ποη[φόρους
> κ]ήπους· τὸ δὴ νῦν γνῶθι.
>
> But please, my dear, don't grudge it if I go
> under the arch, through the gates;
> I'll dock at the grass borders,
> be sure of that.

Is this an indication that whilst not compromising the woman by calling at her house, the poet will nevertheless install himself close by? Such a reading is viable. It is, however, interwoven with a secondary meaning, arising from the fact that the whole sentence also functions as a kind of extended metaphorical reassurance that when they meet, the poet will be satisfied with an onanistic alternative to copulation.

Now it might be thought that the sentence in question is better described as allegorical than as metaphorical. However, it is somewhere between the two. Allegorical meaning is normally a form of linguistic disguise. We recognize it only through knowledge of a context external to the text itself. But Archilochus' progress 'under the arch, through the gate' to 'dock at the grass borders' serves to develop the *already established* theme of alternatives to the 'sacrament'. The nature of this progress, indeed, is further contextualized in the climax of the fragment (fr. 196a.42–53 West):

> παρθένον δ' ἐν ἄνθε[σιν
> τηλ]εθάεσσι λαβὼν
> ἔκλινα· μαλθακῆι δ[έ μιν
> χλαί]νηι καλύψας, αὐχέν' ἀγκάλῃς ἔχω[ν,
> δεί]ματι παυ[σ]αμένην
> τὼς ὥστε νεβ[ρὸν ἐκ φυγῆς

μαζ]ῶν τε χερσὶν ἠπίως ἐφηψάμην
ἧι πα]ρέφηνε νέον
ἥβης ἐπήλυσιν χρόα
ἅπαν τ]ε σῶμα καλὸν ἀμφαφώμενος
θερμ]ὸν ἀφῆκα μένος
ξανθῆς ἐπιψαύ[ων τριχός.

And laying her down in the flowers,
with my soft textured cloak
I covered her; my arm cradled her neck,
while she in her fear like a fawn
gave up the attempt to run.
Gently I touched her breasts, where the young flesh
peeped from the edge of her dress,
her ripeness newly come,
and then, caressing all her lovely form,
I shot my hot energy off,
just brushing golden hairs.

Given this onanistic outcome, Archilochus' earlier progress 'under the arch, through the gates' to 'dock at the grass borders' can be seen as a loosely metaphorical anticipation of it. The stealthy and cautious securing of place functions as an analogue to the qualified sexual fulfilment which later ensues. Indeed, it is also a reconnoitre—a simultaneous testing of the ground and act of reassurance *vis-à-vis* the woman. By preparing the way in advance through hinting at a limited rather than total sexual goal, Archilochus 'softens up' the opposition.

This metaphorically based strategy exemplifies Archilochus' more general tendency to assimilate sexual goals to the securing of position. For it involves a stealthy arrival and safe installation in a potentially hostile or resistant place. In other Archilochean fragments, the metaphorical linkage of sexual goals and occupation of place is even more explicit. In exultant terms, for example, Archilochus declares that 'I used to explore your rugged glens in my full-blooded youth' (fr. 190 West: καὶ βήσσας ὀρέων δυσπαιπάλους, οἷος ἦν ἐφ' ἥβης). More significantly, in the fairly extensive iambic fragment 23, Archilochus again addresses reassuring words—this time to a woman who has already responded positively to his overtures. Consider this passage (fr. 23.17–19 West):

πό]λιν δὲ ταύτη[ν ἣν σὺ νῦν ἐ]πιστρέ[φεα]ι

οὔ]τοι ποτ' ἄνδρες ἐξε[πόρθη]σαν, σὺ δ[ὲ
ν]ῦν εἷλες αἰχμῆι κα[ὶ μεγ' ἐ]ξήρ(ω) κ[λ]έος
This citadel that you are walking in
was never sacked by any man, but now
your spear has conquered it, yours is the glory.

Here the metaphor of secured place is used as the illumination of a generally concealed (or at least understated) power relation. Woman-as-object-of-desire-for-man is a notion which is often understood simply in terms of sexual gratification provided by the former for the latter (and elsewhere, of course, Archilochus fully embraces this possibility). However, in the last quoted passage the poet foregrounds a different dynamic. His desire itself is the citadel which the woman has taken. Note how the intensity of this conquest is underlined by the reversal of customary metaphorical associations even as they are juxtaposed with a rather forced analogy. For it is the woman who has entered the man. She has symbolically appropriated and used the phallic spear. In so doing (and this is the rather forced analogy) she has effected an emotional conquest which finds no parallel in the agonistics of the poet's physical combat with rivals in battle.

Archilochus' use of martial metaphor extends, of course, far beyond the sexual realm. In a fragment from one of Archilochus' iambic poems (fr. 128 West), such metaphor is used to illuminate a more general existential crisis and, through clarifying it, to provide a more secure vantage point from which to survey the travails of existence:

Heart, my heart, with helpless, sightless troubles now confounded,
up, withstand the enemy, opposing breast to breast.
All around they lie in wait, but stand you firmly grounded,
not over-proud in victory, nor in defeat oppressed.
In your rejoicing let your joy, in hardship your despairs
be tempered: understand the pattern shaping men's affairs.

This extended congruence of martial metaphor and existential position finds its most concentrated and forceful statement in the following lines of elegiac (fr. 2 West):

On my spear's my daily bread, on my spear my wine
from Ismaros; and drinking it, it's on my spear I recline.

This fragment is fraught with ambiguity. However, one viable reading of it is as follows. Archilochus metaphorically links the flesh- and blood-spattered spear—the stuff of life and death in combat—to the means of material subsistence and gratification. The fruits of combat earn him the basics of life. Interestingly, however, the poet—in reclining on his spear and drinking highly reputable wine—introduces a complex metaphor which both energizes and distances itself from the notion of battle as his means of material subsistence and gratification. The energizing dimension hinges on a metaphorical drinking of blood which depends on the support of the spear; the distancing element consists of the simultaneous reading of this as an image of luxurious consumption and repose. It is through his life as a warrior that Archilochus finds the means and motive to reflect and savour. Little wonder, then, to find a couplet (fr. 1 West) in which Archilochus declares:

> I am a servant of the lord god of war
> and one versed in the Muses' lovely gifts.

Let us now consider this analysis in relation to the theory of metaphor outlined in Section I. Any act of cognition or judgement is given its character by the relation between the immediate object of such an act and a broader latent field composed of the object's hidden aspects, its relation to other perceptible items, and its position within the personal experience and values of the cognizing subject. The power of metaphor consists in its capacity to elucidate a given term by evoking aspects of its latent field.

In the case of Archilochus, both the subjective and objective dimensions of this field are manifestly evoked. His treatments of love, sex, and existential situations are, as we have seen, not just narratives but ones whose metaphorical content and development are formed by factors which are not immediately present, namely his life and particular experiences as a travelling warrior. This experiential field strikingly defines the way in which he addresses themes which are not themselves intrinsically martial. In Archilochus, therefore, metaphor and its positioning within the specific poem discloses a more general truth about how individual moments of experience are created at the intersection between that which is immediately addressed and a personal sense of past, future, and counterfactual alternatives, which surround it as a latent field. The personality of the creator here discloses the creation of personality itself.

It is this creative subjective dimension which also energizes the objective aspect of the latent field. In human and animal communities, coexistence and the pursuit of mates are fraught with rivalries, competition, conflict, and stratagems. They also involve the traversal and inhabiting of specific places and regions. All these factors (and many others besides) weave in and out of all coexistence and courtship. In our ordinary linguistic descriptions, it is hard to evoke the complexity of this objective field of interactions and locations: Archilochus' metaphors, however, situate us coherently within it. His experience as a warrior, and gifts as a poet, enable him to link love and courtship, for example, to those martial or strategic elements which surround their pursuit and enjoyment. The particular metaphors chosen are ones which link a given situation to an element or elements in the encompassing social or physical field, thus enabling the reader imaginatively to traverse the space between them. Poetic form and format mean that the metaphor is not simply absorbed into the world of immediate verbal interactions—thence to be lost, or end up as a dead metaphor. Rather it is given renewed life through its position within the poem, through the poem's position within the artist's oeuvre, and through that oeuvre's role in the synchronic and diachronic development of the traditions of poetic form. And these factors all play off one another, of course, within a general sense of the species' ongoing historical development.

I am arguing, then, that Archilochus' use of metaphor discloses fundamental philosophical insights concerning constants in both the ontological structure and the content of human experience. This possibility is inherent in all literary metaphor: Archilochus enables us to discern it in a particularly heightened way. There is also a further level of decisive objective significance to his work. This term pertains to a constant in poetic form, rather than experience *per se*.

To explain. The origins of poetry probably lie in a formalization of language (*vis-à-vis* such features as trope and metre) for objective social purposes bound up with ritual and religious belief. Here, the articulation of metaphor would be closely tied to such purposes, and attention would focus, accordingly, on issues of the metaphor's use more than on the poetics of its articulation. Such ritual functions mark out the objective pole of the poetic idiom—the point where it touches or is absorbed by its societal contexts.

Archilochus' use of metaphor, in contrast, is an element within a poetic idiom which helps define the opposite logical extreme. In strictly historical terms he inaugurates a recurrent tendency towards an aggressive and worldly subjectivism which finds an echo in figures such as Omar Khayyám (if we read the *Rubáiyát* in non-allegorical terms), François Villon, and the John Donne of the Sonnets. Archilochus thus creates a defining *logical* moment in the development of poetry as a symbolic form. His imagery, and its patterns of development and deployment, fully articulate poetic form's capacity for expressing constant elements in the subjective dimension of experience. Archilochus' metaphors are the most concentrated achievement of this.

III

In this discussion then, I have argued that the form of metaphor discloses key structural features which are involved in all cognition. For this disclosure to occur effectively, metaphor must be articulated in a mode wherein we are invited to attend to *how* it achieves its effects. The literary artwork offers the most basic instance of this. In such a work, attention focuses on the stylistic means whereby the creator articulates his or her subject-matter.

Archilochus exemplifies these points in a particularly illuminating way. His metaphors elucidate their principal subjects through reference to a latent field which gravitates around both recurrent factors in human experience, and the poet's own highly distinctive personal perspective on them. Indeed, his personal perspective is so emphatic as to define the subjective logical extreme of poetic form itself. He opens out a space of meaning which establishes itself as a possible idiom for others.

In an analysis such as the present one, the function of metaphor is described. In Archilochus and, indeed, *all* literary discourse, metaphor is *realized* as part of the fabric of a created aesthetic object. In recognizing the metaphorical connection between principal and secondary subject, we are invited—by the tensional gap between the two—to traverse it in imaginative terms. The latent field which is a precondition of language's articulation of perception, is here brought directly into play. We are also invited to enjoy the novelty of this connection, or its place in the structure of the poem as a whole. What results is not so much full-blown philosophical understanding, as an empathic enjoyment of the relation between individual creative awareness and the structure and possibilities of being human as such. We enjoy aesthetically-grounded philosophical insight. This is the supreme achievement of metaphor in its artistic context.

6
The Problem of Metaphor: Chinese Reflections

G. E. R. LLOYD

I start from the tension between two positions—or rather between one assumption and one observation—both of which seem at first sight sound enough. The first is an assumption that is commonly made by commentators with widely differing theoretical positions on the thorny issues of the analysis of metaphor, namely that metaphor (however we understand it) is a universal feature of all language, a feature that we can accordingly expect to find exemplified in every natural language, living or dead. The second is the observation that our own notions of metaphor have a history, one that ultimately goes back to the Greeks. It is well known that *μεταφορά*, transfer, is far from being an exact equivalent to our 'metaphor'. Nevertheless, as a first approximation, it is fair to say that our notion goes back to Aristotle's introduction of the contrast between terms used *κατὰ μεταφοράν*, and those used strictly, *κυρίως*. Of course Aristotle owed much to Plato, in this as in so much else, but while Plato had much to say about the use of *εἰκόνες*, images, *ὁμοιότητες*, likenesses, and *παραδείγματα*, models, in a variety of contexts,[1] and while he could, on occasion, use *λόγος* and *μῦθος* as antithetical terms (though elsewhere they may be interchangeable), he did not propose a literal/metaphorical dichotomy as such. That was the fateful step that Aristotle (as a first approximation) may be said to have made.

The question is: was that an invention or a discovery? Those who claim or assume that metaphor is a universal feature of language may well favour the idea that the identification of

[1] See Pender in this volume.

metaphor as such was a discovery—even while they may dissent from features of Aristotle's analysis. Metaphors, on this view, had been there all along, just waiting for the Aristotelian initiative to label them as such—even though questions to do with the correct analysis of metaphor and its relations both with literality and with other tropes remain, no doubt, problematic.

Yet against that a case can be made for treating it as an invention rather than a discovery. An examination of the historical context of Aristotle's work in this area goes to show that his introduction of the contrast between the strict and the transferred use of terms was anything but just a piece of purely abstract linguistic analysis. As I tried to show in *Demystifying Mentalities* (Lloyd 1990: chapter 1), that dichotomy plays an important polemical role in allowing a certain type of challenge to be mounted. If we encounter a piece of mythology, or poetry, or someone else's philosophy, we can press the question as to how precisely the terms are used. When the theologians speak of everything coming from Night, say, or Empedocles invokes a cosmic principle of Love (*Φιλία*), how exactly are we to understand this? Is this literally night, literally love? In which case how are we to relate what is said to what we ordinarily mean by those terms? But if not literally intended, what are the metaphors metaphors *for*?

This dichotomy is one of the tools Aristotle uses to contrast his own highest style of philosophizing with other, inferior, not to say deviant, modes of discourse. Metaphors are repeatedly criticized in the logical and physical works as obscure. They should not be used in definition, for 'every metaphorical expression is obscure' (*Topics* 139^{b}34 f.). Nor in explanation. Empedocles' characterization of the salt sea as the sweat of the earth is dismissed: 'perhaps to say that is to speak adequately for poetic purposes—for metaphor is poetic—but it is not adequate for understanding the nature of the thing' (*Meteorology* 357^{a}24 ff.). Similarly Plato's entire theory of Forms is rejected with the remark that 'to say that [the Forms] are models and that other things share in them is to speak nonsense and to use poetic metaphors' (*Metaphysics* 991^{a}20 ff.).

We are to understand that while metaphor may be all right in poetry, it will not do in philosophy. It certainly will not do in syllogistic, and so not in strict demonstration either, for the validity of a deduction is immediately compromised by any departure from univocity. Quite how far Aristotle imagined he could apply the strictest model of demonstration, elaborated in the *Posterior Analytics*, in practice is another, interestingly complex, question—for it is evidently not the case that his own scientific and metaphysical investigations have been completely purged of the transferred use of terms. Yet negatively or destructively, the literal/metaphorical dichotomy proves to be, in Aristotle's hands, a powerful tool to put down rivals, whether poets, or mythologists, or other philosophers, and to stake out claims for his own high style of philosophizing.

I appreciate, of course, that there are philosophical issues at stake in this area that an empirical study of existing or recorded natural languages will not resolve. Yet such a study can throw light on what different ancient or modern societies have found useful in the matter of the analysis of how language works. In many modern cultures, for sure, there has been seepage, or contamination, from European ideas, themselves the heirs of Graeco-Roman and sometimes specifically Aristotelian theories. But one particularly well-documented ancient society where no such influence has been at work is China. True, China too underwent external influences from a different quarter from about the third century CE onwards, I mean from Indian, specifically Buddhist, ideas. But already before that influence began to be felt, there are considerable reflections on the nature of language which provide an interesting point of comparison and contrast with ancient Greece. The question I wish to pursue here is whether the Chinese developed anything like the literal/metaphorical dichotomy. If not, how did they manage without it? What did they believe to be the important features in the analysis of different modes of discourse or of language itself? Having sketched, admittedly all too briefly, just some aspects of how these questions figure in a Chinese perspective, I shall return to the philosophical issues at the end.

One topic that seems, at first sight, rather promising is *zhengming*, conventionally rendered the rectification of names. We might think, that is, that what we have here is a set of normative rules for the use of language, comparable, perhaps, with Aristotle's privileging of the strict use of terms. Yet such an expectation is defeated as soon as we get beyond that conventional rendition. The key point is that *zhengming*, which covers in fact a wide diversity of doctrines,[2] is, in origin, essentially a matter of the ordering of social roles and statuses.

Admittedly the interpretation of the text in the *Analects* (13.3) which may mark the first introduction of the topic is disputed. Confucius, asked by Zilu what he would do if the prince of Wei entrusted the government to him, replies: 'rectify names', and he goes on to explain that as essential for good government, including the due conduct of ceremony and music and the due application of punishments. Confucius' advice here, it is generally agreed, is specific to the situation of the Lord of Wei, but it is not clear which aspects of the situation it is meant to apply to. The traditional view, which has the support of many of the ancient Chinese commentators, is that he has in mind the lack of filial piety on the part of the young prince Zhe, who had been named Lord of Wei, but who should have renounced this position in favour of his exiled father.[3] But an alternative interpretation is that Confucius refers to the situation in the previous reign and to the confusion, then, of *jun* and *chen*, master and servant, lord and minister.[4] Yet be that as it may, it is already clear from the continuation in the *Analects* itself, with its reference to good behaviour and punishments, that the rectification in question is not a matter of language in general, but of particular roles and relationships.

The fullest early discussion of the topic, in *Xunzi* 22, shows further that the concern is not with language as such. Xunzi opens with some approving remarks about how the later kings had fixed the names of things, for legal terms following the practices of the Shang (dynasty), for the names of ranks and titles the Zhou, for the names of ceremonies ritual practice. What is here at issue is ancient authority not so much for terminology, as for the norms of conduct that that terminology refers to. 'If a true king were to appear now, he would surely set about reviving the old names, and creating new ones as they were needed. To do so, he would have to examine carefully to see why names are needed, how to go about distinguishing between things that are the same

[2] See e.g. Gassmann (1988); Djamouri (1993); Lackner (1993); Levi (1993); Vandermeersch (1993).

[3] See Vandermeersch (1993), 11 ff.

[4] See Gassmann (1988); cf. Lackner (1993), 77 ff.

and those that are different . . .' When arbitrary names are introduced, 'then the relationships between names and realities will become obscured and entangled, the distinction between eminent and humble will become unclear, and men will no longer discriminate properly between things that are the same and those that are different . . . There will be a real danger that the ruler's intentions will not be properly communicated and understood.'[5]

Stress is indeed laid on correct language, but this is not, of course, because of some problem that arises from transferred or metaphorical usage. Rather it is that correct language is just one sign of uprightness: deviation from the terminology that had been laid down is a source of moral and political disorder and confusion. Of course degenerate speech was a sign of degeneracy also in ancient Greece, as in Thucydides' famous denunciation of the warping of language that was one of the products of political *στάσις* in the Peloponnesian War (3.82). Yet that was not a matter of the 'metaphorical' or figurative use of terms either. The Chinese rectification of names is not an invitation to an investigation in the philosophy of language. Rather a perceived or threatened lack of correspondence between names and the things they designate is the occasion for the promulgation of a political and moral agenda.

Yet other Chinese reflections do relate more to language use as such, first their admittedly limited explorations of certain grammatical distinctions, then their poetics, and thirdly certain other contexts in which types of discourse are distinguished and comments on their use and effectiveness are made.

Thus in Chinese grammar we find a contrast drawn between solid or full (*shi*) terms, and empty (*xu*) ones. However this does not correspond to a distinction between strict and derivative uses—as when the same term can be used *κυρίως* and *κατὰ μεταφοράν*. Rather it serves to mark two classes of terms themselves: very roughly, the empty (*xu*) terms correspond to particles, the *shi* to 'content' words.[6]

Chinese poetics brings us closer to the topics we are centrally concerned with here. The Book of Odes contains poems grouped

[5] *Xunzi* 22.11 ff. in the Harvard-Yenching edition. My translations follow those in Watson (1963). Cf. Knoblock (1988–94), iii. 128 ff.

[6] See esp. Harbsmeier (1998), 130 ff.

into three main classes, *Guofeng*, *Erya*, and *Song*. The first are 'folk' or popular poems related to different regions of China. The second, subdivided into *daya* and *xiaoya*, are poems mostly by particular individuals and are meant for a different kind of musical accompaniment from that of *Guofeng*. The third, the *song*, are intended as accompaniments to ceremonials of various types. In the Great Preface (*daxu*) to the Mao edition of the Odes, in the introductory comments on the first poem of all, *guanju* (crying ospreys), these three types of poetry are mentioned, but so too are other aspects or principles that correspond, rather, to stylistic traits. We have here the origin of the three poetic modes labelled *fu* (descriptive/expository), *bi* (comparative/analogical), and *xing* (elevated/evocative). There is, however, considerable disagreement, already among the ancient commentators, as to the interpretation of all three, and especially of *xing*.[7] The boundaries between them appear, in any case, to be rather fluid, even though, so far as *bi* is concerned, it is clear that there is much in classical Chinese poetry that can be said to make use of both explicit and implicit comparisons, and analogies of different kinds.

According to the tradition of poetics that stems from this discussion, comparison is a feature that marks out poetry of a particular type. Yet the fact that this is just one of the general characteristics that poetry may exhibit makes it clear that we are not dealing with any attempt to contrast poetic composition as such with prose, let alone with any suggestion that poetry as such exploits a non-strict or deviant use of language. There is no criticism made or implied in the use of comparison in poetry: rather it is, if anything, a virtue to be cultivated in one style of poetry.

It is not just in connection with poetics that we have self-conscious analysis of modes of language use in ancient Chinese texts. One of the 'mixed chapters' in the *Zhuangzi* compilation draws a distinction between three kinds of 'sayings' (*yan*), and one of the three, *yu yan*, has often been cited as equivalent to metaphor, and in many of the older translations of *Zhuangzi* is actually rendered 'metaphor' or the equivalent in other Euro-

[7] See e.g. Liu (1975), 109 ff.; Cheng (1979), 63 ff.; Jullien (1985), 67 ff., 175 ff.; Yu (1987), 57 ff., 168 ff.

pean languages.[8] Yet this has to be said to be radically misleading.

Zhuangzi's three types are *yu yan*, *zhong yan*, and *zhi yan*, that is, to adapt Graham's translations,[9] 'lodge sayings', 'weighty sayings', and 'spill-over sayings'. Their characterizations are, admittedly, anything but transparent. 'Saying from a lodging-place', we are told at the outset, 'works nine times out of ten, weighty saying works seven times out of ten. Spillover saying is new every day, smooth it out on the whetstone of Heaven.' 'Saying from a lodging-place' is then explained as 'borrowing a standpoint outside to sort the matter out'. The traditional view has it that this refers to the expression of ideas through imaginary conversations, a common convention, but Graham has challenged this. The context here implies, he claimed, that the lodging-place is the standpoint of the other party in debate. You temporarily 'lodge' at the other person's standpoint to win him over. Zhuangzi, on this interpretation, 'seems to be referring to persuasion by *argumentum ad hominem*, the only kind of victory in debate which would have any point for him'.[10]

'Weighty sayings', next, are 'what you say on your own authority', for example, to follow Graham's lead again, the aphorism with the weight of the speaker's experience behind it. 'Spill-over sayings' are interpreted as taking their name from a kind of vessel that is designed to tip and right itself when filled too near the brim. 'Use it to go by', the text says, 'and let the stream find its own channels: this is the way to last out your years', which Graham glosses: 'it is the speech proper to the intelligent spontaneity of Taoist behaviour in general, a fluid language which keeps its equilibrium through changing meanings and viewpoints.'

Though much in this account is obscure, both the terms themselves and the illustrations and explanations given, it is evident first that 'lodge sayings' is some way away from the root idea of the metaphorical in Greek, as the transfer of a term from a

[8] See e.g. Legge (1891), 142 ff., which receives a measure of endorsement from Lin (1994), 53 n. 17. Cf. most recently Mair's translation (Mair 1994: 278 ff.).

[9] *Zhuangzi* 27.1 ff. in the Harvard-Yenching edition (cf. *Zhuangzi* 2.90 ff. and *Zhuangzi* 33.65 ff.), Graham (1989), 200 f.; cf. Graham (1981), 106 ff.

[10] Graham (1989), 201.

primary context to a secondary, derivative, one. Moreover it is not as if the other two categories between them yield anything that can be taken to correspond to the strict, or literal, use of terms. Zhuangzi is indeed interested in evaluating different types of sayings for different purposes in different contexts, and in suggesting their appropriateness for particular functions. But it is not that he makes any attempt to restrict discourse to one particular, privileged, type, even within a particular given context. He certainly did not need to do so, as Aristotle did, for the sake of a formal analysis of the conditions for valid deduction—given, of course, that there was no Chinese interest in formal logic as such at all, and Zhuangzi is obviously not concerned with any such analysis in the first place.

We have clear evidence in ancient Chinese texts before the end of the Han of a range of interests in language and in language use. But to see any of those interests as concerned with anything like the metaphorical/literal dichotomy is a gross example of the violence done to Chinese thought in the name of the imposition of Western categories. The ancient Chinese, it seems, were innocent of any such concerns and got along perfectly well without any such explicit dichotomy.

Yet the hardliner might still say, first, that that just shows up the shortcomings of their philosophy of language, and secondly, that we can still diagnose *their* metaphors, even though they did not have a word for them. So I turn back, now, to the question of what they might have needed any such category for, and finally to the philosophical issues of whether indeed metaphor is what we should be diagnosing as a universal feature of any natural language.

So, first, as to whether the Chinese missed out because of what the hardliner would consider a lacuna in their philosophy of language. If we turn back to the actual use that Aristotle put his dichotomy to, that, we said, was in part a polemical tool serving to demarcate areas of expertise and to claim superiority for his high style of philosophizing, one that would secure truth and, indeed, via the strictest demonstration, incontrovertibility. I have argued in *Adversaries and Authorities* (Lloyd 1996*a*) that there is a difference in style in the way in which the criticism of others is conducted in China, acknowledging, of course, that there is such criticism, even though it is a less pervasive feature of Chinese than of Greek thought. Whereas we can find Greek philosophers, scientists, doctors, even, saying that the whole of the rest of the world has got it wrong, the form that Chinese criticisms take is often *not* that their opponents had *none* of the truth (or rather, as they would say, the Way), but rather that they did not have all of it.[11]

This should not be put down merely to psychology, as if the Chinese were somehow more polite, or less aggressive, than the Greeks in polemic. We have to understand the contexts in which argumentative exchanges typically took place. There is far less face-to-face confrontation, in public or even in private debate, in China than there is in Greece. The debates set out in such texts as the *Yan Tie Lun* (*Discourses on salt and iron*) and *Bohutong* (*White Tiger Hall*) are stylized literary representations of exchanges of view, rather than actual records of arguments as they occurred. In any event, the person you most wanted to persuade was the prince or ruler (one of the standard forms of Chinese philosophical and scientific treatises is the *zou* or presentation to the throne). In that context, it did not pay to be too critical of your rivals. You were often not in a position to know how far they already had the ear of the prince, nor how long your own favour would last. No amount of complacent Greek-style reflection on the strength of your case—of the incontrovertibility of your arguments—was any kind of guarantee of success. The difference from the open debates familiar from Greek philosophical and medical schools is considerable.

So on this score, then, the polemical role of metaphor, as in some of Aristotle's uses, was not called for, at least not to anything like the same degree. There was no war between philosophy and poetry in China, nor between λόγος and μῦθος.

But then, secondly, it might be thought that the lack of the literal/metaphorical dichotomy would carry with it certain disadvantages, or penalties, with regard to the clarification of meanings and the avoidance of misunderstandings. To be sure, having such a dichotomy available is going to be no guarantee of transparency in communication. But to see whether there was any particular problem, on this score, the best thing to do is to review

[11] This is a standard move, found, for example, in Sima Qian, *Shiji* 130, and in *Zhuangzi* 33: cf. Lloyd (1996*a*), 24 ff.

some of the ways in which ancient Chinese actually went about the clarification of meanings in particular contexts.

One particular area where we can follow this up is in the matter of definition in the field of mathematics, where I can draw on the work of a recent Cambridge Ph.D. thesis, by Dominic O'Brien,[12] which took as its subject the comparative analysis of definition in Chinese and Greek mathematics. The chief ancient Chinese mathematical classics, dating from a hundred years either side of the millennium, are the *Zhoubi suanjing* (*Arithmetic Classic of the Zou gnomon*), and the *Jiuzhang suanshu* (*Nine Chapters of the Mathematical Art*), together with the commentary tradition, on the latter especially, beginning with Liu Hui in the third century CE.[13]

The Chinese did not engage in definitions *per genus et differentiam*. Nor did they aim to secure definitions as one type of self-evident indemonstrable primary premisses along the lines of Aristotle's analysis of demonstration in the *Posterior Analytics*. But they were perfectly capable of being precise about the way in which certain terms are to be understood. Take the introduction of particular terms for particular procedures in Liu Hui's commentary on the first section of the *Nine Chapters*, where the problem tackled is that of the addition of fractions. Liu Hui shows that $a/b + c/d = (ad + bc)/bd$ is correct. But to do this he first gives names to the two procedures involved, first the multiplying of denominators by numerators that do not correspond to them (as in the two cases ad and bc in the equation that I have just set out), and secondly the multiplication of the denominators by one another (as in the new denominator bd in the equation). To quote his text: 'Every time denominators multiply a numerator that does not correspond to them, we call this homogenize (*qi*). Multiplying with one another the set of denominators, we call this equalize (*tong*).'[14]

The terms introduced here with specific meanings are both ones that otherwise had a range of general uses. This *qi* (radical 210) means even, level, uniform: this *tong* is used of similarity, sameness, as well as equality, and further of sharing, association,

[12] O'Brien (1995).

[13] See Qian Baocong (1963); Cullen (1996); Chemla (forthcoming).

[14] Liu Hui in Qian Baocong (1963), 96; cf. Chemla (1994), 44 ff.

together. Yet they are now used, by Liu Hui, as the names of well-defined procedures.

What we have here is a classic case of the way in which technical vocabulary may grow, whether in mathematics, philosophy, medicine, technology, or any other domain. This happens not just by the coinage of brand new terms (though some of these may be compounds that owe something to the original meanings of their main elemental components), but just as often by the redeployment of existing terms, where, of course, the relationship between the new and older usages may be more or less close. The new usage, if it is indeed new, will be derivative, and may be 'figurative' or 'metaphorical'. But that certainly does not imply that there will be any unclarity or imprecision in its new acceptance: quite the contrary, in a new technical use, it can be as strict as you like.

Liu Hui marks his new usage absolutely clearly. With the expression *wei* (we call this) he signals the introduction of a term in a technical application he explains precisely. If we choose to puzzle over whether or how far this is a figurative use, this would be rather to miss the point. He could, if he had wished, surely have introduced a variety of possible terms here: the sense, in any event, is given by the two explanations, and there is a mutual dependence of the senses of the terms explained and those of the terms doing the explaining.

Actually there is more to this very example than I have yet let on. I chose it to show how Liu Hui builds up a technical vocabulary for his mathematical work, in this case the validation of an algorithm. But he does not do so out of nothing, of course. I used the terms 'denominator' and 'numerator' in my translation of the two sentences that give the meanings of *qi* and *tong*. But the terms I so translated are *mu* and *zi*, and *mu* ordinarily means 'mother' and *zi* 'son'. But so familiar and well understood are their uses, in context, of the denominator and numerator of fractions that Liu Hui does not bother to explain them.

One can go further. The term for 'multiply', *cheng*, means: ride, mount, avail oneself, but that too causes not a moment's pause.[15] Nor are we dealing with a peculiarity of Chinese, to be

[15] Of course it is not as if there are no problems, no possible room for confusion, in the use of the mathematical terms in question. Right at the start of his commentary on chapter 1, the problem of the area of the rectangular field, Liu

sure. Plenty of examples can be given of Greek terms that start life with concrete meanings related to physical objects, and are then given derivative, precise, mathematical ones, or of terms that have technical applications there. Euclid's circle is not a band or ring, nor any other of the three-dimensional objects of which *κύκλος* may be used: his *σφαῖρα* is not one that Nausicaa could have played with. *Ἀνθυφαίρεσις* might seem to refer to any kind of taking away instead of or in turn (*ἀντί*), but 'reciprocal subtraction' is given a precise technical sense with regard to side and diagonal numbers.

Now faced with the text of Liu Hui what are we to say? The Aristotelian hardliner would no doubt have a field day. None of the chief terms is used *κυρίως*: 'every time mothers avail themselves of (ride) sons reciprocally (*hu*) we call this level: when the crowd of mothers avail themselves of (ride) each other (*xiang*) we call this equal.' Actually a good deal of research in Morohashi[16] would be required to determine the original sense of many of the standard terms used in Chinese mathematics, though with mothers and sons that is not in doubt.

Now I am surely not going to deny that the resonances of highly polyvalent terms are important: we should, no doubt, always consider the full range of possible senses and associations of every phrase, and not just in poetry. But the mistake of the hardliner, as it seems to me, is to take everything other than the literal as metaphorical, everything other than the strict as derivative. Those dichotomies, I remarked, allow, indeed they force, issues to be pressed: what is your precise meaning, even when meanings are not and cannot be precise.

Rather than stay with the Aristotelian dichotomy, the analysis for which I argued, though admittedly rather briefly, in *The Revolutions of Wisdom*,[17] is in terms of the notion of semantic stretch. I argued that that is preferable for two main reasons. First, it allows the differences we recognize to be differences of degree, rather than matters of alternatives construed as mutually exclusive (as the Aristotelian dichotomy and those based on it

Hui says that the product (*ji*) of the breadth and length is the area (*mi*) of the field. But later commentators, Li Chunfeng and his associates, complain that 'product' and 'area' do not have the same sense (Qian Baocong 1963: 93).

[16] Morohashi (1955–60) is the major 13-vol. Chinese dictionary.

[17] Lloyd (1987), ch. 4, referring to Porzig (1934).

regularly, even if not always, are). Secondly, it allows that every term has *some* stretch, even, at the limit, those terms deemed to be univocal.

This is not to say that there is a metaphorical element in the use of every term, nor to collapse the literal into the metaphorical, or to treat it as a null class. Rather it is to overhaul the terms in which the alternatives are put in the first place. For as I argued, to escape from the forcing of issues that so bedevil the analysis, it is essential *not* to continue to work within the schemata of the alternatives as they are generally presented, *either* literal *or* metaphorical, *either* strict *or* derivative.

So far from commiserating with the ancient Chinese for failing to develop and use the literal/metaphorical dichotomy, and for allegedly getting into terrible trouble in their practice and analysis of language as a consequence, we may rather say that there was a positive advantage in their not using that or any other of the related dichotomies we are so familiar with. We cannot exactly congratulate them for avoiding a pitfall they were evidently entirely unaware existed: nor of course did they arrive at their reflections on language by pondering on the problems that stem from the adoption of the Aristotelian framework. But we may remark that those reflections allow for a pluralism that suits the non-exclusivity of their appreciation of others' points of view very well. *Yu yan* works: but so too does *zhong yan*, and as for *zhi yan*, 'let the stream find its own channels: this is the way to last out your years'. To my way of thinking, all three make room for what I call semantic stretch, while incorporating also some recognition of the pragmatics of any communication situation.

To look for, and to fail to find, metaphor in ancient Chinese thought is to be hopelessly Eurocentric, a typical example of the disastrous parochialism that stems from the imposition of Western categories. To complain that, for lack of the literal/metaphorical dichotomy, the Chinese laboured under a serious handicap, with dire consequences for clarity and precision, is to add naïveté to Eurocentricity. Let us be clear that ambiguity and vagueness are possible, indeed there to be exploited, in any language. Nor are Chinese philosophy and science any different from ancient Greek, or modern, philosophy and science, in their need to call on terms with exceptional semantic stretch. At the same time technical senses are hammered out with perfect lucidity—without any indication of a demand that all language should approximate the technical. Chinese writers, and not just poets, indeed often show great talent in making the most of the resonances of the language they use, and of the full range of the associations of terms: but it is only those with hearts of Aristotelian stone who would deplore that: and even then there is so much more to Aristotle himself—and the practice of Aristotelian science, indeed—than is allowed for by many of those who invoke the dichotomy he so fatefully introduced.

Glossary of Chinese Terms

bi	比	song	頌
chen	臣	tong	同
cheng	乘	wei	謂
daxu	大序	xiang	相
daya	大雅	xiaoya	小雅
fu	賦	xing	興
guanju	關雎	xu	虛
hu	互	yan	言
ji	積	yu yan	寓言
jun	君	zhengming	正名
mi	冪	zhi yan	卮言
mu	母	zhong yan	重言
qi	齊	zi	子
shi	實	zou	奏

7
Metaphor and Metonymy: Aristotle, Jakobson, Ricoeur, and Others

MICHAEL SILK

> One would imagine that, after two thousand years of post-Aristotelian literary activity, his views on poetics, like his views on the generation of animals, could be re-examined in the light of fresh evidence.
>
> (Northrop Frye)

> The literary critic . . . must be on his guard . . . against any premature or irrelevant generalizing.
>
> (F. R. Leavis)

Much of the world's significant theorizing about metaphor, and metonymy, has been conducted by philosophers or, in recent times, by philosophically influenced specialists in semantics or semiotics. In what follows, I shall for convenience refer to all such theorists as *philosophical* theorists and to the products of their theorizing as *philosophical* theory. The three theorists named in my title are all, in this sense, philosophical theorists. In the discussion that follows, I shall be taking issue with all three, as individual, but also as representative, theorists: with Aristotle, with Jakobson, with Ricoeur.

My thanks to members of the Oxford audience for helpful responses to this chapter in its original form, and especially to Myles Burnyeat and Tania Gergel for subsequent comments on the revised written version.

I

Thanks to the discussions in his *Poetics* and *Rhetoric*,[1] Aristotle is certainly the most influential theorist of metaphor before the modern age. It is Aristotle who, in the *Poetics*, designates *metaphora* as a special, even unique, phenomenon of poetic language, and associates this uniqueness with the logical basis of all metaphors, the principle of similarity or analogy. After a review of various kinds of poetic usage, he writes (*Poetics* 22, 1459ª5–8):

πολὺ δὲ μέγιστον τὸ μεταφορικὸν εἶναι. μόνον γὰρ τοῦτο οὔτε παρ' ἄλλου ἔστι λαβεῖν εὐφυΐας τε σημεῖόν ἐστι. τὸ γὰρ εὖ μεταφέρειν τὸ τὸ ὅμοιον θεωρεῖν ἐστιν.

Much the most important [feature of poetic language for the composer of poetry to use] is metaphorical [usage]. This alone cannot be learnt from anyone else and is a sign of natural gifts, in that to use metaphors well is to discern similarities.

Metaphora is first introduced as follows (*Poetics* 21, 1457ᵇ1–2):

ἅπαν δὲ ὄνομά ἐστιν ἢ κύριον ἢ γλῶττα ἢ μεταφορὰ ἢ . . .[2]

Every word is either standard or a loan-word or a metaphor or . . .

Here 'standard' is defined as 'a word in communal use' (*λέγω δὲ κύριον μὲν ᾧ χρῶνται ἕκαστοι*: *Poetics* 21, 1457ᵇ3–4), from which (and from the position of 'standard' in the list) one infers that, essentially, usages are either standard or non-standard, with (as becomes apparent) *metaphora* the most important of the non-standard.

In this notion of the 'non-standard' a fundamental principle is latent: whatever is not 'standard' is *deviant* usage, and *metaphora*, implicitly, is the most important kind of deviation. On that notion of deviation, later antiquity constructs the theory of *tropes*, which is not to be found in Aristotle.[3] In his system, however, *metaphora* itself is seen to subsume what will subsequently

[1] In *Poetics* 21–2, and *Rhetoric* 3.2–3 and 3.10–11. The other main theoretical texts cited in this essay are: Jakobson (1956) and (1960); Ricoeur (1978). I refer also to two of my own discussions, Silk (1974) and (1996).

[2] The rest of the list has no direct bearing on the present argument.

[3] The theory of tropes is assumed to be Hellenistic. See e.g. Russell (1981), 143–7, esp. 144 on the Stoic affinities of the 'basic eight' tropes. Cf. n. 25 below.

be distinguished as several different tropes, of which metaphor is one, and (again) the most important one. (Aristotle's *metaphora*, then, is and is not 'metaphor'; and though it will often be convenient to call it metaphor, the two terms are not strictly interchangeable.) In a celebrated fourfold classification, Aristotle defines *metaphora* thus (*Poetics* 21, 1457^{b}6–24):[4]

μεταφορὰ δέ ἐστιν ὀνόματος ἀλλοτρίου ἐπιφορὰ ἢ ἀπὸ τοῦ γένους ἐπὶ εἶδος ἢ ἀπὸ τοῦ εἴδους ἐπὶ τὸ γένος ἢ ἀπὸ τοῦ εἴδους ἐπὶ εἶδος ἢ κατὰ τὸ ἀνάλογον. λέγω δὲ ἀπὸ γένους μὲν ἐπὶ εἶδος οἷον "νηῦς δέ μοι ἥδ' ἕστηκεν"· τὸ γὰρ ὁρμεῖν ἐστιν ἑστάναι τι. ἀπ' εἴδους δὲ ἐπὶ γένος, "ἦ δὴ μυρί' Ὀδυσσεὺς ἐσθλὰ ἔοργεν"· τὸ γὰρ μυρίον πολύ ἐστιν, ᾧ νῦν ἀντὶ τοῦ πολλοῦ κέχρηται. ἀπ' εἴδους δὲ ἐπὶ εἶδος οἷον "χαλκῷ ἀπὸ ψυχὴν ἀρύσας" . . . ἐνταῦθα γὰρ τὸ . . . ἀρύσαι ταμεῖν . . . εἴρηκεν· ἄμφω γὰρ ἀφελεῖν τί ἐστιν. τὸ δὲ ἀνάλογον λέγω, ὅταν ὁμοίως ἔχῃ τὸ δεύτερον πρὸς τὸ πρῶτον καὶ τὸ τέταρτον πρὸς τὸ τρίτον· ἐρεῖ γὰρ ἀντὶ τοῦ δευτέρου τὸ τέταρτον ἢ ἀντὶ τοῦ τετάρτου τὸ δεύτερον . . . οἷον ὁμοίως ἔχει . . . γῆρας πρὸς βίον, καὶ ἑσπέρα πρὸς ἡμέραν· ἐρεῖ τοίνυν τὴν ἑσπέραν γῆρας ἡμέρας, ἢ ὥσπερ Ἐμπεδοκλῆς καὶ τὸ γῆρας ἑσπέραν βίου . . .

Metaphora is the transfer [to one thing] of a word that belongs to another thing, either from genus to species, species to genus, species to species, or by analogy. By 'genus to species' I mean (e.g.) 'here stands my ship' [*Odyssey* 1.185], because lying at anchor is a [kind of] standing. Species to genus, 'ten thousand fine deeds Odysseus has accomplished' [*Iliad* 2.272], because 'ten thousand' is many, and [Homer] uses it here instead of 'many'. Species to species, (e.g.) [?Empedocles'] 'skimming off a life with bronze' [sc. a bronze weapon] . . . because here he has said 'skimming off' for 'cutting', both being [kinds of] removing. By 'analogy' I mean [instances] when *b* is to *a* as *d* is to *c*: [a poet] will say *d* instead of *b*, or *b* instead of *d* . . . Old age is to life as evening is to day; so [a poet] will call evening 'the day's old age' or, like Empedocles, call old age 'life's evening' . . .

Metaphora, then, subsumes not only Empedocles' striking metaphors, but also Homer's less than striking metonymy ('ten thousand')—the kind of metonymy that later antiquity would call *hyperbole*.[5] Regrettably, *metaphora*, in Aristotle's usage, also

[4] Excerpted in the interests of concentration on the clearer examples. The ἀρύσας example (apparently from a hexametric poem) is likely to be by Empedocles: cf. Lucas (1968), ad loc.

[5] See below, p. 124, with n. 26. An operational explication of this instance as metonymy (pp. 132–4) might be: 'Odysseus has accomplished many fine deeds, a measurable tally even on a scale of one to ten thousand.' Quintilian's representative discussion of hyperbole (8.6.67–76) includes both metonymic and metaphorical examples.

subsumes non-deviations, like the cited Homeric use of ἕστηκεν ('stands') of a ship at anchor. This use of the verb might or might not be helpfully described as 'dead metaphor'; it would in any case be better categorized as a straightforward instance of 'standard' usage (ὄνομα κύριον).[6] Here begins a long, and mostly deplorable, tradition of confused responses by theorists to the relationship, real or supposed, between one-off literary usage and secondary but established idiom within a language.[7]

From this same *Poetics* passage another premiss of Aristotle's theory is apparent. For him, metaphor and other tropes are essentially *substitutions*. Homer said 'ten thousand' *instead of* 'many': he *could* have said 'many'; 'ten thousand' is a substitution for 'many'. A poet *could* say *b*; *instead*, he says *d*; *d* is a substitution for *b*. As a hermeneutic tool for the elucidation of metaphor, the substitution principle has been challenged long and hard in twentieth-century philosophical theories of metaphor, most strenuously in the theory of Max Black. Black, in particular, is associated with an alternative model, an 'interactional' theory of metaphor, from which metaphor emerges as a more complex phenomenon, maybe centred on a single word, but affecting a whole statement and giving it a new cognitive significance, through the 'interaction' of two separate frames of reference. Metaphor is seen thus to confer an 'insight' and to 'organize our view' of the original subject.[8] The principle

[6] On the issues involved, practical and theoretical, see Silk (1974), 27–56, 211–23, 228–31. ἵστασθαι of raised inanimates is standard usage, and especially well attested in the Ionic tradition: thus (e.g.) *Iliad* 4.263 (δέπας), 9.44 (νῆες: similarly *Odyssey* 4.426, 24.299, 308); *Odyssey* 2.341 (πίθοι); *Hymn to Aphrodite* 267 (δρύες); Herodotus 1.14.2 (κρητῆρες), 2.91.2 (ἀνδριάντες), 4.15.4 (δάφναι); Thucydides 6.55 (στήλη: likewise used on, and of, tombstones from the 7th cent. BC: *CEG* 1.144.1, 1.58.2); Hippocrates, *Prognosticum* 8 (οἰδήματα); *Internal Diseases* 29 (τρίχες); Aristotle, *Generation of Animals* 777^{b}32 (θάλαττα).

[7] See below, pp. 146–7 with n. 82. Aristotle himself does on at least one occasion seem to grasp the principle that historically secondary usage may be standard. In *Poetics* 22 (1458^{b}21) he calls ἐσθίειν of a cancer κυρίου εἰωθότος [ὀνόματος] (see Silk 1974: 52 with n. 2; for ἐσθίειν of disease see the Hippocratic evidence cited there in n. 3). Ricoeur (1978: 290–1 with n. 66) does, however, credit Aristotle with more clarity on the whole issue than he deserves. Over antiquity as a whole, understanding of the principle comes and goes: Silk (1974), 52 (with n. 5), 228–30.

[8] See primarily Black (1962); also (1977); (1979). For the phrases cited, see Black (1962), 38, 41, 237. Black's position has been criticized by, among others,

might be illustrated by Heraclitus' famous image of life (22 B52 DK):[9]

> αἰὼν παῖς ἐστι παίζων, πεσσεύων
> Life is a boy playing *pessoi* ('backgammon').

Here the metaphor as a whole (one might indeed agree) tends to offer an insight into 'life' (the original subject, or tenor), even to modify our 'view' of 'life' by bringing life into simultaneous relation with 'a boy' (the vehicle of the image).[10] And that kind of capability, certainly, is not suggested by substitutional language. It is, on the other hand, not so easy to feel that any 'insight', exactly, is offered by a metaphor like Pindar, *Pythian* 1.75,[11]

> Ἑλλάδ' ἐξέλκων βαρείας δουλίας
> *Dragging out* Greece from *heavy*/grievous servitude

or by either, or both, of the two distinct metaphors in a bit of Shakespeare once handsomely discussed by F. R. Leavis:[12]

> those honours *deep and broad*, wherewith
> Your majesty *loads* our house.

We may (or may not) agree that substitutional talk is unhelpful in any of these cases. We may (or may not) decide that interactional talk is, as corollary, appropriate.[13]

Donald Davidson (1979) (to which Black 1979 is a reply). For some sensible criticism of Davidson, see Soskice (1985), 27–31, 90–3. Regarding Black's 'interaction', and to avoid any possible misunderstanding, I should stress that his use of the word and mine in Silk (1974) are entirely different. On Black and Davidson, see below, n. 13.

[9] Black has evidently given thought to the question, *which* examples would be good ones (cf. n. 77 below), but himself tends to use trivial examples (like 'man is a wolf'), for which he is rightly castigated by Ricoeur (1978: 88). The given English translation of the Heraclitus is only a feeble equivalent (αἰών is elusive—see n. 37 below—and the 'logic' of the progressive assonantal sequence from παῖς to παίζων to πεσσεύων is lost), but the main point is unaffected.

[10] On 'tenor' and 'vehicle', see Silk (1974), 6–14.

[11] The metaphor is in *my* terms 'interactive', because βαρείας belongs to both terminologies (tenor and vehicle): Silk (1974), 129.

[12] See *Macbeth* I. vi with Leavis (1948), 77–8, 115–16.

[13] I am not concerned here to argue for or against substitutional or interactional theories, except insofar as they seem either experientially justified or an aid to sensitive perception. Certainly, the substitutional model is not usually in accordance with experience of successful metaphor (cf. below, p. 127 with n. 35). Black's interactional theory, however, brings with it a no less counter-

II

As a significant figure in the development of Russian Formalism and then, decades later, one of a select group of theoretical linguists who exercised some measurable influence on the first phase of structuralism, Roman Jakobson is assuredly one of the most remarkable figures in twentieth-century literary theory. His two celebrated contributions to the debate on metaphor belong to the later, structuralist, period of his work: a discussion entitled 'Two Aspects of Language and Two Types of Aphasic Disturbances' and another called 'Linguistics and Poetics'.[14] In these essays Jakobson departs from Aristotelian tradition in two notable ways. First, he sets up metaphor, not as a single special phenomenon, but as a contrastive member of a polarity: *metaphor*, centred on analogy or similarity, is opposed to *metonymy*, centred on association or contiguity. Secondly, metaphor and, now, metonymy are treated not simply as local devices within poetry, or literature more widely, but as typifications of two fundamental modes of discourse as a whole. More specifically: in 'Two Aspects', Jakobson discusses language disorders (aphasia) and classifies them, differentially, as impairments of the faculty of selection/substitution or else as impairments of the faculty of combination/contexture. These two groups of impairment are then duly related to metaphor (selection/substitution) and metonymy (combination/contexture), and metaphor and metonymy, in turn, are reinterpreted as two large contrastive categories of language *tout court*. In 'Linguistics and Poetics',

experiential abstraction, 'metaphorical meaning' (writ large in Ricoeur 1978, esp. 216–56), which seems, *inter alia*, to confuse the semantic load of the vehicle with the supposed point of the tenor/vehicle transaction as a whole. (Such confusion is common: 'metaphor', in many theorists' discussions, oscillates awkwardly between reference to the part and the whole.) Davidson's critique (Davidson 1979) fails to identify the mechanical cause of confusion here, and further complicates matters by a denial (seemingly subject to the same confusion) that metaphor has any 'specific cognitive content'. The scope of this denial turns out to be more limited than at first appears: Davidson is happy to invoke metaphor's 'hidden powers' (1979: 45) and to agree that metaphor 'provokes or invites a certain view of its subject' (43). Unhelpfully, however (like Black and others), he assumes without argument the privileging of the analogical force of metaphor ('aptness': 45).

[14] Jakobson (1956) and (1960) respectively.

again, Jakobson expands the metaphor/metonymy polarity into the large opposition between verse ('metaphorical') and prose ('metonymic'). Such an enlargement of the significance of metaphor, and indeed of metonymy, has no precedent.

Paul Ricoeur is among those who have mounted a challenge to Jakobson's system. Ricoeur, whose philosophical observations have taken him to fields as diverse as hermeneutics and political science, is one of the least classifiable of literary theorists, just as his classic treatise, *La Métaphore Vive*,[15] must be one of the most elusive contributions to the long debate about metaphor. Yet while the intricate arguments of this book certainly resist easy reduction, it may be summarily noted that, though not uncritical of Aristotle, Ricoeur takes more radical issue with Jakobson's dyarchy of metaphor and metonymy and seeks to re-establish the special status of metaphor itself. In an interactional spirit, however, Ricoeur sees in metaphor the power to redescribe reality and a significance that goes far beyond poetry. Metonymy, by contrast, is turned back into the modest thing the ancient tropologists took it to be: a limited literary device and a substitution of a simple kind, whereas metaphor is not a substitution at all. As an interactionist, Ricoeur rejects the Aristotelian association between metaphor and substitution; but while rejecting this link, he does tend to vindicate the principle of deviation, successfully demonstrating that the notion of substitution is not, as widely supposed, entailed by the notion of deviant usage.[16]

In my own attempt now to assist the debate, I shall in part be revisiting territory I have visited before, and in part reworking arguments or examples I have used before.[17] There seems, however, to be a sufficient lack of recognition of certain points that I wish to insist on, and of the overall position that I believe to be necessary, to justify a modicum of self-repetition in what I hope will be seen as a good cause.

[15] Originally published in 1975, but cited here in Czerny's translation (*The Rule of Metaphor*) = Ricoeur (1978).

[16] See p. 145 below.

[17] In Silk (1974) and (1996).

III

I begin with the essential concept of *trope*. A trope is a deviant usage—that is, a known word or phrase used, in context, deviantly from any normal usage of that word or phrase. For myself I would be happy to say that a trope is deviant usage and that all deviant usage is tropical—that therefore 'trope' subsumes even what some would classify as solecisms or mistakes or private usage. This is not what most theorists would say; and ancient theorists, in particular, are careful to distinguish tropes, on the one hand, from solecisms and mistakes on the other: I would prefer to note that some tropes will be found to be more successful than others (and the ones we associate with solecisms or mistakes will probably be unsuccessful).[18] The relevance of notions of value to our discussion should certainly be acknowledged at the outset, if only because much theorizing has been bedevilled by reference to inadequate examples. And let us also acknowledge here that only a wide and sensitive experience of literature in general, and poetry in particular, will let us know when and why examples are adequate or inadequate. It is in poetry that adequate and successful examples characteristically occur; it is there that the potentialities are made good.

The suggested definition of trope may be glossed in operational terms. Operationally, 'normal usage' is: an established usage of a word or phrase such as you would expect to find in a compendious dictionary of current usage; and/or such as you would think a foreigner learning the language on a comprehensive scale ought to know; and/or such as you would expect to be able to call to mind if presented with the word/phrase out of context, and were called on to list all its different uses. There is, for instance, no Greek use of *παῖς*, 'boy', that would accommodate Heraclitus' *αἰὼν παῖς ἐστι* . . . ('Life is a boy . . .'),[19] nor any

[18] Cf. Quintilian 1.5.5, but contrast 8.6.1: 'tropus est verbi vel sermonis a propria significatione in aliam *cum virtute* mutatio'.

[19] In metaphors taking this kind of '*a* is *b*' shape, world literature provides at least one example of a negative version, Donne's 'No man is an island'. Here the requisite deviation (of 'island') is in the implied positive ('A/every man is . . .'). Cf. (on this example) Davidson (1979), 40: 'the negation of a metaphor seems always to be a potential metaphor' (that 'always' must be philosophical, not experiential: cf. pp. 141–7 below) and Cohen (1975), 671.

Greek use of ἐξέλκειν, 'drag out', that would accommodate Pindar's Ἑλλάδ' ἐξέλκων . . . δουλίας ('Dragging out Greece from . . . servitude'), nor any English use of 'deep' and 'broad' that would accommodate Shakespeare's 'those honours deep and broad'. Any usage that in a specified linguistic sequence is not normal in the given sense is deviant and therefore involves a trope. Any usage not thus deviant is not (or 'does not involve') a trope.[20] For instance, in English usage 'birds *build* nests' is not deviant and thus is not a trope, whereas 'the birds had their *buildings* in the tree' *is* deviant and *is* a trope.[21] Again, in current English, chairs have 'legs' and to speak of the *leg* of a chair involves no trope; but when Gerard Manley Hopkins says, of God, 'Over again I feel thy finger', there *is* a trope, because in current English (and/or nineteenth-century English) God does not have 'fingers'.[22] Again, in twentieth-century English, dawn may (for instance) *break*; it cannot, in normal usage, 'burst'. Hence, when Yeats (in 'The Tower') speaks of 'bursting dawn', there is a trope. Many things, in normal usage, may burst—bubbles, balloons, blood-vessels, water-pipes, seed-cases—but not 'dawn'. In all such cases one can *feel* the difference between the deviant and the normal, irrespective of how interesting (or not) or how impressive (or not) the deviation may be.[23] The essence of deviation is that it is *perceptible* deviation. If the deviation is somehow *not* perceptible as such, it cannot be deviation at all. The effect, the experience, of deviation, evidently, is determinative. 'Birds build nests' does not *feel* deviant, therefore cannot be a trope. The same goes for 'leg' of a chair and for Aristotle's ἕστηκεν (of a ship). The same, too, holds good for a scientific phrase like 'electric current' or theological phrase like 'kingdom of heaven' or rustic phrase like the Latin *laetas segetes* ('fruitful crops') or poetic phrase like the Greek

[20] 'Is not/does not involve': the word 'trope', like the word 'metaphor', is used either of the deviant word(s) or of the wider transaction (cf. n. 13 above).

[21] Example from Silk (1974), 30.

[22] Myles Burnyeat asks me if it is a fact (*a*) of the English language or (*b*) of belief that God does not have 'fingers'. The answer (presumably) is *both*, but (*a*) relevantly, irrespective of (*b*). The existence of finger-ful images of God like Michaelangelo's does not directly bear on (*a*)—though it might on (*b*).

[23] Or—needless to say?—how deliberate (or not). In literary stylistics (as opposed to, say, speech-act theory), invoking intentions is usually inconsequential: cf. briefly Silk (1974), 59–63.

ἄνθος ἥβης ('young manhood').[24] None of these are tropes. It follows, since metaphor is a kind of trope, that none of these are metaphors.

The ancient literary theorists bequeathed to their successors an unwieldy apparatus of tropes, of which most can be safely jettisoned.[25] Following Jakobson, I assume two fundamental tropes, metaphor and metonymy, with all others best regarded as versions of one or other of those two.[26] Metaphor may be defined as a trope whose logical basis is one of analogy or comparison or similarity, irrespective of whether that 'logical basis' is central or peripheral to the instance in question. In metaphor, the deviant item or sequence (the vehicle) is distinct from the non-deviant sequence in its vicinity (the tenor) terminologically, and the relation between the two terminologies, in whole or part, is one of analogy, comparison, or similarity. As an operational definition of metaphor, I suggest: a deviantly used word or sequence of words whose adequate explication (sc. explanation by paraphrase or expansion) into non-deviant usage involves overt analogy, comparison, or simile.[27] If one sought an explication of 'the birds had their buildings in the tree', one would have to say something like: 'the nests—in some way unspecified—were *like* human habitations or architectural constructions'. If one sought an explication of 'bursting dawn', it might be: 'dawn, when it breaks, is, or might be, *as* violent/*as* sudden/ *as* shocking/*as* full of potential as something unspecific (like . . .?)

[24] *Laetas* and ἄνθος: see respectively Cicero, *Orator* 81, and Silk (1974), 100, 102. The words are conventionally mistranslated 'cheerful' and 'flower of' (*vel sim.*), as if deviant.

[25] D'Alton (1931), 106–9, remains a wonderful cautionary tale for anyone innocently disposed to believe there was any thought-out coherence to ancient tropology.

[26] As catachresis and allegory (when a trope at all) are versions or subtypes of metaphor, and synecdoche, enallage, and hyperbole versions or subtypes of metonymy. See variously Silk (1974), 6, 210–11; Ricoeur (1978), 48–64, 134–72. Allegory (when a trope) is extended metaphor without an explicit tenor, though the tenor may be alluded to interactively (by 'explanation' or intrusion: Silk 1974: 122–7, 144–9). On hyperbole, cf. above, p. 117 with n. 5.

[27] It in no way follows (with e.g. Quintilian 8.6.8, see McCall 1969: 229–30) that metaphor *is* a condensed simile. On the differences between metaphor and simile, see the lucid discussion by Nowottny (1962: 50–68), and cf. the useful remarks by Davidson (1979: 36–7) and Ricoeur (1978: 24–7, 183–7). On the 'terminological' aspect of the argument here, cf. Silk (1974), 6–14.

bursting'. And if one sought an explication of Pindar's 'Dragging out Greece . . .', one might begin by saying: 'the process of liberating Greece . . . was difficult, perhaps dangerous: *imagine* the difficulty and the danger of *dragging* something (unspecific but concrete) out of . . . that's how difficult and dangerous it was.' Such explications tend to be (the suggested explications certainly are) clumsy and inadequate: that is neither here nor there. The point is that some such explication is always available for a metaphorical trope, and for no other trope. Such explication may, if one chooses, also be applied to non-deviant usages like 'birds build nests' and 'electric current', on the grounds that such usages carry hidden, but still latent, analogies. That proposal, which was given its classic formulation by Nietzsche, and which has more recently been argued by a variety of modern theorists,[28] has its point—but also its dangers, and chiefly that it tends to squander the great Formalist insight and blur the difference between the familiarizing and the *de*familiarizing.[29] At all events, if our concern is with deviant (defamiliarizing) usage, the possibility of applying any kind of equivalent diagnostic analysis to non-deviant (non-defamiliarizing) usage is (again) neither here nor there.

In Aristotle's *Poetics*, which pre-dates the formation of the theory of tropes, *metaphora* is given special weight within a somewhat random-seeming set of types of 'exotic' linguistic usage (22, 1458^{a}22–3):

ξενικὸν δὲ λέγω γλῶτταν καὶ μεταφορὰν καὶ ἐπέκτασιν καὶ πᾶν τὸ παρὰ τὸ κύριον.

By 'exotic' I mean loan-words, metaphors, lengthenings, and anything that diverges from the standard.

The weighting Aristotle gives to metaphor is, as we have seen, attributed by him to its logical basis—to the analogy, similarity, or comparison on which, in logical terms, it rests (*Poetics* 22, 1459^{a}5–8):

πολὺ δὲ μέγιστον τὸ μεταφορικόν . . . τὸ γὰρ εὖ μεταφέρειν τὸ τὸ ὅμοιον θεωρεῖν ἐστιν.

[28] See n. 82 below.

[29] On the principle, see briefly Silk (1995), 119.

Much the most important is metaphorical [usage] . . .[30] to use metaphors well is to discern similarities.

Given that Aristotle formulates this principle within his *Poetics* as part of a theory of poetry (περὶ ποιητικῆς αὐτῆς),[31] it is important to stress that in the poetic usage of metaphor, in Greek as elsewhere, the (ana)logical basis, though always a reality, is rarely of central importance. Nor is it the reason (*pace* Aristotle) for the special status of metaphor: that special status is due rather to the combination of powers held by this trope and reflected in its multiplicity of functions.

The functions of metaphor in actual literary usage, which I have discussed elsewhere in connection with ancient usage, fall into three groups:[32]

(*a*) to make clearer, as through a diagram;
(*b*) to make immediate, as if to the senses;
(*c*) to exploit the associations, including the contrary associations, of the vehicle (i.e of its given terminology), beyond any limited point or ground of comparison.[33]

All three functions may, and often do, coexist, but in any given image, in context, only one is likely to be dominant. Of the three functions, (*c*), by definition, foregrounds the new vehicle, and does so without special reference to the logic of analogy. Early in Aeschylus' *Agamemnon* (40–1) Menelaus is 'Priam's great *adversary at law*' (Πριάμου μέγας ἀντίδικος). The implication is that the Trojan War is in some unspecified sense a legal event,

[30] With a looseness characteristic of the *Poetics*, the items of which 'the metaphorical' is 'the most important' are referred to again and now include compounds ('double names': 1459ᵃ5).

[31] The first words of the treatise (*Poetics* 1, 1447ᵃ8). It is true that the discussion of metaphor (*Poetics* 21–2) takes place within an overall section on *lexis* ('verbalization': see Silk 1994: 109–10), whose remit at first seems to cover what Aristotle calls 'all *lexis*' (*Poetics* 20, 1456ᵇ20), i.e. verbal usage in (the Greek) language *tout court*. However, throughout the discussion of types of ὀνόματα in *Poetics* 21–2, it is apparent that the focus has returned to poetry: see e.g. 1457ᵇ33–4, 1458ᵃ23–4, 1458ᵇ7, and esp. 1459ᵃ8–16 (immediately after the passage under discussion).

[32] See Silk (1996), 967, which the discussion that follows recycles at various points. For the triadic schema, cf. Nowottny (1962), 64.

[33] In this I include the *unlikeness* of an image and all its significant consequences: Silk (1974), 5–6.

and this implication prefigures the way that the whole cycle of conflict is eventually resolved at the end of *Eumenides*. That is unquestionably the main point of the image, and (or though) it has no bearing on the logic of analogy between *this* tenor and *this* vehicle at *this* point. Function (*b*) foregrounds the tropicality of the vehicle and its corollary that any literal terms of reference (*all* literal terms, not some specific terms for which the vehicle is 'substituted') are suppressed. This is less a matter of making anything *clear* than of defamiliarizing and thereby making the listener or reader experience anew: he or she is given 'two shots at the target' and gets a *sense* of the target from the composite perspective.[34] When Yeats writes of 'bursting dawn', we have an instant impression of what (on this projection) the coming of the dawn *feels* like, though not exactly what it feels *like*: we are neither invited nor even permitted to think that the coming of the dawn is being compared with damaged blood-vessels but not with opening seed-cases, or with opening seed-cases but not with damaged blood-vessels—or whatever. We *are* aware of an underlying analogy, but not of exactly what it is (if only for which reason, substitutional talk *is* clearly unhelpful), and for the efficacy of the image that inexactness may be—exactly—what we need.[35]

Alternatively, the tenor may be made in some way clearer through its implicit analogical (etc.) relationship with the vehicle: function (*a*). It is only here that the analogy (or similarity or comparison) is foregrounded, and—as far as metaphor is concerned—this function is rarely dominant, and certainly not in the literature of antiquity. There—and I quote now, for convenience, from my own earlier discussion—'the function is chiefly associated with epic simile . . . or simile or analogy in scientific or philosophical contexts: Plato's long comparison (*Ion* 533de) between the inspirational power of poetry and the

[34] See Nowottny (1962), 59.

[35] 'The inimitable mark of the poet . . . is his ability to control realization to the precise degree appropriate in the given place . . . it is in the incomplete realization of the metaphors that the realizing gift of the poet and the "realized" quality of the passage are manifested': Leavis (1948), 77–8. The 'inexactness' in such a case as Yeats' also helps to make clear why substitutional talk ('bursting' is a *substitute* for 'breaking'?) is so inappropriate. 'Bursting' is indeed no more a *substitute* for 'breaking' than 'dawn' is for 'daybreak'. (And try playing the game with Hopkins' 'Over again I feel thy *finger*' . . .)

magnet, and Lucretius' analogy (5.1056–90) between human speech and animal communication, are representative'. With metaphor in literature—in antiquity and in the Western traditions in general—the function is 'rarely dominant except where the goal is imagery that expresses the inexpressible, as when Plato (*Republic* 509e) uses the very word εἰκόνες ('images') to express the relation between sense-objects and ideal reality'—or likewise when Aeschylus (*Agamemnon* 218) sees Agamemnon '*put on the strap* of necessity' (ἀνάγκας ἔδυ λέπαδνον).[36] Something of a clarificatory effect might provisionally be ascribed to a metaphor like Heraclitus', in that 'life' (αἰών) is something of an inexpressible mystery, and the metaphor expresses something of the inexpressible. On the other hand, it is notoriously not the case that modern interpreters, at least, have any clear sense of the underlying ground of this particular comparison; and one might equally well argue that the metaphor makes 'life' seem more mysterious, not less. On reflection, it might be better to associate the example with functions (*b*) and (*c*), not with (*a*) at all. And it is certainly the case that, though function (*a*) deserves its place in the trinity, examples that promise to give it pride of place often let us down when we pay closer attention.[37]

Immediacy, function (*b*), is altogether commoner and more commonly dominant in poetic usage in particular. This aspect of metaphor is first discussed by Aristotle, this time in the *Rhetoric*, under the heading of *energeia*, 'actuality',[38] which is further

[36] Silk (1996), 967. A case might be made for the proposition that in certain periods of certain literary traditions, function (*a*) is, if not predominant, at least more commonly in evidence: see e.g. the discussion offered by Tuve (1947: 251–381), of the 'logical functions' of images as used in English Renaissance poetry.

[37] My own discussion of the Heraclitus (1996: 967)—where the example is too confidently assigned to function (*a*)—is a case in point. The elusiveness of this image is partly due to the fact that αἰών itself could be construed as 'time' (as I myself translated it at 1996: 967) or 'lifetime' as well as 'life'. See e.g. the range of views discussed at Marcovich (1967), 493–5; Kahn (1979), 227–9; and (for the word αἰών itself) see most recently Johansen and Whittle (1980), 2.45–6 on Aeschylus, *Suppliants* 46. See further n. 47 below.

[38] 'ἐνέργεια [for Aristotle] . . . is principally shewn in animation, literally and metaphorically . . . This sense [of ἐνέργεια] is borrowed [by Aristotle] from the metaphysical use of the term, to express "realization", as opposed to δύναμις' (Cope and Sandys 1973 on *Rhetoric* 3.10.6, 1410^{b}36).

associated with the notion of 'setting things *before the eyes*' (πρὸ ὀμμάτων). Aristotle writes (3.11.2–3, 1411^{b}24–1412^{a}2):[39]

λέγω δὴ πρὸ ὀμμάτων ταῦτα ποιεῖν, ὅσα ἐνεργοῦντα σημαίνει. οἷον τὸν ἀγαθὸν ἄνδρα φάναι εἶναι τετράγωνον μεταφορά . . . ἀλλ' οὐ σημαίνει ἐνέργειαν, ἀλλὰ . . . ὡς κέχρηται Ὅμηρος πολλαχοῦ τῷ τὰ ἄψυχα ἔμψυχα λέγειν διὰ τῆς μεταφορᾶς. ἐν πᾶσι δὲ τῷ ἐνέργειαν ποιεῖν εὐδοκιμεῖ, οἷον ἐν . . . "αἰχμὴ δὲ στέρνοιο διέσσυτο μαιμώωσα".

'Setting things before the eyes', I would say, is achieved by expressions indicative of actualizing. For instance, to call a man 'squared-off' [Simonides, fr. 542.3 West] is a metaphor . . . but it is not indicative of actuality . . .

and Aristotle goes on to contrast the way Homer uses 'animating' metaphor:

Homer often uses metaphor to speak of inanimate things as animate. In all [such cases] it is by achieving actuality that he distinguishes himself, as in . . . 'Through his breast the spear shot, *straining*' [*Iliad* 15.542].

This kind of effect, with its concomitant defamiliarizing, is a striking and central feature of most of the metaphors cited in this discussion so far—not only Yeats' 'bursting dawn', but equally Pindar's 'dragging out', Hopkins' 'finger', and (more mutedly) Shakespeare's 'deep and broad'. On reflection, Heraclitus' *pessoi*, too, partly belongs here, working rather like some Homeric similes, in which the extended vehicle creates a compelling vignette of such interest that the immediate analogy is overshadowed (even though it is only and precisely the knowledge that there *is* an analogy that gives the vehicle its licence to act). While giving due credit to Aristotle for first formulating the principle, we should also note the wholly unhelpful limitation built into his operative phrase, 'before the *eyes*'. As a host of modern critics have pointed out,[40] there is nothing especially visual about metaphorical (or any other kind of) actualization—and, with the given examples to hand, one might point to the Hopkins, the Pindar, the Shakespeare, as obvious testimony to the point. Indeed, Aristotle's own example of Homer's μαιμώωσα ('straining') bears out the point as well.[41] His

[39] As elsewhere, I have excerpted the Greek to avoid irrelevant complications associated with awkward examples.

[40] None more comprehensively than Furbank (1970).

[41] On μαιμάω see Johansen and Whittle (1980) on Aeschylus, *Suppliants*

insistence on the visual, one imagines, reflects not so much his experience of metaphor, as his philosophical concern with mental activity and his own view of vision as 'the paradigm of mental process'.[42]

If the implicit analogy is in practice often subordinated to the effect of immediacy, it is often, again, subservient to the exploitation of the associations of the vehicle: function (*c*). Consider another example, the metaphor at the beginning of Pindar's *Olympian* 2 (1–2), an ode in honour of Theron, tyrant of Acragas:

> *ἀναξιφόρμιγγες ὕμνοι,*
> *τίνα θεόν, τίν' ἥρωα, τίνα δ' ἄνδρα κελαδήσομεν;*
>
> O *lords* of the lyre, hymns,
> Which god, which hero, and which man shall we sing?

If we ask the question 'What is the basic analogy here?' we will no doubt come to the conclusion that Pindar's 'hymns' are lords of the lyre, because (as commentators say) Greek words dominate Greek music.[43] But coming to terms with metaphors within poetry is not a matter, exactly, of 'asking questions' and 'coming to conclusions', but of responding with a more open mind or, rather, sensibility. Responding to words in context is a start, and if we respond to Pindar's words in context we become aware that the chief function of *ἀναξι-* is to introduce the poem as a whole and, in particular, the three parallel items of the next verse: god, hero, man. In Greek usage *ἄναξ* is a normal honorific term for gods, and then again for heroes—but not for ordinary men.[44]

895. It might be supposed that Aristotle also took *διέσσυτο* as 'animating' metaphor. Animating it may be; metaphor it surely is not. (*δια*)*σεύεσθαι* looks to be standard usage of inanimate things from Homer to Ionic prose (the word does not exist in Attic prose): of *αἰχμή* again, *Iliad* 5.661, so *Iliad* 21.167 (*αἷμα*), 13.142 (*ὀλοοίτροχος*); Bacchylides, fr. 20b.7 Snell (*κύλικες*); Hippocrates, *Diseases of Women* 2.201 (*πνεῦμα*), 2.138 (*νοσήματα*), cf. 1.36; similarly (in non-Ionic verse) Aeschylus, *Seven Against Thebes* 941 (*σίδηρος*); likewise (with other compounds) *ἐπισεύομαι* (of *πῦρ*, *Iliad* 17.737; of *κῦμα*, *Odyssey* 5.314; of *πνοιή*, *Odyssey* 6.20), *ἐκσεύομαι* (of *οἶνος*, *Odyssey* 9.373); *ἀνασεύομαι* (of *αἷμα*, *Iliad* 11.458); cf. *ἀπο-/ἐπι-σεύομαι* (v.l.) of *αἷμα*, [Hippocrates], *Acute Diseases* [Appendix], 10.

[42] Norman (1979), 95.

[43] So e.g. Willcock (1995), 142.

[44] See the evidence in LSJ s.v. When, in the classical period, the word *is* used of 'ordinary' men (at the height of their standing), it is used pointedly—either in a pride-goes-before-a-fall context (e.g. of Xerxes at Aeschylus, *Persians* 5) or

Theron, however, is no *ordinary* man, but a great man—on a par even with . . .? At the very outset of the poem, then, the metaphorical compound proposes the problematic that underlies Pindar's poetic ideology as a whole: 'nearly every poem of Pindar is a metaphor, the terms of which are the victor and the heroes. The likeness is never fully pressed, since to say openly that contemporaries resemble demigods touches impiety.'[45] In addition, we might note, the lyre is itself 'lord' of Greek music—it is, after all, the 'golden' instrument of Apollo[46]—and indeed lyres (φόρμιγγες) are themselves right 'for lords' (τοῖς ἄναξι). That is: the opening metaphor—strictly, the free play of associations of its vehicle—creates an explosion of suggestions and connections, one of which, in particular, is momentous for the poem and far outweighs the importance of the notional point of comparison. In this instance, certainly, there is little sensuous charge, and diagrammatic logic is virtually a pretext for associative effect.

Even if it is not the 'point' of a metaphor, an associative force is often its most striking feature. In the Heraclitus, more striking than the ground of comparison—something to do with randomness, or non-randomness: 'life is a boy playing *pessoi*'—is the paradox that 'life' (and the Greek *αἰών* has clear connotations of life-*span*, i.e. *age*) should be a 'boy'.[47] And while the Heraclitus aphorism seemingly claims a kind of self-sufficiency and, as such, contains the cues to an appropriate response within it, one should be alive to the dangers of divorcing an image from an enabling context. The Pindar example just considered would look quite different if quoted out of its epinician context, including the epinician sentence it introduces. Could it be that even an example like, say, Empedocles' 'life's evening' would seem less analogy-heavy in context, whatever that context might be?[48]

with a yes-he-*is*-very-special implication (e.g. of a son of Euagoras, who himself is said to deserve the label θεὸς ἐν ἀνθρώποις, Isocrates, *Euagoras* 72).

[45] The probing formulation comes from an unjustly neglected book: Finley (1955), 40.

[46] χρυσέα φόρμιγξ, Ἀπόλλωνος . . . κτέανον: Pindar, *Pythian* 1.1–2.

[47] See n. 37 above. My formulation implies that the age/youth paradox is part of the point of the image—under function (*c*)—but not part of its 'logic' under function (*a*). Contrast e.g. Marcovich (1967), 495: 'a mature or aged man is just as foolish as is a child', wherewith the paradox has been shifted into function (*a*).

[48] See above, p. 117.

IV

Metonymy may be defined as a trope whose logical basis is one of association or contiguity. An operational definition might be: a word or sequence of words whose explication can be made to use all the tropical items untropically but without any similarity marker ('like', 'as', or whatever). If you are faced with a deviant usage wherein each word is *literally* possible in an expanded context in a sense approximating to that of its given use, you have metonymy. Take the metonyms at the beginning and end of the *Aeneid*.[49] In the opening words of the first line, *arma virumque cano* ('*Arms* and a man I sing'), 'arms' might for instance be expanded to 'the final phase of the Trojan war, and the subsequent war in Italy, in both of which *arms* were literally and relevantly used'. In Aeneas' tortured words, as he avenges himself on Turnus for the killing of young Pallas—*Pallas te hoc vulnere, Pallas* | *immolat* ('With this *wound Pallas, Pallas,* makes you his sacrificial offering': 12.948–9)—'Pallas' might be expanded to 'I, Aeneas, on behalf of Pallas', and 'wound' to 'this weapon which I, Aeneas, am holding, through which I am in the process of, or am just on the point of, inflicting a wound'. The cumulative effect of these metonyms (as I have noted elsewhere) is a remarkable composite image: 'the absent Pallas is "there" in the weapon's stroke to avenge his own "wound" and Aeneas' too'.[50]

Or take this sequence from Eliot's *The Waste Land*:

> *Footsteps* shuffled on the *stair*.
> Under the firelight, under the brush, her hair
> Spread out in fiery points
> *Glowed into words*, then would be savagely still.
> 'My nerves are bad to-night. Yes, bad . . .'

'Footsteps' is metonymic here, as is 'stair'. It is clear that *footsteps* were literally heard on at least one, no doubt more than one, *stair*, also that more than one foot literally *shuffled* on at least one *stair*. It might in fact be more helpful to see both *footsteps* and *shuffled* (quite apart from *stair*) as metonymic—as if the given

[49] Here again I borrow from my discussion in Silk (1996).
[50] Silk (1996), 967–8.

sequence were a portmanteau, a compressed version, of a longer non-tropical sequence: footsteps ⟨were heard, as person or persons unspecified⟩ shuffled ⟨with their feet⟩. One might note—as a marker for the discussion to come—that what we have here presents itself as a selection and recombination of associated elements, where the elements selected and recombined look to be (among other things) the most sensuously evocative. 'Glowed into words', meanwhile, works in much the same way. Under the firelight, her hair literally *glowed*, while her neurotic state of mind was such that we might (and perhaps she did) put it *into words* as follows: 'my nerves . . .'. In the compressed moment one grasps this implication as part of the overall, instantaneous, effect.

Or take this, from Sophocles' *Oedipus Tyrannus* (179–81):

> *ὧν πόλις ἀνάριθμος ὄλλυται·*
> *νηλέα δὲ γένεθλα πρὸς πέδῳ*
> *θαναταφόρα κεῖται ἀνοίκτως.*

The Thebans are dying of the plague:

> Whereof *city* unnumbered perisheth.

It is, no doubt, *citizens*, not city, who are literally 'perishing', and dying, or dead, citizens who are literally 'unnumbered'; and an expansion along such lines is readily available. One notes in passing here how the chilling singularity of ἀνάριθμος serves to defamiliarize the countlessness of the dying. And now:

> *Pitiless*, children on the ground,
> Carrying death, lie without lamentation.

Tidily, but arbitrarily, commentators assure us that νηλέα means 'unpitied', which is something that (all the evidence suggests) the Greek word νηλής never means.[51] 'Unpitied' is implicit in ἀνοίκτως ('without the ritual of pity', therefore 'without lamentation'), but νηλέα is 'pitiless', 'ruthless'. 'Pitiless', however, is only too apt—once we accept it as the metonym it is, in terms of the drastic recombination it effectively involves. The *gods* of the city (not mentioned here, but a pervasive presence in the ode to which the lines belong) are clearly pitiless; so, in particular, is

[51] See LSJ's evidence (but *not* their interpretation) s.v. On the impropriety of their procedure in such cases see Silk (1983).

(the god of) *death*, implicit in the adjective θανατaφόρα and associated with the epithet νηλής in epic.[52] And this ascription of a lack of pity to those who, above all, deserve to receive, but do not receive, pity themselves, painfully conveys a mocking inversion of all propriety. The effect is reminiscent of (but shorter and sharper than) Thucydides' famous account (2.51–3) of the shocking consequences of the plague at Athens. How powerful, then, a simple-seeming metonymy can be: feel its effect. And how questionable, within the diverse range of tropical effects as a whole, the unqualified priority traditionally given to metaphor should now seem[53]—just as questionable as the unqualified priority traditionally given to logical efficacy within the range of functions of metaphor itself.

V

My discussion assumes and accepts Jakobson's privileging polarity of metaphor and metonymy, and the examples cited represent the way the two tropes are characteristically used in poetic contexts—whether heightened verse, or poetic prose, of which the Heraclitus is representative. And there is a special propriety here in using an example of 'poetic prose' like the Heraclitus, because it is Jakobson who (with some plausibility) insists that an understanding of poetry depends on an under-

[52] Hades is referred to (as ἑσπέρου θεοῦ) immediately before the words ὧν πόλις κ.τ.λ. (178). The association between νηλής and death is established by the epic formula νηλεὲς ἦμαρ, *Iliad* 11.484 (τὴν χαλεπὴν ἡμέραν, τούτεστι τὸν θάνατον: scholia ad loc.), *Odyssey* 8.525 etc. Irrespective of its actual etymology, the word was undoubtedly taken to be connected with ἔλεος throughout antiquity (cf. Hainsworth, in Heubeck, West, and Hainsworth 1988, on *Odyssey* 8.525).

[53] There have been regrettably few sustained attempts by literary critics to make anything of metonymy, and those there have been have tended to be theoretically muddled. In the classical arena, a case in point is Stoneman (1981), which uses an admirable range of theoretical reference to construct a bizarre argument that: (*a*) metonymy works by substitution; (*b*) Pindar's metaphors characteristically work by substitution; (*c*) therefore Pindar's metaphors (so-called) are really metonyms. Here both (*a*) and (*b*) are deeply suspect—for (*a*) see below, pp. 140–3—though even if both (*a*) and (*b*) were somehow sound, the conclusion (*c*) would not necessarily follow. On a larger canvas, compare Lodge (1977). At 73–124, having accepted Jakobson's ideas fairly uncritically, Lodge is reduced to ineffectually worrying at the appropriate application of the terms 'metaphor' and 'metonymy' to some random specimens of modern poetry and prose.

standing of the functions of language as a whole and insists, again, that if we theorize about poetry, we should strictly be theorizing about the 'poetic function' of language. For Jakobson, 'poetry' of course exists and has its characteristic features, but its characteristic features are visible in varying degrees throughout various realms of language-use, with their most complete realization in what we call poetry itself.[54]

I see no great difficulty about accepting Jakobson's concept of the 'poetic function' of language, nor in accepting his polarity of the two tropes, metaphor and metonymy. Jakobson himself, however, makes metaphor and metonymy players on an altogether bigger stage, associating metaphor primarily with verse, metonymy with prose. This arises from his interest in mounting explorations on a deep structural level in search of possible connections between seemingly separate aspects of poetry and of discourse as a whole—and then his willingness to give those abstracted connections a determinative place within his system.

Central to Jakobson's argument is a distinction, first adumbrated by Saussure, between selection and combination, which are taken to be processes fundamental to all linguistic usage; *selection* is then identified with *metaphor*, on the implicit grounds that metaphor involves a *substitution*; on the other side, *combination* is identified with *metonymy*, on the grounds that metonymy involves *contiguity*.[55] Finally, an audacious connection is posited between metaphor and formal parallelism, for instance rhyme.

This welter of abstractions and equivalencies may or may not impress. It is worth stressing, in any event, that Jakobson's arguments, though accompanied by concrete instances, give the impression of being driven by principles which are not, seemingly, open to experiential challenge. The crucial passages are as follows. First, from the discussion of aphasia, a bold vignette of his theoretical claims, together with suggestions about why

[54] Jakobson (1960), 356–9.

[55] Jakobson (1960), 358. For whatever reason, Jakobson tends not to advertise the Saussurian basis of his theory: Saussure does not figure in the bibliographies of Jakobson (1960) or (1956). For the Saussurian antecedents of 'selection' and 'combination', see Saussure (1916), 170–84, where the polarity is implicit: 'combinaisons' belong to 'rapports syntagmatiques' (170) and 'notre choix' (as among synonyms) to 'rapports associatifs' (179).

metonymy (if really as important as metaphor) should have been so long neglected:[56]

Similarity in meaning connects the symbols of a metalanguage with the symbols of the language referred to. Similarity connects a metaphorical term with the term for which it is substituted. Consequently, when constructing a metalanguage to interpret tropes, the researcher possesses more homogeneous means to handle metaphor, whereas metonymy, based on a different principle, easily defies interpretation. Therefore nothing comparable to the rich literature on metaphor can be cited for the theory of metonymy. [Furthermore . . .] since poetry is focused upon the sign, and pragmatical prose primarily upon the referent, tropes and figures [have been] studied mainly as poetic devices. The principle of similarity underlies poetry, [witness] the metrical parallelism of lines, or the phonic equivalence of rhyming words . . . Prose, on the contrary, is forwarded essentially by contiguity.

Then, from 'Linguistics and Poetics', Jakobson's formulation of the 'poetic function', his restatement of Saussure, and his reformulation of the metaphor/metonymy distinction in its widest application, in terms of a grand general principle about poetry, often enunciated since:[57]

What is the empirical linguistic criterion of the poetic function? In particular, what is the indispensable feature inherent in any piece of poetry? To answer this question we must recall the two basic modes of arrangement used in verbal behaviour, *selection* and *combination.* If 'child' is the topic of the message, the speaker selects one among the extant, more or less similar, nouns like child, kid, youngster, tot, all of them equivalent in a certain respect, and then, to comment on this topic, he may select one of the semantically cognate verbs—sleeps, dozes, nods, naps. Both chosen words combine in the speech chain. The selection is produced on the base of equivalence, similarity and dissimilarity, synonymity and antonymity, while the combination, the build-up of the sequence, is based on contiguity. *The poetic function*

[56] Jakobson (1956), 95–6, Earlier in the same discussion, Jakobson offers less sweeping and more helpful characterizations about the occurrence of 'similarity' and 'contiguity' in practice. We learn that 'in Russian lyrical songs . . . metaphoric constructions predominate, while in the heroic epics the metonymic way is preponderant' (91), and also that metaphor is predominant in romantic and symbolist literature (sc. poetry), and metonymy in realism (sc. realist prose) (91–2). Here too, however, the broad brush is evident, and in any case the assertions quoted in the text undermine even these qualifications.

[57] Jakobson (1960), 358.

projects the principle of equivalence from the axis of selection into the axis of combination. Equivalence is promoted to the constitutive device of the sequence. In poetry one syllable is equalized with any other syllable of the same sequence; word stress is assumed to equal word stress, as unstress equals unstress; prosodic long is matched with long, and short with short . . . (Jakobson's italics)

And for his unexpected analogy between metaphorical 'equivalence' and aural-metrical 'equivalence' Jakobson draws support from—of all unlikely theorists—the poet Gerard Manley Hopkins and his youthful reflections on poetic parallelism:[58]

Hopkins, in his student papers of 1865, displayed a prodigious insight into the structure of poetry: 'The structure of poetry is that of continuous parallelism . . . But parallelism is of two kinds necessarily—where the opposition is clearly marked, and where it is transitional rather or chromatic. Only the first kind, that of marked parallelism, is concerned with the structure of verse—in rhythm, the recurrence of a certain sequence of syllables, in metre, the recurrence of a certain sequence of rhythm, in alliteration, in assonance and in rhyme . . . To the marked or abrupt kind of parallelism belong metaphor, simile, parable, and so on, where the effect is sought in likeness of things, and antithesis, contrast and so on, where it is sought in unlikeness.'

And, as a gloss to that last proposition, Jakobson adds:[59]

Equivalence in sound, projected into the sequence as its constitutive principle, inevitably involves semantic equivalence, and on any linguistic level any constituent of such a sequence prompts one of the two correlative experiences which Hopkins neatly defines as 'comparison for likeness' sake' and 'comparison for unlikeness' sake'.

One notes, with mild astonishment, the appeal to 'experiences' here. By way of taking Hopkins' admittedly arresting ideas onto a yet more exalted plane, Jakobson is intent on arguing, *not only* that there is an analogy between the two forms of 'equivalence' (because both forms involve crypto-comparison)—*but also* that metaphor (etc.) is in some sense the product or consequence or corollary of the poetic facility for aural equivalence—*and also*

[58] Jakobson (1960), 368: see Gerard Manley Hopkins in House and Storey (1959), 84–5 (from an 1865 undergraduate essay on 'Poetic Diction').

[59] Jakobson (1960), 368–9. The Hopkins phrases cited this time come from a different 1865 composition, dealing (in part) with the same subject, a 'Platonic Dialogue' entitled 'On the Origin of Beauty' (House and Storey 1959: 106).

that something of this dazzle of relationships is perceptible as such. To come down to earth: Jakobson's claim about aural parallelism and comparison (and Hopkins' idea that prompts it) is not, as a general claim, defensible. In *veni, vidi, vici* (to use one of Jakobson's own examples) one does indeed respond to aural parallelism as to reinforcement of a set of given *comparanda*. In Hopkins' own avant-garde rhyme in 'Felix Randal' (to use another), no such response is remotely possible:

Felix Randal the farrier, O is he dead then? my duty all ended,
Who have watched his mould of man, big-boned and hardy-*handsome*,
Pining, pining, till time when reason rambled in it *and some*
Fatal four disorders, fleshed there, all contended?

Here the rhyme does not invite us to 'compare'—in any relevant sense of the word—*handsome* and *and some*, nor is it apparent how we could. The rhyme serves quite different ends, partly to do with a deference but also challenge to a poetic tradition, in the name of 'natural' speech-rhythms. One may readily grant that the rhyme, like rhyme in general, 'means' something, that it has semantic force (a point that Jakobson himself insists on),[60] but not that this force has anything to do with comparison. A more helpful, in fact a classic, statement about the semantic force of sound patterning (not cited by Jakobson) was formulated by William Empson: 'its most important mode of action is to connect two words by similarity of sound so that you are made to think of their possible connections'.[61]

'Possible connections': this principle holds in varying degrees for most instances of aural parallelism, from alliteration to rhyme, and it tends to subvert Jakobson's whole construction. Poetry is all about parallelism (maybe); parallelism is all about similarity; and—But no: parallelism is at least as much about *connection*, which points not to the sphere of similarity, but to the sphere of contiguity. And if Jakobson's own terms of reference suggest that poetry has at least as much to do with contiguity (the basis of metonymy) as with similarity (the basis of metaphor), the high-sounding claim that metaphor, but not metonymy, is at the heart of the poetic function is shown to be bogus.

'The poetic function projects the principle of equivalence from the axis of selection into the axis of combination.' That is,

[60] Jakobson (1960), 367. [61] Empson (1947), 12.

poetry (or, strictly, verse) favours rhyme and other forms of parallelism: yes, conspicuously. And metaphor involves a kind of equivalence: yes, no doubt. But where does this pairing of two, in themselves, unexciting truths get us? It gets us, I suggest, to a place sufficiently remote from actual poetry, actual metaphor, actual rhyme, for Jakobson's next steps—and his grand correlations and his master principle—to sound acceptable. And all this, notwithstanding his admirable willingness to give actual examples. I take issue with Jakobson, not so much because of the abstractness or even the wrongness of his argument, but essentially because of the remoteness of his abstract correlations, which necessarily puts him at an unsatisfactory distance for coming to terms with the poetic usage which purports to be, and is, and must be, at the centre of his discussion. The theory to which these correlations lead is free to ignore or contradict the very experience of poetry on which it should be building—without, as it seems, any compensatory hint that, or how, the theory could be stimulating any helpful understanding of poetry in its stead.

VI

Jakobson's theory is critically discussed by Ricoeur. Jakobson's argument is open to criticism, and Ricoeur identifies particular weaknesses in it. What he fails to do, however, is diagnose the root cause, the deeper weakness—and not surprisingly, because he shares the weakness with Jakobson himself. Ricoeur writes:[62]

> Thanks to his famous ['Aphasia'] article . . . the coupling of metaphor and metonymy has been linked permanently with the name of Roman Jakobson. It was his stroke of genius to have connected this properly tropological and rhetorical duality with a more fundamental polarity that concerns the very functioning of language . . . [But] by generalizing the distinction between metaphor and metonymy far beyond tropology . . . [he] strengthened the idea that substitution and resemblance are two inseparable concepts . . . The new linkage of the metaphorical and metonymic . . . builds on a distinction (to be found in . . . Saussure) between two ways in which signs are arranged—combination and selection . . . Now, where there is selection between alternative terms, there is the possibility of substituting one for the other . . . Selection and

[62] Ricoeur (1978), 174–5.

substitution, accordingly, are the two faces of a single operation. All that remains is to link up combination and contiguity, substitution and similarity . . . From this point on, the correlation with tropes presents no difficulty, if it is granted that metonymy rests on contiguity and metaphor on resemblance . . .

But now Ricoeur distances himself from Jakobson's system, and on several grounds.[63] *Inter alia*, he questions the equivalence of metaphor and the 'meta-linguistic operations' of aural parallelism:[64]

The first makes use of a virtual resemblance inscribed in the code and applies it in a message, whereas the equational definition, for example, talks only about the code. Can the use of resemblance in discourse and a totally different operation requiring a hierarchy of levels be put into the same class?

But above all it is Jakobson's equation of selection and substitution that worries him. That equation falls foul of the interactional insight into metaphor, so that, in Jakobson's theory,[65]

metaphor settles into the status of substitution of one term for another, just as in classical rhetoric . . .

and at this point, undercutting Jakobson, Ricoeur proposes that metaphor and metonymy are not equals after all, because metonymy is substitutional, where metaphor is interactional, which makes it something else or something more:[66]

It is legitimate to ask whether metonymy is not a substitution, more precisely a substitution of names, rather than metaphor.

In all this, symptomatically, it does not occur to Ricoeur to use experience of metaphor or metonymy in action to query Jakobson's appropriation of Saussure's terms of reference. Just try and *realize* Jakobson's association of selection with metaphor and combination with metonymy: does (for instance) Yeats' use of 'bursting' *feel* any more selectional than his non-metaphorical

[63] I leave out of account other criticisms offered by Ricoeur, for instance concerning Jakobson's elision of synecdoche into metonymy (with which eliding I agree: 'nec procul ab hoc genere [sc. synecdoche] discedit metonymia', Quintilian 8.6.23): Ricoeur (1978), 178–9.

[64] Ricoeur (1978), 179.

[65] Ricoeur (1978), 179.

[66] See Ricoeur (1978), 4–6 (in summary) and 173–256 (in detail); the quotation occurs at 179.

use of 'dawn' (and so on)? If anything does *feel* at all selectional, it would be metonymic usage. Experience suggests that discussion of metonymic 'selection' arises unforcedly, as it did in my own account of Eliot's 'Footsteps shuffled on the stair':

> [W]hat we have here presents itself as a selection and recombination of associated elements, where the elements selected and recombined look to be (among other things) the most sensuously evocative.[67]

But here, it seems, selection and (re)combination are themselves conjoined, not opposed. One might well conclude—provisionally: but other instances would point the same way—that the whole Saussurian apparatus serves no useful purpose in this connection at all.

VII

Ricoeur's objections to Jakobson are significant and substantial, and yet (it seems to me) they miss the point. We are discussing the poetic use of language. Jakobson is, explicitly. Aristotle is, if only (though not only) by virtue of situating one of his pioneering discussions in his *Poetics* and cramming the other (in his *Rhetoric*) with instances from poetry. And Ricoeur too, presumably, is, though in his case the focus is (like much else in his discussion) elusive. At all events he, like Jakobson and Aristotle, should be, because (in his own, oddly grudging, words) metaphor 'supposedly embodies the fundamental characteristics of poetic language'.[68] However, if knowledge of poetic language is available only through experience of poetry and sustained attention to the effects of poetry, any theory of poetic language must be based on that experience and that attentiveness, and though theory may legitimately be abstract, the more remote it is from poetic actualities, the more precarious it must be.

[67] Above, p. 133.

[68] Ricoeur (1978), 152. In principle, Ricoeur regards only live ('living') metaphor as metaphor (hence the impeccable statements, 'there are no metaphors in dictionaries' at 170, and 'dead metaphors are no longer metaphors' at 290) and, seemingly as corollary, associates 'living metaphor' with 'true poetry' (284). At times, though, he seems to ignore these terms of reference by, for instance, distinguishing 'the philosopher's metaphors' from 'those of the poet' (e.g. 310). 'Supposedly . . . language' is presumably a gesture towards Jakobson, among others.

As a student of poetry, Jakobson is right to privilege metaphor and metonymy, but he looks for reasons outside poetry and its effects to explain and interpret the insight, and duly ends up in the perverse position of dissociating metonymy from poetry as a matter of principle. Ricoeur is right to subject Jakobson and his theory to criticism, but to his—and our—disadvantage his critique is substantially based on arguments unrelated to poetry and the effects associated with poetry. In this, Jakobson and Ricoeur are true heirs of Aristotle himself, who, like them, fails to keep his eyes and ears on poetry. In the *Poetics* Aristotle insists that metaphor in poetry is important. So it is—but not for his reason, which stresses metaphor's logical aspect at the expense of all others. In the *Rhetoric* he rightly associates poetic metaphor and sensuous immediacy—which, however, he limits to visual efficacy.[69] In both cases the eventual direction of Aristotle's thought is, frankly, determined by philosophical (pre)conceptions at the expense of the experience of poetry itself.[70] Arguably the same is true of Aristotle's intermittent confusion about metaphor and standard usage.

Ricoeur's attempt to mediate between Aristotle and Jakobson (and others) is worth a closer look. Commending the interactionist view of metaphor, he explores the idea of language as classification and metaphor as reclassification:[71]

> Can one not say that the strategy of language at work in metaphor consists in obliterating the logical and established frontiers of language, in order to bring to light new resemblances the previous classification kept us from seeing?

One can glimpse the attractiveness of such a proposition, if one thinks back to Heraclitus' 'Life is a boy playing *pessoi*', or again to (say) L. P. Hartley's anthology quotation, 'The past is another country: they do things differently there', or to one of Ricoeur's

[69] Unlike, say, Cicero, who, while deferring to Aristotelian prejudice, properly acknowledges that metaphor has a more general sensory force ('omnis translatio, quae quidem sumpta ratione est, ad sensus ipsos admovetur, maxime oculorum, qui est sensus acerrimus': *De Oratore* 3.160).

[70] I leave it to the reader to ponder if, and how far, Aristotle's capacity for inattention to poetic metaphor, in the very act of discussing it, implies at bottom the same negative attitude as is evinced by the dismissive phrase, *κενολογεῖν . . . καὶ μεταφορὰς λέγειν ποιητικάς* (of Plato's formulation of the theory of forms) at *Metaphysics* A.9 (991ª21–2).

[71] Ricoeur (1978), 197.

own examples, from Baudelaire, 'La nature est un temple . . .', or indeed to Donne's 'No man is an island, entire of itself'.[72] But think back to Pindar's ἐξέλκων, or Yeats' 'bursting dawn', or Shakespeare's 'honours deep and broad', or Hopkins' 'I feel thy finger': for such cases Ricoeur's formulation is inappropriate, unhelpful, or impossible. In simple terms, Ricoeur has forgotten to remember that metaphor comes in many different shapes, and has arbitrarily privileged one of the less common ones: 'Life is a boy', '*a* is *b*', 'the tenor is a vehicle'.[73] His argument at this point is remote from poetic actuality.

The same unfortunate remoteness characterizes Ricoeur's comprehension of metonymy. In contradistinction to metaphor (says Ricoeur), metonymy is merely 'one name for another name'.[74] But look at the examples. The given formula no doubt works for Virgil's *arma* or his *Pallas*; it is hardly a helpful comment on Sophocles' ἀνάριθμος or νηλέα; and it is simply inapplicable to Eliot's 'glowed into words'. Ricoeur's rejection of Jakobson results in a majestic characterization of metaphor: 'the metaphorical *is* at once signifies both *is not* and *is like*', so that (where metonymy is just 'deviant denomination') metaphor is 'impertinent predication'.[75] Not only does this conclusion idly presuppose that all metaphor has, or at least is convertible to, a 'Life is a boy' shape; it ignores the fact that metonymy too is perfectly capable of assuming that same predicational shape. Take another example from Hopkins:[76] 'I am gall. I am heart-burn.' The 'heartburn' is metaphorical: 'I' am suffering from the psycho-spiritual *equivalent* of . . . The 'gall' part is metonymic: 'I have the *gall* to . . .' or 'I *am* full of *gall* in its established sense of bitterness or rancour, and so . . .'. One might as well say: 'the metonymic *is* at once signifies both *is not* and *is in the same semantic field as*'. Or maybe not.

[72] Hartley: from the prologue of *The Go-Between*. Baudelaire: from *Les Fleurs du mal*, 'Correspondances', no. 4 (see e.g. Ricoeur 1978: 247). Donne: from *Devotions upon Emergent Occasions*, 'Meditation XVII'. Cf. n. 19 above.

[73] Cf. Soskice (1985), 18–19.

[74] Ricoeur (1978), 198.

[75] Ricoeur (1978), 7, 4.

[76] Hopkins, 'Wreck of the Deutschland', stanza 4.

VIII

Aristotle, Jakobson, Ricoeur: all three theorize without consistent reference to the poetry and the experience of poetry which indeed will not, by itself, be sufficient, but which is plainly necessary for any adequate theory. All three, and many others, construct their theories as if a little exemplification and a lot of thought would see them home. In this spirit, it is sadly common for philosophical theorists in the modern era, not just to settle, arbitrarily, on particular-shaped metaphors ('Nature is a temple . . .'), but to switch, arbitrarily, from what are at least real witnesses (like Baudelaire's) to fabricated instances which necessarily lack any context and, therefore, any potential range of functions, and, worst of all, to instances which are either vacuous or not even metaphors at all, but normal usage (often in the form of colloquial currency): 'she's a witch', 'you are a pig'.[77]

It is part and parcel of an experientially founded theory of metaphor and metonymy that it should accommodate, and even provoke, operational definitions that facilitate identification of the different tropes *in practice*: such definitions merely sum up something of a real response to real instances. Conversely, it is characteristic of philosophical theorists that they seem to be remarkably blasé about such identification. Ricoeur, unusually, does discuss this issue, and his discussion is revealing. He himself distinguishes what he calls structural and operational approaches, and actually commends the operational approach for distinguishing real (living) tropes from normal usage (dead ones):[78]

By approaching the phenomenon from the operational side and not only from that of structure, one can distinguish from dead figures other figures in the process of being born.

[77] The two examples occur on a single page (41) of Davidson (1979). As Black points out (1962: 33), 'in default of an authentic context of use, any analysis is liable to be thin, obvious, and unprofitable'. One notes that Aristotle was, once again, first in line here, both with examples of normal usage (like *νηῦς δέ μοι ἥδ' ἕστηκεν*: above, pp. 117–18 with n. 6) and with fabricated instances: *ἐρεῖ τοίνυν τὴν φιάλην ἀσπίδα Διονύσου καὶ τὴν ἀσπίδα φιάλην Ἄρεως* (*Poetics* 21, 1457^{b}21–2) smells of invention. (I plead guilty myself to one fabricated instance for a limited purpose: the 'buildings' example on p. 123 above.)

[78] Ricoeur (1978), 201. The 'phenomenon' under discussion here is in fact metonymy, but might as well be metaphor.

At this point Ricoeur seems almost to see the issue as a classic choice between an empirical ('operational') understanding of tropes (the word 'figures' is unhelpful, but can be ignored here) and an apriorist ('structural') understanding, and in these terms acknowledges that the former has the advantage of identifying the 'phenomenon' in question. The fact that he should need to conduct this argument at all speaks volumes, as does his failure to ponder the value of a theory that can't accommodate the distinctions essential to it.

In marked contrast, Ricoeur spends time and energy identifying theoretical problems associated with the principle of deviation. Deviation (not that Ricoeur makes the point) is something we can experience: we recognize deviation in theory *because* we can feel it in practice. Accurately and perceptively, Ricoeur disentangles the necessary notion of deviation from the suspect notion of substitution, which (unlike deviation) is not confirmed by experience:[79]

> The fact that the metaphorical term is borrowed from an alien domain does not imply that it substitutes for an ordinary word which one could have found in the same place. Nevertheless, it seems that Aristotle himself was confused on this point and thus provided grounds for the modern [e.g. interactional] critiques of the rhetorical theory of metaphor.

As Ricoeur points out, the confusion goes back to Aristotle, who articulated the notion of deviation in the word ἀλλότριος, 'alien' (*Poetics* 21, 1457^{b}7, 31), but simultaneously read into that term additional notions:[80]

> The Aristotelian idea of *allotrios* tends to assimilate three distinct ideas: the idea of a *deviation* from ordinary usage; the idea of *borrowing* from an original domain; and the idea of *substitution* for an absent but available ordinary word.

At the same time, however, Ricoeur involves himself in an argument against the principle of deviation on the grounds that it implies an impossible notion of 'degree zero' normal usage as its contrastive point of reference.[81] As so often, it is the conceptual problem that is felt to be paramount.

79 Ricoeur (1978), 19.
80 Ricoeur (1978), 20.
81 Ricoeur (1978), 138–43.

IX

Metaphor and metonymy are fundamental to poetic language, or (as Jakobson prefers to call it) the poetic function of language, and to no other: they are among the chief textual determinants of the poetic function in the first place. In its interest in metaphor, and its lesser interest in metonymy, philosophical theory seems to presuppose poetic usage, even to trade on poetic usage, and yet to ignore poetic usage at will. Aristotle, Jakobson, and Ricoeur all rely on poetry to know that metaphor is special, or that metonymy also may be special, even to know that these tropes exist at all—and yet they treat poetic usages as if they were merely the scaffolding behind which and through which they can mount their own constructions. But poetic usages are not their scaffolding: they are their bricks.

My criticism of the theorists does not mean I am unaware of major differences between them—especially between philosophers proper and semioticians. Nor does it mean that I am impertinent enough to question the stature of an Aristotle, or indeed to deny the insights or, in general, the importance of any of these thinkers and the arguments they present. However, theirs are too often insights or arguments which are subject to experiential corroboration which the philosopher tends to be unwilling, or unable, to provide, or else insights and arguments of a different order, like those associated with the exposure of concealed analogies and premisses in all discourse.[82] At

[82] The starting point of this tradition of thought is Nietzsche's magnificent aphorism, 'Was ist also Wahrheit? Ein bewegliches Heer von Metaphern, Metonymien, Anthropomorphismen . . .': 'What then is truth? A mobile army of metaphors, metonymies, anthropomorphisms—in short, a sum of human relations which, poetically and rhetorically intensified, become transposed and embellished, and which after long usage by a people seem fixed, canonical, and binding on them. Truths are illusions which one has forgotten *are* illusions' (Nietzsche, 'Über Wahrheit und Lüge in aussermoralischen Sinne' (1873) in Colli and Montinari 1967– : 3.2, 374–5). Other notable contributions have been made by: Heideggger (1957); Derrida (1974); and Ricoeur (1978), esp. 280–95. The whole tradition is summed up in the work of Lakoff and Johnson (1980). It will be gathered that, while accepting the value of such discussions, I see no reason to privilege them; cf. the sensible remarks at Soskice (1985), 67–83 (she relates this largely Continental tradition of thought to Wittgensteinian and other arguments). If nothing else, word derivation, as Soskice (at 81) notes, is not the same as word meaning.

which point, preoccupation with legs of chairs, electric currents, kingdoms of heaven, and Aristotle's ἕστηκεν does have its place.

Such preoccupations, however, have little in themselves to contribute to the understanding of metaphor, or metonymy, in their poetic usage, and *without* that understanding—*without* a constant sense of, and a constant reference back to, poetic practice—thinking about metaphor, or metonymy, will be constantly misdirected or constrained. In this sphere, if you think without, you are probably thinking too much. What was it the wise man said? *Denk nicht, sondern schau*: don't think—look.[83]

[83] Wittgenstein, *Philosophical Investigations*, 1.66 (with due apologies for allowing myself a visual-sounding emphasis).

PART II
Allegory

8
Figures of Allegory from Homer to Latin Epic

ANDREW LAIRD

1. Problems of defining 'allegory'

'Si parva licet componere magnis', non incommune carmina poetarum nuci comparabilia videntur; in nuce enim duo sunt, testa et nucleus, sic in carminibus poeticis duo, sensus litteralis et misticus; latet nucleus sub testa: latet sub sensu litterali mistica intelligentia; ut habeas nucleum, frangenda est testa: ut figurae pateant, quatienda est littera; testa insipida est, nucleus saporem gustandi reddit: similiter non littera, sed figura palato intelligentiae sapit. Diligit puer nucem integram ad ludum, sapiens autem et adultus frangit ad gustum; similiter si puer es, habes sensum litteralem integrum nullaque subtili expositione pressum in quo oblecteris, si adultus es, frangenda est littera et nucleus litterae eliciendus, cuius gustu reficiaris. His itaque aliisque pluribus modis tam Graecorum quam Latinorum poemata possunt commendabilia probari . . . (*Super Thebaiden* 180–1 Helm)[1]

'If one may put small with big', the songs of poets seem comparable to an unshelled nut; for there are two parts to a nut, the nutshell and the nut itself, the 'nucleus'. So too there are two parts to poetic songs: the

Earlier versions of this chapter were presented at Boulder, Harvard, New York University, Newcastle, and Princeton, as well as to the seminar on metaphor and allegory at Corpus Christi College Oxford on which the present volume is based. I would like to thank those present on all occasions for comments and criticisms, particularly Michèle Lowrie, Philip Mitsis, Gregory Nagy, and Richard Thomas.

[1] The sole manuscript of the *Super Thebaiden* surviving in a 13th-cent. copy attributes authorship to Fulgentius, Bishop of Ruspe; it is not among the Carolingian manuscripts of Fulgentius Planciades, author of *Content of Virgil*, who lived in the 6th cent. Although the *Super Thebaiden* has community of diction and approach with the *Content of Virgil*, Whitbread (1971: 235–6) presents the arguments for a later date of composition.

> literal sense and the hidden one. As the nucleus is concealed under the shell, so a hidden understanding lies below the sense of the letter. If you want the nucleus, you have to break the shell—so too the literal meaning must be shaken off for the figures to be revealed. The nutshell is flavourless but the nucleus gives back flavour to whoever tastes it—correspondingly, it is not the letter, but the actual figure which gives its flavour to the palate of understanding. A boy likes a whole nut to play with, whilst a wise adult will break it to eat it. Correspondingly, if you are a boy, you take pleasure entirely in the literal sense without it being pressed for a more subtle exposition, but if you are an adult, the letter must be broken up and the nucleus of that literal meaning must be extracted for you to be refreshed by its taste. In ways like this and very many others, the poems of the Greeks and Romans can be approved and deemed commendable . . .

This passage is from a Christian interpretation—which probably dates from the tenth century AD—of Statius' *Thebaid*. The unusual use of the word *super* ('beyond') in the transmitted title of the essay, *Super Thebaiden*, is significantly suggestive: the word *de* ('on' or 'about') is far more customary in the titles of Latin treatises. *Super Thebaiden*, then, indicates concern with things *over and above* Statius' epic poem and not just the poem itself. And indeed the remarks quoted here from the introduction to that treatise describe what is often called *allegorical* interpretation of poetry: the literal meaning of a poem being discarded, even 'broken up', for the latent nucleus of the hidden 'figures' to be understood. Simultaneously, that introduction could be seen to illustrate the kind of process it discusses in providing a transparent example of that process (by likening a poem to an unshelled nut). The writer thus cracks and decodes his own 'figure' of allegory for the reader, even as he presents it. However, no word for allegory (such as *allegoria* and its cognates) is used in this excerpt, or in the material that follows.

Like many technical terms, the words 'allegory' or 'allegorical' appear to be reassuringly specific. Scholars seem to have little difficulty in isolating allegorical figures, allegorical passages, allegorical texts, allegorical interpretations, allegorical genres, and even periods of cultural history in which allegory is supposed to be prominent as a form of expression or interpretation. Impressions that allegory can be more or less straightforwardly recognized as a mode of literary communication derive more directly from medieval theories and practices of interpretation than they do from ancient ones.[2] The diversity of definitions of what we call 'allegory' suggested by disparate usages in Graeco-Roman antiquity is fairly daunting; and where modern and contemporary accounts are concerned the issues involved become even more confusing.[3]

In dealing with allegory, we are not only faced with the customary problem of definition. There is also a problem with our usual recourse in such situations—adducing instances from which to put together a profile of allegory. But finding an example of allegory is no less difficult than settling on a definition. Examples of allegory are like Macavity the Mystery Cat: it is very hard to tell whether or not they were really there. This is in fact a more serious problem than that of definition, because it directly affects interpretation of ancient texts. For instance, if we hold with Denis Feeney that personification allegory proper in epic was 'fully realised in Statius and . . . was to rule in post-classical literature', do we assume that it is not 'officially' there in Virgil or Homer?[4] It is not necessary to oppose Feeney's particular view, only to emphasize that the recognition of allegory (of any kind) is not like the recognition of a hexameter, nor even like the recognition of a metaphor. The detection of allegory is really a subjective issue, or to be more accurate, a question of ideology. Someone's detection of an allegory is more likely to be determined by culturally induced expectations than by any personal perspective.

This chapter has three basic objectives: (i) to show how allegory can be understood as an intrinsic part of epic communication: something which can be conceived as being 'built into'

[2] Dante's *Epistle* 10 to Can Grande della Scala on allegory and the polysemous quality of the *Commedia* has had a particular influence on modern discussions. See e.g. Bolgar (1954) and Curtius (1953), as well as works cited in the following note. Toynbee (1966) is a text of the *Epistles*.

[3] For ancient conceptions and important bibliography, see Trapp (1996), and Tate and Hardie (1996). Russell (1981: 95) highlights the numerous senses of ἀλληγορία and its cognates in 'Heraclitus' alone. See also Russell and Innes in this volume. Lewis (1936), Fletcher (1964), and Frye (1971), 91 and (1974) are standard discussions for Anglo-American critics; Benjamin (1977) engages with (e.g.) Goethe, Schopenhauer, and Coleridge in debating the role of allegory in European cultural history. See also Todorov (1973), 68–9. Clifford (1986) is a contemporary application of allegory.

[4] Feeney (1991), 242–3.

rather than 'read into' epic; (ii) to show why ancient interpreters might be excused for their apparently loose and disparate conceptions of allegory in poetry, as well as for their apparent intentionalism in frequently attributing their own allegorizations of poems to the poets themselves; (iii) to examine poetry in order to demystify allegory. This third objective is part and parcel of (i) and (ii): allegory is a facet of many kinds of text and many kinds of language—there is a strong case for regarding it as only speciously different from other forms of interpretation.

One cannot accomplish these objectives by running around after all the ancient definitions and applications of *allegoria*, *huponoia*, and metaphor and then attempting to collate or somehow organize them. Such an endeavour would be flawed by two possible drawbacks. *Either* one would be tempted to privilege a particular ancient definition or set of definitions which were consistent with each other, to the exclusion of further definitions which would still be pertinent and important. *Or* this process of collation would involve applying (at some level) one's own preconceived notion of what allegory really is. Instead it is better to accomplish the objectives given above by using another more original method. This is to look in primary poetic texts for figures of allegory itself, and to see what they might teach us.

There is an additional reason for adopting such an unusual point of departure. It is the unappetizing fact that one cannot give an account of any instance of allegory in a particular text without producing what could legitimately be regarded as a further allegory. The further allegory tends to be of a bland and unspectacular nature: it usually suggests that the part of the text examined is concerned, on a secondary level, with signification itself. This suggestion is virtually unavoidable and generally goes unnoticed. Here is a specific example to illustrate this (Prudentius, *Cathemerinon* 9.141–4):

> O tortuose serpens,
> qui mille per meandros
> fraudesque flexuosas
> agitas quieta corda.

O twisting serpent who agitates peaceful hearts through a thousand meandering turns and through sinuous deceits.

We 'understand' that the serpent that agitates peaceful hearts is not a real snake—if only because the diction here indicates the metaphorical nature of that serpent. We may also 'understand' that the serpent stands for temptation or something similar by bringing to bear a basic knowledge of Scripture and Christian symbolism: the serpent in this text, we may say, is an allegory. None the less it remains the case that, when we say Prudentius' serpent *stands for* temptation, we are also presupposing that the business of 'standing for' is somehow 'in' Prudentius' text—even though Prudentius' text actually says nothing whatsoever about signification of any kind. Thus to claim that Prudentius' serpent 'stands for' anything is also to say something (potentially allegorical) about the status of Prudentius' *text* and how it means. Just as simple description of a text collapses into interpretation of that text, so interpretation collapses into allegory even more rapidly and regularly, though this is a process which it is not popular to scrutinize. Given that accounts of an allegory in a text tend to lead to a further allegory of how that text works, my approach will be to give this recursiveness full play, and deliberately to concentrate, as far as it might be possible, on allegories of allegories.

2. Epic messenger scenes as figures of allegory

Allegory—however it is conceived—is very much bound up with meaning and verbal communication. The conventions of epic poetry are likely to provide a good hunting ground for such 'meta-allegories'. By epic conventions, I mean those distinctive features of epic, like invocations to Muses, catalogues, ekphrases of artworks, similes, and reported poems. I am keen on them because they not only give a signal of the genre they belong to; they also have a quality of reflexivity. They call attention to and help determine the ways the text they help constitute communicates to its audience. That is the real business of genre. The dynamic role of those epic conventions, which were once deemed as inert parts of the furniture, is now widely acknowledged. However, the dynamic role of one well-known epic convention can still be further interrogated. This is the convention—which seems to be as old as poetic narrative itself—of the messenger scene in which a celestial god dispatches a minion to convey his words to the world below.[5] Although current communications technology has reduced the need for messages to be conveyed by individuals, the term 'message' is used in modern theories of language and communication to indicate the content of an utterance: the notion of *what* is said. That notion is far from unproblematic: the nature of the relationship between the message (content, substance, or *res*) and its medium (as form, style, or *verba*) has long been a central issue for debate in fields like linguistics, rhetoric, philosophy, and theology.[6] Umberto Eco's account of 'message' as a technical term in semiotics in fact has a disturbing resemblance to some notions of allegory:[7]

> I am not saying that a single code can produce many messages, one after the other, for this is a mere truism; I am not saying that the contents of many messages can be conveyed by the same kind of sign-vehicle, for this too is a truism; I am saying that usually a single sign-vehicle conveys many intertwined contents and therefore what is commonly called a message is in fact a *text* whose content is multilevelled *discourse*.

Elsewhere I have shown that the epic convention of messengers who receive and then deliver messages can be seen as a paradigm for the whole process of communication with all its complexities.[8] The following discussion will review some examples of this convention to a rather different end: to show first how the messenger scene may serve as an allegory for allegory, and to expose a Roman view of the generally allegorical nature of Homeric epic.

Mud thrown up by the legacy of structuralist criticism tends to stick to endeavours of this kind. For instance, Tzvetan Todorov's reading of Henry James notoriously showed that his tales were 'metaliterary stories, stories devoted to the constructive principle of the story'.[9] Following such leads, much recent criticism has allegorized ancient and modern literature in this fashion, presenting individual works as being, in whole or

[5] Greene (1963) is the fullest treatment of the convention.

[6] Barthes (1971).

[7] Eco (1976), 57. Cf. e.g. the accounts of allegory at Fletcher (1964), 2 and Todorov (1973), 68–9.

[8] Laird (1999), ch. 7 reviews speech presentation in the messenger scene in Augustan, Flavian, and Renaissance Latin epic.

[9] Todorov (1971). Todorov's reading of James is discussed at Jefferson (1986), 105–7.

in part, *thematically* devoted to concerns in poetics.[10] Such claims sometimes risk being foolishly misconceived as well as uninteresting. But it is not my aim here to harp callowly on about all poetry being about poetry. There are some justifications for treating the epic messenger scene as reflexive allegory: Plato's *Cratylus* for instance provides some independent evidence for a conception of such scenes as a *mise-en-abyme* or allegory for verbal communication—and for the symbolic nature of epic itself. In Plato's dialogue, Socrates argues that names are formed by composition from other words. He thus replies to Hermogenes, who has asked Socrates to examine the name of Hermes, because he was prompted by curiosity about his own name (*Cratylus* 408a):

Well then this name 'Hermes' seems to me to have to do with speech; he is an interpreter (ἑρμηνεύς) and a messenger, is wily and deceptive in speech, and is oratorical. All this activity is concerned with the power of speech. Now, as I said before, εἴρειν denotes the use of speech; moreover, Homer often uses the word ἐμήσατο, which means 'contrive'. From these two words, then, the lawgiver imposes upon us the name of the god who contrived speech and the use of speech—εἴρειν means 'speak'—and tells us: 'Ye human beings, he who contrived speech (εἴρειν ἐμήσατο) ought to be called Eiremes by you.' We, however, have beautified the name as we imagine, and call him Hermes. Iris also seems to have got her name from εἴρειν, because she is a messenger.

Here we find etymologies and allegorizations for both Hermes and Iris, who happen to be the standard messengers of the Olympian gods in the *Iliad* and the *Odyssey*.[11] But the fact that Homer is not explicitly mentioned at least means that nobody can accuse Socrates, as we might accuse the allegorist 'Heraclitus', for example, of attaching inappropriately alien meanings to the texts.[12] Socrates is talking about language not poetry, and if his 'lawgiver' imposed names prior to the usage Socrates claims to correct, then it follows that Socrates is holding

[10] Barthes' *S/Z* (1970: 216) for instance, characterized Balzac's story *Sarrassine* as 'representing the very confusion of representation'. For classical literature, the essays in Roberts, Dunn, and Fowler (1997) show, mainly successfully, how *closure* might be thematized in a wide range of ancient texts.

[11] On Iris in Plato, see Arendt (1978), 142.

[12] See Russell (1981), 96–7, and further in the present volume, on the allegory of 'Heraclitus'.

that these allegorical etymologies are pre-Homeric, and thus, perhaps, 'built into' Homeric poetry.

However, Socrates next becomes more directly concerned with the specific nature of poetry rather than of language in general (*Cratylus* 408cd):

[SOCRATES:] You know that speech signifies all things (*πᾶν σημαίνει*) and always makes them circulate and move about, and is twofold, true and false.
[HERMOGENES:] Certainly (*Πάνυ γε*).

Well the true part is smooth and divine and dwells aloft among the gods, but falsehood dwells below among common men, is rough and like the tragic goat (*τραγικόν*); for tales and falsehoods are most at home there in the tragic, goatish life (*περὶ τὸν τραγικὸν βίον*).

Certainly (*Πάνυ γε*).

Then Pan, who declares and always moves (*ἀεὶ πολῶν*) all, is rightly called goat-herd (*αἰπόλος*), being the double-natured son of Hermes, smooth in his upper parts, rough and goat-like in his lower parts. And Pan, if he is the son of Hermes, is either speech or the brother of speech, and that brother resembles brother is not at all surprising.

Before developing his image into the figure of Pan, Socrates fuses the notion of the false poetic *μῦθοι* with the crude, misleading nature of mortal speech in general, by exploiting the two senses of *τραγικόν* (as both 'tragic' and 'goatish'). Significantly the Homeric Hymn to Pan lays an extraordinary amount of emphasis on *Hermes* as Pan's father.[13] Indeed this Hymn first mentions its subject patronymically ('Tell me Muse of the dear son of Hermes'). This could suggest that Socrates' elaboration of Pan's qualities here may not be purely speculative—it is possible they could have been corroborated by a tradition which already existed.[14] Whatever the case, this visual characterization of speech as something reaching down from heaven to earth has as much bearing on the epic messenger scene as the discussion of Hermes and Iris which preceded it.

The questions of truth and falsity in poetry and in speech are very much at issue in the very first scene in classical literature in which an Olympian god dictates a message to be delivered

[13] For an account of the etymologies of Pan which specifically pertain to this Hymn, see Càsola (1975), 362–3.

[14] Sedley (1998) argues convincingly that Plato did hold the etymologies offered by Socrates in the *Cratylus* to be 'exegetically correct'.

to a mortal. Here neither Hermes nor Iris is involved: Zeus summons a Dream (Ὄνειρος) to go to Agamemnon at the opening of the second book of Homer's *Iliad* (2.8–15):

'Go, wicked dream, to the swift ships of the Achaeans. When you come to the hut of Agamemnon, son of Atreus, tell him everything truly, as I bid you. Order him to arm the long-haired Achaeans speedily, for now he may take the broad-wayed city of the Trojans: the immortals who possess homes on Olympus are no longer disputing: for Hera's supplications have converted them all, and woes hang over the Trojans.'

The Dream finds Agamemnon asleep and appears to him in the likeness of Nestor, announces to the chief that he is Zeus' messenger, and delivers the message just as he has been instructed. Then follows the revelation from the Homeric narrator that the content of the dream is untrue (*Iliad* 2.35–8):

So, having spoken, the Dream went away and left Agamemnon there pondering in his heart things which were not going to happen. For he thought he would capture the city of Priam on that day. Foolish man: he did not know what deeds Zeus planned.

If the Dream faithfully and truthfully reports a message from Zeus which is in itself false, this is an unsettling prototype for the epic messenger scenes to follow—both in the *Iliad* and in subsequent poems. Such a scene, if it is regarded as an allegory of epic communication, may have a kind of programmatic significance coming as it does so early in the poem, suggesting the truth status of epic discourse is bound to be unreliable. Consider in conjunction with this, the poet's own claim that what he tells us is mere 'repute' (κλέος)—the Muses alone know everything (*Iliad* 2.484–90):

Now tell me Muses who possess homes on Olympus—for you are goddesses, you are present and know everything, while we hear only repute and do not know anything—who were the leaders and lords of the Danaans: I would not be able to tell or name the host, not even if I had ten tongues, ten mouths, and an unbreakable voice and a heart of bronze.

It remains to show how the implicit status of the messenger scene in Homer as an allegory of epic discourse can be exposed by the transformations of this convention in Latin epic. The fourth book of Virgil's *Aeneid* has long been examined for the changes it rings on the conventional Homeric messenger scene, particularly in the famous episode in which Jupiter dispatches Mercury to Aeneas, ordering him to leave Carthage and Dido. Various parallels and contrasts have been established between this episode involving Mercury and the one which precedes and prompts it involving Fama, the female personification of Rumour.[15] According to ancient traditions, Fama is a divinity of perverted speech; whilst Mercury was consistently allegorized as 'the unperverted word'.[16] Recently, critics have cautiously identified Fama with the epic poet himself. This kind of identification is not only to be discerned in Virgil's *Aeneid*. In Ovid's *Metamorphoses*, Fama becomes more specifically a personification of Homer's epic discourse.[17]

Since antiquity, the physical form of Virgil's Fama has intrigued commentators (*Aeneid* 4.176–83):[18]

mox sese attollit in auras
ingrediturque solo et caput inter nubila condit.
illam Terra parens ira inritata deorum
extremam, ut perhibent, Coeo Enceladoque sororem
progenuit pedibus celerem et pernicibus alis,
monstrum horrendum, ingens, cui quot sunt corpore plumae,
tot vigiles oculi subter (mirabile dictu),
tot linguae, totidem ora sonant, tot subrigit auris.

She soon lifts herself up into the air; she advances on the ground and hides her head among the clouds. Mother Earth bore her as a last daughter in rage against the gods, so they say, a sister for Coeus and

15 Parallels: Mercury responds to Jupiter's command, as Fama responds to the prompting of events; both go to Libya (*Aeneid* 4.173, 257); both fly (e.g. 176–7, 223, 226, 241, 246) and make their flight between heaven and earth (184, 256); both are compared to birds. Contrasts: Fama spreads truth and untruth on earth (188–90), while Mercury is the true messenger of heaven; Fama never closes her eyes to sleep (185), while Mercury gives and takes away sleep, and closes the eyes of the dead.

16 Hardie (1986), 278. The best assembly of evidence for Hermes as an embodiment of *λόγος* or *λογισμός* is at Buffière (1956), 289–96.

17 Hardie (1999), 97. See also Zumwalt (1977).

18 Page (1894, ad loc.) doubted whether so many abstract qualities could be expressed in a physical form: 'conception of a bird with an equal number of tongues and ears becomes ludicrous'. Servius (ad loc.) explains that this description is not *narratio* but *argumentatio*. Dyer (1989) states that the 'eyes, tongues, mouths and ears belong, not to the underside of Fama's body, but to those who are prying and gossiping on earth as she flies'.

Enceladus. She is swift on her feet and quick on her wings, a huge and horrible monster, and as numerous as the feathers under her body are the vigilant eyes underneath her—strange to tell!—as numerous are the tongues, so many mouths that sound and an ear always pricked.

Fama walks on the ground with her head in the clouds; she also flies above the organs of perception and communication which may or may not constitute her. The figure is thus in possession of at least two kinds of physical attributes which are clearly distinct, if not contrary. There is a remarkable similarity between this image of Fama, incorporating the chattering inhabitants of earth, and Socrates' more anthropomorphic iconization of speech as Pan in the *Cratylus*. Like Fama, Pan has a body which stretches from heaven to earth; he too moves about and blends truth with falsity. The image of Pan, like that of Fama, is not easy to visualize either. Pan's lower parts, like Fama's underside, dissolve into a symbol of false terrestrial discourses which include poetry and stories. Fama too has various connections with poetry and stories. First, Servius' remark on *ut perhibent* in line 179 points out the significance of Fama as a figure of allegory for Virgil's own discourse:

Whenever the poet states something of a mythical nature, he usually brings in the phrase *fama est*. So it's marvellous that just when he's talking about Fama herself, he says 'so they say'.

Virgil's description of Fama also shows that she has much in common with the poet of the *Aeneid* (*Aeneid* 4.188–94):[19]

> . . . tam ficti pravique tenax quam nuntia veri.
> haec tum multiplici populos sermone replebat
> gaudens, et pariter facta atque infecta canebat:
> venisse Aenean Troiano sanguine cretum,
> cui se pulchra viro dignetur iungere Dido;
> nunc hiemem inter se luxu, quam longa, fovere
> regnorum immemores turpique cupidine captos.

She clings on to her lies and distortions as often as she tells the truth. At that time she rejoiced in plying peoples with talk on many levels, she was singing facts and fictions mixed in equal parts: how Aeneas sprung from Trojan blood had come to Carthage and how the beautiful Dido was thinking it fit to join herself with him as husband; how they were

[19] Here it is possible to advance on observations (made in different ways) in Feeney (1991), and Hardie (1999: 98).

even now indulging themselves and keeping each other warm the whole winter through forgetting about their kingdoms and had become captured by foul lust.

Like the poet, Fama *sings* her story. The subject matter of her rumour is the very subject matter of the fourth book of the poem. In fact everything she reports is just as it has already been narrated. Virgil says that Fama was dealing in *multiplici sermone* ('talk on many levels') and mixing fiction in equal part with fact. In this respect, poetry is very much like rumour: after all, in the *Ars Poetica* Horace characterizes the ideal epic poet as someone who 'lies and mixes truth with falsehood' ('ita mentitur, sic veris falsa remiscet').[20] So Fama may have a reflexive significance for the *Aeneid*: She is not only a character in the story; she is recurrently a formal component in the narrative of the whole poem. The appearance of Fama in the *Aeneid* always marks a change of scene or turning point in the actual construction of the poem's plot.

Some might challenge any identification between Fama and the poet in *Aeneid* 4 by claiming that the value judgements in Fama's (allegorical?!) account of the union between Aeneas and Dido ('luxu, quam longa, regnorum immemores, turpique cupidine captos') explicitly condemn their behaviour up to this point in the poem. However, even before the appearance of Fama, the narrator was far from benign about those events.[21] More importantly, Fama's message programmatically determines subsequent events in *Aeneid* 4, as much as it records what has gone before: Iarbas' prayer to Jupiter, the message Jupiter dictates to Mercury, the text Mercury delivers to Aeneas, and even Aeneas' apologetic speech to Dido can all be seen to reconfigure what was first described by Fama. Fama thus becomes a figure of allegory for the narrative of *Aeneid* 4, which is almost entirely constituted by successful or unsuccessful exchanges of communication.

In Ovid's *Metamorphoses* 11, Juno sends a message to Alcyone: the goddess wants to respond to the prayers Alcyone has made for her husband's life. The prayers cannot be granted because Ceyx has already drowned in a storm at sea, so Juno acts only to stop Alcyone praying in vain. Her communication

[20] Horace, *Ars Poetica* 151.

[21] See *Aeneid* 4.169–72.

involves Iris, Somnus, and Morpheus in succession as intermediaries. Juno's instructions to Iris are given in only four verses (*Metamorphoses* 11.585–8):

> 'Iri, meae' dixit 'fidissima nuntia vocis,
> vise soporiferam Somni velociter aulam,
> exstinctique iube Ceycis imagine mittat
> somnia ad Alcyonen veros narrantia casus.'

'Iris,' she said, 'messenger most faithful to my words, go quickly to the drowsy home of Sleep and bid him send, in the image of dead Ceyx, dreams narrating the true state of events.'

Forms of the adjective *fidus* ('faithful') are elsewhere used in Ovid to convey the fidelity of discourse to an idea or event.[22] Iris' delivery turns out to be very faithful indeed to Juno's words (*Metamorphoses* 11.623–9):

> 'Somne, quies rerum, placidissime, Somne, deorum,
> pax animi, quem cura fugit, qui corpora duris
> fessa ministeriis mulces reparasque labori,
> somnia, quae veras aequant imitamine formas,
> Herculea Trachine iube sub imagine regis
> Alcyonen adeant, simulacraque naufraga fingant.
> imperat hoc Iuno.'

'O Sleep, rest of all things, Sleep, most placid of the gods, peace of the soul, from whom cares flee, who calms bodies weary of their hard ministries and refreshes them for work, bid your dreams, which equal true shapes in their imitations, to adopt the image of the king and approach Alcyone in Hercules' city of Trachis. Then let them forge a likeness of the shipwreck. Juno orders this.'

Here Iris orders Sleep to instruct his dreams; in Juno's speech Iris herself was ordered to instruct Sleep. Iris' insistence that the dreams should forge a *likeness* of the shipwreck implies that more artifice is involved than Juno's hope that the dreams would recount what really happened (588) had suggested. For Iris, a dream which tells the truth is still just a convincing deception.[23]

[22] *fidissima* ('most faithful') is comparable to Jupiter's use of the word to address Mercury in *Metamorphoses* 2.837. Ovid addresses his verse letter as 'a faithful servant of speech' in *Tristia* 3.7.1. Cf. *Tristia* 3.4.40 and *Amores* 1.11.27.

[23] This paradox is ironized by Ovid in 11.666–8 when Morpheus posing as Ceyx claims not to be an *ambiguus auctor*. Agamemnon's dream in the *Iliad* is of course the prototype for a (false) dream dispatched from heaven.

This must be so if 'dreams equal true shapes in their imitations'. Sleep passes on the instruction to Morpheus (647–8), who is told to adopt the form of Ceyx. The 'true events' are then presented to Alcyone in her sleep at 658–70 by Morpheus–Ceyx: her prayers have been in vain, and she should not expect his return. The content of the dream is then borne out by Alcyone's discovery of Ceyx' corpse.

The complicated structure of this messenger scene still bears on the nature of epic communication. The words of both Juno and Iris refer to, or re-present what has happened in the story: the shipwreck and the death of Ceyx. Both speakers present and re-present what will happen next in the story: how Alcyone is to know of her husband's death. Of course the informing of Alcyone is also the end to which both these speeches are given. This message is about a message. But Juno, as the speaker of the dictation speech, is also a dictator of events. A god or goddess in epic who rules in the story also has power over the outcome of the story. No less than the poet-narrator, Juno knows the truth about Ceyx' death: this is the epic 'content' or 'message' which we have already heard. As the 'most faithful mouthpiece of Juno', it is Iris who translates this truth into epic form. And in being a conventional symbol (a messenger), Iris herself also embodies that epic form.

The elaborate structure of this messenger scene shows how Ovid's unusual techniques of fictional construction mediate the more traditional epic realm. There may be only one truth (*veros . . . casus*) in the epic story, but there are many forms into which it can be fashioned, as Iris is well aware (see 11.625–6 quoted above). It is Morpheus who does this fashioning by speaking to Alcyone in the guise of her dead husband (*Metamorphoses* 11.666–8):

non haec tibi nuntiat auctor
ambiguus: non ista vagis rumoribus audis:
ipse ego fata tibi praesens mea naufragus edo.

It is not an ambiguous author who announces these things to you: you are not hearing them from vague rumours. I am myself the very victim of the shipwreck uttering my fate to you.

Morpheus is only pretending to be the ghost of Ceyx, yet the account of Ceyx' death which he makes up conforms precisely to what is 'true' in the world of the story. Indeed Morpheus' fictional embedded narrative appears to impact on 'real' events: his words seem to prompt Alcyone to discover Ceyx' corpse. This final link in the chain of speeches by which Juno communicates to Alcyone is explicitly signalled as being false and fictional. Yet Morpheus' speech influences what happens in the story. It also re-presents the 'official' story of Ceyx no less convincingly (and in greater detail) than the poet's presentation and the speeches of Juno and Iris. This must question the status of the preceding dictation and delivery speeches—traditional components of epic messenger scenes—as presentations of 'what happened'. None the less, this story still retains a 'message' in the technical sense. The notion of truth in epic is not actually threatened here: the allegory of this scene simply draws attention to the ultimate indiscoverability of that truth, however faithfully Iris or any other interpreter may seek to pronounce it.

At this stage I hope to have shown that the scenes I have examined are allegories of epic, but it remains to show just how they are allegories of allegory, or, at least, allegories of epic as allegory. It remains to show more explicitly how epic itself might be innately allegorical. These passages from Virgil and Ovid do seem to suggest this: so it will be necessary to review the ways in which they transform and implicitly comment on Homeric material. After that, I shall consider an independent testimony on the interpretation of epic from Horace. The implication of all these passages will be that Homer can be intelligently and automatically conceived as allegory.

3. Epic as allegorical discourse

A feature of Virgil's Fama already discussed illustrates the way in which she might be an allegory, not just of epic, but of epic as a form of allegory. It is the conjunction of numerous mouths and numerous tongues—together with the possibility of these mouths and tongues belonging to the human beings who simultaneously transmit and constitute Fama. A conjunction of numerous mouths and tongues occurs later in the *Aeneid* when the Sibyl says to Aeneas, at the end of her account of Tartarus (*Aeneid* 6.625–7):

'non, mihi si linguae centum sint oraque centum,
ferrea vox, omnis scelerum comprendere formas,
omnia poenarum percurrere nomina possim.'

'If I had a hundred tongues and a hundred mouths and a voice of iron, I could not encompass all their different crimes or run through names of all their punishments.'

The trope of *adunaton* emphasizes the sheer ineffability of the numbers of crimes and names of their punishments. The ultimate source of this passage is well known: Homer's assertion (*Iliad* 2.284–90 quoted in the previous section) that even with ten tongues he could not name all the leaders of the Danaans.

However, it is also worth looking at the whole context of the Sibyl's speech in *Aeneid* 6. The speech is closed by her emphasis on ineffability. Aeneas had asked the priestess about the grim noises emanating from the citadel of Tartarus (*Aeneid* 6.560–2):

'quae scelerum facies? o virgo, effare; quibusve
urgentur poenis? quis tantus plangor ad auras?'
tum vates sic orsa loqui . . .

'What kinds of criminal are here? Tell me virgin. What punishments are inflicted on them? Why is there so much lamentation in the air?' Then the prophetess began to speak as follows . . .

Such a succession of questions addressed to a maiden with divine power does rather resemble the way epic narratives begin—not least the proem of the *Aeneid* itself. Indeed there seems to be a play on the word *vates* used in the very next verse to designate Aeneas' respondent: it connotes a role of poet as well as prophetess for the Sibyl. In her reply, she says that when Hecate put her in charge of Avernus, the goddess herself 'taught me the punishments of the gods and led me through them all'. The Sibyl emphasizes that she has seen and been led through everything. But her narrative cannot be comprehensive: as she says at the end, she cannot run through it all again. Even if she had a hundred tongues and mouths, she could not recount the ineffable things Hecate the goddess could teach. So instead what we have is an epitome, spiced with *praeteritio*, in which particulars serve to point to a general truth, which cannot ever be directly communicated.

The evocation of proemic dialogue between poet and Muse in this dialogue between Aeneas and the priestess could suggest a certain sort of relationship between poetry and reality; the former can only convey the latter symbolically. Incidentally, another link between poetry and ineffability is forged in the first line of Aeneas' embedded epic in *Aeneid* 2.3. If, as it seems to me, this verse is haunted by the first line of the *Iliad*, with *regina* corresponding to Homer's θεά, then the word *infandum* has more than just a rhetorical significance. Aeneas' narrative to Dido, no less than the Sibyl's to Aeneas, is poetically framed. No less than the Sibyl, Aeneas is compelled to convey the general by means of the particular, or, putting it more cautiously, to convey *x* by means of *y* where *x* is greater than *y*. This is of course a weak sense of allegory.

The context of what I take to be the ultimate source for Fama's tongues and mouths in *Iliad* 2 gives us something to chew on. Homer addresses the Muses as being present and knowing all things, whereas mortals he says have heard only the κλέος and know nothing. Provided we are not misled by the frequent English glossing of the personified Fama as 'gossip', after φήμη it would be hard to find a word that corresponds more closely to the Latin word *fama* than κλέος. This reinforces the suggestion that Virgil's Fama has a debt to this passage. Reading this passage of Homer through the spectacles of Virgil gives us something like the following: we cannot have knowledge—all we have is κλέος, so the status of Homer's poem can be no more than that; the hypothetical ten tongues and mouths, like those on the underside of Fama, must be human and not divine; to Virgil, Homer is saying that even if he possessed these extra resources he would not be able to give a full account or the right account without the help of the Muses; Homer's poem might be conceived as being like the delivery speech in a messenger scene where we have no access to the divine dictation speech; Homer's poem can only be an inadequate reproduction of what the Muses know (pointing to that knowledge, as the formulaic repetition of 2.484 in the *Iliad* does on three separate occasions) but never a comprehensive communication of it. So Homer too conveys *x* by means of *y* where *x* is greater than *y*. As I remarked, this is only a weak definition of allegory with which most ancient and modern accounts would easily harmonize. I shall advance on this below (p. 170f.) but what I hope to have shown is still pretty substantial: Fama is an allegory of epic as allegory. The Virgilian intertextuality exposes a general allegorical signification in Homer's discourse.

Ovid's messenger scene also takes us to the second book of the *Iliad*. The dream sent to Alcyone recalls that sent by Zeus to Agamemnon. The bearing of this on the Alcyone story can be dealt with much more briefly. That dream sent to Agamemnon is the first example in the *Iliad* of a celestial dispatching a minion to convey his words to a mortal: Zeus instructs the dream to tell Agamemnon that he can now take the city of Troy. It is notable that in this first instance of the convention in Homer, the message dictated is completely false, as Homer's narrator underlines in 2.35–8. The Ovidian handling of the false dream strongly suggests that such a dream is conceived as a paradigm for the poem in which it appears. There is a paradox detected in Homer which Juno's elaborate embassy to Alcyone develops to the full: a false dream can still be truly emblematic of epic discourse, which itself awkwardly confuses truth, fiction, and falsity.

I now turn to a more explicit interpretation of Homeric epic by another Augustan poet. This is the well-known discussion of the *Iliad* and *Odyssey* which begins Horace, *Epistles* 1.2. It has a very important bearing on epic as allegory, but perhaps not in the way we might be conditioned to expect. The epistle begins as follows (1.2.1–7):

> Troiani belli scriptorem, Maxime Lolli,
> dum tu declamas Romae, Praeneste relegi;
> qui, quid sit pulchrum, quid turpe, quid utile, quid non,
> planius ac melius Chrysippo et Crantore dicit.
> Cur ita crediderim, nisi quid te detinet, audi.
> Fabula qua Paridis propter narratur amorem
> Graecia Barbariae lento collisa duello.

I have been rereading the writer of the Trojan war, Maximus Lollius, at Praeneste, whilst you are declaiming in Rome. He says what is decent, what is base, what is useful, what is not, more plainly and better than Chrysippus and Crantor. Why I have come to think so, do hear, unless something else is occupying you. The story, in which it is related how, on account of Paris' love, Greece clashed in tedious conflict with a barbarian power.

The word *relegi* is ironic: Italo Calvino defined literary classics as books of which people say, 'I am rereading . . .' and never 'I am reading . . .'.[24] Horace's idea of an *Homère moralisé* is of course no more spontaneous: the naming of Chrysippus and Crantor, who used poetry to illustrate their doctrines, shows the poet is fully aware of the long-standing tradition of allegorizing Homer. Moreover, the selection of Rome and Praeneste as locations is no more accidental than the juxtaposition of those words in the verse. Rome is a busy place where people declaim and do *negotium*. Praeneste was a villa resort by Augustus' time: a place for *otium*. It is also a fitting place to read Homer. According to Plutarch (*Parallel Stories* 316 AB), Aristocles related that Telegonus, Odysseus' son by Circe, founded Praeneste.

So, the prima facie casual opening of this poem is actually craftily contrived. Halfway through the poem, Horace abandons Homer to moralize without him. The moral allegorizing of Homer serves only as a point of departure for Horace's own ethical precepts. Yet for that moral allegorizing of Homer and for the poem as a whole to be effective, Horace had to begin by setting the scene and putting his preaching in the context of a symbolic scenario in verses 1–4. The ethical direction of Horace's own poem is dependent on that scenario for its mediation. That would still be the case even if you did believe that Horace really was reading Homer in Praeneste whilst Lollius was declaiming in Rome.

This epistle is far more complicated than it first seems. We are unlikely to take Horace's allegory of Homer, dare I say it, literally. On the other hand, we should not necessarily regard its writer as a jovial academic colleague who rehearses trite moral allegories of Homer as a *jeu d'esprit*. The verses opening the poem weave a plausible autobiographical fiction, designed to assist the moral argument of the poem. That fiction could certainly be called allegorical. And that fiction frames the allegorizing of Homer which follows. So again we have a meta-allegory. The more one examines this epistle, the clearer it becomes that it is expanding the range of our responses to Homer rather than limiting them. The epistle is a mimetic narrative, a rhetorical display, and a philosophical sermon. Any reader who acknowledges the polysemous quality of this little poem is more than likely to concede the same to Homer's monumental epics.

24 Calvino (1987), 125.

The presentation of Homer in this last example is very different in nature from that of the Homeric intertexts in the reflexive allegories in the *Aeneid* and the *Metamorphoses*. But together these Latin epics provide a picture of Homer (and of epic in general) which is remarkably coherent. A very crude and very reductive summary for the sake of clarity goes like this. The examination of Virgil suggests that epic is a vehicle inadequate for its message. The examination of Ovid is similar but more aporetic: epic is a kind of vehicle in which the relationship between message and medium is hopelessly convoluted. The examination of Horace demonstrates by discussion and example that epic is polysemous and that, whatever other dimensions it has, epic can convey philosophical truth. In sum then, epic is symbolic, enigmatic, polysemous, and instructive. These qualities suggest epic is allegorical—at least according to many contemporary definitions of allegory.

This unexciting-sounding position is something to be pleased with for two reasons. First, we got to this modern verdict only by looking at passages of Augustan poetry. The fact that I referred to those passages as allegories does *not* mean my argument is circular. I could have called those passages anything and still produced the same close readings of them.[25] Secondly, this does make a case for allegory—at least in the limited sense of conveying *x* by means of *y*—as being something which is built into rather than read into epic. This seems to apply not only to Latin epic (as might be expected from some recent studies) but also to Homer.[26] What I mean by being 'built into' epic should soon become clearer. However, simply saying that epic is allegorical in our terms does not yet do anything to fulfil my other major objective. That was to excuse those ancient interpreters we call 'allegorists' for the content of their moral or philosophical interpretations which look so far-fetched and for their frequent

[25] I am aware that no Roman poet uses or discusses any ancient nomenclature for allegory. But Horace (in *Ars Poetica* 151 and 391 f.) clearly presupposes what is now understood by the term. Here I am only venturing to tease out from the poets' practice ways in which allegory can be seen to work in Roman literature and its antecedents.

[26] Feeney (1991) and Hardie (1986) and (1999); Vessey (1973) for Latin epic. On allegory and Homer, see Lamberton (1986), and Lamberton and Keaney (1992). Thalmann (1988) exemplifies one way in which Homer may now be read for the moral of the story.

insistences that the poets shared and intended the interpretations they put on their poems. This will be the issue which leads to the general conclusion to this chapter.

It should be noted that, irrespective of the practice of ancient 'allegorical' criticism, discussions in ancient rhetorical theory present *allegoria* as a trope or figure.[27] For the rhetoricians, allegory is in company with metaphor, metonymy, synecdoche, antonomasia, catachresis, and metalepsis. Quintilian's chief discussions of allegory in the eighth book of the *Institutes of Oratory* can serve as an example. This part of the work is concerned with *elocutio* and specifically deals with tropes. Tropes, Quintilian says in 9.1.4, involve the transference of expressions from their natural signification to another ('in tropis ponuntur verba alia pro aliis')—generally they involve only a few words. Allegory is presented as something more drawn-out than a short turn of phrase. It can extend to whole passages or even to a whole poem like Horace, *Odes* 1.14 (the 'ship of state' poem: see *Institutes* 8.6.44):[28]

Allegoria, quam inversionem interpretantur, aut aliud verbis, aliud sensu ostendit, aut etiam interim contrarium. Prius fit genus plerumque continuatis tralationibus, ut:

> O navis, referent in mare te novi
> fluctus; o quid agis? fortiter occupa
> portum

totusque ille Horatii locus, quo navem pro re publica, fluctus et tempestates pro bellis civilibus, portum pro pace atque concordia dicit.

Allegoria, which [Latin speakers] understand as *inversio*, expresses something in words which actually has another sense, and sometimes a sense which is actually contrary to the meaning of the words. The first type is usually brought about by sustained metaphors, as in this example:

> O ship, new waves will take you back to sea;
> O what are you doing? Resolutely make for
> harbour

and in the rest of this passage of Horace, in which he uses 'ship' to stand for the state, 'waves' and 'storms' for civil wars, and 'harbour' for peace and concord.

The general picture is that the speaker (or writer), his addressee

[27] Lausberg (1998: 398–403) assembles ancient rhetorical discussions and definitions of *allegoria*. See also Innes in this volume.

[28] See Lowrie (1995), 129–37, on the allegorical background to this poem in Alcaeus.

(or reader), and the context make pretty clear what his allegory conveys. Like our modern notion of metaphor, allegory for the ancients is patently a feature of style or verbal expression. Again, it should be emphasized that among those ancient writers who are now called 'allegorists' (with the conspicuous exception of 'Heraclitus'), uses of the term 'allegory' or terms like it seem to be rather rare.

This is a large claim to make, but ancient writers often seem to confuse the study of what we would call the general meaning of texts with the study of the meaning of figures or words. Thus we can be exasperated by the laborious discussions of diction in scholia and rhetorical criticism which seem to us to be irrelevant to the real meaning of the literary texts they treat. At the other extreme, we see ancient 'allegorists' imposing interpretations on texts which seem to have no empirical basis. Donald Russell sums up the modern perception of the problem:

> Ancient interpreters assumed that the authors they were expounding first formulated their message, and then gave it allegorical dress. This is to neglect a difference between allegory and 'symbolism', which is commonly stated in modern times. No one in antiquity seems to have had the idea that, instead of beginning with a message and embodying it in fiction, one might begin with a story and treat it as a symbol of the happenings or truths which have some formal resemblance to it. And this is odd.[29]

The scientific quality of ancient rhetorical criticism and the evolution of literary criticism have perhaps conditioned our own expectations. Ancient philosophical interpretations of poetry could be seen as deriving from broader, philosophical interpretations of language. The various and abundant pre-Platonic notions of the autonomy of logos have received a great deal of scholarly attention.[30] If, as the Presocratic Heraclitus said of Apolline oracles, poetry 'does not speak out nor conceal, but indicates', then to construct the import of a poem and to assume this construction to be the real meaning of the poem is pardonable, if not inevitable.[31] We do this all the time when we interpret ordinary speech. The American philosopher of mind Donald

[29] Russell (1981), 97.

[30] See (e.g.) Kerferd (1981), 68–110.

[31] See 22 B93 DK. Kahn (1979: 123–4) discusses the implication of this fragment for the presentation of Heraclitus' own thought.

Davidson, in an influential essay on mental events, offers some remarks which imply that he would have more sympathy with ancient 'allegorists' than most classicists:

> The problem . . . is given centre stage by appeal to explicit speech behaviour. For we could not begin to decode a man's sayings if we could not make out his attitudes towards his sentences, such as holding, wishing or wanting them to be true. Beginning from these attitudes, we must work out a theory of what he means, thus simultaneously giving content to his attitudes and to his words. In our need to make him make sense, we will try for a theory that makes him consistent, a believer of truths, and a lover of the good (all by our own lights, it goes without saying). Life being what it is, there will be no simple theory that meets these demands. Many theories will effect a more or less acceptable compromise, and between these theories there may be no effective grounds for choice.[32]

We should bear these points in mind before deriding the efforts of those ancient interpreters whom we call allegorists. The pertinence of Davidson's observations for our attempts to understand ancient poetry can be illustrated with an example. If we discern an echo of a Homeric source in Virgil, the detection of that echo is an act of interpretation, not plain description. It may indeed be the case that ancient readers of Virgil preoccupied with *aemulatio* comment extensively on Virgil's imitation of Homer, but this observation obscures the basic point. The basic point is that apprehension of Homeric influence in Virgil cannot be an inevitable or even the proper response to reading Virgil. Our identification of Homer as a key intertext for 'understanding' Virgil leads us to assume that any properly informed reader would have to share that apprehension. That identification as well as the ensuing assumption is actually ideological: we ascribe to our beliefs the status of knowledge of objective truth. Medieval readers did just the same when they 'allegorized' Virgil in availing themselves of theological 'facts' and gave priority to intertexts from Holy Scripture. It is important to note that the term 'allegorize' usually conveys a negative value-judgement in modern accounts of such interpretative practices.

[32] Davidson (1980), 222.

4. Conclusion: Allegory as a function of interpretation

Allegorization in the end boils down to interpretation, and interpretation amounts to allegorization. Metaphor and other tropes must be essentially distinct from allegory (*pace* Quintilian) because they are features of diction which are part of the internal fabric of a text. They are, as it were, scientifically detectable. The attribution of the term allegory only to certain forms of interpretation, on the other hand, is no less ideological than the general business of interpretation itself. Both those who regard allegory as a trope and those who regard allegory as a misguided, deviant form of interpretation are subject to a form of false consciousness.[33] In this connection, Walter Benjamin's observations about allegory in *The Origin of German Tragic Drama* are all the more striking because they were written in the 1920s, before he embraced Marxism:

> Even great artists and exceptional theoreticians . . . still assume that an allegory is a conventional relationship between an illustrative image and its abstract meaning . . . That is, to put it briefly, the denunciation of a form of expression, such as allegory as a mere mode of designation. Allegory, as the following pages will serve to show is not a playful illustrative technique but a form of expression, just as speech is expression, and, indeed, just as writing is.[34]

The assumption of the 'conventional relationship' which Benjamin questions here relates to our perceptions of ancient interpretative practices, noted in Donald Russell's remarks quoted earlier. That assumption is also exemplified, strikingly, by the illustration from the *Super Thebaiden* which opened this discussion. The idea that allegory involves the conceit of 'a hidden understanding [which] lies below the sense of the letter', as this medieval writer put it, has no less currency today than it did eighty years ago. The conceit is a seductive one, but it invokes a metaphysics of presence which is hard to defend.[35] The

[33] Discriminating allegory from lexical figures is not to insist that the use and interpretation of such figures did not always have larger political and ideological significance: Ahl (1984) considers the ways in which ancient writers used 'figured speech' as a tactful way of securing free expression.

[34] Translated as Benjamin (1977), 162.

[35] The critique of the 'metaphysics of presence' has been derived principally from Heidegger, *Being and Time* 1.1.5.35 (1962: 211–14).

fact of the matter is that hidden understandings are really *constructed from* the sense of the letter by readers—or listeners—and not implanted by authors—or speakers.

Benjamin's likening of allegory to both written and spoken expression is also salutary in serving to reinstate allegory as a basic function of communication and interpretation. This is not a modern flight of fancy. An important discussion by Andrew Ford demonstrates that the earliest allegorical exegesis of Homer was bound up with conditions of performance and epic recitation well before the fifth century BC.[36] It is also pertinent that Horace's allegorization of Homeric epic in *Epistles* 1.2 emphasizes that poetry is a medium which is oral as well as literary: Homer is referred to as *scriptorem*, the *writer*, of the Trojan war; Horace recounts that he has *read* (*perlegi*) a poet who also *speaks* (*dicit*), and asks his reader to *listen* (*audi*) to an epistle which is *de facto* written.

My discussion of messenger scenes in epic as figures of allegory was intended to show how allegory is reflexively built into epic, and then to show by implication how allegory is built into other kinds of discourse, insofar as all discourse yields to interpretation. Allegory is thus an essential feature of *any* text—but a feature which, like the 'message' in the semiotical sense, is actualized in various ways according to the nature of the relation between text and reader, or between speaker and addressee. It is for this reason that allegory has an ideological dimension which metaphor and other lexical tropes cannot in themselves possess.

[36] Ford (1999).

9
Allegory and Exegesis in the Derveni Papyrus: The Origin of Greek Scholarship

DIRK OBBINK

1. Introduction

Exegesis has a long history in the Greek tradition. ἐξηγέομαι means simply to narrate, hence explain, a process: to lead one through a difficult way, the thickets of reasoning, a text. It always has something of an after-the-fact, dependent connotation: something must already exist, be a tradition, in order to be explained: for example, alternative names of a plant or hero are given already in Homer.

Disguised in this is the fact that something is made up or produced in the process. The literary commentary in the Greek tradition makes its way from its roots in the aftermath of the Presocratic era to late antique and medieval theories of allegory. It provides a history of the origin of Greek scholarship which turns out, surprisingly, to have dimensions of social and religious history as well as linguistic and philological. The *Oxford Dictionary of the Christian Church* defines 'exegesis' as the act of explaining a text, in theology a sacred text, including translation, paraphrase, or commentary on its meaning.[1] Its purpose may be either to describe the author's meaning or to apply that meaning to a contemporary situation. But in practice, I argue, it is always the latter aim that we find in the early history of these phenomena.

One of the things that is produced is commentary, another is myth. Commentary might be defined as a unified field theory of

[1] Cross and Livingstone (1997), 585.

literature in which all literature is other literature, and every utterance demands its own gloss. In writing, it has been suggested, commentary can exist at the most basic, minimal form as punctuation in a text, delineating a text into its construable and hence comprehensible units. Since these can consist even in the blank spaces placed between words or cola in ancient manuscripts to indicate punctuation, commentary at its most minimal can consist of nothing at all.[2]

It has also been suggested that the commentary tradition as we know it sprang into existence due to the widespread exportation of papyrus as a writing material from Egypt beginning in the eighth and seventh centuries BC. But we know full well that exegesis and commentary in the Greek tradition existed in an oral form early on: the rhapsodic performative tradition included the notion of explaining or expounding upon the texts performed. The Homeric rhapsode Ion of Plato's dialogue, who not only recites Homer but claims to be able to expound on the meaning of the texts of Homer, Hesiod, and Archilochus is an obvious example.[3] Much expansion and variation in oral composition is a function of this time of exegesis. A character in Aristophanes' earliest play, known to us only in a fragment, asks another character the significance of a word in Homer (*Banqueters*, fr. 233 *PCG* iii. 2). By the third century, the beginning of Hellenistic times, at least, it is associated with the book: in the *Phoenicides* of the comic poet Strato, the cook uses archaic Homeric words for commonplace things, and his desperate master is obliged 'to take the books of Philetas and look each word up to find its meaning' (*ὥστ' ἔδει | τὰ τοῦ Φιλίτα λαμβάνοντα βυβλία | σκοπεῖν ἕκαστον τί δύναται τῶν ῥημάτων*: *PCG* vii, fr. 1). This passage was familiar enough to figure already in a schoolbook in the later third century BC, by which time exegesis of this sort was kids' stuff. The version we get from the D-scholia and the Alexandrian scholars is simply a more elaborate, tour de force version, designed to dazzle the children of the king and delight at dinner parties.

Already by the end of the fifth century, however, explanation of traditional poetry (including oracles and hymns) was

[2] See Montanari (1997). Examples in Hansen (1997); Saenger 1998.

[3] Commentary *ante litteram*: Lamedica (1991), (1992). Earliest Greek commentaries: Pfeiffer (1968), 212.

becoming tied to the book. It is perhaps no mistake that the oldest extant exegetical commentary in the Greek tradition dates from this period, or shortly after: the commentary on an Orphic theogony from Derveni in Thessaloniki. The only one known to me of anywhere near equivalent antiquity is the recently identified one on Plato's *Phaedo* (*CPF* iii. 7, 203–20 = *P.Heid G. inv.* 28 + *P.Graec.Mon.* 21) which dates from the early third century BC. This is the era in which the first known commentaries on Plato were written, presumably because around 300 BC the first generation of students brought up speaking the new *koine* began to flood the philosophical schools. The *koine* was the linguistic medium from which the new Hellenistic philosophical terminologies were now starting to emerge. For the first time, Attic Greek will have seemed antiquated, and must have made much less easy and less palatable reading to students than hitherto. In a climate in which Plato's writings were struggling to retain their supremacy against the new philosophical idioms, the kind of study aid offered by a commentary makes obvious sense.[4] The fourth-century Academic Crantor is described by Proclus (*Commentary on Plato's Timaeus* i. 76.1–2 Diehl) as 'the first commentator on Plato' (though Xenocrates and others before him had offered exegesis of individual Platonic passages). Later, Cicero read Crantor's work, presumably the first systematic exegesis of an entire Platonic dialogue, in the manner of the great commentaries on philosophical works of later antiquity and modern times.

2. The Derveni book

Not long after the discovery of the Derveni papyrus,[5] Rudolf Pfeiffer, arguing that elementary explanatory notes, consulted

[4] Sedley (1996 and 1997) questions the commentary format of *CPF* iii. 7, suggesting a critique by Strato of Plato's arguments for the immortality of the soul in the *Phaedo*.

[5] For the Greek text, see *Zeitschrift für Papyrologie und Epigraphie* (*ZPE*), 47 (1982), after 300. References to *P.Thessaloniki* correspond to the order of the columns in the English translation in Laks and Most (1997). Recently on the social context: Carpenter (2000) (art on the vase found with the papyrus); Janko (1997). On the philosophical background: Laks (1997); Most (1997*a*); Hussey (1999). On the authorship: Janko (2001).

by Callimachus, must have long accompanied the text of the Homeric poems and finally became the basis for our D-scholia, speculated that the 'ὑπόμνημα on the Orphic Theogony in the new Dervéni papyrus' was a 'specimen of just such a pre-Alexandrian "commentary"'.[6] And this is likely to be true, at least in part, though highly ironic, in light of the author's combined unity of conception and eccentricity. Certainly some of the exegetical techniques invoked by the commentator derive from a shared early stage of critical activity dating to the late fifth century. Thus it is clear that from early on in the Greek tradition there existed different types of allegory, and not only allegory but also etymology, metaphor, simile, polyonymy, analogy.[7] There is a desire for recourse to extended forms of metonymical explanation involving multiple correspondence as early as the early fifth century, that is to say *ὑπόνοια* and allegory in the specific and restricted (rather than the later general) sense: for example, Metrodorus of Lampsacus (61 DK), an extreme form of systematic allegory which suggests that we should see the gods each as different parts of the human body, with the heroes as parts of the universe. The model for the allegory is the biological organism, with its target being to relate parts to the whole, microcosm to macrocosm—although exactly what Metrodorus was trying to explain, whether about the text of Homer or the nature of the world (or both), is far from transparent, as is almost the rule in allegory of the specific and restricted sense.[8] This aspect of allegory is a function of its being one step toward abstraction, from concrete example to abstract idea. And as de Tocqueville put it: 'An abstract term is like a box with a false bottom: you may put in it what you please, and take them out again without being observed.'[9]

Metrodorus was a 'pupil' or follower of Anaxagoras. According to 59 A1 §11 DK, Metrodorus developed Anaxagoras' view 'that Homer's poetry was about virtue and justice' (i.e. allegory on the moral level). The claim is remarkable in ancient literary criticism and rhetoric, which (at least until the Neoplatonic movement) has decided difficulty in speaking about whole works

[6] Pfeiffer (1968), 139 n. 7.
[7] See Dawson (1992).
[8] Cf. Richardson (1975), esp. 69–70.
[9] Tocqueville (1840), ii. 1.16, 482.

or issues important to modern critics, such as unity, textuality, programmatic imagery, or meaning beyond the level of the word, phrase, or gloss. Failure to find ways of speaking about whole texts may be due to the difficulty of turning the papyrus roll back and forth in order to compare different passages in a text, and also to the custom of teaching and explicating works of poetry line by line (as in commentaries and scholia) as the preferred form of exegesis. No practising poet or prose-writer ever protests against this tradition, though there are of course antecedents in Plato (e.g. the demand for unity in the *Phaedrus*). The young Socrates certainly toyed with allegory (under the rubric ὑπόνοια) in the specific, restricted sense as a possible method of explanation, that is, hermeneutic, at least until he read Anaxagoras' book and gave up, disappointed, turning to a search to prove the Delphic oracle wrong about his own wisdom. At least Plato told these stories of Socrates' second sailing in order to express his own disdain for allegory as any more a reliable method of explanation (so *Phaedrus* 229c–230a on Boreas and Oreithyia; *Republic* 378b–e)[10] than etymology turns out to be in the *Cratylus*.[11] One may compare Plato's more general dismissal of the value of the interpretation of poetry (by poets or anyone else) in *Protagoras* 347c ff., *Hippias Minor* 365cd, *Apology* 22bc, *Meno* 99cd, and his view of inspiration as irrational (in the *Ion*, *Phaedrus*, etc.).

Allegory as a programmatic method of inquiry or explanation hardly fares better in the Hellenistic period. That the terminology is shifting betrays lack of trust in the methodology. While Socrates' term is ὑπόνοια (according to Plato), by Longinus' time the preferred term is ἀλληγορία/-ησις. See for example Longinus, *On the Sublime* 9.7:

ἀλλὰ ταῦτα φοβερὰ μέν, πλὴν ἄλλως, εἰ μὴ κατ' ἀλληγορίαν λαμβάνοιτο, παντάπασιν ἄθεα καὶ οὐ σῴζοντα τὸ πρέπον. Ὅμηρος γάρ μοι δοκεῖ παραδιδοὺς τραύματα θεῶν στάσεις τιμωρίας δάκρυα δεσμὰ πάθη πάμφυρτα τοὺς μὲν ἐπὶ τῶν Ἰλιακῶν ἀνθρώπους ὅσον ἐπὶ τῇ δυνάμει θεοὺς πεποιηκέναι, τοὺς θεοὺς δὲ ἀνθρώπους. ἀλλ' ἡμῖν μὲν δυσδαιμονοῦσιν ἀπόκειται "λιμὴν κακῶν ὁ θάνατος", τῶν θεῶν δ' οὐ τὴν φύσιν, ἀλλὰ τὴν ἀτυχίαν ἐποίησεν αἰώνιον.

Terrible as these passages [sc. *Iliad* 21.388 and 20.61–5: Aidoneus fears that Poseidon might split the earth asunder in the *theomachia*] are, they

[10] See Tate (1929). [11] Cf. Sedley (1998).

are utterly irreligious and breach the canons of propriety unless one takes them allegorically. I feel indeed that in recording as he does the wounding of the gods, their quarrels, vengeance, tears, imprisonment, and all their manifold passions Homer has done his best to make the men in the *Iliad* gods and the gods men. Yet, if we mortals are unhappy, death is the 'harbour from our troubles', whereas Homer has made their miseries rather than their divine nature immortal.

Longinus' dating is unclear, but a parallel in Philodemus (*On Piety, P.Herc.* 433 fr. 2 ii + 1088 fr. 1) suggests that he should not stray far from the traditional late Republican/early Imperial dating:[12]

Ὅμηρ[ος καὶ Πείσαν]δρος [μετὰ συμφορῶν] καὶ μ[όχθων τοὺς θεοὺ]ς ἐκπεπομ[φότες πανταχ]όθεν, κ[αθάπε]ρ̣ ταλαιπωρ[οτ]έ̣[ρους] τῶν ἐχ[όντ]ων, [ἔφυ]ρον αὐτοὺς καὶ [κακ]ὰς ὑ[π]ολήψεις [πε]ρὶ αὐ̣τῶν· οἱ μὲ[ν γὰρ ὄν]τες θνητοὶ πα[ρ]αγρά[πτ]ους ἔχου[σ]ι τὰς κακοπαθίας, οἱ δ' ἀεὶ ζῶντες αἰωνίους ἀναδεχόνται τὰς συμφοράς.

Homer and Pisander, having sent out the gods amid sufferings and labours from all sides, have confused them and debased ideas about them, as if the gods were more wretched than people who have these troubles. For the latter have sufferings which are limited, since they are mortal, whereas the gods, because they live forever, endure woes that last for all eternity.

This seems to be corroborated by an echo in Virgil (*Aeneid* 12.879–80, the Lament of Iuturna):

quo vitam dedit aeternam? cur mortis adempta est
condicio? possem tantos finire dolores
nunc certe, et misero fratri comes ire per umbras!
immortalis ego?

Why did he (sc. Iuppiter) bother to grant me eternal life? Why am I not eligible for the safety-clause of death? Especially when it could now bring an end to such woes, and I could accompany my brother (sc. Turnus) through the shades. Immortal, am I?

Philodemus' own (derisive) term for such allegories is not *ἀλληγορία/-ησις*, but *συνοικείωσις*, rendered *accommodare* by Cicero (*On the Nature of the Gods* 1.39–41):

In secundo autem volt Orphei Musaei Hesiodi Homerique fabellas accommodare ad ea quae ipse primo libro de dis inmortalibus dixerat.

[12] Cf. Cassius Longinus (later 3rd cent. AD) F10f Brisson and Patillon, with Heath (2000), 63–4.

In book 2 [of *On Gods*], he [sc. Chrysippus] speciously accommodates the myths of Orpheus, Musaeus, Hesiod, and Homer with his own theology as expounded in book 1.

Chrysippus and the Stoics try to 'accommodate' the poets' meanings to substantiate their own doctrines.[13] Demetrius, *On Style* (dating also uncertain, but his four-style theory is known already to Philodemus in his *Rhetoric*)[14] at 101 still knows this restricted, specific sense of ἀλληγορία:

What is implied always strikes more terror, since its meaning is open to different interpretations, whereas what is clear and plain is apt to be despised, like men who are stripped of their clothes. This is why the mysteries are revealed in allegories (ἀλληγορίαι), to inspire the shuddering and awe associated with darkness and night. In fact, allegory is not unlike darkness and night.

(He goes on to note that a succession of allegories, if not avoided, becomes a riddle, αἴνιγμα.) But Cicero, who actually explains ἀλληγορία by a Latin etymology in *Orator* 94,[15] simply thinks of it as 'a continuous stream of metaphors' (*fluxerunt continuae plures tralationes*). This is the sense which Quintilian (8.6.44) calls the most common, and 'Heraclitus' (see Russell in this volume) can use ἀλληγορία, -ησις in a weak and non-specific sense to describe any bold and progammatic metaphor, like Alcaeus' 'ship of state'. It is clear from Philodemus (*On Rhetoric* i. 181.18 (col. 23) Sudhaus) that ἀλληγορία already in Republican times had a wider meaning.

But the commentator of the Derveni papyrus by all indications seems to have been a card-carrying member of the hard-core variety of allegorist. What was he allegorizing, and why?

The author of the Derveni commentator belongs to an earlier, though not unrelated era, closer to the Presocratics and a developing interest in causes and the soul that flourished in Plato's treatment. Early Greek exegesis of traditional texts, like

[13] See Henrichs (1974).

[14] Philodemus, *On Rhetoric* i. 165 Sudhaus (col. 4), summarizing a four-style theory that implies knowledge of and a terminus ante quem for Demetrius, *On Style*: see Grube's translation (1961) with notes at 53–5; cf. Innes at Halliwell, Fyfe, and Innes (1995), 313, 315 n. 10, 330. I note that Radermacher (1899: 361 n. 1) restores μ[εσότητ' ἢ] rather than Sudhaus' μ[έγαθος ἢ].

[15] Cicero, *Orator* 94: *alia plane fit oratio*. Here *alia . . . oratio* is meant as an etymology for ἀλληγορία.

the Orphic theogony expounded by the Derveni commentator, shows the application of the latest scientific theories of the day in order to derive meaning and extension from the text, drawing it into the sphere of the author's own interest, namely religion and cult. I argue that the Derveni commentator saw his elucidation of cosmology as instruction for mystic initiates. The Derveni commentator's poetic text can be seen as part of a series of tomb texts whose conception of the next world derives at least in part from mystery ritual, in which an eschatological myth associated with the mysteries is combined with a dominant concern about relations between elements (fire, air, earth, water, and their mixtures). The Orphic poem which the commentator expounds is said to be *αἰνιγματωδής*. There are said to be 'riddling' references to cosmological elements: Zeus is interpreted as air (col. xvii.5), Moira as *τὸ πνεῦμα* (xviii.3), Okeanos is said to be air (xxiii.5), an interpretation of a verse which called Okeanos 'broadly flowing'; according to the commentator, this verse was immediately followed in the Orphic poem by a verse about Achelous which is also quoted by the Homer commentary *P.Oxy*. II. 221, ix. 1–2 (composed by a poet whose text of the *Iliad* did not have 21.195). The sun is said to be a generative element (*P.Thessaloniki*, col. xvi.1–11):

[αἰδοῖ]ον τὸν ἥλιον ἔφ[η]σ̣εν εἶναι δε[δήλω]ται. ὅτι δὲ
ἐ̣κ τῶν ὑπαρχόντων τὰ νῦν ὄντα γίνεται λέγει·
"πρωτογόνου βασιλέως αἰδοίου, τῶι̣ δ' ἄρα πάντες
"ἀθάνατοι προσέφυμ μάκαρες θεοὶ ἠ̣δ̣ὲ θέαιναι
"καὶ ποταμοὶ καὶ κρῆναι ἐπήρατοι ἄλ̣λα τε πάντα.
"[ὅ]σσα τότ' ἦγ γεγαῶτ', αὐτὸς δ' ἄρα μοῦ̣νος ἔγεντο."
"[ἐ]ν̣ τού̣τοις σημαίνει ὅτι τὰ ὄντα τὰ ὑπῆ[ρ]χεν ἀεί, τὰ δὲ
ν[ῦ]ν ἐ̣ό̣ντα ἐκ τῶν ὑπαρχόντων γίν[ετ]αι. τὸ δὲ
"[αὐ]τ̣ὸς δὲ ἄρα μοῦνος ἔγεντο", τοῦτο δὲ [λ]έγων δηλοῖ
[αὐ]τ̣ὸ̣ν Νοῦμ πάντων ἄξιον εἶ̣ναι μόν[ο]ν ἐόντα
[ὥσπερ]εἰ μηδὲν τἆλλα εἴη· οὐ γὰρ [οἷόν τε τα]ῦτα εἶναι.

It has been made clear that he called the sun a genital organ (or 'reverend': *aidoion*). And he says that the things that now exist have come to be from existing things:

Of the first-born king, the reverend one.
And onto him all the immortals grew, blessed gods and goddesses
And rivers and lovely springs and everything else
That had been born then; and he himself was alone.

In these verses he indicates that the things that exist always existed and that the things that exist now have come to be out of existing things. The phrase 'and he himself was alone': in saying this he makes clear that Mind itself being alone is worth everything, just as if everything else were nothing. For it is not possible for these things to be . . .

Demeter, Hera, Rhea are said to be earth (*P.Thessaloniki*, col. xxii):[16]

πάν̣[τ' οὖ]ν ὁμοίω[ς ὠ]νόμασεν ὡς̣ κ̣άλλιστα ἠ[δύ]ν̣ατο
γινώσκ̣ων τῶν ἀνθρώπων τὴμ φύσιν, ὅτι οὐ̣ πάντες
ὁμοίαν ἔχουσιν οὐδὲ θέλουσιν πάντες ταὐτά·
κρατιστεύοντες λέγουσι ὅ τι ἂν αὐτῶν ἑκάστωι
ἐπὶ θ̣υμὸν ἔλθηι, ἅπερ ἂν θέλοντες τυγχάνωσι,
οὐδαμὰ ταὐτά, ὑπὸ πλεονεξίας, τὰ δὲ καὶ ὑπ' ἀμαθίας.
Γῆ̣ δὲ καὶ Μήτηρ καὶ Ἥρ̣η ἡ αὐτή. ἐκλήθη δε
Γῆ μὲν νόμωι, Μή̣τηρ δ' ὅτι ἐκ ταύτης πάντα γ[ίν]εται.
Γῆ καὶ Γαῖα κατὰ [γ]λ̣ῶσσαν ἑκάστοις. Δημήτηρ̣ [δὲ
ὠνομάσθη ὥσπερ̣ ἡ Γῆ Μήτηρ, ἐξ ἀμφοτέρων ἓ[ν] ὄ̣νομα·
τὸ αὐτὸ γὰρ ἦν. ἔστι δὲ καὶ ἐν τοῖς Ὕμνοις εἰρ̣̣[η]μένον·
"Δη̣μήτηρ [Ῥ]έα Γῆ Μή̣τ̣ηρ Ἑστία Δηι̣ωι". καλε[ῖτ]αι γὰρ
καὶ Δηιὼ ὅτι ἐδηι[ώθ]η ἐν τῆι μείξει. δηλώσει δ . [. .]α̣ν
κ̣ατὰ τὰ επ . γε̣ . [. . .]· Ῥέα̣ δ' ὅτι πολλὰ καὶ̣ . . .[ ]
ζῷ̣ια ἔφυ [c.11] ἐ̣ξ αὐτῆς. Ῥέα κα .[
κα[c.17]. ηδεκ[

Therefore he (sc. Orpheus) named (i.e. in his poem) everything likewise in the noblest possible way, knowing the nature of mankind, that not all of them have the same nature nor do they all want the same things. When they are in a position of power they say what they desire, whatever they happen to be wishing, never the same things, sometimes through greed, sometimes through ignorance. Ge, Meter, Rhea, and Hera: they are all the same she. She was called Ge by custom; Meter because everything comes from her. Ge and Gaia according to each people's dialect. She was named Demeter just as if she is Ge-meter: one name from both. For it was the same thing. And it was also said in the Hymns:

Demeter, Rhea, Ge Meter, Hestia, Deio.

For she is called Deio too because she was cut asunder (i.e. ravaged) in the mixture (or: 'in sexual intercourse'). And he will make clear that, according to the (verses? epic poems?) . . . And Rhea because many and . . . creatures were born . . . from her. Rhea (was called?) . . .

[16] Col. xviii at *ZPE* 47 (1982), 10 (following 300).

It is not only the mystic text which has for the Derveni commentator a hidden meaning. The Eumenides, to whom *μύσται* ('initiates') sacrifice, are in fact souls (col. ii.6–10). People are overcome by pleasure and remain ignorant of what is of concern in the next world (col. v).

P.Thessaloniki, col. xx in particular[17] shows the author appearing to be criticizing traditional ritual and religious practice:

[τούτους ὅσοι μὲν]
ἀνθρώπω[ν ἐμ] πόλεσιν ἐπιτ̣ελέσαντες [τὰ ἱε]ρὰ εἶδον,
ἔλασσον σφᾶς θαυμάζω μὴ γ[ι]νώσκειν (οὐ γὰρ οἷόν τε
ἀκοῦσαι ὁμοῦ καὶ μαθεῖν τὰ λ̣εγόμενα), ὅσοι δὲ παρὰ τοῦ
τέχνημ ποιουμένου τὰ ἱερά, οὗτοι ἄξιοι θαυμάζεσθαι
καὶ οἰκτε[ί]ρεσθαι, θαυμάζεσθαι μὲν ὅτι̣ δ̣οκοῦντες
πρότερον ἢ ἐπιτελέσαι εἰδήσειν ἀπέρχονται ἐπι-
τελέσαντες πρὶν εἰδέναι οὐδ' ἐπανερόμενοι ὥσπερ
ὡς εἰδότε̣ς̣ τ̣[ι] ὧν εἶδον ἢ ἤκουσαν ἢ ἔμαθον· [οἰ]κ̣τε⟨ί⟩ρεσθαι δὲ
ὅτι οὐκ ἀρκε[ῖ] σφιν τὴν δαπάνην προανηλῶσ̣θαι ἀλλὰ
καὶ τῆ̣ς̣ γνώ̣μ̣ης στερόμενοι προσαπέρχονται.
πρὶν μὲν τὰ [ἱε]ρὰ ἐπιτελέσαι ἐλπίζον̣[τε]ς εἰδ̣ήσειν
ἐπ̣[ιτελέσ]αν[τες] δ̣ὲ στερηθέ̣ντες κ̣α̣[ὶ τῆ]ς ἐλπί[δος] ἀπέρχονται̣.
τ . [c.10].υοντ[. . .]λ̣ογοσ̣ . . [. .]ται̣[. . . . .] . να
. [c.20] . υ̣ο . ⟦ c.10 μ]ητρὶ μὲν
[c.10] ἀδελφῆς [c.10]ο[c.10]ωσ εἶδε ⟧

[About all those (i) who] after performing a public rite in the cities have seen the holy things (i.e. have been initiated), I wonder less that they fail to attain knowledge, since it is impossible to listen to what is being said and learn it simultaneously. But all those (ii) who have learned (i.e. been initiated) from one who makes a craft of the holy rites deserve to be wondered at and pitied. They deserve (ii*a*) to be wondered at because, thinking before the ceremony that they will attain knowledge, they go away after being initiated before they have understood, without even asking additional questions, as though because they understood (i.e. thinking that they have understood) something of what they have seen or heard or learned. And they (ii*b*) must be pitied because it is not enough that their money is spent, but they go off deprived even of their judgement.

Hoping before performing the holy rites to gain knowledge, nevertheless they go away after being initiated deprived even of their expectation . . .

[17] Col. xvi at *ZPE* 47 (1982), 9 (following 300); translated at Laks and Most (1997), 18–19.

The author draws a distinction between those who have seen *τὰ ἱερά* after performing a public rite in the cities and those who do so after going to a private professional priest (*παρὰ τοῦ τέχνημ ποιουμένου τὰ ἱερά*). He is not surprised to hear about the first, but the second group evokes pity from him because these people intend to gain knowledge before the ceremony but go away without asking additional questions and without understanding what they have seen or heard or learned. They have spent their money too soon, and as a result have lost their judgement (*γνώμη*). I argue that the Derveni commentator sees himself as answering in his commentary on the Orphic poem this critique of mystery initiation. Unlike those who go away without understanding what they have seen or heard or learned, the Derveni commentator asks questions about the Orphic poem, engaging in procedures of interpretation that use instruction in cosmology and mythology as a form of initiation, that is, by engaging in a remythologizing[18] of the Orphic poet's originally conceptual insights. This remythologizing is paralleled in the texts of the Orphic gold leaves.[19]

The author thus invokes contemporary scientific research on causes and particle theory (in particular that of Diogenes of Apollonia) to make his target text seem modern and up to date, while exercising his real concern for private mysteries and social moralizing. Ironically enough, the Orphic theogony on which he comments, a hexameter product of the late fifth century, may have been written for exactly this purpose.[20]

There are few complaints in the later philosophical tradition about the rise of this new exegesis. Epicureans and allied sceptics from the third to the first centuries BC charge that such commentators (and the Stoics who adopted the procedure) reduce the

[18] So Burkert (1968).

[19] Ritual exegesis: Oliver (1950); Jacoby (1949), ch. 1; Clinton (1974); Persson (1918). Cf. Cleidemus, 323 fr. 14 Jacoby (= Athenaeus 409f), from his *Exegetikon*, on libation and sacrifice in funeral cult.

[20] i.e. an 'Attisch-eleusinische Hymnensammlung': Wilamowitz (1884), 339; Graf (1974), 151 ff. Cf. Baumgarten (1998). An 'altattische Dionysos-Hymnen' quoted in *P.Thessaloniki*, col. xxii: Obbink (1994). (To the evidence cited there, add Athenaeus 653b = Crates fr. 109 Broggiato—cf. Latte (1968), 623–4—in a discussion of Attic diction: *ἐν τοῖς ὕμνοις τοῖς ἀρχαίοις φάσκων ἀντὶ τοῦ βότρυος τὴν σταφυλὴν κεῖσθαι*. Private communication from A. C. Cassio via W. Burkert.) Dated to before 411/409: Burkert (1994).

gods to some entity or principle, or equate one or more of them with some other divinity. The confusion resulting from such reductionism, they charge, would make it impossible in our conceptions for individual gods to exist as people have always thought of and described them. Calling air Zeus or Demeter Earth is deemed not only an abuse of language, but equivalent to atheism. By the second century we get a new terminology to describe this kind of reductionism, *συνοικείωσις*, *συνοικειόω*, rendered as *accommodare* by Cicero (*On the Nature of the Gods* 1. 41). The poets too 'accommodate', 'assimilate' the gods in their conceptions to lifeless, objectionable things, or to other gods. Thus exegesis is characterized as a kind of accommodation that negotiates the boundaries of sense and reference emanating from the poetic text and opening the way for later theories of allegory.

To conclude, as far as we know, the earliest form of scholarly exegesis in the Greek tradition derives not from grammarians in museums but from the sphere of ritual and religion.

10

The Stoics' Two Types of Allegory

G. R. BOYS-STONES

> In book 2 [of his work *On the Gods*, Chrysippus] wants to make the stories in Orpheus, Musaeus, Hesiod, and Homer conform with what he himself had said in book 1 about the immortal gods, so that even the most ancient poets, who wouldn't so much have suspected any of it, would appear to be Stoics.
>
> (Cicero, *On the Nature of the Gods* 1.41)

The Epicurean criticism of Stoic allegorical exegesis—the suggestion that it is ad hoc in its procedure and disingenuous in its appropriation of the poets—still resonates in discussions of allegory in ancient philosophy. In particular, it is often assumed that the ancient philosophical practice of allegorical exegesis operated more or less independently of any theory dealing with the reasons why an author might have wanted to write in allegory to start with. Reasons of course might be found; but none that would have any impact on the exegesis. What was important was finding the message; the medium hardly mattered.

This assumption, I want to argue, is wrong. And its wrongness is quickly apparent in the work of the Stoics—the only major philosophical school of the Hellenistic period with an interest in allegory at all. For, to start with, at least, they made the surprising assertion that the material on which they exercised their exegesis had never been *intended* allegorically. The

This chapter builds on and overlaps with my discussion of Stoic allegory in Boys-Stones (2001), chapters 1–3, where a fuller account of some aspects of the questions not dealt with here will be found. It has benefited from the exposure of earlier drafts to audiences in Oxford (at the Corpus Christi seminar where the present collection had its genesis), in Bristol, in Lund, and at the Vrije Universiteit in Amsterdam (with special thanks there to Gert-Jan van Dijk).

Epicureans were right: the ancient poets did not have the slightest suspicion of the value or nature of the material they were conveying—and they certainly were not Stoics. In order to justify this position, it turns out that the Stoics had a highly sophisticated theory about the origins of their material—a theory intrinsically bound up with their exegetical strategies. To understand the allegorical 'message' of their material in this first sense of 'allegory' is very much a matter of understanding how it came to be allegorical in the first place.

This is not, however, all there is to be said. For the later Stoics came to believe that they could discern a second type of allegory in traditional theology—a strand of allegory that was, after all, 'deliberate', woven together with the unintended form of allegory identified by their predecessors. But given the theoretical background against which we can now see this development occurred, it is inconceivable that it might have occurred in isolation from reflective thought about its significance. Once one is used to the idea that allegory is something that *happens* to material, it is actually surprising to discover it being done deliberately. And in this case, the Stoics' reflections on why it happens turn out to raise important questions about the scope and nature of 'ordinary' philosophical discourse.

I

That the Stoics—the earlier Stoics, at least—believed there to be no authorial intention behind the 'allegorical' material they recovered from the ancient poets is clear from the distinction made in our evidence between the 'subtle physical theory' they found within these texts and the superstitious and 'foolish' activity of the poets themselves in writing them (cf. Cicero, *On the Nature of the Gods* 2.63). Useful they might be; but considered as the work of the poets, they were fit only to be 'repudiated with contempt' (*On the Nature of the Gods* 2.70–1).[1] From the perspective of the later tradition of allegorical exegesis, as practised by Philo of Alexandria, or by Neoplatonist and Christian exegetes, this comes as something of a surprise: a

[1] Cf. also *SVF* ii. 1076, p. 315.17–19: '*Childishly* (παιδαριωδῶς) the gods are spoken of and written of and depicted as human in form . . .'. See esp. Long (1992), the seminal paper in this field.

theory of authorial intention is central to their explanation for the allegorical nature of their texts; indeed, one might wonder what sense it makes to say that, as a matter of objective fact, a text could *communicate* something more interesting than its author had intended or realized. But the Stoics had good precedent for a theory according to which allegory might emerge in a tradition without ever becoming apparent as such to the channels through which the tradition passed: such a theory is found already in Aristotle.

According to Aristotle, human civilization has, over the course of the eternal history of the world, been repeatedly developed to its highest level—and repeatedly destroyed again by one of the devastating cataclysms which periodically ravage the earth. Obviously some humans survive these cataclysms; but there would not, Aristotle supposed, tend to be philosophers among them. (Philosophers belong at the heart of the civilizations which are destroyed.) Nevertheless, it is likely that those who do survive might carry over with them at least fragments of the technical insights achieved by their lost society; and it is these fragments, so Aristotle supposes, which form the basis for the mythological traditions which grow up in the post-cataclysmic era. Wrenched from their intellectual context, and misunderstood by the men who preserved them, these insights become quite literally mythologized—read not as philosophy, but as the starting-point for bardic invention[2]—and it is only when philosophy becomes re-established in the growth of the new

[2] See esp. *Metaphysics* Λ.8, 1074^{b}1–14: 'Fragments of the thought of the ancient, the very ancient thinkers have been handed down to us in the form of a myth, to the effect that these [sc. planets] are gods, and that the divine embraces the whole of nature. The rest has been added later in a mythological form . . .'. Cf. also *On the Heavens* 270^{b}14–20, *Meteorology* 339^{b}27–30, *Politics* 7.10, 1329^{b}25–9, and fr. 13 Rose for the theory that human civilization is repeatedly developed and destroyed by cataclysm (also for the information that some 'fragments' of antediluvian wisdom are preserved in popular sayings). It might be noted that some of the constituent parts of his theory (if not the theory itself) have Platonic precedents: Aristotle's cyclical view of human history seems to build on the account in Plato, *Laws* 3, for example; and the suggestion that mythology has a core that can be traced back to the very earliest men may find a precedent in *Politicus* 272c, where Plato refers to 'surviving stories' which depict and therefore presumably derive from the period of the 'golden' men who lived in the Cronian Age he is there describing. See further Boys-Stones (2001), 8–14.

civilization that philosophers start to recognize their own. In a tradition ostensibly received as mythological narrative, they could see faded fragments of what their pre-cataclysmic forefathers had thought. Sections of mythology, we might say, are revealed to them for the first time as *effectively* allegorical.

The Stoics, to be sure, did not assent to Aristotle's belief either in the eternity of the world or in the cyclical nature of its internal history. Nevertheless, their own beliefs about the history of the world (and their own understanding of philosophy) led them to agree with Aristotle about one thing, and that is that there must have been people of an earlier historical period who understood the world better than their descendants. A little reflection shows that the very first generations of mankind at least must fall into this case. For if god created men (as the Stoics believed), and if god had providential care for them (as they likewise supposed), then it is unreasonable to think that the first men were created vicious and unhappy. Yet unhappiness and vice were precisely, according to the Stoics, a matter of false belief. It follows quite simply, then, that the first generations of mankind could not have held false beliefs about the world. It is worth noting here the Stoics' insistence that these men could not have been *philosophers* as such, as this is a point which will have some importance for my argument later on.[3] Presumably, the Stoics supposed that philosophy implied a self-conscious attempt to understand the world which could only find its impulse in reaction to the misery and vice which arose at a later stage of human history. Nevertheless, the beliefs which these primitive folk did hold about the world had a particular interest for the philosopher, just insofar as their unaffected and natural purity guaranteed their truth. It is, then, these beliefs which are reflected in later mythology. And while the Stoics did not believe that there was a natural cataclysm to account for the transition from philosophy to mythology, they did believe that a gradual

[3] This position is argued with some vehemence in Seneca, *Epistles* 90 (e.g. 90.36: 'They were not sages—though they did what sages should do'). It cannot, admittedly, be taken for granted that Seneca represents the views of the early Stoa here: attempts have been made (perversely, in my view) to reconcile his position as much as possible with that of the later Stoic Posidonius (who is in fact the object of his attack in this letter): see e.g. Bertoli (1982); Pfligersdorffer (1982). For a fuller defence of my position, see Boys-Stones (2001), 18–27.

slide into decadence led to the loss of the purer world-view possessed by early man. As vice spread, and with it a more distorted view of the world, we must suppose that the insights inherited from earlier thinkers became increasingly unintelligible to later generations. These insights were received, not as (for example) physical accounts of the heavenly bodies, but as amusing fictions (or obnoxious superstition, depending on one's point of view) concerning a pantheon of superhuman deities. In other words, they became allegorical without anyone noticing. The first kind of allegory, identified by the early Stoics, was the result of intensional error, not of intentional craft.

II

It might be supposed that the Stoics' interest in the allegorical exegesis of mythology was motivated by the hope that they would be able to gain from it some support for their own philosophical doctrines (even, optimistically, answers to their own philosophical problems). But it should be noted that their understanding of allegory, as outlined so far, contains no suggestion that mythological allegory will compass only the kinds of insight into nature which are of immediate interest to a philosopher. Later philosophers, working with an intentional theory of allegory, will often make the claim that allegory is (or anyway should be) typically restricted to the higher levels of philosophy and theology: indeed, I shall suggest that the *later* Stoics themselves developed just such a view of allegory. But under the present theory, it is only the fact that philosophy is easily prone to misconstrual that links the insights of the early thinkers to the allegory of the mythographers: there is no theoretical reason why material originating in other fields of thought might not equally be misunderstood and become similarly allegorical. Once a tradition of story-telling exists—a tradition, furthermore, which from its roots involved borrowing material from its surrounding culture and adapting it for ends of its own—there would be a positive incentive for the poets to assimilate more material in this way. And, if the allegorization of such material (that is to say, its assimilation into the tradition) would in this case be more the result of disregarding than of missing its meaning, the effect will be very much the same. In fact, there is evidence from Aetius

(*SVF* ii. 1009, p. 300.13–37) that the early Stoics discerned as many as *seven* sources behind the mythological tradition—seven distinct possibilities for the origin of the traditional depiction of particular gods.[4] A particular god might, we are told, have his or her origins in (1) '[natural] phenomena and the heavenly bodies'. Father Heaven (Uranus) and mother Earth (Ge), the stars, the sun, and the moon are given as examples, and these seem to correspond with aspects of mythology based on the speculation of early man. But again, some gods represent (2) perceived 'benefits' to human beings (examples are Zeus, Hera, Hermes, and Demeter);[5] or (3) perceived 'harms' (examples are the Poenae, Erinyes, and Ares). Some gods are in origin merely (4) 'states of affairs' (πράγματα): e.g. Elpis ('Hope'), Dike ('Justice'), Eunomia ('Civil Order'); some are (5) passions (παθή): Eros, Aphrodite, and Pothos (all, as it happens, forms of *desire*) are given as examples. There are gods in the mythological tradition which resulted from (6) fictive input from the poets themselves, who naturally add to and embroider their material in pursuit of a good story. The example is given here of the gods 'Coeus, Crius, Hyperion, and Iapetus', invented by Hesiod (cf. *Theogony* 134) to plug gaps that he saw in the genealogical narrative he had inherited.[6] Finally, there are aspects of the mythological

[4] *SVF* ii. 1009 as a whole needs to be treated with care, since it groups together as part of a single discussion what are in fact three quite distinct answers to the question it sets, which is: 'From where do men get a concept (ἔννοια) of the gods?' The first answer corresponds to the standard explanation of how we gain a concept, in the technical sense of a 'common concept' (κοινὴ ἔννοια), of *god* at all: *SVF* ii, pp. 299.10–300.8, and cf. Cleanthes *apud* Cicero, *On the Nature of the Gods* 2.13–15; also SE, *M* 9.60. But what follows this reflects an answer to the very different issue of *who* was responsible for the *particular gods* described in traditional theology: see *SVF* ii, p. 300.8–12 (and cf. Varro *apud* Tertullian, *Against the Gentiles* 2.1; but esp. Augustine, *City of God* 6.5). Finally, we are given the list of seven headings with which I am at present concerned: this list once again deals with the origins, not of our concept of god as such, but of the particular representations of god in traditional theology. The issue this time, however, is what these 'gods' represented in their original source-material.

[5] No further explanation is offered. Zeus perhaps is (merely) 'useful' *qua* law (*SVF* ii. 1081). For Hermes as 'reason' see further below on Cornutus; likewise for Demeter as representing grain. Hera is standardly identified as 'air' (ἀήρ); but this seems too fundamental to count as merely 'useful'.

[6] This particular example, however, like almost every particular example in the field, was subject to disagreement: the Stoic Cornutus (of whom more

pantheon which rely on (7) *historical* incidents concerning, in particular, human benefactors. Stories concerning the god Dionysus, for example, might be allegorical reflections of a historical account of the man who discovered wine.[7]

This information is crucial for understanding the scope and nature of the Stoics' exegesis of mythology. Given the complexity of the evolution of the tradition implied by this list of sources, it follows that the Stoics could not *simply* hope to identify the allegorical from the non-allegorical components of mythology on the grounds of a perceived 'fit' between the former and their own philosophical doctrines. Even if they were narrowly concerned only with the excavation of 'philosophical' material (though there is good evidence that this is not all they wanted to do),[8] they would have to embark on a much more sophisticated *Kritik* of the tradition and its sources as a whole in order to do it. In what follows, then, I want to consider the

below) gave these gods an allegorical interpretation: *Introduction to Greek Theology* 17, 30.1–18 Lang (and cf. *SVF* ii. 1086).

[7] For the other examples given here (Heracles and the Dioscuri) cf. e.g. Clement, *Exhortation to the Greeks* 2.26.7. For Clement, 'euhemerism' is characteristic of pagan exegesis, and shows their religion to be devoid of gods altogether. It should be remembered, however, that the present passage is concerned with the sources of mythological images of god, not the nature of divinity. And then, with the exception perhaps of Persaeus (cf. *SVF* i. 448), euhemeristic explanations were used sparingly by most Stoics in any case: 'Dionysus' might be taken to name the man; but it might equally be taken to pick out the 'generative and nourishing *pneuma*' that pervades the universe (as 'the Stoics' at Plutarch, *On Isis and Osiris* 367 C); or to derive from the verb διανύσαι ('accomplish') and refer to the course of the sun (as Cleanthes at *SVF* i. 546).

[8] In the ideal state, according to Zeno, there would be no need for the trappings of conventional religion (e.g. temples at *SVF* i. 264–5); but the Stoics presumably realized that it would be counter-productive to preach against its mythological basis in a community of fools. One of their concerns, then, was to use the exegesis of mythology to instil a rational understanding of traditional theology, and remove the superstition which threatened to obscure the piety for which it was a vehicle. Cf. Cornutus, *Introduction* 35, 76.9–16 Lang, in a retrospective summary of his purpose in writing the work: 'You will accept our ancestral traditions and the complete account concerning them [sc. the symbols and 'enigmas' of mythology], and concerning the cultivation of the gods and things properly done to their honour; but only in such a way that the young are led thereby to piety without superstition, and are taught to sacrifice, and pray, and worship, and swear oaths in due form, and as appropriate in the circumstances.' To have a rational understanding of mythology is to combine piety and patriotism without superstition.

methods of exegesis employed by the Stoics in this light. For, although we have rather poor evidence on the matter from the surviving fragments of the earlier Stoics, we do have an entire surviving work from a later Stoic—Lucius Annaeus Cornutus, writing in the first century AD[9]—which we might take to be good evidence for the way they approached the matter.[10] (As we shall see, something else has started to happen in Cornutus as well: from his exegesis emerges evidence for a *second* type of allegory, a level of philosophical allegory in mythology which someone after all intended as such—but more of that in its place.)

III

It has struck some commentators on Cornutus as surprising that he spends as much time as he does on etymology, and so little time on the examination of 'extended episodes in early Greek poetry'.[11] But to be surprised at this is to misunderstand the nature of the task he faces. Given the Stoics' understanding of mythological allegory, Cornutus cannot afford to assume as a starting-point that any given passage of mythology is allegorical in any sense at all: it could be pure fiction; it might blend allegory with fiction; it might well blend allegory derived from different kinds of source-material. In any case, Cornutus needs an exegetical framework in terms of which he can make some sort of independent assessment, and an examination of the *dramatis personae* is the obvious first step towards doing this. Indeed, one of the most important routes into the study involves something more fundamental even than etymology properly speaking—namely, establishing the original *reference* of the words employed as character-names by the poets.[12] These will reveal very quickly

[9] For Cornutus generally, see esp. Most (1989).

[10] Cf. e.g. *Introduction* 35, 76.6–7 Lang for a modest acknowledgement of the 'fuller and more systematic' works of his predecessors. Very occasionally the source of particular conclusions (if not for the theoretical approach by which they were reached) can be located quite precisely: at least part of his account of Atlas, for example, seems to derive from Cleanthes (cf. *Introduction* 26, 48.15–17 Lang with SVF i. 549; the more striking if the aspirated MS variant ὁλοόφρονα is read in Cornutus; cf. Boys-Stones 1998: 171–2 n. 10).

[11] So Long (1992), 54.

[12] I make a distinction between establishing the original reference and the etymological meaning of the name not least because there are cases where it is

something of the nature of the poets' sources. Consider, for example, the following headings (which correspond, respectively, to sources (1), (6), and (7) in the list cited above from Aetius):

Primitive accounts of nature. By establishing the reference of divine names, we can quickly see that one source which fed into the poetic tradition involved speculation about the heavens. This would explain, for example, the presence of 'Uranus' (*οὐρανός*, i.e. heaven) in the mythological pantheon (see *Introduction* 1).

Poetical fabrication. Some of the poetical 'divinities' might be just that—poetic invention. As it happens, Cornutus does not, in this case, name names, but he refers to the general principle. Speaking of the Hesiodic genealogy in particular, he says that Hesiod 'received some things from the ancients, but, more in the manner of a story-teller, added others on. In this way,' Cornutus goes on, 'most of the ancient theology has been corrupted' (*Introduction* 17, 31.12–17 Lang).

Historical figures. Cornutus refers at length to at least one historical figure who made his way into myth as a 'god', namely Heracles (see *Introduction* 31 and further below).[13]

From this humble, but significant starting-point, Cornutus can start the process of reconstructing the various sources transmogrified into mythology. It is here that etymology properly speaking can help: as the study of word derivation (rather than simply of reference) it can reconstruct the thought-processes which led to the creation of the names in the first place. Having established, for example, that 'Uranus' referred in the poets' source-material to the 'heavens', we can ask what their source had in mind when it named the heavens this way. The

possible to establish the former while struggling over the latter. So, at least, in the case of 'Athena': Cornutus is sure that the name refers, in origin, to divine intelligence and, as such, providence (*Introduction* 20, 35.6–9 Lang; also, then, the wisdom in which philosophers share: cf. 20, 39.12–40.4 Lang quoted below in the text), but confesses the name hard to etymologize 'because of its antiquity': 20, 36.1–2 Lang.

13 As an adjunct to this heading, one might consider the possibility that other forms of 'historical' speculation have crept into mythology as well. Cornutus, for example, countenances (although in the end he seems to reject) the possibility that the name Dionysus derived from Mt Nysion, where Zeus first revealed the grape-vine (*Introduction* 30, 58.4–6 Lang).

answer Cornutus suggests is that the poets' ultimate source believed the heavens to be the limiting boundary of nature (οὖρος: 1, 1.4 Lang); or perhaps, that heaven 'tends' or 'guards' what exists (ὡρεῖν/ὠρεύειν: 2.1–2 Lang).

Nor does the value of etymology stop at teasing out theories implicit in the use of individual words: associations *between* words suggested by the mythological evidence can often be accounted for in etymological terms, and provide a valuable addition to the reconstruction of source-material. Typically, then, Cornutus, having looked at the *name* of a mythological personage, goes on to consider (in this order): the epithets normally associated with this character; their relationship (genealogical or otherwise) with other mythological characters; and finally their iconographical attributes.[14] In chapter 16, for example, the mythological name 'Hermes' is established as having referred, in the original source, to 'reason'. This identification is supported by its etymology, which gives us further information on the view of reason held by the original source: it viewed reason as a matter of 'contriving speech' (ὠνόμασται δὲ ἀπὸ τοῦ ἐρεῖν μήσασθαι: 20.21–2 Lang),[15] or perhaps as being the 'bulwark and fortress' of human life (ἢ ἀπὸ τοῦ ἔρυμα ἡμῶν εἶναι καὶ οἷον ὀχύρημα: 20.23 Lang). But then the fact that the name is

[14] I say 'finally', although in practice Cornutus often returns to consider further epithets after a discussion of attributes. Clear examples of this pattern include the discussions of Zeus in ch. 9, and of Hermes in ch. 16; other (usually shorter) discussions are readily seen to be abbreviations or variations of this archetype: see esp. on Poseidon in ch. 22; Aphrodite in 24; Eros in 25; the Seasons in 30. Cornutus' interest in the allegorical potential of iconographical attributes shows, of course, that he is interested in the theological tradition at large, not merely its literary reflections (cf. Most 1989: 2023–6).

It should be noted that the poets are not, of course, perfectly consistent in their transmission of genealogy, or their portrayal of character: so (to use examples I shall pick up further below) the poets give epithets to Poseidon which appear to contradict each other (e.g. 'Earth-Shaker', but also 'Earth-Holder': see *Introduction* 22, esp. 42.1–3 and 21–3 Lang); they disagree whether Enyo was mother, daughter, or nurse of Ares (*Introduction* 21, 40.15–17 Lang); and they disagree over the parentage of the Graces (15, 18.14–19.9 Lang; also over their number at 19.17–20.5 Lang). Cf. more generally *Introduction* 17, 27.19–28.2 Lang for the poets' (mis)treatment of divine genealogies. Nevertheless, they presumably have less motive to innovate in this than in, for example, the retelling of the stories involving their characters.

[15] This etymology is found already in Plato: see *Cratylus* 408a, quoted by Laird above, Ch. 8, p. 157.

linked (to take one example) with the epithet διάκτορος tells us in addition that the source thought that reason is 'piercing (διάτορος) and clear' (21.1–2 Lang); or, perhaps, that (as encompassing speech) it 'leads (διάγειν) our thoughts into the souls of those near by'. Hermes' mythological parentage is revealing as well: that his mother is given as Maia hints at an original belief that reason involves investigation and inquiry (implicit here is a connection with the verb μαίομαι, to search: see 23.6–11 Lang). And finally, the representation of Hermes by square statues (i.e. 'herms') points to a belief in the stability of reason (23.11–25.2 Lang for the full story).[16]

In this way, then, it is possible to see how the additional information adduced from the association of different names, epithets, and so on, takes Cornutus from a simple starting-point to a rich and increasingly complex framework of reconstruction. Of course, this framework will always be open to modification as it is required to deal with more material; but at the same time it will become more and more robust as Cornutus' researches progress and broaden—robust, indeed, to the point where it can be used in its turn to assess the nature of apparently related mythological material according to its consistency with the general picture emerging. What we know of Hermes in terms of

[16] At this stage too, it might be noted, there is a possibility of making some deductions about the historical stage at which different parts of the tradition were incorporated. If it is right to suppose that the purity of thought among the very first generations would keep them from arriving at false conclusions, then it is clear that less reliable sources must be more recent. One example of this would be the source which led to the mythological story of Athena's birth from the head of Zeus which, according to Cornutus, represents an association of intelligence with the head (cf. *Introduction* 20, 35.9–12 Lang): neither the earlier nor the later Stoics believed that the head was the seat of intelligence (see e.g. Posidonius F146 EK; and cf. Chrysippus at *SVF* ii. 911, pp. 252.20–253.18 for a more spirited attempt to reconcile the myth to orthodox Stoic belief. Cornutus, to be sure, says that the story is 'ancient'—ἀρχαῖος; but this word need not point us to the *primitive philosophers*, as is shown when it is used at *Introduction* 20, 37.14–17 Lang of what is already an interpretation of a pre-existing mythological passage). For another example of the input of later, less reliable speculation about the world (or, in this case, the divine), compare Cornutus' discussion of the darker theology surrounding Hecate: the epithets and practices on which this is based clearly do not derive from the earliest stages of the tradition (see *Introduction* 34, 72.15–73.7 Lang: note especially ἤρξαντο, 'they began . . .' at 72.29 and προσανεπλάσθη, 'the fiction was added that . . .', at 72.20).

this framework, for example, enables us to explain his pastoral associations as a later contamination which occurred within the mythological tradition through the confusion of *νόμος* ('law', with which 'reason' is intimately connected) and *νομός* ('pasture', with which it is not: see *Introduction* 16, 25.18–22 Lang). Cornutus' researches into Heracles likewise bring him to the conclusion that the poets have blended two separate bodies of source-material: one philosophical source (which requires 'Heracles' to be an allegorical representation of divine *logos* as lending strength to the universe: *Introduction* 31, 62.23–63.7 Lang), and one historical source (referring to the homonymous *hero:* 63.7–64.17 Lang).

The exegete is, ironically, helped by the fact that the transmission of the mythological tradition is itself not simple: that different sub-traditions exist, whose differences and outright contradictions draw attention to the different directions in which the poets of various traditions have developed their common material.[17] Strabo, in fact, has left us an explicit theoretical description of an approach which is implicit in the work of his younger contemporary Cornutus (*Geography* 10.3.23. We can overlook for now the fact that Strabo is dealing with what he sees as cases of *deliberate* allegory; the problem he faces and the exegetical strategy he adopts is the same):

> The whole study of the gods examines ancient opinions and myths, since ancient men stated their natural conceptions about the state of the world enigmatically, and always applied myth to their accounts. It is not easy to solve all of these enigmas accurately, but if the bulk of mythological narratives are set out in the open, some consistent with each other, others contradictory, one might more easily make a conjecture about the truth from them.

In the results of Cornutus' use of such a method, we can see that in some cases it will be simply impossible to decide which (if any) of the various sub-traditions has changed its original material the least (as perhaps in the case of the parentage of the Graces at *Introduction* 15, 18.14–19.9 Lang)—although at least one is alerted by the differences themselves to the fact that the source-material has somewhere been changed. In other cases the discrepancies simply will not matter, since the various

[17] Another source of divergence is noted at *Introduction* 17, 30.11–13 Lang: dialectal variation (the 'god' *Κοῖος* is merely an Ionic form of the word *ποῖος*).

alternatives all point in the same direction (as explicitly over the question of whether Enyo was mother, daughter, or nurse of Ares: *Introduction* 21, 40.15–17 Lang). In other cases again, the disagreement will turn out to be more apparent than real—for example if it arises from material treating of the same thing from different points of view (*Introduction* 22, 42.21–43.2 Lang on Poseidon not as Earth-Shaker, but Earth-Holder). A more interesting and substantial example in Cornutus—which involves the analysis now of an extended passage of narrative—involves disagreement within the corpus over which 'god' was responsible for bringing the arts to mankind (*Introduction* 18–19, 33.6–12 Lang): Prometheus, who is, perhaps, best known in this role; or Hephaestus and Athena, championed by a competing tradition?[18] The wider pattern of reconstruction that is emerging provides a context for deciding the case: for Cornutus will go on to show that there are mythological narratives supporting the suggestion that Athena, identified with reason and providence (or 'foresight'), brought men together in communities—and this meant providing them with philosophy and technology. The fact that Prometheus also represents 'foresight' explains his intrusion into an account which originally involved Athena working in consort with Hephaestus (representing fire, the material precondition for technological advance).[19]

The scope for allegorical exegesis to recover the source-material (and so the allegorical meaning) of substantial areas of mythology through the *internal* investigation of the tradition is

[18] The tradition is more complicated than Cornutus suggests: at Plato, *Protagoras* 320c–322d (esp. 321de), Prometheus is said to have *passed on* the gifts of Athene (i.e. wisdom) and Hephaestus (i.e. fire); and in *Homeric Hymn* 20 it is Hephaestus alone who is responsible for the benefactions.

[19] An association between philosophy and technical progress is something that Cornutus shares with Posidonius against the earlier Stoics. For Posidonius (and his disagreement on this point with Seneca, representing, as I have argued, the earlier Stoics: note 3 above), see Seneca, *Epistles* 90 *passim* (but esp. 90.21 for agriculture); also *Epistles* 88.21–3 (for the link between invention and an understanding of causality). For Cornutus, note the connection between the invention of grain cultivation at Eleusis (*Introduction* 28, 55.4–56.5 Lang) and the establishment of the Mystery rites by philosophers there (56.22–57.5 Lang and further below). All of this in turn is essentially bound up with the philosophers' role in the development of human communities (which, in the passages just cited, the discovery of grain makes possible and the Mysteries celebrate; cf. also *Introduction* 16, 25.18–22 Lang; 20, 39.12–40.4 Lang; 28, 56.14–20 Lang).

clearly very great. But the exegete has another powerful resource he can bring to bear on his material. He can also engage in a comparative analysis of mythology across cultures: the diverse subtraditions within the Greek tradition through which common material is developed in different directions turns out to be only a small-scale (and presumably a rather later) example of a process which started in the earliest days of the tradition (*Introduction* 17, 26.7–12 Lang):

> Many and varied myths about the gods were woven among the ancient Greeks, just as many arose among the Magi, many among the Phrygians, and again among the Egyptians, Celts, Libyans, and other races . . .

The similarities (as well as the differences) between different theological systems had of course been noted, and identifications and syncretizations between the gods of different cultures expounded as early as Herodotus.[20] However, the later Stoics (and here, it might be noted, we enter territory for which there are no attested precedents in the earlier Stoa) seem to have been the first analysts of mythology to develop this observation into what we might call a proper science of comparative mythology. Cornutus, for example, does not just note similarities or dependencies between different theological systems,[21] he also notes differences between them, making use of cross-cultural comparison as a means of isolating shared elements, of stripping away accretions whose peculiarity to particular traditions marks them out as the result of later development, and so to reconstruct a stage of traditional theology closer to its ultimate origins with the primitive philosophers. An interest in the religious practices of other peoples and the forces which can cause them to vary is evinced already, for example, in his note on the special cultivation of Ares by the 'Thracians and Scythians and suchlike races'

[20] Cf. esp. *Histories* 2.49–50; also 2.104 for the shared practice of ritual circumcision among the Colchians, Egyptians, Ethiopians, Phoenicians, and the 'Syrians of Palestine'. Closer to Cornutus' own time, cf. Varro, esp. *Divine Antiquities* 16, 150 Cardauns, and *Latin Language* 5.57–74 with Boyancé (1955), 58; Pépin (1958), 298; Hengel (1974), 160.

[21] For examples of this, see 6, 6.11–14 Lang for the Syrian Atargatis, representing the same as the Greek Rhea (also 6.14–19 Lang for the epithet 'Phrygian' applied to her as being particularly worshipped by the Phrygians); and cf. 2, 3.10–11 Lang for the (Roman) Δεός.

(*Introduction* 21, 41.12–15), and in the kind of explanation he offers: these are people 'among whom the exercise of military skills and disregard for justice is esteemed'. A more substantive example, and one with more direct implications for the understanding of Greek theology, comes in Cornutus' discussion of the myth of the Rape of Kore (*Introduction* 28, 54.12–21 Lang):

There was a myth that Hades kidnapped the daughter of Demeter which came about because of the disappearance of the seeds under the earth for a certain time. But the dejection of the goddess and her search throughout the cosmos were made up and added on later. For among the Egyptians, Osiris, who is sought and rediscovered by Isis, suggests the same sort of thing. Among the Phoenicians, there is Adonis, who is alternately above the ground and below the ground for six-month periods (Demeter's produce being thus called 'Adonis' from the fact that it 'pleases' [ἁδεῖν] men).

The details of Cornutus' argument here are (as often) not easy to reconstruct:[22] perhaps the most satisfactory gloss involves making the explanatory clause ('For among the Egyptians . . .') refer back to Cornutus' interpretation of the myth as a whole ('We know that the myth of Demeter and Kore contains elements of ancient wisdom—referring, as it happens, to the crop-cycle—and we know *this* because the Egyptians and the Phoenicians have traditional stories with much the same narrative structure'). But in any case, what is really important is what is beyond any doubt: that Cornutus is inviting us to compare mythologies from different cultures in an attempt to uncover their shared source; that this passage introduces us to a method of comparative mythology which can be used to identify the presence of primitive elements within the mythical structures that have grown up around them

The significance of this insight, both for its theoretical implications, and for its historical influence, cannot be exaggerated. It

[22] Cornutus can hardly be saying (on the reading of the passage that otherwise seems to me most natural) that the Egyptian and Phoenician narratives prove that the 'grief of Demeter and her search through the cosmos for her daughter are fictional accretions to the original myth': Isis did grieve and search for Osiris; and, although no search was necessary for Adonis, his death was certainly grieved (witness Bion's *Lament for Adonis*; Theocritus, *Idyll* 15, esp. 100–44).

represents, in particular, an approach to the allegorical exegesis of mythology which had been adopted into the heart of Platonism within two generations of Cornutus' death[23]—but for which we find *no* direct evidence earlier than Cornutus: that is to say, we have *no* examples of this kind of exegesis before Cornutus at all, and no evidence even for the general approach earlier than the Stoics of the generation immediately preceding him.[24] And the lure of the theory should be obvious: for it allows another check on the nature of the development of its source-material by the mythological tradition—and a check that is all the more valuable for the early stage of the tradition to which material held in common between the various theologies must be ascribed. Indeed, it may be possible to go further than this. Depending, presumably, on the antiquity of the separation between the two traditions, it might well be possible to suppose that cross-cultural comparison of mythology will allow the exegete to reconstruct (and ultimately, of course, to understand the content of) not just *early* source-material for the mythological traditions, but actually, in particular, the *earliest* material of all: the wisdom of the primitive philosophers.

[23] Cf. e.g. the 2nd-cent. Platonist Numenius, who advocated in the realm of theology a comparative study that is anchored in Plato and Pythagoras, but which opens out to include the traditions of the Brahmans, Jews, Magi, and Egyptians (fr. 1a des Places). (Significantly enough, Numenius is placed by Porphyry within a tradition of exegesis at the head of which stands Cornutus with his Stoic contemporary Chaeremon: *Against the Christians* fr. 39 von Harnack = Chaeremon Test. 9 van der Horst.) For a good example of the method in use, cf. Plutarch, *On Isis and Osiris* esp. 369 D–371 C, in which Plutarch's theory of cosmic dualism is supported by an exegetical comparison of Egyptian, Persian, Chaldaean, and Greek theology.

[24] As arguments *ex silentio* go, a good case is provided by the 2nd-cent. ethnographical writer Apollodorus, who hardly seems to have mentioned non-Greek theologies at all in his work *On the Gods*—an extensive and highly influential work that was used by Cornutus himself. We have a good number of fragments (*FGrH* 244: cf. in particular frr. 95–9, 126, and 135–6 for material in Cornutus), but only *one* (fr. 104) mentions gods of only *one* other race (the Egyptians); and even here Apollodorus mentions them only to euhemerize them out of existence. And this from a man interested enough in other peoples to write a twelve-book ethnographical commentary on Homer's Catalogue of Ships (frr. 154–207).

IV

The creative process through which the mythological tradition developed involved the assimilation of non-fictive material into a fictive environment; the allegorical exegesis of mythology in consequence involves separating out the various strands of the tradition and reconstructing their original meaning. I have outlined some of the sources identified by the Stoics' mythological *Quellenforschung*, and surveyed some of the techniques that they used to isolate them. But in Cornutus, at least, it turns out that not all of the allegorical sections of mythology (in the sense of 'allegory' that I have so far been discussing) are derived from discussions originally conducted in more 'literal' terms. The historically derived sections do; there may be sections deriving from later speculation about the world which do as well.[25] But the material which derives from the earliest thinkers turns out, according to Cornutus, to have been allegorical in its expression already—and in this case, I mean by 'allegory' something *deliberately intended as such* by its authors. The myth of Demeter, examined above as an example of a narrative shared (in its essentials) across cultures and therefore of great antiquity, turns out not to be an allegorized assimilation of agricultural theory originally set out more plainly by its inventors. Cornutus is quite clear that the inventors themselves expressed their discovery in allegorical terms. Indeed, they even established a special setting appropriate to their special mode of expression: the Eleusinian mysteries (*Introduction* 28, 56.22–57.5 Lang):

> While doing philosophy they began to celebrate the mysteries [to Demeter], rejoicing in the discovery of things useful for life and in the great festival, using it as proof that they had stopped fighting with one another over necessities,[26] and were *sated* (μυσίαν), that is, were filled.[27] It is plausible that the 'mysteries' (τὰ μυστήρια) took their name from this . . .

[25] See again n. 16.

[26] For the historical progression from barbarity to civilization and virtue by means of philosophy (and the concomitant invention of the arts of which the cultivation of grain was acknowledged the most important), see further below.

[27] κεκορῆσθαι: the etymological meaning of 'mystery' thus converges with the etymological origin of Kore, who plays a central role in the Eleusinian rites.

We have, in passing, seen already that Strabo assumes that the primitive wisdom in which he was interested was expressed in 'enigmatic' form; there is no reason to suppose (especially given the conceptual availability of the alternative notion of allegory) that this is a rash and ungrounded assumption. If the antiquity of the Eleusinian mysteries is not proof enough of the supposition, it might gain some confirmation through Cornutus' comparative research. For if this method really might allow the exegete to reconstruct something of the most primitive stage of the mythological tradition, the fact that so much material subsists which shares not just the same philosophical content, but actually the same narrative structure, might be taken to provide evidence that the narrative structures themselves were adopted with the original source-material. It might, in other words, be taken to provide evidence that the primitive philosophers already expressed themselves in a way which could be taken as fictive by anyone not a philosopher. But why might Cornutus have thought they did this?

One reason immediately suggests itself: it is at the very least a striking coincidence that the primitive allegorists are, in Cornutus' account, actually themselves *philosophers*. As I noted above, the early Stoics were careful to say that the insights they reconstructed from their 'allegorical' reflections in the mythological tradition derived (at best) from men who lived at a historical period when the human race had not yet been corrupted—not that it derived from *philosophers*. Indeed, the early Stoics seem to have thought that philosophy, as a self-conscious attempt to understand the universe, and a means towards straightening out one's distorted rationality, would be something that could only arise once the innocent purity of the first generations had been lost. Insights preserved by the poets were not, then, fragments of an ancient *philosophy* as such, but elements of an understanding of nature thrown up incidentally as the arts for manipulating nature were developed.

What changed matters, in some quarters at least, seems to have been the intervention of the later Stoic writer Posidonius. For Posidonius crucially denied one fundamental premiss of the earlier Stoics' account of early man—namely, that mankind in its natural, created state would have no impulse to vice which might require the development of philosophy. According to the earlier

Stoics, the human soul was entirely and simply rational: so, as no causes existed which could engender false beliefs, people were safeguarded from the possibility that they might become vicious. But according to Posidonius, human psychology was more complex than this, in particular because it contained non-rational as well as rational forces which governed and explained human motivation.[28] In this case, the appearance of vice in a person might not have to wait upon *external* corruption, but tended to have an *internal* source as well. Right from the start, according to Posidonius, all human beings were inclined by their non-rational impulses to pursue pleasure and honour in a way that might compromise the demands of their rational selves. Galen tells us that Posidonius criticized the early Stoics precisely on the basis that if, as they thought, the only source of vice were external, there would be *no* way of explaining the decline from the Golden Age at all.[29] If these external influences are powerful enough to overcome our own motivation towards virtue, he says, then we would all be evil in any case; but if on the other hand, our psychological motivation towards the good is stronger than any external influences could be, then 'who persuaded the first human beings to be conquered by the weaker force?'[30]

Posidonius does not think either that vice comes in afterwards to human beings from outside, without a root of its own in our minds, starting from which it sprouts and grows big, but the very opposite. Yes, there is a seed even of evil in our own selves; and we all need not so much to avoid the wicked as to pursue those who will prune away and prevent the growth of our evil.

[28] See F142–8 EK and generally, for the difference between Posidonius and Chrysippus, Glibert-Thirry (1977). The difficulty is to know quite where these 'forces' (δυνάμεις) were located: Galen tempts us to compare them to the 'parts' of the soul as described by Plato, but Posidonius explicitly rejects terminology that could have this implication, and it seems more likely that he described them, very roughly, as different *kinds* of desire, rather than the desires of different *parts* of the soul. But see on this Kidd (1971), 203–6, and especially Cooper (1998) (cf. also Gill 1998). For the historical question of the relationship between Posidonius' psychological theory and that of Plato, see Vander Waerdt (1985).

[29] See F35 EK with commentary at Kidd (1988), 174–8. And cf. F169.35–48 EK with Kidd (1971), 206–8.

[30] F35.5–7 EK. The passage that follows is the translation by Kidd (1999: 93) of F35.18–24 EK.

The final consequence of this revolution in Stoic psychological theory was that, if mankind was ever to have lived in conformity with nature (and, indeed, with their own natures), it would be necessary to provide some additional *external* force for the good which might counter-balance the internal force they now possessed for the bad. Humans would, in other words, need philosophy right from the start. And under the assumption that god would not create a race that would always be strictly imperfect, Posidonius asserted precisely that there were philosophers among early men—indeed, that the first human communities were founded when men living a solitary and rude existence were brought together through the agency of philosophy and the arts that it discovered (Seneca, *Epistles* 90.7). The age during which these philosophers ruled was known as a 'Golden Age', not least because the philosophers were able to restrain the innate impulses of people at large towards vice (*Epistles* 90.5):

> They were restrained in their own actions, and protected the weaker from the stronger . . . And no one had the inclination or the excuse for injustice: they were good subjects under good rulers, and a king could threaten nothing worse against someone who was disobedient than that they should be ejected from the kingdom.

It is clear that Cornutus was deeply influenced by Posidonius' account. Like Posidonius, he believed that the *very* first of our ancestors were brutal, violent, and antisocial, people, but that philosophers, in inventing the various arts, allowed thereby the formation of communities. Compare *Introduction* 28, 56.22–57.5 Lang (quoted above); also 16, 25.18–22 Lang; 28, 56.14–20 Lang; but especially 20, 39.12–40.4 Lang, where Cornutus derives from the myth of the Giants an account of the formation of communities, and the central role played in it by philosophy:

> It has been handed down that Athena distinguished herself in the battle against the Giants, and was accordingly called Giant-slayer. Now it is likely that the first men, born from the earth, were violent and hot-tempered in their dealings with each other, being utterly incapable of reaching an agreement or of fanning the spark of community spirit which was in them. But the gods, as if spurring them on and putting them in mind of their rational concepts, prevailed, and the cultivation of reason utterly subdued them and brought them into line—to the extent that you might have thought it had routed and destroyed their

old natures. After the change, they and their offspring became different people, living together in communities, thanks to Athena, Guardian of Cities.

The Giants represent human life without philosophy; and the impossibility of such an existence (let alone its incompatibility with a providential account of the world) is Cornutus' argument (as it was also Posidonius') for the existence of a highly developed philosophy, derived from a privileged source, among the earliest generations of men. If the later Stoics believed that insights from the earliest people became preserved in mythology as the earlier Stoics had done, it would now be precisely the insights of *philosophers* preserved. And so it seems to be *because* they were philosophers that, Cornutus thinks, they expressed themselves in allegory:

The ancients were no ordinary men, but capable of understanding the nature of the cosmos and *inclined to use symbols and riddles in their philosophical discussions of it* (συνιέναι τὴν τοῦ κόσμου φύσιν ἱκανοὶ καὶ πρὸς τὸ διὰ συμβόλων καὶ αἰνιγμάτων φιλοσοφῆσαι περὶ αὐτῆς εὐεπίφοροι).

But the question has now, of course, been altered, not answered. For if the claim is that it is somehow *natural* for philosophers to want to express their thought in allegory, we need to ask: Why so?

As it happens, the history of the philosophical exegesis of allegory in antiquity contains a large range of suggestions for why a philosopher might choose to write in allegory. Occasionally, indeed, the answer is given that allegory is an essentially *stylistic* choice: the choice, for example, that a philosophical *poet* would make (e.g. 'Heraclitus', *Homeric Problems* 24), or that the fashion of the time might demand (so Dio of Prusa, *Oration* 53.3); or that is an appropriate reflection of the grandeur of the subject-matter (so Demetrius, *On Style* 99–102 with Innes, above, p. 19; cf. Hermogenes, *On Types* 246). However, an explanation that went no further than this would sit oddly with the strong contrast that Cornutus (like all Stoics) wished to draw between the early thinkers, on the one hand, and the poets, on the other: there cannot have been 'poetical' considerations before there was poetry. And indeed, Cornutus seems to go out of his way to avoid describing (what I have called) the allegories of the early philosophers in terms which might be mistaken for the terms of rhetorical tropology: he does not even use the word *allegory* (here or anywhere else in the *Introduction*): like Strabo in the passage quoted, he talks rather of the early philosophers' tendency to express their thought through *symbols and enigmas* (τὸ διὰ συμβόλων καὶ αἰνιγμάτων φιλοσοφῆσαι).[31]

More to the point, perhaps, are those accounts of allegory which attempt to make its choice not merely decorative, but part of the philosophical project itself. In particular, a common theme in allegorical commentaries—from Derveni to the latest Neoplatonist writers—is the value of concealment. Allegory, by making obscure the wisdom communicated, is a way of restricting that wisdom to a particular audience, to those initiates (literally or figuratively speaking) who have the 'key' to its decoding (as apparently the Derveni Papyrus col. 7 Tsantsanoglou; cf. Philo of Alexandria, e.g. *On the Cherubim* 48; also Origen, *Philokalia* 13). As such, it is a means of protecting the wisdom discussed from the abuse of those who would not understand it (e.g. ps.-Plutarch, *On the Poetry of Homer* 2.92; Numenius, fr. 55 des Places); or, conversely, to protect the public at large from a dangerously superficial acquaintance with the deeper truths of god and of nature (cf. Varro *apud* Augustine, *City of God* 4.31). There is evidence for this kind of explanation in the Stoa. Chaeremon of Alexandria, a rough contemporary of Cornutus, and himself an Egyptian priest,[32] said of the ancient Egyptian scribes that they employed symbolic modes of exposition as a means of *concealing* their wisdom (fr. 12.6–9 van der Horst). Quite why they wished to conceal their wisdom is not explained in this fragment; but if it is to be made consistent with what we are told in Test. 12 van der Horst ('the Egyptians . . . wanted to teach the great and lofty things to the uninitiated by means of allegories and myths'), then presumably the idea is that they found in allegory a pedagogical vehicle which precisely made discriminations in its audience, revealing more to those capable of understanding it, but (through the construction of

[31] The word ἀλληγορία is, however, known to Strabo (cf. *Geography* 1.2.7, of Homer πρὸς ἐπιστήμην ἀλληγορῶν); it also seems to be attested for Cornutus, but (significantly) in one of his *rhetorical* works. See his *Art of Rhetoric* 85, 17.13–16 Graeven.

[32] See again n. 23. For Chaeremon generally see Frede (1989); fragments in van der Horst (1987).

surface narratives relatively easy to grasp) something at least to those of more limited philosophical attainment. A person would get out of their allegories exactly as much as—but no more than—they were intellectually capable of profiting from.

This, however, does not seem to be the end of the story. If it were, indeed, it might argue for the end of allegorical exegesis itself, since the exegete would risk spoiling the game he has identified if he makes clear a level of meaning that was meant to be concealed: the process of exegesis itself would deny (or ignore) the need for allegory posited by its practitioners.[33] But with suitable refinement, this problem can be avoided—namely, if we view allegorical exegesis as not so much a matter of *translation* (from the darkness of allegory to the light of plain speech), as a matter instead of *commentary*. The idea would be that successful allegorical exegesis performed on the most serious allegorical texts will give you a way into their understanding, but not an explicit account of all you can learn from them. There is some evidence that this is an appropriate response, because it seems that the Neoplatonists, at least, believed that it was, properly, *impossible* to give an explicit account of all that an allegory expresses: a philosophical allegory might contain the truths that it does only *when and because* it is allegorical. And, given that we are talking here about the deepest discussions of the structure of nature, a reason for this quickly suggests itself. After all, the world revealed to our senses conceals truths available only to the intellect in a way suggestively analogous to the structure of allegory, which presents the reader with a superficial narrative concealing within it truths not immediately apparent. This, in any case, is what we are told by the fourth-century Neoplatonist philosopher Sallustius. Discussing why 'the ancients' expressed their philosophical views in 'myth' (that is to say, allegorically), he inverts and so strengthens the analogy I have outlined, saying the following (*On the Gods and the Universe* 3):

> It is possible to call the universe itself a myth, since bodies and objects are apparent in it, while souls and intellects are hidden.

And Sallustius is by no means alone in thinking of allegory in these terms. When Dio of Prusa compares the universe to a

[33] Cf. Numenius, fr. 55 des Places, quoted by Leidl in this volume at Ch. 3, n. 29.

temple of initiation (*Oration* 12.34; cf. Plutarch, *On Tranquillity* 477 C), he suggests something very similar: that understanding the structure of reality reflects the process of initiation (to which, it should be noted, allegory was thought particularly appropriate). The philosopher/initiate proceeds from perception of the apparent/symbolic to understanding of the underlying reality/symbolized meaning.[34] Or again, to pick out another aspect of the comparison hinted at in the passage of Sallustius just quoted, an allegory may be compared to a complex of body and soul: the more important component is housed (and of course hidden) in a vehicle that is readily accessible to perception.[35]

Such models, then, are clearly important for the Platonist understanding of philosophical allegory. It might, however, be objected that they are inappropriate for understanding the work of Cornutus or the later Stoics more generally: Platonists, after all, believed in a way that the Stoics did not that the world of the senses coexisted with a distinct level of being accessible by the intellect and inaccessible, even in principle, to the senses;[36] the Stoics, on the other hand, specifically denied the existence of any such metaphysical realm or layer of being. However, if the Stoics would have to explain the model in slightly different terms from those used by the Platonists, it does not follow that they might not have used it—or even originated it. Indeed, far from imply-

[34] Cf. perhaps also Josephus, *Antiquities* 1.9, but esp. 24, where 'the whole [Law] has a structure harmonious with the universe, the lawgiver shrewdly hinting at some things, solemnly setting out others in allegory, but revealing in literal terms those things it is expedient to say plainly'.

[35] So e.g. Philo, *On the Contemplative Life* 78 (a passage quoted with approval by Eusebius, *Ecclesiastical History* 2.17.20): 'Exegesis of the holy scriptures comes about through hidden meanings in allegories (δι' ὑπονοιῶν ἐν ἀλληγορίαις): for the whole Law seems to these men [the Therapeutai] like an animal, having literal prescriptions as its body, and as its soul the unseen meaning laid up within the words.' At *On the Migration of Abraham* 93, Philo uses the analogy to explain why we should observe the letter of the Law despite understanding its allegorical significance (it is, he says, for much the same reason as we take care of the body, as being the abode of the soul). Later in the Neoplatonist tradition, cf. e.g. Olympiodorus, *Commentary on Plato's Gorgias* 46.2; for Origen (who deploys an analogy based on the threefold distinction of body, soul, and spirit), see Edwards in this volume (Ch. 12).

[36] Hence Plato himself was able to describe the visible world as an 'image' (εἰκών: or 'metaphor'? cf. Pender in this volume at Ch. 4, pp. 55–7) for the intelligible: *Timaeus* 92C5–7.

ing a model of allegory alien to Stoical thought, it is possible that we have evidence for its use, in a disputed fragment of Chaeremon (15D van der Horst):

> The point of view of the Egyptians (for I am interested in that too) is not wholly clear, but everything is symbolic. For they have sphinxes and ibises and some spherical forms stored away in treasuries, and some other things of which the outward appearance does not transcend sense-perception, but they claim that, by means of these things, they are making an image of intelligibles (διὰ τούτων εἰκονίζειν τὰ νοητά).

Chaeremon's modern editors have tended to view this fragment as straightforwardly contradictory with his views on metaphysics as we know them from elsewhere—and have on this basis rejected the attribution of the fragment to Chaeremon altogether. Taking τὰ νοητά as a reference to an 'intelligible world', van der Horst, for example, argues that it contradicts (his) fr. 5, where we are told that Chaeremon did not believe in the existence of anything beyond the 'visible worlds'.[37] But whatever reasons there might be to reject the ascription of the fragment to Chaeremon,[38] it turns out that this cannot be one of them. The reason is very straightforward: the phrase τὰ νοητά does not (or need not) after all mean 'intelligible *world*': it merely means 'intelligibles'. A more literal, and perhaps a more natural, translation of the word might be something like 'objects of understanding', and the Stoics did, of course, believe that there were objects of understanding. In a different way from the Platonists, they nevertheless did agree that to *see* the world was a different thing from *understanding* it, and used this very word to help express the distinction.[39] The Stoics did not indeed believe that anything existed beyond (what Chaeremon calls) the visible worlds: they did away with 'intelligible substances' (νοηταὶ οὐσίαι).[40] But if objects of thought do not, according to the Stoics,

[37] Van der Horst (1987), 64—although he is in fact only spelling out the reasons for Schwyzer's dismissal of the fragment (1932: 61).

[38] It might be noted, for example, that the fragment does not name Chaeremon; although it is clearly related in subject-matter and approach to named citations.

[39] Cf. e.g. SE, *M* 7.359–60 (= *SVF* ii. 849), distinguishing between a non-rational 'power' of the soul to perceive sensible objects (αἰσθητά) from a rational 'power' which is affected by intelligible objects (νοητά).

[40] So *SVF* ii. 108: the qualification is important: the Stoics did away with intelligible *substances*, not 'intelligibles' as such.

have substantial existence as part of the furniture of the universe, they subsist none the less as propositions *about* the furniture of the universe.[41] And if the Stoics could maintain this distinction between what is seen and what is understood, then they could very easily have shared the view of allegory we find in later Platonist, or Platonist-influenced texts: that allegory is a mode of discourse peculiarly adapted to philosophical accounts of the world, because it is a mode of discourse that in some sense shares its structure with the world as it reveals itself to a rational being. As the philosopher (even the Stoic philosopher) works from the evidence of the senses towards a rational understanding of the rational structure of the world, so the truths expressed in an allegory are manifested to the reader in a superficial narrative.

This way of viewing allegory is not incompatible with the need for allegory as a means of concealment: rather, it complements that account, and to some extent helps to remove the difficulties I identified in it. For what it says is that one might try to spell out in less obscure terms the meaning of a philosophical allegory, but that in doing so one immediately loses the context in which it made philosophical sense. The Stoics' spiritual ancestor in physics, Heraclitus, famously said that 'nature loves to hide'.[42] If so, then of course an account of nature that did not express its hiddenness would be a defective account; and, worse than this, an attempt to drag these deeper truths out into the glare of plain speech would, understandably, make them look absurd and denuded. Exegesis must function for this type of allegory like commentary not like translation, it must give just enough information to draw us into the text, without giving enough to alienate us from its meaning.[43] These allegories both conceal and

[41] 'Intelligibles' are, for example, the primary bearers of truth-value: SE, *M* 8.10 (= *SVF* ii. 195).

[42] 22 B123 DK. This fragment is used by Neoplatonist commentators precisely in the context of explaining the need for allegorical myth: cf. e.g. Proclus, *Commentary on Plato's Republic* ii. 107.5–7 Kroll = Porphyry 182F.66–70 Smith (*καὶ ὅτι τὸ πλασματῶδες τοῦτο κατὰ φύσιν πώς ἐστιν, διότι καὶ ἡ φύσις κρύπτεσθαι φιλεῖ καθ' Ἡράκλειτον*). It goes without saying that, this mode of expression being necessary for certain areas of philosophy, Proclus supposes that it is to be found in Plato; also, of course, that this in no way contradicts Plato's strictures against the baser fables to be found in the poets. In addition to the wider context of the passage just cited, see Proclus, *Platonic Theology* 1.4.

[43] It is in this context, then, that we should understand Numenius' dream (cf.

adorn; but not for the sake of concealment or for the sake of adornment. The philosophers' purpose in using them is simply to express the truth—because they are the only way of expressing the highest truths. And this, I suggest, is why the later Stoics could assume that the earliest philosophers (the most perfect philosophers who have lived or could now live) were inclined to express themselves in symbols and enigmas.

V

The Stoics' understanding of traditional theology was at all times a highly sophisticated account of the evolution of a tradition. They never viewed mythology as an authoritative philosophical account of the gods, taken either literally or (in either sense discussed) allegorically; and we find evidence for a complex examination of received theology understood as a product of its culture—or, rather, an expression of the entire history of that culture, traced back to the philosophy of the very first men, and taking in elements of later history, speculation, and sheer invention as the tradition developed. There is a great deal that could be said about this as a view of theology; but for the purposes of this chapter, what is most significant is the view—or rather views—of allegory which developed in the course of the Stoics' investigations into that tradition. By the time later Stoics such as Cornutus were writing, we find two types of allegory, both of tremendous historical significance: a notion of 'allegory' which looked back to the work of the earlier Stoics, and through them to Aristotle, by which historical and speculative material representing every period of Greek cultural development became incorporated into the tradition; and a notion of allegory which looked forward to the allegorical exegesis of Platonists and Christians, which is associated with the most truly philosophical accounts of the world. Neither of these kinds of allegory, to pick up a point I have made in the Introduction to this volume, answers very closely to the definition of allegory found in rhetorical texts—despite attempts by later writers to use the technical terms of the orators as a basis for their own

n. 33): it was not the fact that he engaged in allegorical exegesis that caused offence, but that he went too far in doing so.

accounts.[44] The first kind of allegory involves the accidental obscuring of a narrative whose meaning was originally—and is most appropriately—expressed in literal terms; the second kind of allegory is deliberate in its formulation, but also inextricably linked as such with its subject-matter. This latter kind of allegory represented, in a sense which was to be further spelled out in the Platonist and Christian traditions, the very language of creation.

[44] Cf. 'Heraclitus', *Homeric Problems* 2.5; but further Russell in this volume (Ch. 11) for the intellectual location of the author.

11

The Rhetoric of the *Homeric Problems*

DONALD RUSSELL

We know nothing about this 'Heraclitus', the author of the *Homeric Problems*.[1] That this was his name, and something like this the title of his book, is generally accepted on the evidence of the *subscriptio* in the Codex Ambrosianus B 99 (M) (cf. Oelmann 1910, p. xxxvii). Nor, of course, do we know when he lived. There are, however, two general reasons for a date not later than the second century AD. One is the absence of any of the metaphysical or Neoplatonist allegorizations that are so common later.[2] The other, much less cogent, is the pretentious, highly metaphorical, and distinctly non-Atticizing style.

More important, what sort of person was the author? Grammarian, rhetor, or philosopher? Something, perhaps, of all three. He possesses a good deal of scholarly learning: etymologies (e.g. ὠκεανόν at 22.7 [33.13]), mythology, Homeric antiquities. He was attractive enough as a purveyor of such traditional scholarship to be copied out in medieval scholia on Homer (see Buffière 1962, pp. xlvii–liv). He also has a good deal of philosophical knowledge, mainly about physics, not attributable to any one school, but with a large element of Stoic material. Thus he speaks (25.2 [38.9]) of 'the most reputed of the philosophers' as holding the view that the preponderance of one

[1] References to the work in this chapter are given to chapter and section, as in Buffière (1962), and to page and line numbers of the Societatis Philologae Bonnensis Sodales (SPB) edition (introduction by F. Oelmann), which gives much more information about the text. (When both are used, the latter appears in square brackets.)

[2] Heraclitus is a model of what Bernard (1990: 11–21) calls 'substantive allegory'.

or other of the elements, destroying the harmony of the whole, leads to conflagration (*ἐκπύρωσις*) or cataclysm. Again (at 72.15 [95.14]) he speaks of 'the philosophers' who distinguished the 'conceived' from the 'spoken' word (*ἐνδιάθετος* and *προφορικὸς λόγος*). His turn of phrase implies that he does not claim to be a philosopher himself (ps.-Longinus, *On the Sublime* 44.1 offers a parallel for a writer distancing himself from philosophers). He once makes a 'concession' to the Peripatetics (23.12, [36.8]) in the matter of the 'fifth body'; and he holds back his invective against Plato (a main theme of his argument) out of 'respect for the name of Socratic wisdom' (79.1 [104.15]). But, thirdly, he is a rhetor, making a case, not afraid of paradox in doing so, and organizing his material with care. It is this third aspect that I want to explore here. I shall do this in Sections II–IV by means of a detailed study of the Prologue (chapters 1–5) and the Epilogue (chapters 76–9), which are closely, and very artificially, bound together. First, however, let us see what comes between, so as to form a view of the evidence mustered in support of Homer's innocence.

I

Heraclitus claims (6.1 [9.4]) to follow the order of the epics, and to find allegorical statements about the gods 'in each *rhapsodia*' by means of 'refined knowledge' (*διὰ λεπτῆς ἐπιστήμης*).[3] In fact, some episodes are treated at much greater length than others, and there is a large gap in the treatment of the *Odyssey* (nothing between books 11 and 20), which is due to the loss of some part of the text at the end of 74 [98.14].

We begin (chapters 6–16) with a lengthy discussion of the plague in the first book of the *Iliad*. This hinges on our being convinced that Homer knew the identification of Apollo with the sun (7.3 [10.1]) which Heraclitus establishes by a study of epithets: *Φοῖβος*, *ἑκαέργης*, *Λυκηγενέτης*, *χρυσάορος*. Granted this, the way is open for a purely rational account of events. The plague was a 'spontaneous calamity' (*αὐτόματος φθορά*). It happened in hot weather, when plagues do occur. It was summertime, as we can tell from a variety of circumstances: the long battles of the later books imply long hours of daylight;

[3] Cf. 7.3 [10.12]; 29.4 [44.12]; 56.5 [78.6].

Hector would never have bivouacked by the ships if it had been cold weather; and, even if the barbarians (9.9 [15.18]) had been stupid enough to campaign in the winter, the more prudent Greeks would surely not have sent scouts out at night in a season when a snow-shower or a heavy rainstorm might have swept Odysseus and Diomedes away. All this (whatever its source) is a typically rhetorical argument from 'times' and 'persons' (including national characteristics), the sort of thing used in exercises of 'construction' and 'destruction' (ἀνασκευή and κατασκευή) concerning the 'probabilities' of mythical stories.[4] Some of the details of the events, however, need a different approach: the noise of Apollo's arrows (12.2 [19.8]) is meant to represent the heavenly music of which even Homer's enemy Plato was aware (Heraclitus cites *Republic* 10, 617b); and, if Apollo 'moved like the night' (νυκτὶ ἐοικώς at *Iliad* 1.47), this is because a dark, cloudy sky is associated with times of plague.

This is the 'first allegory' (16.5 [25.8]). It is followed (17–20 [25–31]) by a discussion of the more straightforward case of Athena's appearance to Achilles (*Iliad* 1.194–200). Here, a side-issue can be raised against Homer's chief prosecutor, Plato. He can be charged with plagiarism, or rather 'ingratitude' (ἀχαριστία: 17.2 [26.5]). This is very much a declaimer's move: the Action for Ingratitude (δίκη ἀχαριστίας/*actio ingrati*), may have had some basis in real procedure, but was predominantly a theme of the schools.[5] The ground here is that Plato took his tripartite psychology—and the location of the three faculties, reason in the head, spirit (θυμός) round the heart, and desire (we are told: cf. *Timaeus* 70de) in the liver—straight out of Homer. Other passages of Homer are adduced: Odysseus beats his chest (*Odyssey* 20.17), 'thumping as it were on the door of that house of Abhorrence of Evil, his heart' (καθάπερ οἶκόν τινα τῆς μισοπονηρίας θυροκρουστῶν τὴν καρδίαν: 18.2 [28.5]). Tityos' liver (*Odyssey* 11.578) is appropriately the object of the vultures' attention: the guilty organ is punished 'just as lawgivers cut off the hands of those who assault their fathers' (18.7 [28.17])—

[4] Cf. e.g. Aphthonius, *Progymnasmata* 5–6 on the story of Apollo and Daphne.

[5] Cf. Seneca, *On Benefits* 3.6.1 with Bonner (1949), 87–8. For the alleged real law in Persia and at Athens and Marseilles, cf. Valerius Maximus 2.6.7; 5.3, ext. 3.

another piece of declaimers' law,[6] and so another hint of our author's rhetorical background. Athena's actions thus become intelligible. Achilles has been in doubt, and debating 'in his mind and his heart' (*κατὰ φρένα καὶ κατὰ θυμόν*) whether to kill Agamemnon or calm himself. He has drawn his sword. At this point, Athena takes him by the hair (20.1 [30.10]) so that the seat of reason becomes involved, Achilles' anger having cooled and his 'boldness in the face of any danger' (20.6 [30.17]) taking fright and retreating before 'the repentance of reason'. Of course, if she could have managed it, Athena would have stopped his anger altogether; but she only represents human reason, great passions do not yield at once, and she contents herself with stopping the violence but allowing hard words. But Athena is doing nothing wrong, and there is no need for allegory as a defence of impropriety. Heraclitus does not make this explicit; in fact, to show allegory in innocent contexts (as we shall see) strengthens the case for seeing it where it is needed to counter the charge of impiety. Perhaps he does not see this. The transition (20.12–21.1 [31.11–15]) is suggestive:

> So let the episode of Athena, whom he represented as a mediator in Achilles' anger, be thought to deserve allegorical interpretation by itself,[7] but there is a very heavy charge against Homer, one deserving every condemnation, if he made up the story, as we find it in the sequel, that 'the other Olympians wanted to bind' the ruler of all [cf. *Iliad* 1.399–404].[8]

The Binding of Zeus, then, merits not only Homer's expulsion from Plato's Republic, but banishment 'beyond the pillars of Heracles and the impassable Ocean sea'. The charge is carefully built up. Zeus was conspired against, not by Titans and Giants, but (much more disgraceful) by his sister and wife Hera, by his brother Poseidon, and by Athena, the child to whom he was both father and mother. He was then rescued by unlikely and unworthy aid: Thetis and Briareus (21.4–6 [32.6–17]). The answer is that this is a cosmological allegory: Zeus, the most powerful of the elements, is attacked by air, water, and earth, and the confusion is ended by Thetis, who sets things right, and the great power of Briareus (25.6–11 [39.1–14]). To make this

[6] Cf. Theon, *Progymnasmata* ii. 130 Spengel: ὁ πατροτύπτης χειροκοπείσθω.

[7] Reading αὐτῆς with M and Buffière; but ταύτης τῆς (O) or τοιαύτης (SPB) is possible.

[8] Reading ὅτι for ὅτε at 31.15 SPB.

plausible, it has to be shown that the doctrine of the elements is foreshadowed in Homer, and that he was the source of everything that Thales, Anaxagoras, and others taught. So what seemed an 'inescapable accusation' can be dealt with by scientific allegorizing (25.12 [39.15–16]).

The story of Zeus throwing Hephaestus down from heaven (chapters 26–7) is objectionable in two ways: Hephaestus is lamed and nearly perished. He represents, it seems, earthly fire, not heavenly; he is lame by comparison, and perhaps also because he needs sticks to keep him going; and he goes out if you do not keep him supplied with fuel. This interpretation is rendered plausible by the fact that Homer elsewhere (*Iliad* 2.426) uses 'Hephaestus' as a metonymy for fire: 'They put the offal on spits and held it over Hephaestus.' No more recondite explanation is needed, and an elaborate one of Crates is summarily dismissed (27.2–4 [42.9–43.4]).

In most of what follows, Heraclitus can be seen to have a preference for moral explanations: scientific ones are reserved for hard cases, and are not always necessary even then. Thus in his discussion of the Theomachy (chapters 52–8), the hardest case of all, he advances a theory that the battle symbolizes the coincidence of all seven planets in one zodiacal sign, which would signify total destruction; but he does not really believe this—it has more 'plausibility' than 'truth' about it—and he puts it in only 'to show us that he is aware of it'.[9] Much clearer, and much more in keeping with Homer's wisdom, is the moral explanation, that it is essentially a battle between folly (Ares) and wisdom (Athena), or between forgetfulness (Leto) and reason (Hermes). Scientific explanation only comes in with Poseidon and Apollo (water fighting fire), and Hera and Artemis (the dark air eclipses the moon). Similarly, the explanation of Poseidon's destruction of the Greek wall (chapter 38) also has two stages, one purely rationalistic, in which the god represents rain and flood, and one more recondite, in which his trident stands for three different kinds of earthquake (see 38.6 [56.2–6]), the 'shaker', the 'gaper', and the 'tilter' (*βρασματίαν καὶ χασματίαν καὶ κλιματίαν*). This is another 'refined' explanation, and claimed as such (*λεπτῶς* at 38.5 [55.20]).

[9] For this way of dismissing but demonstrating knowledge, cf. Quintilian 3.6.28: *quae ne praeterisse viderer, satis habui attingere.*

The Shield of Achilles, discussed at chapters 43–51, is very special. Here there is a long tradition of cosmogonical explanation to follow (see Hardie 1985; 1986: 340 ff.). Hephaestus is now a demiurgic fire (it does not matter that he was ordinary fire in chapters 26–7) and he works at night, because Night and Chaos are at the beginning of things, to fashion the four elements (gold is aether, silver air, bronze water, and tin earth) into his marvellous artefact. The shield is spherical (43.14 [66.1]), and so we have to show in a digression (*ἐν παρεκβάσει*) that Homer consistently holds the view that the universe is spherical. The evidence, etymological and grammatical, is given at length (chapters 44–48.1). The details of the shield then all fit in. Homer himself speaks of earth, sky, sea, and heavenly bodies as represented on it. The cities at peace and war represent Empedocles' Love and Strife. The five layers of the shield stand for the five zones of the Earth. This again is not an 'impious' passage: it does not need to be explained away in order to defend Homer against the main charge. Rather, it shows that he contains levels of wisdom for which one has to dig under the surface. The value of this argument for the defence is, again, that once we accept such things about the shield, we have a good excuse for seeking deeper meanings anywhere, including the places where we find the surface meaning offensive.

In the interpretations of the *Odyssey* also, ethical lessons predominate. Athena, advising Telemachus in Book 1, represents allegorically his growing realization that he should not acquiesce in the suitors' debauchery (61.1–2 [81.10–17]). Even more plainly, the person who provides Telemachus with a ship (*Odyssey* 2.386) is Noemon ('thoughtful'), son of Phronios (suggesting 'prudence'), whose name reveals an allegory (*ὁ τῆς ἀλληγορίας ἐπώνυμος*: 63.7 [84.8–11]). Athena plays the same role with Odysseus in the closing part of the poem (chapter 75). The wandering (chapter 70) and Circe's temptation (chapter 72) are also interpreted in an ethical sense. There are, however, scientific allegories too, sometimes in innocuous places—Aeolus' twelve children are the months, and he is the year (chapter 71)—but especially when defence is needed. The outstanding problem is of course the story of Ares and Aphrodite (69.1–4 [89.9–90.2]):

Let us pass over all the rest, and turn to the continual angry accusations noisily repeated by the false accusers. They are forever declaiming against what they call the impious fiction of the tale of Ares and Aphrodite. 'He has given citizen rights in heaven to Immorality, and has felt no embarrassment about attributing to the gods behaviour which is punished by death when it occurs among humans: adultery.

> The love of Ares and fair-garlanded Aphrodite,
> How first they came together in Hephaestus' house
> [*Odyssey* 8.267–8]

—and then the chains and the gods' laughter, and Poseidon's plea to Hephaestus.'

Despite the fact that the story is told to the pleasure-loving Phaeacians, Heraclitus maintains that it is not just fun, but conceals a philosophical lesson, more precisely the Empedoclean theory of Strife and Love, represented by Ares and Aphrodite, now brought together in harmony. No wonder the gods laugh—they are not laughing *at* the pair, but taking pleasure at seeing them no longer in conflict, but in peace and concord together (69.11 [90.13]: ὁμονοοῦσαν εἰρήνην ἀγόντων). There is another possibility too: it may all be an allegory of the smith's craft, Ares being the iron which Hephaestus softens 'by fire, with loving art' (69.15 [90.20–1]: διὰ πυρὸς μαλάξας τὸν σίδηρον ἐπαφροδίτῳ τινὶ τέχνῃ), and Poseidon, who asks Hephaestus to release his prisoner, nothing other than the water in which the hot iron is dipped.

The central part of the treatise ends (75.12 [100.5]) with the words: 'Having thus assembled all these things together, we find the whole poem (ποίησις) full of allegory.' This is a point to be stressed. If allegory can be seen to be present everywhere, it can plausibly be adduced to defend objectionable passages; one is not seen to be giving them special arbitrary treatment.

II

Let us then take up the Prologue (chapters 1–5), in which the principles of the defence are established.

(1.1) Great and grievous is the case brought against Homer from heaven for his contempt of the divine

(the words μέγας ἀπ' οὐρανοῦ are echoed in the Epilogue (76.1

[100.8]), where Homer is 'the great hierophant of heaven and gods' (*ὁ μέγας οὐρανοῦ καὶ θεῶν ἱεροφάντης*)),

for he was impious in all things, if he meant nothing allegorically.

So, if we take this strictly, it is necessary only to prove that there is some allegory, and if we cannot do this, Homer is impious through and through. In fact, as we have seen, the defence will go further than this, and prove pervasive allegory in the poems—though not, of course, structural allegory, for Heraclitus makes no attempt to interpret the whole plot of either epic as an allegory. There is a likeness here to the passage of ps.-Longinus (*On the Sublime* 9.7) where the Theomachy is said to be 'terrifying, but altogether impious and improper unless taken allegorically'. This is, we shall see, not the only parallel between the two commentators.

(1.2) Sacrilegious fables, full of blasphemous folly, rage madly (*μεμήνασιν*) through both poems (*σωμάτια*).

The word *σωμάτιον*, to mean one of the epics, is found in ps.-Longinus (of the *Iliad* at *On the Sublime* 9.13), and *μαίνομαι* is the verb in a Homeric line which ps.-Longinus applies to Homer himself (9.11).

(1.3) And consequently, if one were to believe that it was all said simply as a piece of poetical tradition without any philosophical theory and with no underlying allegorical trope, Homer would be a sort of Salmoneus or Tantalus, with 'tongue uncontrolled, most shameful sickness' [Euripides, *Orestes* 10].

Salmoneus despised the gods, Tantalus betrayed them. If Homer cannot be acquitted, he deserves punishment. This too is taken up in the Epilogue (78 [104.2 ff.]), where it is Homer's chief prosecutor who deserves the fate of 'Tantalus and Capaneus', and has the same passage of Euripides applied to him.

(1.4) And so I have come to be very surprised that the religious (*δεισιδαίμων*) life, devoted to[10] temples and precincts and the annual festivals of the gods, has embraced Homer's impiety so affectionately, chanting his foul tales from memory.

[10] Reading *προστρεπόμενος* (Schow), comparing Plutarch, *Against Colotes* 1117A: *ἐπιθειάσεις αἷς προστρέπεσθε*, and deleting *ἐν ταῖς* (O^2); but the text remains unsure.

The word δεισιδαίμων in a favourable sense is a classical usage (cf. Xenophon, *Agesilaus* 11.8; *Cyropaedia* 3.3.58), but uncommon later, though there are instances in Diodorus and Josephus. It is perhaps another sign that Heraclitus is not in any Atticist fashion. His pretence of being 'surprised' is a figure; from his opponent's point of view it is of course paradoxical that the pious should 'embrace' Homer.

(1.5) From the very first age of life, the infancy of children just starting to learn is nurtured on teaching in his school. We are in effect swaddled in his poetry and nourish our minds with it as though it were milk to drink. (1.6) And then, as each child grows,[11] Homer stands at his side; as he gradually grows to manhood, he shares his youth,[12] and then his adult life; even in old age, we have not had too much of him; when we stop, our thirst begins again; (1.7) the only end of Homer for a human being is the end of life.

Here again the points are taken up in the Epilogue (76.3 [100.14–19]). The theme is a familiar one, well expressed in Dio Chrysostom's—untypical and conceivably inauthentic—*Oration* 18, which gives advice to an ambitious man on what to read to improve his oratory and public image: 'Homer is first, middle, and last, for every child and man and elder; he gives each of us as much as we can take' (18.8). And again there is a ps.-Longinus parallel: 'virtually swaddled' (μόνον οὐκ ἐνεσπαργανωμένοι) from childhood onward, in a sort of slavery (*On the Sublime* 44.3).

(2.1) For these reasons, it is, I think, plain and obvious to all that no stain of polluted myth is sprinkled[13] over his poem. Pure and innocent of all foulness are, first, the *Iliad*, and next the *Odyssey*, each of which raises its voice in unison to proclaim its own piety.

Two examples follow from the *Iliad*—6.129, and 15.104 (not quite exact)—so an *Odyssey* line, or two, must be missing: one might guess that it was 4.78, 'No mortal man would contend against Zeus.'

The next section (2.2–5) demonstrates Homer's piety in two ways: first, by his descriptions of individual gods—Zeus, shaking the world by an imperceptible nod, Poseidon making mountains and forests tremble, Hera causing Olympus to quake

11 αὐξομένῳ (Wyttenbach).

12 συνηβᾷ (O²), a necessary conjecture.

13 ἐνέσπαρται Mehler.

as she moves on her throne, Athena's grim eyes, Artemis as she appears hunting on Taygetus and Erymanthus; and secondly, by the epithets he applies to the gods as a whole: 'blessed', 'with undying thought', 'givers of good things', 'living in ease'. The second point is almost identical with ps.-Plutarch, *Life and Poetry of Homer* 2.112 (55 Kindstrand); the references in the first part are all obvious and traditional.[14] Heraclitus' trick is to put them together to lead us up to his conclusion:

(3.1) In the face of this, who dares call Homer impious?

> Zeus, greatest, most glorious, in dark cloud dwelling in *aether*,
> Sun, who seest all things and hearest all things,
> rivers and earth, and you who punish the dead below,
> whoever swears a fake oath:
> be witnesses

to Homer's pious intention, that he honours (νεωκορεῖ) the divine with extraordinary expressions of emotion (πάθεσιν ἐξαιρέτοις) because he is divine himself.

This climax of the argument, in which the Homeric passage is woven into the author's own thought—compare ps.-Longinus, *On the Sublime* 9.8—raises some problems. The quotation is a conflation of *Iliad* 2.412 and 3.277–80; it is repeated in 23.4 [35.5–10], where 'dwelling in *aether*' of *Iliad* 2.412 is actually used to make the point required. So it is not an accidental memory slip, but a conflation with some history behind it. The word νεωκορεῖ is to be noted: it means 'worships', 'serves the temple'. In Cornutus, Hestia 'is served' (νεωκορεῖται) by virgins because she is a virgin herself (*Introduction to Greek Theology* 28, 52.16–17 Lang). The point here is similar: Homer 'serves' all divine powers because he is divine (θεῖος) himself—as of course conventionally he is.[15] The word πάθεσιν seems to mean 'emotional passages' (as at ps.-Longinus, *On the Sublime* 9.13); the vague ἐξαιρέτοις, 'extraordinary', 'exceptional', is a favourite of Heraclitus (he has it, or the adverb, nine times).

The work continues as follows:

(3.2) If some ignorant persons fail to recognize Homeric allegory, and have not descended into the recesses of his wisdom, if their judgement of the truth is made hastily without being put to the test, and they snatch

[14] *Iliad* 1.528, 13.18, 8.199, 1.199–200, 6.102–4.

[15] e.g. Aristophanes, *Frogs* 1034; Plato, *Phaedo* 95a.

quickly[16] at what he seems to have intended as a fact because they do not know what has been said in a philosophical sense—away with them! (3.3) Let us who have been hallowed within the sacred enclosure track down the noble truth of the poems by due procedures![17] (4.1) Away too with Plato, the flatterer and slanderer of Homer, who dispatches him out of his Republic, an honoured exile, garlanded with white wool, and with his head drenched with costly perfume!

This is the first mention of Plato, though the attack on him is to be intensified later. The reference is to *Republic* 3, 398a. He is a 'flatterer' (κόλαξ) because he seems to honour Homer even in sending him away, but there may also be an allusion to his relationship with Dionysius, which is certainly in mind at 78.6 [104.6], where Plato's haunting the doors of tyrants and also his being sold into slavery are used against him.

(4.2) Nor need we trouble about Epicurus, who cultivates his undignified pleasure in his own garden, and spurns all poetry as a lethal bait or fable. (4.3) Against these men, I may well sigh deeply and cry [*Odyssey* 1.32]:

Ah me, how mortals blame the gods!

(4.4) And the bitterest part of it is that both these philosophers found the basis of their doctrines in Homer, and are thus ungratefully impious towards the very person from whom they have gained most of their knowledge.

This looks forward both to the Epilogue, where Epicurus' hedonism is derived from Odysseus' words to the Phaeacians (79.2 [104.15]), and to the passage in 17 [26.5 ff.] where Plato's tripartite psychology is derived from Homer. Nothing original in all this: ps.-Plutarch, *Life and Poetry of Homer* 2.122, 128–9 (60 ff. Kindstrand) makes much the same points.

Let us summarize the argument so far:

1. Without allegory, Homer must be guilty of impiety.
2. But his popularity with religious people—and indeed with all ages of man—gives the lie to this.
3. In fact, both epics contain clear, truthful utterances about the gods, individually and collectively.
4. Therefore people who only look on the surface of the story

[16] προαρπάζουσιν Wyttenbach.

[17] Or 'under the guidance of the poems', taking ὑπὸ νόμῳ τῶν ποιημάτων together.

are 'ignorant', because their superficial interpretation would often be inconsistent with Homer's piety as 'proved' by (2) and (3).

5. And we need take no notice of Plato and Epicurus, both of whom are ungrateful pupils of Homer, who are very wrong to abuse him.

III

The second part of the Prologue (5 [5.11–8.20]) is described as a short 'technical' account—that is, a grammatical or rhetorical discussion of what 'allegory' (ἀλληγορία) is. It gives a standard definition, based on the literal meaning of the word: 'It is a trope which says one thing but signifies something other than what it says.' Something very like this, and the same Alcaeus example (fr. 326 Lobel–Page) is in Cocondrius (at iii. 324 Spengel); the same thing—*aliud verbis aliud sensu ostendi*—in Quintilian (8.6.44), with Horace, *Odes* 1.14 doing duty for Alcaeus.

The essential point for Heraclitus to show is that Homer *intended* his hearers to look for an underlying sense. Without this, the defence would not be possible. He does it indirectly, first, by showing that other writers clearly use allegory intentionally. His first example is Archilochus, who compares war to a storm at sea (fr. 105 West); his second, the compulsive allegorist Alcaeus, of whom he quotes two passages (the second is fr. 6 Lobel–Page), commenting that 'the islander spends all too much time at sea (κατακόρως θαλαττεύει) in his allegories' (5.9 [7.10]). His third example is Anacreon's portrayal of the girl as a 'Thracian colt' who needs breaking in (fr. 417 Page—known only from this passage). But of course these instances prove nothing about Homer's intentions. That can only be done by finding a certain example in the epics. So:

(5.13) Homer himself is sometimes found using allegories which are neither ambiguous nor still to be looked for; (5.14) he has taught us (παραδέδωκε) this type of expression very plainly in the passage where Odysseus, enumerating the evils of war and battle, says:

(5.15) Whereof the bronze spills most straw on the ground,
But the harvest is least, when Zeus inclines the scales.
[*Iliad* 19.222–3]

(5.16) What is spoken of (τὸ λεγόμενον) is farming, but what is thought of (τὸ νοούμενον) is battle. But he has also indicated the real meaning (τὸ δηλούμενον) by means of mutually contradictory things.

This raises considerable difficulties. I have translated Heyne's ἐπεῖπεν 'he has indicated'; the paradosis ἐπείπομεν can scarcely be right; but the solution has perhaps not been found. The scholia on the Homeric passage quoted here class it as a 'mixed' allegory, that is to say one in which both terms are named. 'When Zeus inclines the scales', they say, makes it clear that this is no ordinary harvest. In fact the antecedent of 'whereof' (ἧς), which is 'strife' (φυλόπιδος), has already left no doubt in the hearer's mind. Wrenched from its context, in the form Heraclitus gives it, the passage is just usable as proof that Homer wants to show us how allegory works; but, especially if you include the previous line, it does not prove that he can use it without giving a clear signal. Of course Heraclitus is in a dilemma here. He needs 'signalled' passages to show the possibility of allegory; but the mere fact that they are 'signalled' detracts from their value as evidence of 'unsignalled' allegories.

And just what does the last sentence mean? The first words (πλὴν ὅμως) are, to judge from other occurrences (e.g. 9.1 [14.16]; 60.2 [81.3]), not strongly adversative but more a formula of transition. *Τὸ δηλούμενον* is the thing really meant (as in 5.7 [7.3]: *Μύρσιλος γὰρ ὁ δηλούμενός ἐστι*) but is it the same as *τὸ νοούμενον*? Farming and fighting are very different, but are they truly 'contradictory' (ἐναντία)? As symbolizing peace and war, perhaps; but the only real antithesis in the passage is between 'most straw' (πλείστην καλάμην) and 'least harvest' (ἀμητὸς ὀλίγιστος): greatest waste for least return. If these are the 'opposites', the δηλούμενον is not 'battle' but the wastefulness of war—which is the whole point of Odysseus' speech.

This concludes the Prologue. Taking it as established that all writers are familiar with allegory, and that Homer has shown he knows about it, Heraclitus now (at 6.1 [9.1–3]) sees no reason why we should not use the 'therapy' of this defence to meet any criticisms of what is thought to be wrong in Homer's attitude to the gods. And he embarks on his book-by-book survey—discussed in Section I above.

IV

And so to the Epilogue (chapters 76–9 [100–6]).

(76.1) After all this, does Homer, the great hierophant of heaven and the gods, who opened up for human souls the untrodden and closed paths to heaven, deserve to be condemned as impious? (76.2) Were this vile and unholy verdict to be given and his poems destroyed, dumb ignorance would spread across the world; (76.3) no help would come to the band of little children who drink in wisdom first from Homer as they do milk from their nurses; (76.4) nor would adolescents, or young men, or old age that has passed its prime any longer derive pleasure. (76.5) Life's tongue would be ripped out, and it would all go on in dumb silence. (76.6) So let Plato banish Homer from his Republic as he banished himself from Athens to Sicily. (76.7) It is Critias who ought to have been driven from that Republic, for he was a tyrant, or Alcibiades, who was disgustingly effeminate as a boy, and a precocious adult as a lad, the mocker of Eleusis at dinner, the loser of Sicily, the founder of Decelea.

The rhetor surely shows through here. Plato's visits to Sicily are represented as a voluntary exile. Anti-Platonic tradition represented them generally as motivated by flattery or the desire for a luxurious life (cf. Riginos 1976, chapter 7), and this is the charge answered in the *Seventh Letter*. Alcibiades is a favourite with the declaimer, and this mannered summary of his career makes all the points with exemplary sharpness. It is not easy, however, to see how it advances the case. We shall see (79.1 [104.15]) that Socrates is a good thing; perhaps therefore there is some point in suggesting that Plato ought to have turned against the two alleged disciples whose villainy was used as a handle to attack their master.

(76.8) Yet while Plato banished Homer from his private city, the whole world claims to be Homer's sole country:

> (76.9) Of what land shall we enrol Homer as citizen—
> Homer, to whom all cities extend their hand? [18]

(76.10) And above all Athens, which denied Socrates as a citizen to the point of giving him the poison, yet prays only to be thought

[18] *Greek Anthology* 16.294, one of a large group (16.292–304) of epigrams on these themes.

Homer's native land! (76.11) But how could Homer himself have tolerated living under Plato's laws, when the two of them are divided by such contrary and conflicting positions? (76.12) Plato recommends common marriages and children, while both Homer's poems are sanctified by chaste marriages; (76.13) the Greeks have gone to war for Helen, Odysseus goes on his wanderings for Penelope. (76.14) Again, the most righteous principles of all human life are the basis of society in both Homer's poems; (76.15) Plato's dialogues, on the other hand, are disgraced throughout by pederasty; there is not a passage in which he is not bursting with desire for a male partner.

(76.16) Homer invokes the Muses, virgin goddesses, for the most brilliant of his heroes' achievements when there is a really noble command to give them, worthy of Homer's divine nature, (76.17) no less when men are marshalled by cities than in the individual exploits of the great heroes.[19]

(77.1) Thus he often, as it were, stops on his home ground of Helicon and says:

> (77.2) Tell me now, you Muses whose home is on Olympus,
> Who were the leaders and princes of the Danai?
> [*Iliad* 2.484–5]

(77.3) Or again, when he begins the heroic deed of Agamemnon, by praising the hero who has a likeness to three gods:[20]

> (77.4) Tell me now, you Muses whose house is on Olympus,
> Who was it who first came face to face with Agamemnon?
> [*Iliad* 11.218–19]

(77.5) On the other hand, our wonderful Plato, in his beautiful *Phaedrus*, at the start of that very moral distinction of the kinds of love, had the hardihood, just like Ajax in the maiden-chamber of the most holy goddess, to pour a libation of filth over the Muses and summon those chaste goddesses to aid his wicked works, saying: (77.6) 'Come ye Muses, whether it is for the nature of your song that you were called clear-voiced, or because of some musical nation,[21] help me in this tale that I have to tell' [*Phaedrus* 237a]. (77.7) What tale, I would ask, O most wonderful Plato? A tale of heaven and the universe, or of earth and

[19] I punctuate after *ἄξιον* (102.4 SPB) and read *διαταττομένων ἤ* (Polak). The meaning anyway is clear: invocations (which are imperatives directed to the Muses) are used for whole armies (as in *Iliad* 2.484) and for individual actions (as in 11.218).

[20] i.e. to Zeus, Ares, and Poseidon: *Iliad* 2.478. In combination with 11.218, Heraclitus emphasizes the grandeur of the occasions for which Homer reserves these invocations.

[21] 'Clear-voiced' = *λίγειαι*; the 'musical nation' refers to the Ligurians (*Λίγυες*).

sea? (77.8) No; nor one of sun and moon and the motions of fixed stars and planets. (77.9) What the goal of his prayer is I am ashamed even to report: (77.10) 'Once upon a time there was a beautiful boy, or rather young lad, who had many lovers, and one persuasive one who had convinced him that he did not love him, though in fact he did, and said, one day, when asking for his favours . . .' [*Phaedrus* 237b]. (77.11) In such naked language[22] did he reveal his wickedness on the rooftop, as it were,[23] not so much trying to conceal the disgrace of the thing by a decent pretence.

(78.1) So it is only natural that Homer's discourse should be the life of heroes, and Plato's dialogues the love of young men. (78.2) In Homer, everything is full of noble virtue: (78.3) Odysseus is wise, Ajax brave, Penelope chaste, Nestor invariably just, Telemachus dutiful to his father, Achilles totally loyal in his friendships. (78.4) And what is there of this in philosopher Plato? Unless indeed we are to say that there is practical use[24] in the solemn twitterings (*τερετίσματα*) of the Ideas, which his pupil Aristotle laughs at.[25]

(78.5) He was rightly punished, I am sure, for his words against Homer; it is he who has 'tongue uncontrolled, most shameful sickness' [Euripides, *Orestes* 10], like Tantalus, like Capaneus, like all who have suffered innumerable disasters because of their looseness of tongue. (78.6) Often did he journey wearily to tyrants' doors; born free, he endured the chains of slavery, even to the point of being sold. (78.7) Everyone has heard of Pollis the Spartan to whom ⟨he was surrendered⟩, and how he was saved by the mercy of a Libyan and valued, as a poor quality slave, at 20 minae.[26] (78.8) And this was the due reward ⟨he received⟩ for the impieties against Homer of his unbridled and unfenced tongue.[27]

(79.1) There is more that I could say against Plato, but I let it pass, out of respect for the reputation of Socratic wisdom. (79.2) But the Phaeacian philosopher Epicurus, the horticulturalist who grew

[22] *ὀνόμασι* Muenzel, for *ὄμμασι*: 'eyes'.

[23] i.e. as in a brothel: see Gow and Page (1965), 2.267 on Dioscorides 37.4 = *Greek Anthology* 11.363.4.

[24] *βιωφελῆ φήσομεν* Oelmann.

[25] See *Posterior Analytics* 83^{a}32–4: *τὰ γὰρ εἴδη χαιρέτω· τερετίσματά τε γάρ ἐστι, καὶ εἰ ἔστιν, οὐδὲν πρὸς τὸν λόγον ἐστίν*. Not that Heraclitus knew Aristotle's logical works; the colourful phrase will have come down in common tradition.

[26] The Libyan is Anniceris. For these stories, see Riginos (1976), ch. 8.

[27] I assume ⟨*παρεδόθη*⟩ at 104.9 SPB (hiatus permissible at colon-end), and *τιμωρίαν* ⟨*ὑπέσχε*⟩ at 104.12 SPB. The closing words are an unadvertised reminiscence of Aristophanes, *Frogs* 838 (*ἀχάλινον ἀκρατὲς ἀθύρωτον στόμα*) with the variant *ἀπύλωτον* favoured by most of the secondary tradition (see Dover 1997 ad loc.).

pleasure in his private Garden, who took a bearing on all poetry, not only Homer, by looking at the stars[28]—did he not steal ignorantly and shamefully from Homer the only doctrine which he passed on to mankind? (79.3) What Odysseus said falsely, unwisely, and hypocritically at the court of Alcinous, Epicurus proclaims as the goal of life, and claims to be speaking the truth:

(79.4) When joy possesses the whole people,
and the feasters in the house are listening to the singer,
that seems to me in my heart to be the best thing of all.
[*Odyssey* 9.6–7, 11].

For the use of this latter passage of the *Odyssey*, see also ps.-Plutarch, *Life and Poetry of Homer* 2.150, where it is also said that Odysseus said these things to please his pleasure-loving audience, and Epicurus was deceived by them—just as Odysseus' varied life of hardship (the beggar's rags and wallet) and luxury (to bed with Calypso) led Aristippus both to embrace poverty and to indulge himself. Whether Epicurus actually quoted these lines (as Asmis 1991; Obbink 1995*b*: 208) seems to me not quite certain. It may indeed be argued that Heraclitus could not honestly have made the point that Epicurus disregarded the circumstances of Odysseus' speech unless he had actually quoted it. But Heraclitus is not all that honest; it remains possible that he (or some predecessor) took these lines as a convenient summary of Epicurus' hedonism which could be neatly used against him. It is worth observing that Heraclitus happily uses the contextual argument here, and totally neglects it when he needs a passage for his own purposes. At 69.7, for example, he takes the tale of Ares and Aphrodite as deserving allegorical defence; yet it too was told to the Phaeacians: he admits as much, but only to dismiss the point (90.2 SPB).

(79.5) Odysseus says this—not the Odysseus who fought heroically at Troy, not the Odysseus who destroyed cities in Thrace, not the Odysseus who sailed past lotus-eating pleasure, not the Odysseus who was greater than mighty Cyclops, (79.6) who travelled the whole earth

[28] *ἄστροις σημήνασθαι* (104.17 SPB) is proverbial for 'making a guess from a distance' (Diogenianus 2.66), or making a long journey without landmarks. Epicurus has 'put to sea' and is out of sight of poetry. There is perhaps an allusion to his advice to 'take your boat out and get away from all education': *παιδείαν δὲ πᾶσαν, μακάριε, φεῦγε τἀκάτιον ἀράμενος* (fr. 163 Usener = Diogenes Laertius 10.6).

on foot and sailed the Ocean sea, who as a living man beheld Hades— (79.7) that is not the Odysseus who said these things, but the poor relic of Poseidon's anger, the man whom the dreadful storm washed up to be pitied by the Phaeacians. (79.8) He feels compelled accordingly to approve what was thought honourable by his hosts, (79.9) for he had only one prayer which he prays in his misery:

> Grant me to come to the Phaeacians as a friend to be pitied.
> [*Odyssey* 6.327]

So he was forced by necessity to speak well of bad practices which he could not mend by teaching. (79.10) But Epicurus, in his ignorance, made Odysseus' temporary necessity the basis of his own doctrine of life, planting in his famous Garden the things that Odysseus had declared most beautiful in Phaeacia. (79.11) But let us let Epicurus go his way. He had even more ills of soul than of body. (79.12) Homer's wisdom, on the other hand, all eternity (*αἰών*) has made divine,[29] and, as time goes on, so his charms grow young, and there is no one who has not opened his mouth in praise of him. (79.13) We are all alike priests and attendants on his divine poetry:

> Let them go to their ruin, the one or two who take counsel
> apart from the Achaeans; no success shall be theirs.
> [*Iliad* 2.346–7]

This eloquent conclusion, with the final development on the theme of Homer 'the divine' displays the rhetor in Heraclitus at his best. The final artificiality is to end with a quotation. This is not common: Plutarch, *On Monarchy* 827 C may be a parallel, but is probably a fragment. Certain examples are Aristides, *Oration* 33 ('On those who criticize him for not declaiming') and two speeches of Dio Chrysostom: 52, *On Aeschylus, Sophocles, and Euripides*, and, most notably, 12, the great *Olympicus*.

[29] We may again compare ps.-Longinus, *On the Sublime* 35.2 for 'all eternity' (*ὁ πᾶς αἰών*) giving the prize of victory to great writers.

12

Origen on Christ, Tropology, and Exegesis

MARK EDWARDS

Origen (AD 185–254) is generally regarded as the founder of philosophical theology and also of the mystical tradition in Christianity.[1] Only his name, not his influence, was effaced by his condemnation at the Second Council of Constantinople in 553. Today it is not the critics but the eulogists of Origen who multiply his heresies and exaggerate his dealings with philosophy.[2] Freedom of speculation, within the bounds prescribed by sacred writings, is the hallmark of theology in our era, so that equal admiration is accorded to Origen's (qualified) indifference to tradition and his (absolute) fidelity to the text. At one point, however, praise stops short: hardly any scholar or theologian finds it possible to approve of his characteristic method of scriptural exegesis. Then, as now, that method was described as allegorical by his detractors; sometimes then, and often now, the prohibited way of allegory is contrasted with the true way of typology, the first being represented as pagan, the second as a monopoly of the Church. Even the apologists for Origen have argued that he combined the old pagan with the new Christian principle, and by this they imply of course that a valid contrast can be drawn, and that typology is the better of the two.

Definitions of allegory are always hard to come by. For Marius

I am grateful to the British Academy for a post-doctoral fellowship which enabled me to undertake preliminary research for this and other studies on ancient hermeneutics.

[1] The tradition of treating Origen as a philosopher begins (for English readers) with Bigg (1913); on Origen and mysticism see Louth (1981), 52–74.

[2] Though an exception must be made for the greatest modern authority, Henri Crouzel, who presents an orthodox hero in his *Origen* (1989).

Victorinus it is present whenever 'one thing is said, and another is intended' (*Commentary on Galatians* 4.24, 54 Locher), which hardly serves to distinguish it from irony or some instances of lying. For C. H. Dodd, an incomparable exponent of typology in the New Testament (e.g. Dodd 1952), allegory is merely the *ignis fatuus* of the Catholic tradition, and therefore casts no spell upon the natural and unprejudiced perceptions of a twentieth-century British Nonconformist (Dodd 1938). Hostility to allegory has been reinforced by the classical description of it as an extended metaphor; for metaphor, though it may be the stuff of poetry, is conventionally regarded by theologians as a dangerous imperfection in human speech. The dogmatician hesitates to admit that his terms are metaphors; the liberal writes as though the class of metaphors were a shocking discovery of the modern era;[3] both, if they are obliged to use one, urge that it is not a simple metaphor, but a symbol, an analogy, or a myth.

But allegory has now revived in the estimation of literary theorists, who never shared the theologian's fear of metaphor. So pervasive indeed is the latter for the followers of Roman Jakobson that metaphor and metonymy divide the whole of literature between them (Jakobson 1956; cf. Silk in this volume). While Jakobson's doctrines rarely find their way into theological discussion, they have helped to confirm the prejudice that allegory is the left hand of discourse, as antithetical to typology as error to truth or poetry to prose. In Section I of this chapter, I shall argue that ancient allegory, embracing as it did the three great tropes of rhetorical theory, had no dominant affinity with metaphor. In the rest, I shall maintain that the application of these tropes to Origen's exegetic theory will reveal that his three levels of understanding are all equally typological,[4] in that the first is related metaphorically, the second metonymically, and the highest synecdochically to the threefold being of Christ.

[3] Cf. e.g. most contributors to Hick (1977).

[4] An association of typology with metonymy is proposed by Frye (1982), where it is said that theology 'carries the typology of the Bible on in history and adapts it to what we have called second-phase or metonymic language'. The first, or metaphorical, phase, is represented in myths which are interpreted by reference to a lost past rather than a hidden future.

I

The distinction between typology and allegory has its origins in the fourth century, when Christians of the Antiochene school conceived a distaste for allegory, and therefore needed another term for the mode of reading scripture that was endorsed by Paul in his letter to the Galatians.[5] The interpretation of passages from the Old Testament as prefigurements of Christ, his Church, and his Kingdom was henceforth to be called typology; unlike its older sibling, this did not reduce historical to generic propositions, but revealed the continuity between the mysterious providence of God in former ages and his manifest operation in the present. Typology and literal exegesis shared the premiss that both Testaments made up a linear narrative, from creation to the founding of the Church; allegory, by contrast, took whatever came to hand from the pagan sciences to disrobe both texts and authors of the accidents entailed by flesh, locality, and time.

We might say that the difference between typology and allegory is that one sees truth fulfilled in time and the other seeks truth outside it, treating time, in Plato's words, as the 'moving image of eternity'. Following Jakobson, we might have said that the former works by contiguity, the latter by substitution; and this would be a fair judgement on the notorious occasions when the allegorist discards the literal meaning of his text. If we were to persist with Jakobson's terms, we should conclude that allegory is metaphorical and typology metonymic; this consequence, however, would be as false to ancient practice as it is trite to modern ears. As Aristotle and Paul Ricoeur (1978: 173–215) admonish us, the substitution of terms creates a metaphor only where there is resemblance, or at least analogy. Yet figures of similitude in literature were not called allegories, then or now, in the majority of instances, but only when they possessed the length, the detail, and the obliquity of reference that characterizes myth.

Thus myth, though not the only, was by far the most frequent matter of allegorical exegesis. The relation between the myth

[5] Chrysostom states that the term ἀλληγορούμενα ('allegories') at Gal. 4: 24 is used 'catachrestically' for typology: *Homilies on Galatians* 73 Field.

and what it signified was comparable to that which held in the world between the composite particular and the abstraction that philosophers called its quiddity,[6] substance, form, idea, or *logos*. The plurality of terms is unavoidable, for the nature of this relation was a subject of dispute not only between but within the philosophical schools of late antiquity. Plato himself perceived that the particular could not be a simple copy of its idea;[7] but if we say instead that it 'participates' by *methexis*, we have to employ that term in a unique sense which is almost incommensurable with its meaning in the physical domain.[8] In rhetorical parlance, the mimetic principle corresponds to metaphor, the methectic to synecdoche—a helpful term, ignored by modern criticism, which designates the use of part for whole. The metonymic relation holds in Platonism, not between the particular and the ideal, but between the material body and the ambivalent, not quite corporeal entity which is called its soul and is often said to be one's proper self (see especially Gerson 1994: 104–5).

The occidental mind has thought in threes since the time of Plato, except in the middle of the twentieth century, when Cartesian France began to cast her spell on other nations. For many critics metaphor and metonymy have become an exhaustive dyad, except where metaphor swallows up metonymy as well; but if we wish to follow the growth of allegory as a hermeneutic procedure, we cannot work with any scheme that is less discriminating than the classical tropology of metaphor, metonymy, and synecdoche. These, according to Pierre Fontanier,[9] are the literary counterparts of resemblance, correspondence, and connection, the three relations holding universally between objects in the world. If philosophy aims to be comprehensive in its description of reality, we can only expect that philosophical allegory will be equally ambitious in its combination of literary tools.

[6] Translating here the Aristotelian term τὸ τί ἦν εἶναι.

[7] See esp. *Parmenides* 132a1–133a3 for the 'Third Man' argument, unceasingly deployed against Plato from Aristotle to the present day. See Meinwold (1992).

[8] See esp. *Parmenides* 130e5–131e7. Fine (1986) makes a good case for the presence of the idea in the particular.

[9] Fontanier (1977). But I rely here on Ricoeur (1978), 48–65, esp. 56.

In the interpretation of myth the principle equivalent to metaphor is analogy: thus one says that, as the day contains twelve hours or the year twelve months, so the twelve labours of Hercules are analogous to the progress of the sun. The correlative to metonymy is personification: when we represent our traits and passions as living characters, we invert the rule whereby we speak of the government as Westminster or the monarch as the Crown. The converse of synecdoche, etymology, was thought to have been commended in the *Cratylus*,[10] and therefore may be regarded as the root of all Platonic allegorizing. It is the converse because the etymologist reads not part for whole, but whole for part; that is to say, the meaning of a name was to be ascertained by resolving it into its elemental characters and sounds. The dominance of one mode or another was determined by the tenor of exegesis. The so-called 'physiologists' made use of analogy and etymology to turn the gods into natural phenomena; heroes lent themselves to moralistic allegorizing, with a metonymic translation of the interest from the person to his virtues, or from the body to the soul. Platonists, for whom actions in the body were a prelude to deliverance from it, learnt to construe the myths of Plato literally and those of the ancient poets metonymically: Odysseus, for Numenius and Porphyry, was no longer a storm-tossed mariner, but the soul of the philosopher laboriously ascending to the intellectual sphere.[11] To explain why the text had a literal meaning different from its true one—which is seldom the case with metaphor—one argued that the text had one significance for insiders and another for outsiders. More concisely, one spoke of it as possessing a soul and body of its own (Porphyry, fr. 416F Smith):

> If discourse be supposed to have a soul and body, the invention of thoughts could justly be called its soul, and the exposition its body.

The body in Plato's dialogues is described as the vehicle (e.g. *Phaedrus* 246a3–b4), instrument (*Alcibiades I* 129e3–130a2), or garment (*Phaedo* 87b2–e7) of the soul; thus it is dispensable to its owner, and so is the surface meaning of the text to enlightened readers. This is again not true of a poet's metaphors, in which the

[10] See Plato, *Cratylus* 396d4–397a1 on Euthyphro, with Hirschle (1979).

[11] See Porphyry, *The Cave of the Nymphs*; Numenius, frr. 30–5 des Places; Lamberton (1986), esp. 318–24 on Numenius; Edwards (1988).

vehicle rather than the tenor is the acknowledged sign of mastery;[12] metonymy and synecdoche, on the other hand, owe their meaning to convention, not the author, and the 'literal' sense is entirely evacuated by the trope. We rightly form no image of the Bench when we are aware that the noun is being used only to indicate the Judge.

To say then that typology is a species of metonymy is not enough to set it apart from pagan, let alone from Christian allegory. In this, as in every other sphere of Christian thought, the difference lies in the content, not the method. Whereas ethics, physics, and theology were all legitimate destinations of allegory, typology pointed nowhere but to Christ. In the case of Origen, however, I shall argue that even this distinction fails, because his threefold exegesis is based on a threefold anthropology peculiar to the Church. Physics, ethics, and the higher mysteries correspond in his theology to the body, soul, and spirit of the human person, all of which were assumed in the incarnation of Christ, the Word of God, who is present to us in every word of scripture. Christianity knows of no salvation without the union of body, soul, and spirit; Origen believed that no theology is complete unless it incorporates the body, soul, and spirit of the text. The three levels of inspiration, like the three parts of the person, are related metonymically to each other, but in different ways to Christ, in whom the Spirit, nature, and humanity are at one.

II

The question of Origen's debt to the philosophers is too often addressed without reference to his own statement of the difference between his doctrines and his methods. The infallible scripture, consisting of both Testaments, was for him the only source of Christian knowledge, and only the elucidation of this, not the creation of new theories, could be furthered by an appeal to pagan wisdom. In his letter to Gregory Thaumaturgus (*Philokalia* 13), he likens the tools of pagan hermeneutics to the treasures of the Egyptians, which, according to a notorious passage in the Book of Exodus, were stolen by the Israelites on

[12] Borrowing the terms (though not the whole theory) of Richards (1936), 96.

the eve of their return from servitude to the promised land. This ingenious application of a dangerous text is an instance of his capacity to make the Bible serve as its own interpreter. In the words of his Jewish teacher, the Bible is a great mansion full of sealed rooms with a key by every door; but since this is often the key to another door, we must have gathered all the keys before we can take complete possession of the house.

Origen steers a middle course between the Platonic method, which sets out to make the text conform to reason, and the fideism of simple-minded Christians—Pauline Christians, as they thought themselves—who held that reason also must give way before the Word. Origen thinks it possible for reason to discover inconsistencies, immoralities, and absurdities on the surface of the canon; and for these he propounds a homoeopathic remedy, applied not so much by the exegete to scripture as by scripture to itself. That is to say, we resolve the difficult passages by looking for the recurrence of the same images elsewhere, in a context that clearly indicates how they ought to be construed (see *Philokalia* 2.3, 72 Robinson). The reflexive Word is the analogue of Christ, the Redeemed Redeemer or self-physicking physician—though 'analogy' would be too weak a term for Origen, who finds in Christ not merely the inspiration, but the unity of the meaning and the substance of the text.

If there is one Christ, the sole Creator, sole redeemer, and sole exemplar of humanity, why is there such diversity among Christians? Some errors, like those of Gnosticizing heretics, were consequences of straying from the canon,[13] but sometimes the concentration of the mind on the flesh of Jesus causes believers to forget that he and the saints belong eternally to a world that we cannot see. His flesh was not, as the Gnostic taught, phantasmal, for had he not lived there would have been no gospel, and had he not died we should still be under the tyranny of Satan.[14] Nevertheless the flesh is not the whole of Christ but a veil through which we must pass to apprehend not only his nature but the fullness of our own (*Against Celsus* 4.15 etc.).

[13] See *Commentary on John* 13.17, i. 264 Brooke, on Heracleon's use of the Preaching of Peter.

[14] Origen appears to be the originator of the theory that Christ's blood was a ransom to the devil: *Commentary on Romans* 2.13.

The human person, according to Paul and Origen,[15] is a triple bond of body, soul, and spirit. No Christian could deny the superiority of spirit, any more than he could deny the resurrection of the body. Origen held both tenets, though even in antiquity he was thought to have predicted the survival of the incorporeal nature without the body. His true position seems to have been that when the present body suffers death its form (εἶδος) is translated to the soul, and that the soul, when purged of its blemishes, assumes the condition of spirit.[16] That neither soul nor body is lost is clear from his recurrent use of the Pauline phrase 'one spirit with the Lord' (1 Corinthians 6: 17), which connotes for him, not a state of disembodiment, but that of Christ himself in his incarnation (*Against Celsus* 2.9). The spiritual body, of which he speaks in his work *Against Celsus* (5.18–23), is not a notional body, but one transparent to the desires of spirit. In this he is at one with Paul and also with Augustine (see *City of God* 22.5 ff.)—except that the latter contemplates a moral revolution unassisted by any physical refinement of the flesh.

Origen held that, after its separation from the corruptible flesh, the soul of the saint will rise, with its tenuous vehicle, through the air and then through all the planetary spheres, the increments in its knowledge keeping pace with the sanctification of the will. When it attains the perfect state, 'to which nothing can be added', it will be a pure spirit in the presence of God (see *First Principles* 3.6.3 and 9 with Edwards 1995). This progress through the three aspects of humanity has already been accomplished in the sublunar realm by Jesus Christ, who through his life, his death, and his resurrection has made it possible for others. As an incarnate man, he was perceived by all, though truly known to few; in the interval between death and resurrection he appeared as a soul to other souls in Hades; restored to his disciples on the third day, he retained a palpable yet elusive body which was visible to the outward eyes of those who had been enlightened by the Spirit.[17] Matter is necessary to our identity in

[15] For Paul, see 1 Thess. 5: 23; for Origen, *First Principles* 4.2.4, *Dialogue with Heraclides*, *passim*; etc.

[16] Expounded by Methodius (*c*. AD 300) in Epiphanius, *Panarion* 64 (AD 376).

[17] For the soul in Hades (cf. 1 Pet. 3: 16), see *Dialogue with Heraclides* 7; for the spiritual body of the resurrection, see *Against Celsus* 2.62–5.

the everlasting kingdom (*First Principles* 1.6.4), but once the 'coat of skins' has been exchanged for a robe of glory, carnal senses see no more of this than of the spirit or the soul.

All this must be taken into account when we read the celebrated passage on the threefold sense of scripture (*On First Principles* 4.2.4):

> In the Proverbs of Solomon we find the following precept with regard to the doctrines in the sacred writings: 'You must write them in a threefold manner in wisdom and knowledge, so that you may respond with words of truth to those who challenge you' [Proverbs 23: 20–1]. Therefore one must inscribe the doctrine of the sacred writings on his soul in a threefold way: that is, so that the simple may be edified, if I may so speak, by the body of the scriptures (for that is what we mean by the superficial interpretation), the one who has advanced a little further by what we might call its soul, and the one who is perfect by the spiritual law . . . For just as man is constituted by body, soul, and spirit, just so is the scripture that God has deigned to bestow for man's salvation.

Had Origen been a Platonist, the discernment of the soul and spirit in scripture would have entailed the dissolution of the superficial meaning. In Christian thought, however, the destiny of the body is not to perish, but to become the fit companion of the soul. This object is most likely to be fulfilled by the perusal of the written word, which functions for us as the body of the Logos. Yet as in the world, so in the word, the body can neither do good nor receive it without the presence of the Spirit. The letter alone, unpurged of outward blemishes, is apt to lead the carnal mind into heresy and sin. If we ask why the Spirit permits these blemishes—these 'stumbling-blocks' (σκάνδαλα) as Origen dares to style them—his answer is that they are there to exercise the intellect, as the troubles of the world are there to exercise our patience and free will. Just as we should not be aware of sin without the trials of our mundane existence, so we should not suspect a deeper mystery in the scriptures if we found its surface wholly free of stains. 'Mystery' is his own word,[18] and well chosen, for the Egyptian, Phrygian, and Eleusinian mysteries were notorious for their obscenities, which expositors defended on the grounds that the mind is more disposed to seek an arcane significance when perplexed by the incongruity of the sign.[19]

[18] Or rather that of Paul at 1 Cor. 10: 11: see *First Principles* 4.2.6.

[19] Iamblichus, *On the Mysteries* 1.11, 61 des Places; Julian, *Hymn* 6 [222cd].

At first sight, this analogy is no more than a well-worn metaphor from Plato. The latter retained the language of the mysteries, while dispensing with the priesthood, arguing that it is only the inward dialogue of reason that can purify the soul. Philosophy is comparable to the mysteries insofar as it is an esoteric discipline, superior insofar as it confers the immortality that is only anticipated in the ritual ablutions.[20] Origen is, even more than Plato, a theologian of the intellect, or rather of the *logos*. He repeatedly says that the inner man has spiritual senses (*First Principles* 1.1.9 etc.), which acquaint him with realities beyond common sight and hearing, and therefore cannot be satisfied by the bread and wine of the eucharist or by outward forms of prayer. Yet only once, in a homily on the enigmatic Song of Songs (at 1.7, 39.17 Baehrens), does he speak of an encounter with the Bridegroom which 'cannot be understood without experience'. Where mystic initiations had three stages—the *δρώμενον*, or 'performance', the *λεγόμενον*, or 'discourse', and the *ὁρώμενον*, or 'spectacle'[21]—he scarcely seems to know of any sacred Christian practice but the reading of the Word.

In this, as in much else, he is a disciple of the Fourth Gospel. Whereas the Book of Genesis has attributed creation to the Spirit, the Fourth Evangelist speaks of it as the sole work of the Logos (1: 1–3); whereas the patriarchs had met with angels, and from time to time with God himself, the Evangelist leaves the angels to themselves and baldly asseverates that 'no man has seen God at any time' (John 1: 18). There is no transfiguration, and the glory of the risen Christ remains invisible even to his followers; only in the future life, when we ourselves have undergone transformation, shall we 'see him as he is' (1 John 3: 3). While the time of vision (the *ὁρώμενον*) is not yet come, that of works, the *δρώμενον*, is past. No material sacrament is instituted, and when the Pharisees challenge Christ to accredit his claim by miracles, he answers that his own words are sufficient testimony.

The Naassene Gnostics of the 2nd cent. had already celebrated the divine virtues of formlessness (*ἀσκημοσύνη*), notwithstanding the Pauline usage of the term at Romans 1: 27: see Hippolytus, *Refutation* 5.7.23–9.

[20] On the purpose and influence of this transposition of terms, see Riedweg (1989).

[21] Peter Kingsley (1995: 230 n. 48) traces back to Empedocles the threefold sequence of *κάθαρσις*, *παράδοσις*, *ἐποπτεία*.

The true believer is not one who has seen or who has done, but one who is visited by 'the Word of God' (John 10: 35).

For all that, it is not without cause that 'mystery' is a term more often connected with the Fourth Gospel than with any other writing of the New Testament. After all, it records the saviour's miracles, and does so expressly to evoke belief. It says in the Prologue 'we have seen his glory' (1: 14b), and subsequently reveals that this is the glory of the Cross (12: 28–33). This last point is the essence of the gospel: it is not that deeds are illusory, but, unlike words, they cannot either interpret or authenticate themselves (cf. 10: 37–8). The written word is now our only evidence of past works or coming glory (20: 31), but even if these were present to us, we could not understand them without divine illumination (9: 39, 14: 26). Add to this that so much in the narrative is obscure, or superficially heretical or inconsistent with the other gospels,[22] and we see that it is itself a sort of mystery, whose exoteric features stand in need of elucidation. The difference is that, being a life of Jesus, the embodied Word, the medium which creates the scandal also affords the means for its relief.

Philo had led the way, to be followed by Clement of Alexandria, in applying the terminology of the mysteries to biblical revelation.[23] Origen is less prone to this, but he does adopt the mystagogic idiom of the Platonists to explain the presence in the Hebrew canon of three books ascribed to Solomon the Wise:[24]

Let us first attempt an investigation of the fact that the Church of God has accepted three volumes as writings of Solomon, with the book of Proverbs in the first place, the one called Ecclesiastes second, while the Song of Songs is assigned to the third. This is what occurs to me at present. There are three general disciplines whereby one arrives at the knowledge of things, which the Greeks call ethical, physical, and theoretical, whereas we can call them moral, natural, and speculative . . . Moral is the name given to the one through which an honest way of life is inculcated upon us, and practices which tend to virtue are

[22] On Origen's dealings with the temporal life of Christ, see Edwards (1998).

[23] David Dawson (1992: 83–126), shows that the Torah retains its primacy for Philo, as the New Testament does for Christians.

[24] *Commentary on the Song of Songs*, proem, 75.2–9, 17–23 Baehrens. Origen knew a Hebrew canon almost identical with the present one: Eusebius, *Ecclesiastical History* 6.25.

inaugurated. Natural is the name given to that by which the nature of every single thing is disclosed, so that nothing in life may be done against nature, but everything may be assigned to the uses that the Creator intended when he produced it. Speculative is the name given to that by which, having transcended things visible, we contemplate something of the divine and heavenly, beholding them with the mind alone because they surpass corporeal vision.

In some accounts of Origen, the last stage is described as the *enoptic* one.[25] But Origen does not use this word, any more than he pursues his own suggestion that there may be a fourth term, logic, to be added to his sequence. Greek knows only the cognate *epopteia*, which found its way into theories of the philosophic life, although the sequence ethics–physics–dialectic is better attested in the schools of the Hellenistic and Roman period (Hadot 1979). Origen, as the above quotation shows, did not regard *theoria* and logic as interchangeable categories, any more than his Alexandrian predecessor Clement, who detected a four-fold pattern in the composition of the Mosaic scriptures (*Stromateis* 1.28.176). Since logic is the science which delineates the parts and tropes of speech, and thereby guides interpretation, we might suppose that its representative book in Origen's scheme would be the so-called Wisdom of Solomon, to which he appeals in other works for canonical pronouncements on the nature of Christ the Word (*First Principles* 1.2 etc.). But the preface to the Song of Songs adheres to the Hebrew canon, dismissing apocryphal works with some asperity (88 Baehrens), and the stages of understanding are therefore limited to three.

Does this triad match the other pattern, which is based upon the trichotomy of body, soul, and spirit? It is clear enough that ethics makes demands upon the body, while enoptic is the climax of a spiritual reading; but can the soul of scripture be equated with the comprehension of natural phenomena? The soul of scripture has generally been characterized as its moral sense: on this account, the two figurative senses have the same referent, human nature, one pertaining generically to conduct, and the other to special objects of belief. This inference, however, is not verified, even if it is not refuted, by Origen's illustration of his theory (*First Principles* 4.2.6):

[25] Greer (1979: 231), following De Lubac (1959–64), i. 1, 205. So far as I can discover, this word does not occur in English or in Greek.

Of what might be called the soul of scripture an example is to be found in Paul's first letter to the Corinthians: 'For it is written,' he says, 'Thou shalt not muzzle the ox that treadeth the corn' [1 Corinthians 9: 9–10]. Then in his explanation he advances the following rule: 'Does God care for oxen? Or does he say it entirely for our sake? Yes, it is written for our sake, meaning that the one who ploughs should plough in hope and the one who winnows in the hope of sharing the fruits.'

Paul expounds this text to prove that ministers of religion have a right to be sustained by contributions. Had Origen made this point, we might have agreed with those who posit an ecclesiastical sense at the second level of exegesis.[26] The adjective is sanctioned by one sentence in the proem to Origen's *Commentary on the Song of Songs*, which applies the sense of that book both to the Church and to the soul; but Origen says nothing here of his threefold hermeneutic, and it may be that both interpretations are spiritual. Laconic as it is, the passage quoted here from the treatise *On First Principles* tells us only that the Bible (or the Old Testament) is occasionally oblique in its commands.

It is reasonable to assume that the second sense, as the soul of scripture, will convey the knowledge proper to the soul of the reader, just as the other two inform his body and his spirit.[27] The knowledge of the soul, however, is neither moral nor ecclesiastical, as Origen makes clear in his discussion of the soul's return to God (*First Principles* 2.11.7):

When, for instance, the saints have arrived at the heavenly places, they will then perceive the rationale of each of the stars and understand whether they are animated or whatever the truth may be. But they will also know the rationale of the other works of God, which he himself will reveal to them. For now he will show them, as his sons, the causes of things and the propriety of his own ordinance, teaching them why certain stars are placed in a certain portion of the sky . . . And thus the rational nature will enjoy gradual increase, not as it increased when flesh or body were coupled with soul, but the mind, augmented by intelligence and understanding, is led in a state of perfection to perfect knowledge, not at all impeded any more by the corporal senses.

The knowledge due to the soul is thus primarily cosmological, though of course it will acquire new moral insight from the

[26] Cf. Origen, *Commentary on the Song of Songs*, proem, 90.4 Baehrens.

[27] The relevance of hermeneutics to the human condition in Origen's thought is discussed by Torjesen (1986), and more particularly (1989). The importance of the body is, however, most strongly emphasized by Dawson (1998).

discovery of God's purpose in creation. As the proem to the Song of Songs also indicates, to know the world is to know our place in it. Confirmation that this was Origen's theory is afforded by Evagrius, the monastic theologian of the fourth century, who commends the practice of encratic virtue as a means to a state of passionlessness (*ἀπάθεια*) which frees the soul for the contemplation of the natural order.[28] The exercise leads eventually to a union with God through perfect knowledge. Thus there are three stages in the ascent to blessedness: first the ethical discipline of the body, then the illumination of the soul by natural science, and finally the consummation of knowledge in the spirit.[29] There is little doubt that Evagrius derived the kernel of his thought from Origen, though in keeping with the humanistic premisses of the fourth century he adopts the tripartite soul of Plato, eschews continuous exegesis of scripture, and does not appear to think of Christ as the necessary mediator of our approach to God.

Evagrius all but ignores the transformation of the body, which, according to Paul, will take placc 'in the twinkling of an eye' (1 Corinthians 15: 52). For Origen this event is the culmination of a journey through the spheres, when, purged of sin and filled with knowledge, the soul enjoys a sudden recollection and understanding of the whole of its previous life. It does not, however, experience this in solitude, or even, as Plotinus says, 'alone with the alone' (*Enneads* 6.9.9). The Christian is a member of a body, knit together with all the saints—perhaps with all humanity[30]—in the God-man, Jesus Christ. If we wish to behold God, we must dwell in Christ, as Moses looked on glory from the shelter of a rock (*Commentary on Song of Songs* 4, 230.23–231.1 Baehrens):

> In this rock which is Christ, there are no tokens of the serpent, that is of sin, as he is the only one who did no sin [1 Peter 2: 22]. Therefore it is under the cover of this rock that the soul arrives at the place before the walls, that is at the contemplation of incorporeal and eternal things.

[28] See *To Anatolius: Texts on Active Life* 70 (104–5 Kadloubovsky and Palmer).

[29] *Instructions to Cenobites and Others* 76–8 (116 Kadloubovsky and Palmer) equates active virtues with the body of the Lord, discrimination with his blood, and theology with the bosom of God (cf. John 1: 18).

[30] On this and other points in this paragraph, see Edwards (1995).

Origen, as usual, is alluding simultaneously to a number of biblical images: Christ as the cornerstone of the present Church and future Temple (cf. 2 Peter 2: 4–7), Christ as the one foundation on which the wise man builds his dwelling (cf. Matthew 7: 24–5 with 1 Corinthians 3: 11 and 10: 4), Christ as the sole and perfect truth who sees all truth in God (cf. John 14: 6). Above all, he is thinking of his favourite verse from Paul, which he seldom fails to cite whenever he speaks of the consummation: the supreme joy that awaits us in the kingdom of the Father is that 'Christ will be all in all' (1 Corinthians 15: 28).[31]

III

What has all this to do with figures of rhetoric?[32] To answer this question we must accept, as Origen would, that rhetoric involves a theory of meaning and not only a taxonomy of forms. That is to say that metaphor, metonymy, and synecdoche are not merely signs but modes of signification, intelligible only by their relation to some object which is not expressed, but could logically replace them in the text. In Origen's theory it might appear that different senses of scripture not only signify in different ways but signify different objects; and that is true, so long as we think only of the indicative relation between an utterance and the truth to which it points. We may also think that 'truth' is a fallacious term if it comprehends at the same time moral precepts, natural laws, and suprasensory revelations; but for Origen, the distinctions that we commonly draw between denotation and content, or prescription and description, are irrelevant when one speaks of sacred matters. The truth that Christians worship is a Person, whom they not only know but imitate and may even, in a certain sense, become. The process may be described under the three rhetorical figures:

1. Ethics is the metaphorical discipline, for it encourages us

[31] The verse is cited in *First Principles* at 120.28, 277.21, 282.6 (Greek at 282.21), 283.1, 285.3, 287.23, and 289.23–4 Koetschau.

[32] Some people would ask what theology ever has to do with rhetoric. They could look for an answer in the eucharistic controversy between Luther and Zwingli: the former maintained that Christ's words 'This is my body' are to be understood synecdochically, the latter applied the trope of *alloiosis*. See Bornkamm (1983), 542–7; Cross (1996).

not only to obey Christ but to imitate his actions during his sojourn in the flesh. He became man both to teach us and to show what we could accomplish; as the whole of his life is a pattern for us, it is necessary for Origen to defend his apparent weakness and duplicity against Celsus and to warn embattled Christians that they too have a Cross to bear (*To the Martyrs* 12). So literally did Origen take this precept that he died of tortures inflicted during the Decian persecution, achieving in his seventieth year the martyrdom that he sought in vain at the age of 17 (Eusebius, *Ecclesiastical History* 6.2).

2. If metaphor is (in Peirce's term) iconic (1955: 102), while metonymy is indexical, a Platonist would say that any knowledge of the natural world is metaphorically knowledge of its divine original. The world, as Plato said, is the 'first-born image' (μονογενὴς εἰκών) of the eternal paradigm (*Timaeus* 92d). For Christians this was heresy: Christ, the Word of God, was the only image of the Father (Colossians 1: 15 etc.) and the world was his creature, not so much a mirror of his essence as a token of his power. 'He made us', as Augustine later found, is the only testimony that the world gives to its Author (*Confessions* 10.6). For all that, the instruction which the soul receives in Origen's second stage cannot fail to enhance its understanding of Christ's role as the second Person of the Trinity—a role in which, after all, he is described by Origen as the soul of God (*First Principles* 2.8.5). Thus the saint adds a metonymic knowledge of Christ's divinity to the metaphorical knowledge of him as man.

3. To know him as both God and man—to know him as he is—one must, as we have already seen, be 'one spirit' with him, and this entails that the spirit in ourselves must take possession of soul and body. As Christ is the head of all redeemed humanity, the relation of the saint to him is that of part to whole. Nevertheless, identity is not lost, nor is any of its elements; and just as spirit comprehends soul and body without annihilating either, so the enoptic climax does not countermand our ethical and physical speculations, but preserves what is most valuable in both. When Christ is 'all in all', the synecdochic relation holds, not only between the saint and his Redeemer, but between the first two levels of exegesis and the third.

Something of the kind appears to be held in Origen's doctrine of the Trinity, where, though all three of the persons or hypostases are eternal and divine, the Godhead resides primarily in the Father. The Son is both the image of the Father and (metaphorically at least) his emanation;[33] the Spirit, who derives from him, is the mediator of gifts, and as it were the material index of the Father's operation through the Son.[34] On earth we know the Father metaphorically through the Son and metonymically through the Spirit; but the final state, when Christ is all in all, is the Father's everlasting kingdom, where cognizance of the Spirit and the Son will be constitutive of, not a substitute for, the knowledge of God himself.

IV

In the Church tradition, Origen is as much a Latin father as a Greek one. Marius Victorinus expounds his concept of the spirit; Jerome's debts to his commentaries on the New Testament are unconcealed; and his threefold scheme is reproduced, without the emendations of Rufinus, by Gregory of Elvira and Ambrose of Milan. Gregory distinguishes the historic, the prophetic, and the figurative,[35] using the second term, as Origen would, to signify the knowledge of every mystery that pertains to the present world.[36] Ambrose shows himself a true disciple when he seeks the hermeneutic key to the Song of Songs in the very words of Solomon: after wandering in the shadows of an uncomprehending literalism, we breathe the precious odours of salvation, and finally are led by the spirit into perfect rest (*On Isaac* 68). De Lubac (1959–64: i. 1, 207–19) even argues that the fourfold exegesis of the Middle Ages, famously expounded in Dante's letter to Can Grande della Scala, has its roots in Origen's theory. Of all Latin authors, only Augustine seems to have been

[33] *First Principles* 1.2.1 and 1.2.5, citing Heb. 1: 3 and Wisd. 7: 25–6 in the latter passage.

[34] *Commentary on John* 2.10. The Spirit acts as the matter of God's gifts to us, when they are dispensed through Christ.

[35] *Tractatus Origenis* 5.1, 34 Bulhart. For *historia*, cf. the Latin of Rufinus at *First Principles* 307.16 Koetschau, defending the literal narrative. For *figuraliter* see *First Principles* 318.28 Koetschau.

[36] On the comprehensive character of prophecy as the knowledge of unseen things in Origen, see Harnack (1918–19), ii. 123.

immune to his influence, for the pattern which he acknowledges—*moralis*, *physicalis*, *rationalis*—appears to have been derived from Platonism through Lactantius.[37] Moreover, Augustine found that in hermeneutics, as in most things, he walked straighter without the crutches of tradition: thus he advanced a different theory of the triple sign, according to which a word has a conventional propensity to engender a certain image in the phantasy or spirit, and this stands in a more permanent, though enigmatic, relation to its interpretant, the idea, which has no perceptible qualities and no other place or substance than the mind.[38]

Scholars have commended this analysis by likening it to that of C. S. Peirce (Markus 1957, esp. 82–3). For our purpose, it suffices to note that Augustine posits a reader who is still united to his carnal body, so that images peculiar to the soul must be phantasmal, rather than belonging to an order of future percepts. No knowledge of Christian doctrine would have been possible without the incarnation, for it is in this form that we find 'without, in humble guise, the one whom we deserted in our pride when he dwelt within' (*quem intus superbiens reliquit foris humilem invenit*: *On Free Will* 3.10.30). Like Origen, Augustine casts aside the Platonic thesis that the present world is a copy of an invisible reality,[39] together with the 'Cratylean' postulate that language has a natural relation to the Ideas.[40] His most conspicuous debt is to the *Categories* of Aristotle, or rather to the Porphyrian interpretation of them, which maintains that words affect the mind by generating an image (φαντασία) in the soul.[41] Porphyry, as a hostile critic of Origen, had denied that Christians had a right to allegory, and they in turn denied that right to him;[42]

[37] For *On True Religion* 16–17 see Bochet (1998).

[38] See *On Genesis Read Literally* 12.15 with Finan (1992), 141–55.

[39] See Augustine, *Confessions* 12.9 and Origen, *First Principles* 2.3.6. Modern readers sometimes fail to distinguish Plato's theory from the Christian (and commonsensical) view that God foresaw what he would make, and also from the belief in invisible spirits.

[40] Reemts (1998), 109–21 ascribes to Origen a belief that language is natural in a different sense, namely, that the concepts fixed by social usage are, or may be, adequate to express the true nature of things.

[41] See Porphyry, fr. 83F Smith, cited from Boethius, *On Interpretation* 2.33.24 ff. This is a comment on Aristotle, *Categories* 16[a]28–9.

[42] For Porphyry against Origen see Eusebius, *Ecclesiastical History* 6.19; for Eusebius against Porphyry, see *Preparation for the Gospel* 3.9, *passim*.

nevertheless he taught Augustine almost all the philosophy that he knew.[43] The theory of signs that the latter borrows from him is not designed for any single text or trope or pedagogic method. Founded as it is upon a threefold anthropology of body, soul, and intellect—not body, soul, and spirit—it describes communication as it occurs between human beings everywhere, even if they have no knowledge of scripture and no faith in Christ as Lord.

Augustine seems to be offering semiotics under the guise of hermeneutics, anticipating the modern view that we ought to read the Bible as we read any other book. We should not suppose, however, that the body is irrelevant to his biblical exegesis; that would be to ignore the implications of the tenet, which he holds in common with Origen and the Cappadocian Fathers, that matter is created by a sovereign act of God. It is not, as Plato may have taught, a crucible into which God pours the Forms; nor is it, as Aristotle argued, an eternal potentiality which coexists with the eternal agent. It is the substrate for every embodied creature, logically prior but brought into being together with it, just as sound is a logical precondition of, but temporally concurrent with, the production of a word (*Confessions* 12.27). The Word—that is, the Word of God—begets not only meaning but the very possibility of meaning; for us, as God's interpreters, the body which he gave us is a necessary instrument for the full determination of his truth. The body was given to us for obedience, and the rule of interpretation for the Christian is charity, the foundation of all obedience in this life and all beatitude in the next (*Christian Doctrine* 3.15 etc.). Plenary exegesis is achieved when we are able and prepared to use the body in accordance with the precepts of the Lord.

Augustine left all other ancient theorists far behind him in his writings on semantics, which ask not only what a term can signify, but how. In his dialogue *The Master*, a preliminary answer is that bodily experience is related synecdochically to our knowledge of the world.[44] To see or hear the sign without experience of the object would add nothing to our awareness; but the nature of most objects is too abstract to be grasped, let alone

[43] By way of Marius Victorinus (*Confessions* 8.3): see Hadot (1968).

[44] See esp. *The Master* 10–11. My summary in these paragraphs is indebted to Stock (1996), 148–62, though I have not pursued the distinction between the written and the spoken word which is a central theme of his admirable study.

conveyed, by bare experience, and we therefore need the sign to help us build or recognize the mental concept. In certain cases—higher goods and virtues, for example—the concept is already part of our intellectual furniture; but to comprehend it fully we corporeal beings must practise the obedience that is enjoined on us by scripture in the present life but consummated only when the soul receives a spiritual body in the next. In the meantime, as Brian Stock expresses it, 'a reformed life is a genre of rewriting: its text is the self'.[45]

Only the strictest pupils of the Reformation now agree with Origen that the Word of God incarnate is the sole key to the Word of God as scripture. The most common complaint against him, that his allegory foists meanings on the text that it was never meant to bear,[46] rests tacitly on two axioms that are modern rather than contemporary. The first is that the intention of an author governs the meaning of his work; the second is that a single meaning is, or should be, the regular concomitant of a certain form of words. According to this position, there ought not to be a plurality of senses, nor can a new one be conjured into being by the capacity of one reader to persuade others of its presence. A book would not be long enough to rehearse the assaults to which such literalism is now exposed. Some hold that in any case religious statements have no meaning, or at least no denotation, since there is no conceivable object to which we might appeal to prove them false or true.[47] Others allege that if a proposition is used consistently by the members of a given 'speech-community', this suffices to prove it meaningful;[48] it follows (though the inference is not always drawn) that if the same community consents to apply a text in several ways, it will have a corresponding variety of meanings. Literary theorists are aware that Christianity is the religion of the Logos, and the prologue to the Fourth Gospel, with its mysterious proclamation of the Word as the author and centre of the world, continues to employ the pens of structuralists, post-structuralists, and others

[45] Stock (1996), 187, with special reference to *The Utility of Belief*, but with the *Confessions* in mind as well.

[46] See Crouzel (1989), 72 on his 'inadequate notion of the part played by the human intellect' in the composition of scriptural books.

[47] For an infamous attack on all metaphysics see Ayer (1936), ch. 1.

[48] A view often traced (rightly or wrongly) to Ludwig Wittgenstein, *Philosophical Investigations* (1963), esp. 53–4 (sections 138–9).

who adhere to the proposition that 'there is nothing outside the text'.[49] Such critics, however, assume that their meditations would be shocking to theologians, who are expected to regard their texts as witnesses, not only to themselves, but to the transcendent realm of meaning that our ancestors called 'truth'.

In fact there are more Derridean, Wittgensteinian, and postmodern theologians than is generally imagined (see e.g. Phillips 1988, and Ward 1997). Like the existentialists and Marxists of a previous generation, they are apt to say that the meaning of a text lies not so much in its lexical content as in the activity (πρᾶξις) that it inspires. Perhaps the best foundation for this position is provided not by Derrida or Barthes, but by the older, Bergsonian school of French philosophy, which held that knowledge and memory are to be valued only as stimuli to action, and that hence there is no true knowledge which is not in some way ingested by the body. According to Merleau-Ponty,[50] the laws of nature consolidate the body and are thus the source of its creative freedom; in the same way the norms of language circumscribe, and therefore constitute, our freedom in writing, thought, and speech.

In the present life, we find ourselves in passive occupation of a body whose constant properties we can only slightly modify by habit, diet, and exercise; our mind seems, by comparison, free, creative, and almost infinitely mobile. Yet Christian theology—or at least the Aristotelian strain which characterizes Origen[51]—has always held that the intellect must belong to an individual who, if he is human, knows himself through the action of his thought upon the perceptions mediated by his body.[52] And just as the body is needed to house the soul, so the letter is needed as the vehicle of the spirit. Origen was perhaps the first to note that the possession of a body is a prerequisite of survival as personal beings apart from God; he was also the first to argue that we have

[49] See Moore (1989), esp. 159–69. But Dawson (1992: 129–45) finds much the same principle in the 2nd-cent. theologian Valentinus, who would no doubt have traced it (correctly) to John 1: 1. For the importance of Derrida to modern theology see Ward (1995).

[50] Merleau-Ponty (1960), 83–111; and see 'Éloge de la Philosophie' at 15–41 for Bergson.

[51] Some of my reasons for holding that he is more an Aristotelian than a Platonist (and a Christian more than either) are given in Edwards (1993).

[52] See Aquinas, *Contra Averroem*, for this interpretation of the active reason in Aristotle's *De Anima*.

spiritual as well as physical senses, yet he never says that the former have any substrate but the written text of scripture. The spirit transcends the letter as it frees itself from the world, not by negating it completely, but by assigning it to its due place in the economy of God.

As an orthodox Christian, Origen held that while revelation may be conveyed to us through bodies, texts, and practices, the truth is not identical with any of its material expressions, but abides eternally and transcendentally in God. Nevertheless, he also held, against scholastics, liberals, and philosophers of religion, that the spirit of revelation is inseparable from the matter; in this sense, it is also true for him that 'there is nothing outside the text'. He agreed that truths are exhibited, in the first instance, through the body of the text; but body for him is a cipher for the soul, while soul and body are the rudiments of spirit. For him, as for Immanuel Kant, we verify the Christian faith by living as though we already knew the truth of it; by a cumulative surrender of the three elements in ourselves to the same three elements in scripture we can hope to attain both unity of insight and integrity of being. My brief conclusion here will be that Origen, by positing a determinate plurality of meanings in the scriptures, is able to endorse much that is said by modern writers against the theory of static meaning, but without violence to the function of the text as a repository of truth.

BIBLIOGRAPHY

I. ANCIENT AUTHORS

Details of Greek texts used in this volume but not listed here will be found in L. Berkowitz and K. A. Squitier, *Thesaurus Linguae Graecae Canon of Greek Authors and Words*. 3rd edn. (New York/Oxford: 1990).

ANONYMOUS, *On Tropes*. L. Spengel (ed.), *Rhetores Graeci*, vol. iii (Leipzig: Teubner, 1856), 227–9.

Anonymous Commentary on Plato's Phaedo = *P.Heid.G. inv.* 28 + *P.Graec.Mon.* 21. A. Carlini (ed.), *CPF* iii. 7, 203–20.

BACCHYLIDES, fragments. B. Snell (ed.), *Bacchylides. Carmina cum fragmentis* (Leipzig: Teubner, 1934), 81–118.

CHAEREMON, fragments. Van der Horst (ed.) (1987).

CHARISIUS, *Art of Grammar*. H. Keil (ed.), *Grammatici Latini*, vol. i (Leipzig: Teubner, 1857), 1–296.

CORNUTUS, *Epitome of the Ars Rhetorica*. J. Graeven (ed.), *Cornuti Artis Rhetoricae Epitome* (Berlin: Weidmann, 1891).

CRATES OF MALLOS, fragments. M. Broggiato (ed.), *Cratete di Mallo: I frammenti* (La Spezia: Agorà Edizioni, 2001).

Derveni Papyrus (i) A full text is printed anonymously at *Zeitschrift für Papyrologie und Epigraphie*, 47 (1982), 1–12 after 300. (ii) Columns 1–7 in the new ordering edited by K. Tsantsanoglou, 'The First Columns of the Derveni Papyrus and their Religious Significance', at Laks and Most (1997), 93–5. (iii) A full translation of the text in the new ordering at A. Laks and G. Most, 'A Provisional Translation of the Derveni Papyrus', in Laks and Most (1997), 9–22.

DIONYSIUS OF HALICARNASSUS, *Opuscules rhétoriques*. G. Aujac (ed. and trans.). 5 vols. (Paris: Les Belles Lettres, 1978–92).

EVAGRIUS, *To Anatolius: Texts on Active Life*; *Instructions to Cenobites and Others*. E. Kadloubovsky and G. E. H. Palmer (edd. and trans.), *Early Fathers from the Philokalia* (London: Faber & Faber, 1954).

FULGENTIUS, *Super Thebaiden*. R. Helm (ed.), *Fabii Planciadis Fulgentii V. C. opera. Accedunt Fabii Claudii Gordiani Fulgentii De aetatibus mundi et hominis et s. Fulgentii episcopi Super Thebaiden* (Leipzig: Teubner, 1898).

GREGORY OF ELVIRA, *Tractatus Origenis*. V. Bulhart (ed.), *Gregorii Iliberritani episcopi quae supersunt* = Corpus Christianorum. Series Latina 69 (Turnhout: Brepols, 1967).

'HERACLITUS', *Homeric Problems*. Societatis Philologae Bonnensis Sodales (edd.), *Heracliti Quaestiones Homericae* (Leipzig: Teubner, 1910).

JOHN CHRYSOSTOM, *Homilies on Galatians*. F. Field (ed.), *Sancti Patris Nostri Joannis Chrysostomi Interpretatio Omnium Epistolarum Paulinarum per Homilias Facta*, vol. iv (Oxford: Parker, 1852).

(CASSIUS) LONGINUS, fragments. L. Brisson and M. Patillon, 'Longinus Philosophus et Philologus. I: Longinus Philosophus', *ANRW* ii. 36.7 (1994), 5241–99 (for fragments 1–13); 'II: Longinus Philologus', *ANRW* ii. 34.4 (1998), 3023–108 (remaining fragments).

MACROBIUS, *Commentary on the Dream of Scipio*. J. Willis (ed.), *Macrobius*, vol. 2 (Leipzig: Teubner, 1970).

ORIGEN, *Commentary on John*. A. E. Brooke (ed.), *The Commentary of Origen on S. John's Gospel*, 2 vols. (Cambridge: Cambridge University Press, 1896).

—— *First Principles*. P. Koetschau (ed.), *Origenes: Werke*, vol. 5 = *Die griechischen christlichen Schriftsteller der ersten drei Jahrhunderte*, vol. 22 (Leipzig: Hinrichs, 1913).

—— *Homilies on the Song of Songs*. W. Baehrens (ed.), *Origenes: Werke*, vol. 8 = *Die griechischen christlichen Schriftsteller der ersten drei Jahrhunderte*, vol. 33 (Leipzig, Hinrichs: 1925).

[PLUTARCH], *Life and Poetry of Homer*. J. F. Kindstrand (ed.), *(Plutarchi) De Homero* (Leipzig: Teubner, 1990).

PORPHYRY, fragments. A. Smith (ed.), *Porphyrius: Fragmenta* (Leipzig: Teubner, 1993).

POSIDONIUS, fragments. L. Edelstein and I. G. Kidd (edd.), *Posidonius*, vol. i: *The Fragments*, 2nd edn. (Cambridge: Cambridge University Press, 1989).

THEOPHRASTUS, fragments. Fortenbaugh, Huby, Sharples, and Gutas (edd.) = FHSG.

VARRO, *Divine Antiquities*. B. Cardauns (ed.), *M. Terentius Varro: Antiquitates Rerum Divinarum* (Mainz: Akademie der Wissenschafte und der Literatur/Wiesbaden: Steiner, 1976).

(MARIUS) VICTORINUS, *Commentary on Galatians*. A. Locher (ed.), *Marii Victorini Afri Commentarii in Epistulas Pauli ad Galatas, ad Philippenses, ad Ephesios* (Leipzig: Teubner, 1972).

2. MODERN AUTHORS

ABBENES, J. G. J., SLINGS, S. R., and SLUITER, I. (1995) (edd.) *Greek Literary Theory after Aristotle: A Collection of Papers in Honor of D. M. Schenkeveld* (Amsterdam: VU University Press).

Ahl, F. (1984), 'The Art of Safe Criticism in Greece and Rome', *American Journal of Philology*, 105: 174–208.

Annas, J., and Waterfield, R. (1995) (edd. and trans.), *Plato, Statesman* (Cambridge: Cambridge University Press).

Arendt, H. (1978), *The Life of the Mind* (New York: Secker & Warburg).

Armstrong, D. (1995), 'The Impossibility of Metathesis: Philodemus and Lucretius on Form and Content in Poetry', in Obbink (1995*a*), 210–32.

Asmis, E. (1991), 'Philodemus' Poetic Theory and *On the Good King According to Homer*', *Classical Antiquity*, 10: 1–45.

Asper, M. (1997), *Onomata Allotria: Zur Genese, Struktur und Funktion poetologischer Metaphern bei Kallimachos* = Hermes Einzelschriften 75 (Stuttgart: Steiner).

Assfahl, G. (1932), *Vergleich und Metapher bei Quintilian* = Tübinger Beiträge zur Altertumswissenschaft 15 (Stuttgart: Kohlhammer).

Austin, R. G. (1953) (ed.), *Quintiliani institutionis oratoriae liber XII*, corrected reprint (Oxford: Oxford University Press).

Ayer, A. J. (1936), *Language, Truth and Logic* (2nd, revised edn. 1946) (London: Gollancz).

Barker, A. (1999), 'Shifting Frontiers in Ancient Theories of Metaphor', *Proceedings of the Cambridge Philological Society*, 45: 1–16.

Barnes, T. J. (1996), *Logics of Dislocation, Models, Metaphors, and Meanings of Economic Space* (New York/London: Guildford).

Barthes, R. (1970), *S/Z* (Paris: Éditions du Seuil).

——(1971), 'Style and its Image', in S. B. Chatman (ed.), *Literary Style: A Symposium* (Oxford: Oxford University Press), 3–15.

Baumgarten, R. (1998), *Heiliges Wort und heilige Schrift bei den Griechen: Hieroi logoi und verwandte Erscheinungen* (Tübingen: Gunter Narr Verlag).

Beissinger, M. H., Tylus, J., and Wofford, S. L. (1999) (edd.), *Epic Traditions in the Contemporary World: The Poetics of Community* (Berkeley/Los Angeles/London: University of California Press).

Benjamin, W. (1977), *The Origin of German Tragic Drama*, English trans. J. Osborne (London/New York: Verso).

Bernard, W. (1990), *Spätantike Dichtungstheorien: Untersuchungen zu Proklos, Herakleitos und Plutarch* (Stuttgart: Teubner, 1990).

Bertoli, E. (1982), 'L'età dell'oro in Posidonio e Seneca', *Quaderni di lingue e letterature*, 7: 151–79.

Bigg, C. H. (1913), *The Christian Platonists of Alexandria* (Oxford: Oxford University Press).

Black, M. (1954), 'Metaphor', *Proceedings of the Aristotelian Society*, 55: 273–94.

Black, M. (1962), *Models and Metaphors: Studies in Language and Philosophy* (Ithaca: Cornell University Press).

——(1977), 'More About Metaphor', *Dialectica*, 31: 431–57.

——(1979), 'How Metaphors Work: A Reply to Donald Davidson', in S. Sacks (ed.), *On Metaphor* (Chicago: University of Chicago Press), 181–92.

——(1993), 'More About Metaphor', in Ortony (1993*a*), 14–41 (a revised version of Black 1977).

Blume, H. D. (1963), *Untersuchungen zu Sprache und Stil der Schrift περὶ ὕψους* (diss., Göttingen).

Blümer, W. (1991), *Rerum eloquentia: Christliche Nutzung antiker Stilkunst bei St. Leo Magnus* (Frankfurt: Peter Lang).

Bochet, I. (1998), 'Non aliam esse philosophiam . . . et aliam religionem (Augustin, *De ver. rel.* 5,8)' in B. Pouderon and J. Dore (edd.), *Les Apologistes Chrétiens et la culture grecque* (Paris: Beauchesne), 333–53.

Bolgar, R. R. (1954), *The Classical Heritage and its Beneficiaries* (Cambridge: Cambridge University Press).

Bonner, S. F. (1949), *Roman Declamation in the Late Republic and Early Empire* (Berkeley: University of California Press).

Bornkamm, H. (1983), *Luther in Mid-Career*, English trans. E. T. Bachmann (Philadelphia: Fortress Press).

Boyancé, P. (1955), 'Sur la théologie de Varron', *Revue des Études Anciennes*, 57: 57–84

Boys-Stones, G. (1998), 'Eros in Government: Zeno and the Virtuous City', *Classical Quarterly*, 48: 168–74.

——(2001), *Post-Hellenistic Philosophy: A Study of its Development from the Stoics to Origen* (Oxford: Oxford University Press).

Braun, E. (1994), *Lukian unter doppelter Anklage. Ein Kommentar* = Studien zur klassischen Philologie 85 (Frankfurt: Peter Lang).

Brink, C. O. (1963), *Horace on Poetry: Prolegomena to the Literary Epistles* (Cambridge: Cambridge University Press).

——(1971), *Horace on Poetry: The 'Ars Poetica'* (Cambridge: Cambridge University Press).

——(1982), *Horace on Poetry: Epistles Book II: The Letters to Augustus and Florus* (Cambridge: Cambridge University Press).

Buffière, F. (1956), *Les Mythes d'Homère et la pensée grecque* (Paris: Belles Lettres).

——(1962) (ed. and trans.), *Héraclite: Allégories d'Homère* (Paris: Belles Lettres).

Burkert, W. (1968), 'Orpheus und die Vorsokratiker', *Antike und Abendland*, 14: 93–114.

——(1994), 'Orpheus, Dionysos und die Euneiden in Athen: Das

Zeugnis von Euripides' *Hypsipyle*', in A. Bierl und P. von Möllendorff (edd.), *Orchestra: Drama, Mythos, Bühne* (Stuttgart: Teubner), 444–9.

Calvino, I. (1987), 'Why Read the Classics?', in his *The Literature Machine,* English trans. P. Creagh (London: Secker & Warburg), 125–34.

Campbell, L. (1867) (ed.), *The Sophistes and Politicus of Plato* (Oxford: Oxford University Press).

Carpenter, T. H. (2000), 'Images and Beliefs: Thoughts on the Derveni Krater', in G. R. Tsetskhladze, A. J. N. W. Prag, and A. M. Snodgrass (edd.), *Periplous: Papers on Classical Art and Archaeology presented to Sir John Boardman* (London: Thames & Hudson), 51–9.

Càsola, F. (1975) (ed.), *Inni Omerici* (Milan: Fondazione Lorenzo Valla).

Chemla, K. (1994), 'Nombre et opération, chaîne et trame du réel mathématique', *Extrême-Orient Extrême-Occident*, 16: 43–70.

—— (forthcoming), *Les Neuf chapitres sur les procédures mathématiques* (Paris).

Cheng, F. (1979), 'Bi et xing', *Cahiers de linguistique. Asie orientale*, 6: 63–7.

Classen, C. J. (1994), 'Rhetorik und Literarkritik', in F. Montanari (ed.), *La Philologie grecque à l'époque hellénistique et romaine* = Entretiens sur l'Antiquité Classique 40 (Geneva: Fondation Hardt), 307–60.

Clemen, W. (1977), *The Development of Shakespeare's Imagery*, 2nd edn. (London: Methuen).

Clifford, J. (1986), 'On Ethnographic Allegory', in J. Clifford and G. E. Marcus (edd.), *Writing Culture: The Poetics and Politics of Ethnography* (Berkeley/Los Angeles/London: University of California Press), 98–121.

Clinton, K. (1974), *The Sacred Officials of the Eleusinian Mysteries* = Transactions of the American Philosophical Society 64.3 (Philadelphia: American Philosophical Society).

Cohen, Ted (1975), 'Figurative Speech and Figurative Acts', *Journal of Philosophy*, 72: 669–84.

Colli, G., and Montinari, M. (1967–), *Nietzsche: Werke, kritische Gesamtausgabe* (Berlin: de Gruyter).

Cooper, J. M. (1998), 'Posidonius on the Emotions', in Sihvola and Engberg-Pedersen (1998), 71–112.

Cope, E. M., and Sandys, J. E. (1973) (edd.), *The Rhetoric of Aristotle* (New York: Arno Press).

Cornford, F. M. (1935), *Plato's Theory of Knowledge: The Theaetetus and the Sophist of Plato Translated with a Running Commentary*

(London/New York: Kegan Paul, Trench, Trubner & Co./Harcourt, Brace and Company).

Cross, F. L., and Livingstone, E. A. (1997) (edd.), *The Oxford Dictionary of the Christian Church*. 3rd edn. (Oxford: Oxford University Press).

Cross, R. L. (1996), 'Alloiosis in the Christology of Zwingli', *Journal of Theological Studies*, 47: 105–22.

Crouzel, H. (1989), *Origen*, English trans. A. S. Worrall (Edinburgh: T. & T. Clark).

Cullen, C. (1996), *Astronomy and Mathematics in Ancient China: The Zhou bi suan jing* (Cambridge: Cambridge University Press).

Curtius, E. R. (1953), *European Literature and the Latin Middle Ages*, English trans. W. R. Trask (New York: Pantheon Books).

D'Alton, J. F. (1931), *Roman Literary Theory and Criticism: A Study in Tendencies* (London: Longmans).

Davidson, D. (1978), 'What Metaphors Mean', *Critical Inquiry*, 5: 31–47.

——(1979), 'What Metaphors Mean' (= Davidson 1978), in S. Sacks (ed.), *On Metaphor* (Chicago: University of Chicago Press), 29–45.

——(1980), *Essays on Actions and Events* (Oxford: Oxford University Press).

Dawson, D. (1992), *Allegorical Readers and Cultural Revision in Ancient Alexandria* (Berkeley/Los Angeles/London: University of California Press).

——(1998), 'Allegorical Reading and the Embodiment of the Soul in Origen', in L. Ayres and G. Jones (edd.), *Christian Origins: Theology, Rhetoric and Community* (London: Routledge), 26–44.

De Lubac, H. (1959–64), *L'Exégèse Mediévale: Les Quatre Sens de l'Écriture*, 2 vols. (Paris: Aubier).

Demandt, A. (1978), *Metaphern für Geschichte: Sprachbilder und Gleichnisse im historisch-politischen Denken* (Munich: Beck).

Deremetz, A. (1995), *Le Miroir des muses: Poétiques de la réflexivité à Rome* (Villeneuve d'Ascq: Presses Universitaires du Septentrion).

Derrida, J. (1974), 'White Mythology: Metaphor in the Text of Philosophy', *New Literary History*, 6: 5–74.

Détienne, M. (1962), *Homère, Hésiode et Pythagore: Poésie et Philosophie dans le Pythagorisme Ancien* (Brussels: Latomus).

Deubner, L. (1902–9), 'Personifikation abstrakter Begriffe', in W. M. Roscher (ed.), *Ausführliches Lexikon der griechischen und römischen Mythologie*, vol. iii. 2 (Leipzig: Teubner), 2068–169.

Dihle, A. (1977), 'Der Beginn des Attizismus', *Antike und Abendland*, 23: 162–77.

Djamouri, R. (1993), 'Théorie de la "rectification des dénominations" et réflexion linguistique chez Xunzi', *Extrême-Orient Extrême-Occident*, 15: 55–74.

Dodd, C. H. (1938), *The Parables of the Kingdom* (London: Nisbet).

——(1952), *According to the Scriptures: The Sub-Structure of New Testament Theology* (London: Nisbet).

Dover, K. J. (1997) (ed.), *Aristophanes' Frogs* (Oxford: Oxford University Press).

Duckworth, G. E. (1933), *Foreshadowing and Suspense in the Epics of Homer, Apollonius and Vergil* (Princeton: Princeton University Press).

Dyer, R. (1989), 'Vergil's Fama: A New Interpretation of Aeneid 4.173 ff.', *Greece and Rome*, 26: 28–32.

Eco, U. (1976), *A Theory of Semiotics* (Bloomington: Indiana University Press).

Edwards, M. J. (1988), 'Scenes from the Later Wanderings of Odysseus', *Classical Quarterly*, 49: 509–21.

——(1993), 'Ammonius, Teacher of Origen', *Journal of Ecclesiastical History*, 44: 169–81.

——(1995), 'Origen's Two Resurrections', *Journal of Theological Studies*, 46: 502–18.

——(1998), 'Christ or Plato?', in L. Ayres and G. Jones (edd.), *Christian Origins: Theology, Rhetoric and Community* (London: Routledge), 10–25.

Eggs, E. (2001), 'Metapher', in G. Ueding (ed.), *Historisches Wörterbuch der Rhetorik*, vol. v (Tübingen: Niemeyer), 1099–183.

Empson, W. (1947), *Seven Types of Ambiguity*, 2nd edn. (London: Chatto & Windus).

Enders, J. (1997), 'Delivering Delivery: Theatricality and the Emasculation of Eloquence', *Rhetorica*, 15: 253–78.

Fantham, E. (1974), *Comparative Studies in Republican Latin Imagery* = Phoenix Supplement 10 (Toronto: University of Toronto Press).

Feeney, D. C. (1991), *The Gods in Epic: Poets and Critics of the Classical Tradition* (Oxford: Oxford University Press).

Finan, T. (1992), 'Modes of Vision in Augustine: *De Genesi ad Litteram* XII', in T. Finan and V. Twomey (edd.), *The Relation between Neoplatonism and Christianity* (Dublin: Four Courts Press), 141–55.

Fine, G. (1986), 'Immanence', *Oxford Studies in Ancient Philosophy*, 4: 71–98.

Finley, J. H. (1955), *Pindar and Aeschylus* (Cambridge, Mass.: Harvard University Press).

Fletcher, A. S. (1964), *Allegory: The Theory of a Symbolic Mode* (Oxford: Oxford University Press).

FONTANIER, P. (1977), *Les Figures du discours*. Containing *Manuel Classique pour l'étude des tropes* (4th edn., orig. pub. 1830) and *Des figures du discours autres que les tropes* (orig. pub. 1827) (Paris: Flammarion).

FORD, A. (1999), 'Performing Interpretation: Early Allegorical Exegesis of Homer', in Beissinger, Tylus, and Wofford (1999), 33–53.

FOWLER, H. N., and LAMB, W. R. M. (1925) (trans.), *Plato, The Statesman, Philebus, Ion* = Loeb Classical Library 164 (Cambridge, Mass./London: Harvard University Press).

FREDE, M. (1989), 'Chaeremon der Stoiker', *ANRW* ii. 36.3: 2067–103.

FRYE, N. (1971), *Anatomy of Criticism* (Princeton: Princeton University Press).

——(1974), 'Allegory', in A. Preminger, F. J. Warnke, and O. B. Hardison (edd.), *Princeton Encyclopaedia of Poetry and Poetics* (Princeton: Princeton University Press), 12–15.

——(1982), *The Great Code: The Bible and Literature* (London: Routledge).

FURBANK, P. N. (1970), *Reflections on the Word 'Image'* (London: Secker & Warburg).

GALE, M. R. (1994), *Myth and Poetry in Lucretius* (Cambridge: Cambridge University Press).

GALLOP, D. (1971), 'Dreaming and Waking in Plato', in J. P. Anton and G. L. Kustas (edd.), *Essays in Ancient Greek Philosophy* (Albany: State University of New York Press), 187–201.

GASSMANN, R. H. (1988), *Cheng ming, Richtigstellung der Bezeichnungen: Zu den Quellen eines Philosophems in antiken China: Ein Beitrag zur Konfuzius-Forschung* = Études asiatiques suisses 7 (Bern: Peter Lang).

GELZER, T. (1979), 'Klassizismus, Attizismus und Asianismus', in H. Flashar (ed.), *Le Classicisme à Rome aux 1ers siècles avant et après J.-C.* = Entretiens sur l'Antiquité Classique 25 (Geneva: Fondation Hardt), 1–41.

GERA LEVINE, D. (1995), 'Lucian's Choice: *Somnium* 6–16', in D. Innes, H. Hine, and C. Pelling (edd.), *Ethics and Rhetoric: Classical Essays for Donald Russell on his Seventy-Fifth Birthday* (Oxford: Oxford University Press), 237–50.

GERSON, L. (1994), *Plotinus* (London: Routledge).

GIBBS, JR., R. W. (1994), *The Poetics of Mind: Figurative Thought, Language and Understanding* (Cambridge: Cambridge University Press).

GILL, C. (1998), 'Did Galen Understand Platonic and Stoic Thinking on Emotions?', in Sihvola and Engberg-Pedersen (1998), 113–48.

GLEASON, M. W. (1995), *Making Men: Sophists and Self-Representation in Ancient Rome* (Princeton: Princeton University Press).

GLIBERT-THIRRY, A. (1977), 'La Théorie stoïcienne de la passion chez Chrysippe et son évolution chez Posidonius', *Revue Philosophique de Louvain*, 75: 393–435.

GOLDSCHMIDT, V. (1947), *Le Paradigme dans la dialectique platonicienne* (Paris: Presses Universitaires de France).

GOODMAN, N. (1976), *Languages of Art: An Approach to a Theory of Symbols*, 2nd edn. (Indiana: Hackett).

GOUDRIAAN, K. (1989), *Over classicisme: Dionysius van Halicarnassus en zijn program van welsprekenheid, cultur en politiek* (diss., Amsterdam).

GOW, A. S., and PAGE, D. L. (1965), *The Greek Anthology: Hellenistic Epigrams*, 2 vols. (Cambridge: Cambridge University Press).

GRAF, F. (1974), *Eleusis und die orphische Dichtung Athens in vorhellenistischer Zeit* = Religionsgeschichtliche Versuche und Vorarbeiten 33 (Berlin/New York: de Gruyter).

GRAHAM, A. C. (1981), *Chuang-tzu: The Seven Inner Chapters and Other Writings* (London: Allen & Unwin).

——(1989), *Disputers of the Tao: Philosophical Argument in Ancient China* (La Salle, Ill.: Open Court).

GREENE, T. M. (1963), *The Descent from Heaven: A Study in Epic Continuity* (New Haven/London: Yale University Press).

GREER, R. (1979), *Origen* (London: SPCK).

GRUBE, G. M. A. (1961) (trans.), *A Greek Critic: Demetrius On Style* = Phoenix Supplementary Volume 4 (Toronto: University of Toronto Press).

HADOT, P. (1968), *Porphyre et Victorinus* (Paris: Études Augustiniennes).

——(1979), 'La Division des parties de la philosophie dans l'Antiquité', *Museum Helveticum*, 36: 201–23.

HAHN, R. (1967), *Die Allegorie in der antiken Rhetorik* (diss., Tübingen).

HALLIWELL, S., FYFE, W., and INNES, D. (1995) (edd. and trans.), *Aristotle*, vol. 23: *The Poetics; 'Longinus', On the Sublime; Demetrius, On Style* = Loeb Classical Library 199 (Cambridge, Mass./London: Harvard University Press).

HANSEN, A. E. (1997), 'Fragmentation and the Greek Medical Writers', in Most (1997*b*), 289–314.

HARBSMEIER, C. (1998), *Language and Logic* = J. Needham (ed.), *Science and Civilisation in China*, vol. 7, part 1 (Cambridge: Cambridge University Press).

Hardie, P. R. (1985), '*Imago Mundi*: Cosmological and Ideological Aspects of the Shield of Achilles', *Journal of Hellenic Studies*, 105: 11–31.

——(1986), *Virgil's* Aeneid: *Cosmos and Imperium* (Oxford: Oxford University Press).

——(1999), 'Metamorphosis, Metaphor and Allegory in Latin Epic', in Beissinger, Tylus, and Wofford (1999), 89–107.

Harmon, A. M. (1921) (trans.), *Lucian*, vol. 3 = Loeb Classical Library 130 (Cambridge, Mass./London: Harvard University Press).

Harnack, A. von (1918–19), *Der kirchengeschichtliche Ertrag der exegetischen Arbeiten des Origenes*, 2 vols. = Texte und Untersuchungen zur Geschichte der altchristlichen Literatur ii. 12.3–4 (Leipzig: J. C. Hinrichs).

Haverkamp, A. (1996), 'Einleitung in die Theorie der Metapher', in his *Theorie der Metapher* = Wege der Forschung 389, 2nd edn. (Darmstadt: Wissenschaftliche Buchgesellschaft), 1–27.

Hawkes, T. (1972), *Metaphor* (London: Methuen).

Heath, M. (2000), 'Longinus, *On Sublimity*', *Proceedings of the Cambridge Philological Society*, 46: 43–74.

Heidegger, M. (1957), *Der Satz vom Grund* (Pfullingen: Neske).

——(1962), *Being and Time*, English trans. J. Macquarrie and E. Robinson (Oxford: Blackwell).

Hendrickson, G. L., and Hubbell, H. M. (1962) (trans.), *Cicero*, vol. 5: *Brutus, Orator* = Loeb Classical Library 342, revised edn. (Cambridge, Mass./London: Harvard University Press).

Hengel, M. (1974), *Judaism and Hellenism: Studies in their Encounter in Palestine during the Early Hellenistic Period*, English trans. J. Bowden (London: SCM Press).

Henrichs, A. (1974), 'Die Kritik der stoischen Theologie im PHerc. 1428', *Cronache Ercolanesi*, 4: 5–32.

Herter, H. (1959), 'Effeminatus', in T. Klauser (ed.), *Reallexikon für Antike und Christentum: Sachwörterbuch zur Auseinandersetzung des Christentums mit der antiken Welt*, vol. iv (Stuttgart: Hiersemann), 620–50.

Hesse, M. (1966), *Models and Analogies in Science* (Notre Dame: Notre Dame University Press).

Heubeck, A., West, S., and Hainsworth, J. B. (1988), *A Commentary on Homer's Odyssey*, vol. 1: *Introduction and Books 1–8* (Oxford: Oxford University Press).

Heydebrand, R. von, and Winko, S. (1995), 'Geschlechterdifferenz in Rezeption und Wertung von Literatur', in H. Bussmann and R. Hof (edd.), *Genus: Zur Geschlechterdifferenz in den Kulturwissenschaften* (Stuttgart: Kröner), 206–61.

HICK, J. (1977) (ed.), *The Myth of God Incarnate* (London: SPCK).
HIDBER, T. (1996), *Das klassizistische Manifest des Dionys von Halikarnaß: Die Praefatio zu De oratoribus veteribus: Einleitung, Übersetzung, Kommentar* = Beiträge zur Altertumskunde 70 (Stuttgart/ Leipzig: Teubner).
HIRSCHLE, M. (1979), *Sprachphilosophie und Namenmagie im Neuplatonismus* (Meisenheim: Hain).
HOLYOAK, K. J., and THAGARD, P. (1995), *Mental Leaps: Analogy in Creative Thought* (Cambridge, Mass./London: MIT Press).
HOSE, M. (1999), 'Die zweite Begegnung Roms mit den Griechen oder: Zu politischen Ursachen des Attizismus', in G.Vogt-Spira and B. Rommel (edd.), *Rezeption und Identität: Die kulturelle Auseinandersetzung Roms mit Griechenland als europäisches Paradigma* (Stuttgart: Steiner), 274–88.
HOUSE, H., and STOREY, G. (1959) (edd.), *The Journals and Papers of Gerard Manley Hopkins* (London: Oxford University Press).
HUSSEY, E. (1999), 'The Enigmas of Derveni', *Oxford Studies in Ancient Philosophy*, 17: 303–24.
INNES, D. C. (1988), 'Cicero on Tropes', *Rhetorica*, 6: 307–25.
——(1989), 'Augustan Critics', in G. A. Kennedy (ed.), *Cambridge History of Literary Criticism*, vol. 1: *Classical Criticism* (Cambridge: Cambridge University Press), 259–67.
——(1994), 'Period and Colon: Theory and Example in Demetrius and Longinus', in W. W. Fortenbaugh and D. C. Mirhady (edd.), *Peripatetic Rhetoric after Aristotle* = Rutgers University Studies in Classical Humanities 6 (New Brunswick: Transaction Publishers), 36–53.
——(1995), 'Longinus, Unity and Structure', in Abbenes, Slings, and Sluiter (1995): 111–24.
JACOBY, F. (1949), *Atthis: The Local Chronicles of Ancient Athens* (Oxford: Oxford University Press).
JÄKEL, O. (1999), 'Kant, Blumenberg, Weinrich: Some Forgotten Contributions to the Cognitive Theory of Metaphor', in R. W. Gibbs, Jr., and G. J. Steen (edd.), *Metaphor in Cognitive Linguistics: Selected Papers from the Fifth International Cognitive Linguistics Conference Amsterdam, July 1997* (Amsterdam: John Benjamins), 9–27.
JAKOBSON, R. (1956), 'Two Aspects of Language and Two Types of Aphasic Disturbances', in R. Jakobson and M. Halle (edd.), *Fundamentals of Language* (The Hague: Mouton), 67–96.
——(1960), 'Closing Statements: Linguistics and Poetics', in T. A. Sebeok (ed.), *Style in Language* (Cambridge, Mass.: MIT Press), 350–77.

JANKO, R. (1997), 'The Physicist as Hierophant: Aristophanes, Socrates and the Authorship of the Derveni Papyrus', *Zeitschrift für Papyrologie und Epigraphie*, 118: 61–94.

——(2001), 'The Derveni Papyrus (Diagoras of Melos, APOPYRGIZONTES LOGOI?): A New Translation', *Classical Philology*, 96: 1–32.

JAUMANN, H. (1995), *Critica: Untersuchungen zur Geschichte der Literaturkritik zwischen Quintilian und Thomasius* = Studies in Intellectual History 62 (Leiden: Brill).

JEFFERSON, A. (1986), 'Structuralism and Post-Structuralism', in A. Jefferson and D. Robey (edd.), *Modern Literary Theory*, 2nd edn. (London: Batsford), 92–121.

JOHANSEN, H. F., and WHITTLE, E. W. (1980) (edd.), *Aeschylus: The Suppliants*, 3 vols. (Copenhagen: Gyldendalske Boghandel Nordisk Forlag).

JOHNSON, M. (1981) (ed.), *Philosophical Perspectives on Metaphor* (Minneapolis: University of Minnesota Press).

JOWETT, B. (1892) (trans.), *The Dialogues of Plato*, 3rd edn., 5 vols. (Oxford: Oxford University Press).

JULLIEN, F. (1985), *La Valeur allusive: Des catégories originales de l'interprétation poétique dans la tradition chinoise: Contribution à une réflexion sur l'altérité interculturelle* (Paris: École française d'Extrême-Orient).

JÜRGENSEN, H. (1968), *Der antike Metaphernbegriff* (diss., Kiel).

KAHN, C. H. (1979), *The Art and Thought of Heraclitus* (Cambridge: Cambridge University Press).

KAPP, V. (1991), 'Zum Begriffspaar männlich/weiblich in Rhetorik und Kunsttheorie', in G. Ueding (ed.), *Rhetorik zwischen den Wissenschaften: Geschichte, System, Praxis als Probleme des 'Historischen Wörterbuchs der Rhetorik'* (Tübingen: Niemeyer), 195–205.

KEARNS, M. S. (1987), *Metaphors of Mind in Fiction and Psychology* (Lexington: University Press of Kentucky).

KENNEDY, G. A. (1991) (trans.), *Aristotle, On Rhetoric: A Theory of Civic Discourse* (Oxford: Oxford University Press).

KERFERD, G. B. (1981), *The Sophistic Movement* (Cambridge: Cambridge University Press).

KERN, O. (1888), *De Orphei, Epimenidis, Pherecydis Theogoniis quaestiones criticae* (Berlin: R. Stricker).

KIDD, I. G. (1971), 'Posidonius on the Emotions', in A. A. Long (ed.), *Problems in Stoicism* (London: Athlone Press), 200–15.

——(1988), *Posidonius*, vol. ii: *The Commentary* (Cambridge: Cambridge University Press).

——(1999), *Posidonius*, vol. iii: *The Translation of the Fragments* (Cambridge: Cambridge University Press).

KINGSLEY, P. (1995), *Ancient Philosophy, Mystery and Magic: Empedocles and Pythagorean Tradition* (Oxford: Oxford University Press, 1995).

KIRBY, J. T. (1997), 'Aristotle on Metaphor', *American Journal of Philology*, 118: 517–54.

KITTAY, E. F. (1987), *Metaphor: Its Cognitive Force and Linguistic Structure* (Oxford: Oxford University Press).

KNOBLOCK, J. (1988–94), *Xunzi: A Translation and Study of the Complete Works*, 3 vols. (Stanford: Stanford University Press).

KUHN, T. S. (1970), *The Structure of Scientific Revolutions* = Foundations of the Unity of Science 2.2 (Chicago/London: University of Chicago Press).

KURZ, G. (1993), *Metapher, Allegorie, Symbol*, 3rd edn. (Göttingen: Vandenhoeck & Ruprecht).

LACKNER, M. (1993), 'La Portée des événements: Réflexions néo-confucéennes sur la "rectification des noms" (*Entretiens* 13.3)', *Extrême-Orient Extrême-Occident*, 15: 75–87.

LAIRD, A. (1999), *Powers of Expression, Expressions of Power: Speech Presentation and Latin Literature* (Oxford: Oxford University Press).

LAKOFF, G., and JOHNSON, M. (1980), *Metaphors We Live By* (Chicago: University of Chicago Press).

—— and TURNER, M. (1989), *More Than Cool Reason: A Field Guide to Poetic Metaphor* (Chicago/London: University of Chicago Press).

LAKS, A. (1994), 'Substitution et connaissance: Une interprétation unitaire (ou presque) de la théorie aristotélicienne de la métaphore', in D. J. Furley and A. Nehemas (edd.), *Aristotle's Rhetoric: Philosophical Essays* (Princeton: Princeton University Press), 283–305.

—— (1997), 'Between Religion and Philosophy: The Function of Allegory in the Derveni Papyrus', *Phronesis*, 42: 121–43.

—— and MOST, G. (1997) (edd.), *Studies on the Derveni Papyrus* (Oxford: Oxford University Press).

LAMBERTON, R. (1986), *Homer the Theologian: Neoplatonist Allegorical Reading and the Growth of the Epic Tradition* (Berkeley: University of California Press).

—— and KEANEY, J. J. (1992) (edd.), *Homer's Ancient Readers* (Princeton: Princeton University Press).

LAMEDICA, A. (1991), 'La terminologia critico-letteraria dal Papiro di Derveni ai Corpora scoliografici', in P. Radici Colace and M. Caccamo Caltabiano (edd.), *Lessici Tecnici Greci e Latini* = Atti del I Seminario di Studi, Accademia Peloritana dei Pericolanti (Messina: Accademia Peloritana dei Pericolanti), 83–91.

—— (1992), 'Il Papiro di Derveni come commentario: Problemi formali', in A. H. S. El-Mosalamy (ed.), *Proceedings of the XIX*

International Congress of Papyrology (1989) (Cairo: Ain Shams University, Center of Papyrological Studies), i. 325–33.

Lane, M. (1998), *Method and Politics in Plato's Statesman* (Cambridge: Cambridge University Press).

Lanham, R. A. (1991), *A Handlist of Rhetorical Terms* (Berkeley/Los Angeles/Oxford: University of California Press).

Laplace, M. M. J. (1996), 'L'ecphrasis de la parole d'apparat dans l'Electrum et le De Domo de Lucien, et la représentation des deux styles d'une esthétique inspirée de Pindare et de Platon', *Journal of Hellenic Studies*, 116: 158–65.

Laqueur, T. (1990), *Making Sex: Body and Gender from the Greeks to Freud* (Cambridge, Mass./London: Harvard University Press).

Latte, K. (1968), *Kleine Schriften zu Religion, Recht, Literatur und Sprache der Griechen und Römer*, ed. Olof Gigon (Munich: Beck).

Lausberg, H. (1998), *Handbook of Literary Rhetoric: A Foundation for Literary Study*, English trans. M. T. Bliss, A. Jansen, and D. E. Orton; ed. D. E. Orton and R. D. Anderson (Leiden: Brill).

Leary, D. E. (1990) (ed.), *Metaphors in the History of Psychology* (Cambridge: Cambridge University Press).

Leavis, F. R. (1948), *Education and the University: A Sketch for an English School*. 2nd edn. (London: Chatto & Windus).

Legge, J. (1891) (trans.), *The Texts of Taoism* = Sacred Books of the East, vols. 39–40 (Oxford: Oxford University Press).

Levi, J. (1993), 'Quelques aspects de la rectification des noms dans la pensée et la pratique politiques de la Chine ancienne', *Extrême-Orient Extrême-Occident*, 15: 23–53.

Lewis, C. S. (1936), *The Allegory of Love: A Study of Medieval Tradition* (London: Oxford University Press).

Lin, Shuen-fu, (1994), 'The Language of the "Inner Chapters" of the Chuang Tzu', in W. J. Peterson, A. H. Plaks, and Ying-Shih Yü (edd.), *The Power of Culture* (Hong Kong: The Chinese University Press), 47–69.

Liu, J. J. Y. (1975), *Chinese Theories of Literature* (Chicago: University of Chicago Press).

Lloyd, G. E. R. (1966), *Polarity and Analogy: Two Types of Argumentation in Early Greek Thought* (Cambridge: Cambridge University Press).

——(1987), *The Revolutions of Wisdom: Studies in the Claims and Practice of Ancient Greek Science* (Berkeley/Los Angeles/London: University of California Press).

——(1990), *Demystifying Mentalities* (Cambridge: Cambridge University Press).

——(1996*a*), *Adversaries and Authorities: Investigations in Ancient*

Greek and Chinese Science (Cambridge: Cambridge University Press).

——(1996*b*), 'The Metaphors of *metaphora*', in his *Aristotelian Explorations* (Cambridge: Cambridge University Press), 205–22.

Lloyd-Jones, H. (1996) (trans.), *Sophocles: Fragments* = Loeb Classical Library 483 (Cambridge, Mass./London: Harvard University Press).

Lodge, D. (1977), *The Modes of Modern Writing: Metaphor, Metonymy, and the Typology of Modern Literature* (London: Edward Arnold).

Long, A. A. (1992), 'Stoic Readings of Homer', in Lamberton and Keaney (1992), 41–66.

Louth, A. (1981), *The Origins of the Christian Mystical Tradition* (Oxford: Oxford University Press).

Lowrie, M. (1995), 'A Parade of Lyric Predecessors: Horace C. 1.12–1.18', *Phoenix*, 49.1: 33–48.

Lucas, D. W. (1968), *Aristotle: Poetics. Introduction, Commentary and Appendixes* (Oxford: Oxford University Press).

Lyne, R. O. A. M. (1989), *Words and the Poet* (Oxford: Oxford University Press).

McCall, M. H. (1969), *Ancient Rhetorical Theories of Simile and Comparison* (Cambridge, Mass.: Harvard University Press).

MacDonald, C. (1976) (trans.), *Cicero*, vol. 10: *In Catilinam I–IV, Pro Murena, Pro Sulla, Pro Flacco* = Loeb Classical Library 324 (Cambridge, Mass./London: Harvard University Press).

McFague, S. (1987), *Models of God: Theology for an Ecological Nuclear Age* (London: SCM).

McReynolds, P. (1990), 'Motives and Metaphors: A Study in Scientific Creativity', in Leary (1990), 133–72.

Mair, V. H. (1994), *Wandering on the Way: Early Taoist Tales and Parables of Chuang Tzu* (Honolulu: University of Hawaii Press).

Marcovich, M. (1967), *Heraclitus: Greek Text with a Short Commentary* (Merida: Los Andes University Press).

Markus, R. A. (1957), 'St Augustine on Signs', *Phronesis*, 2: 60–83.

Mayor, J. E. B. (1872–8), *Thirteen Satires of Juvenal*, 2nd edn., 3 vols. (London: Macmillan).

Meinwold, C. (1992), 'Goodbye to the Third Man', in R. Kraut (ed.), *The Cambridge Companion to Plato* (Cambridge: Cambridge University Press), 365–92.

Meredith, J. C. (1978) (trans.), *Immanuel Kant: The Critique of Judgement* (Oxford: Oxford University Press).

Merkelbach, R. (1967), 'Der orphische Papyrus von Derveni', *Zeitschrift für Papyrologie und Epigraphie*, 1: 21–32.

MERLEAU-PONTY, M. (1960), *Éloge de la Philosophie et autres essais* (Paris: Gallimard).

——(1968), *The Visible and the Invisible*, English trans. A. Lingis (Evanston: Northwestern University Press).

——(1976), *The Phenomenology of Perception*, English trans. Colin Smith with revisions by F. Williams (London: Routledge & Kegan Paul).

MONTANARI, F. (1997), 'The Fragments of Hellenistic Scholarship', in Most (1997*b*), 273–88.

MOORE, S. (1989), *Literary Criticism and the Gospels: The Theoretical Challenge* (New Haven: Yale University Press).

MOROHASHI, TETSUJI (1955–60), *Dai Kanwa Jiten*, 13 vols. (Tokyo: Taishukan Shoten).

MOST, G. (1989), 'Cornutus and Stoic Allegoresis: A Preliminary Report', *ANRW* ii. 36.3: 2014–65.

——(1993), 'Die früheste erhaltene griechische Dichterallegorese', *Rheinisches Museum*, 136: 209–12.

——(1997*a*): 'The Fire Next Time: Cosmology, Allegoresis and Salvation in the Derveni Papyrus', *Journal of Hellenic Studies*, 117: 117–35.

——(1997*b*) (ed.), *Collecting Fragments: Fragmente sammeln* = Aporemata 1 (Göttingen: Vandenhoeck & Ruprecht).

MÜLLER-RICHTER, K., and LACARTI, A. (1996), *'Kampf der Metapher!' Studien zum Widerstreit des eigentlichen und uneigentlichen Sprechens: Zur Reflexion des Metaphorischen im philosophischen und poetologischen Denken* = Sitzungsberichte Österreichische Akademie der Wissenschaften, philologisch-historische Klasse 634 = Veröffentlichungen der Kommission für Literaturwissenschaft 10 (Vienna: Österreichischen Akademie der Wissenschaften).

NEWIGER, H. J. (1957), *Metapher und Allegorie bei Aristophanes* = Zetemata 16 (Munich: Beck).

NISBET, R. G. M. (1999), 'The Word Order of Horace's Odes', in J. N. Adams and R. G. Mayer (edd.), *Aspects of the Language of Roman Poetry* (Oxford: Oxford University Press), 135–54.

NORMAN, R. (1979), 'Aristotle's Philosopher-God', in J. Barnes, M. Schofield, and R. Sorabji (edd.), *Articles on Aristotle*, vol. 4: *Psychology and Aesthetics* (London: Duckworth), 93–102.

NOWOTTNY, W. (1962), *The Language Poets Use* (London: Athlone Press).

NÜNLIST, R. (1998), *Poetologische Bildersprache in der frühgriechischen Dichtung* = Beiträge zur Altertumskunde 101 (Stuttgart/Leipzig: Teubner).

OBBINK, D. (1994), 'A Quotation of Philodemus' *De pietate* in the

Derveni Papyrus', *Cronache Ercolanesi*, 24: 111–35.

——(1995*a*) (ed.), *Philodemus and Poetry: Poetic Theory and Practice in Lucretius, Philodemus and Horace* (Oxford: Oxford University Press).

——(1995*b*), 'How to Read Poetry about Gods', in Obbink (1995*a*), 189–209.

——(1997), 'Cosmology as Initiation vs. the Critique of the Orphic Mysteries', in Laks and Most (1997), 39–54.

OBERHELMAN, S., and ARMSTRONG, D. (1995), 'Satire as Poetry and the Impossibility of Metathesis in Horace's Satires', in Obbink (1995*a*), 233–54.

O'BRIEN, D. (1995), 'Mathematical Definition in Selected Greek and Chinese Texts' (Ph.D. diss., Cambridge).

OELMANN, F. (1910), 'Prolegomena', in Societatis Philologae Bonnensis Sodales (edd.), *Heracliti Quaestiones Homericae* (Leipzig: Teubner).

OLIVER, J. H. (1950), *The Athenian Expounders of the Sacred and Ancestral Law* (Baltimore: Johns Hopkins University Press).

ORTONY, A. (1993*a*) (ed.), *Metaphor and Thought*, 2nd edn. (Cambridge: Cambridge University Press).

——(1993*b*) 'Metaphor, Language and Thought', in Ortony (1993*a*), 1–16.

OWEN, G. E. L. (1973), 'Plato on the Undepictable', in E. N. Lee, A. P. D. Mourelatos, and R. Rorty (edd.), *Exegesis and Argument: Studies in Greek Philosophy Presented to Gregory Vlastos* (Assen: Van Gorcum), 349–61.

PAGE, T. E. (1894), *The Aeneid of Virgil: Books I–VI* (London: Macmillan).

PAXSON, J. J. (1994), *The Poetics of Personification* (Cambridge: Cambridge Univerity Press).

——(1998), 'Personification's Gender', *Rhetorica*, 16: 149–79.

PEIRCE, C. S. (1955), 'Logic as Semiotic: The Theory of Signs', in his *Selected Writings*, ed. J. Buchler (New York: Dover Books), 98–119.

PENDER, E. E. (2000), *Images of Persons Unseen: Plato's Metaphors for the Gods and the Soul* = International Plato Studies 11 (Sankt Augustin: Academia Verlag).

PÉPIN, J. (1958), *Mythe et Allégorie: Les Origines grecques et les contestations Judaeo-Chrétiennes* (Paris: Aubier, Éditions Montaigne).

PERSSON, A. W. (1918), *Die Exegeten und Delphi* = Vorstudien zu einer Geschichte der attischen Sakralgesetzgebung 1 (Lund: Gleerup).

PFEIFFER, R. (1968), *History of Classical Scholarship*, vol. i: *From the Beginnings to the End of the Hellenistic Age* (Oxford: Oxford University Press).

PFLIGERSDORFFER, G. (1982), 'Fremdes und Eigenes in Senecas 90. Brief an Lucilius', in J. Stagl (ed.), *Aspekte der Kultursoziologie: Aufsätze zur Soziologie, Philosophie, Anthropologie und Geschichte der Kultur. Zum 60. Geburtstag von Mohammed Rassem* (Berlin: Reimer), 303–26.

PHILLIPS, D. Z. (1988), *Faith after Foundationalism* (London: Routledge).

PORZIG, W. (1934), 'Wesenshafte Bedeutungsbeziehungen', *Beiträge zur Geschichte der deutschen Sprache und Literatur*, 58: 70–97.

PÖSCHL, V. (1964), *Bibliographie zur antiken Bildersprache* (Heidelberg: Winter).

PRIBRAM, K. H. (1990), 'From Metaphors to Models: The Use of Analogy in Neuropsychology', in Leary (1990), 79–103.

QIAN BAOCONG (1963), *Suanjing shishu* (Beijing: Zhonghua shuju).

RADERMACHER, L. (1899), 'Studien zur Geschichte der antiken Rhetorik IV (Ueber die Anfänge des Atticismus)', *Rheinisches Museum für Philologie*, 54: 351–74

REEMTS, C. (1998), *Vernunftgemässer Glaube: Die Begründung des Christentums in der Schrift des Origenes gegen Celsus* (Bonn: Borengasser).

RICHARDS, I. A. (1936), *The Philosophy of Rhetoric* (New York/London: Oxford University Press).

——(1965), *The Philosophy of Rhetoric*, 2nd edn. (New York: Oxford University Press).

RICHARDSON, N. J. (1975), 'Homeric Professors in the Age of the Sophists', *Proceedings of the Cambridge Philological Society*, 201: 65–81.

——(1980), 'Literary Criticism in the Exegetical Scholia to the *Iliad*: A Sketch', *Classical Quarterly*, 30: 265–87.

RICHLIN, A. (1997), 'Gender and Rhetoric: Producing Manhood in the Schools', in W. J. Dominik (ed.), *Roman Eloquence: Rhetoric in Society and Literature* (London/New York: Routledge), 90–110.

RICOEUR, P. (1978), *The Rule of Metaphor: Multi-Disciplinary Studies of the Creation of Meaning in Language*, English trans. Robert Czerny, with Kathleen McLaughlin and John Costello (London: Routledge).

——(1996), 'Between Rhetoric and Poetics', in A. Rorty (ed.), *Essays on Aristotle's Rhetoric* (Berkeley/Los Angeles/London: University of California Press), 324–84.

RIEDWEG, C. (1989), *Mysterienterminologie bei Platon, Philon und Klemens von Alexandrie* (Berlin: de Gruyter).

RIGINOS, A. S. (1976), *Platonica: Anecdotes Concerning the Life and Writings of Plato* (Leiden: Brill).

Roberts, D. H., Dunn, F. M., and Fowler, D. P. (1997) (edd.), *Classical Closure: Reading the End in Ancient Literature* (Princeton: Princeton University Press).

Robinson, R. (1953), *Plato's Earlier Dialectic*, 2nd edn. (Oxford: Oxford University Press).

Rosen, S. (1995), *Plato's Statesman: The Web of Politics* (New Haven/London: Yale University Press).

Rowe, C. J. (1995) (ed. and trans.), *Plato: Statesman* (Warminster: Aris & Phillips).

—— (1996), 'The Politicus: Structure and Form', in C. Gill and M. M. McCabe (edd.), *Form and Argument in Late Plato* (Oxford: Oxford University Press), 153–78.

Russell, D. A. (1981), *Criticism in Antiquity* (London: Duckworth).

—— and Winterbottom, M. (1972) (edd.), *Ancient Literary Criticism. The Principal Texts in New Translations* (Oxford: Oxford University Press).

Rutherford, I. (1998), *Canons of Style in the Antonine Age: Idea-Theory in its Literary Context* (Oxford: Oxford University Press).

Saenger, P. (1998), *Space Between Words: The Origin of Silent Reading* (Stanford: Stanford University Press).

Santoro L'Hoir, F. (1992), *The Rhetoric of Gender Terms: 'Man', 'Woman', and the Portrayal of Character in Latin Prose* = Mnemosyne Supplementum 120 (Leiden: Brill).

Saunders, T. J. (1970) (trans.), *Plato, The Laws* (Harmondsworth: Penguin).

Saussure, F. de (1916), *Cours de linguistique générale* (Paris: Payot).

Schenkeveld, D. M. (1964), *Studies in Demetrius On Style* (Amsterdam: Hakkert).

—— (1993*a*), '*Pap. Hamburg* 128: A Hellenistic *Ars Poetica*', *Zeitschrift für Papyrologie und Epigraphik*, 97: 67–80.

—— (1993*b*), 'The Lacuna at Aristotle's Poetics 1457b33', *American Journal of Philology*, 114: 85–9.

Schlunk, R. R. (1974), *The Homeric Scholia and the Aeneid: A Study of the Influence of Ancient Homeric Literary Criticism on Vergil* (Ann Arbor: University of Michigan Press).

—— (1993) (trans.), *Porphyry, The Homeric Questions* = Lang Classical Studies 2 (New York: Peter Lang).

Schwyzer, H.-R. (1932), *Chaeremon* (Leipzig: Kommissions-Verlag).

Scodel, H. R. (1987), *Diaeresis and Myth in Plato's Statesman* = Hypomnemata 85 (Göttingen: Vandenhoeck & Ruprecht).

Sedley, D. N. (1996), 'Plato's *Phaedo* in the Third Century BC', in M. S. Funghi (ed.), *ΟΔΟΙ ΔΙΖΗΣΙΟΣ. Le vie della ricerca: Studi in onore di Francesco Adorno* (Florence: Olschki), 447–55.

SEDLEY, D. N. (1997), 'Plato's *Auctoritas* and the Rebirth of the Commentary Tradition', in M. Griffin and J. Barnes (edd.), *Philosophica Togata*, ii: *Plato and Aristotle at Rome* (Oxford: Oxford University Press), 110–29.

——(1998), 'The Etymologies in Plato's *Cratylus*', *Journal of Hellenic Studies*, 118: 140–54.

SHARPLES, R. W. (1985) (ed. and trans.), *Plato: Meno* (Chicago/ Warminster: Bolchazy-Carducci/Aris & Phillips).

SHEPPARD, A. D. R. (1980), *Studies on the 5th and 6th Essays of Proclus' Commentary on the Republic* = Hypomnemata 61 (Göttingen: Vandenhoeck & Ruprecht).

SIHVOLA, J., and ENGBERG-PEDERSEN, T. (1998) (edd.), *The Emotions in Hellenistic Philosophy* (Dordrecht/Boston/London: Kluwer).

SILK, M. S. (1974), *Interaction in Poetic Imagery: With Special Reference to Early Greek Poetry* (Cambridge: Cambridge University Press).

——(1983), 'LSJ and the Problem of Poetic Archaism: From Meanings to Iconyms', *Classical Quarterly*, 33: 303–30.

——(1994), 'The "Six Parts of Tragedy" in Aristotle's *Poetics*', *Proceedings of the Cambridge Philological Society*, 40: 108–15.

——(1995), 'Language, Poetry and Enactment', *Dialogos*, 2: 109–32.

——(1996), 'Metaphor and Simile', in *OCD*[3], 966–8.

SKEMP, J. B. (1952) (trans.), *Plato's Statesman* (London: Routledge & Kegan Paul).

SMITH, J. (1657), *The Mysterie of Rhetorique Unvail'd* (London). Reprinted = Anglista & Americana 124 (Hildesheim/New York: Olms, 1973).

SOSKICE, J. M. (1985), *Metaphor and Religious Language* (Oxford: Oxford University Press).

SPURGEON, C. F. E. (1935), *Shakespeare's Imagery and What It Tells Us* (Cambridge: Cambridge University Press).

STAHL, W. H. (1952) (trans.), *Macrobius, Commentary on the Dream of Scipio* (New York/London: Columbia University Press).

——and JOHNSON, R. (1977) (trans.), *Martianus Capella and the Seven Liberal Arts*, vol. 2: *The Marriage of Philology and Mercury* (New York: Columbia University Press).

STANFORD, W. B. (1936), *Greek Metaphor: Studies in Theory and Practice* (Oxford: Blackwell).

STEEN, G. (1994), *Understanding Metaphor in Literature: An Empirical Approach* (London/New York: Longman).

STERNBERG, R. J. (1990), *Metaphors of Mind: Conceptions of the Nature of Intelligence* (Cambridge: Cambridge University Press).

STOCK, B. (1996), *Augustine the Reader: Meditation, Self-Knowledge, and the Ethics of Interpretation* (Cambridge, Mass./London: Belknap Press).

STONEMAN, R. (1981), 'Ploughing a Garland: Metaphor and Metonymy in Pindar', *Maia*, 33: 125–38.

STRAWSON, P. (1959), *Individuals* (London: Methuen).

TAMBA-MECZ, I., and VEYNE, P. (1979), 'Metaphora et comparaison selon Aristote', *Revue des Études Grecques*, 92: 77–98.

TATE, J. (1929), 'Plato and Allegorical Interpretation', *Classical Quarterly*, 23: 142–54.

—— and HARDIE, P. R. (1996), 'Allegory, Latin', in *OCD*³, 64–5.

TAYLOR, A. E. (1961) (trans.), *The Sophist and the Statesman*, ed. R. Klibansky and E. Anscombe (London: Nelson).

THALMANN, W. G. (1988), 'Thersites', *Transactions of the American Philological Association*, 118: 1–28.

TOCQUEVILLE, A. DE (1840), *Democracy in America. Part the Second: The Social Influence of Democracy* (New York: J. & H. G. Langley).

TODOROV, T. (1971), *Poétique de la Prose* (Paris: Éditions du Seuil).

—— (1973), *The Fantastic. A Structural Approach to a Literary Genre*, English trans. Richard Howard (Cleveland: Press of Case Western Reserve University).

TORJESEN, K. (1986), *Hermeneutical Procedure and Theological Method in Origen's Exegesis* (Berlin: de Gruyter).

—— (1989), 'Hermeneutics and Soteriology in Origen's Peri Archon', *Studia Patristica*, 21: 333–48.

TOYNBEE, P. J. (1966) (ed.), *Dante Alighieri: Epistolae*, 2nd edn. (Oxford: Oxford University Press).

TRAPP, M. B. (1996), 'Allegory, Greek', in *OCD*³, 64.

TUVE, R. (1947), *Elizabethan and Metaphysical Imagery* (Chicago: University of Chicago Press).

VAN DER HORST, P. W. (1987) (ed.), *Chaeremon: Egyptian Priest and Stoic Philosopher*, 2nd edn. (Leiden: Brill).

VANDERMEERSCH, L. (1993), 'Rectification des noms et langue graphique chinoises', *Extrême-Orient Extrême-Occident*, 15: 11–21.

VANDER WAERDT, P. A. (1985), 'Peripatetic Soul-Division, Posidonius and Middle Platonic Moral Psychology', *Greek, Roman and Byzantine Studies*, 26: 373–94.

VAN HOOK, L. (1905), *The Metaphorical Terminology of Greek Rhetoric and Literary Criticism* (diss., Chicago).

VAN NOPPEN, J. P. (1983) (ed.), *Metaphor and Religion* = Theolinguistics 2 (Brussels: VU of Brussels).

VERDENIUS, W. J. (1949), *Mimesis: Plato's Doctrine of Artistic Imitation and its Meaning to Us* (Leiden: Brill).

VESSEY, D. W. T. (1973), *Statius and the Thebaid* (Cambridge: Cambridge University Press).

WARD, G. (1995), *Barth, Derrida and the Language of Theology* (Cambridge: Cambridge University Press).

——(1997) (ed.), *The Post-Modern God* (Oxford: Blackwell).

WATSON, B. (1963), *Hsün Tzu: Basic Writings* (New York: Columbia University Press).

WEINRICH, H. (1967), 'Semantik der Metapher', *Folia Linguistica*, 1: 3–17.

WEST, D. (1969), *The Imagery and Poetry of Lucretius* (Edinburgh: Edinburgh University Press).

WEST, M. L. (1994) (trans.), *Greek Lyric Poetry* (Oxford/New York: Oxford University Press).

WHITBREAD, L. (1971) (trans.), *Fulgentius the Mythographer* (Columbus: Ohio State University Press).

WHITE, R. M. (1996), *The Structure of Metaphor: The Way the Language of Metaphor Works* (Oxford: Blackwell).

WHITMAN, J. (1987), *Allegory: The Dynamics of an Ancient and Mediaeval Technique* (Cambridge, Mass.: Harvard University Press).

WILAMOWITZ, U. VON (1884), *Homerische Untersuchungen* = Philologische Untersuchungen 7 (Berlin: Weidmann).

WILLCOCK, M. M. (1995), *Pindar: Victory Odes* (Cambridge: Cambridge University Press).

WILSON, N. (1983), 'Scolasti e commentatori', *Studi classici e orientali*, 33: 83–112.

WISSE, J. (1995), 'Greeks, Romans, and the Rise of Atticism', in Abbenes, Slings, and Sluiter (1995), 65–82.

WITTGENSTEIN, L. (1963), *Philosophical Investigations*, English trans. E. Anscombe, 2nd edn. (Oxford: Blackwell).

YU, P. (1987), *The Reading of Imagery in the Chinese Poetic Tradition* (Princeton/Guildford: Princeton University Press).

YUNIS, H. (forthcoming), 'Reading and Interpreting Homer, Orpheus, Thucydides, and Plato', in *Writing into Culture: Written Text and Cultural Practice in Ancient Greece* (Cambridge: Cambridge University Press).

ZUMWALT, N. (1977), '*Fama subversa*. Theme and Structure in Ovid, *Metamorphoses* 12', *California Studies in Classical Antiquity*, 10: 209–22.

INDEX OF PASSAGES CITED

Ancient authors

AESCHYLUS
fragments (ed. Radt)
58: 16
281: 17
Agamemnon
40–1: 126
218: 128
Persians
5: 130–1 n. 44
Seven Against Thebes
941: 129–30 n. 41
Suppliants
46: 128 n. 37
895: 129–30 n. 41
ALCAEUS (ed. Lobel–Page)
Z 2: 19
fr. 6: 228
fr. 326: 228
AMBROSE
On Isaac
68: 251
ANACREON (ed. Page)
fr. 417: 228
ANAXAGORAS (59 DK)
A1 §11: 180
ANONYMOUS
On Tropes (ed. Spengel)
iii. 228–9: 7 n.
iii. 228: 15 n. 16
Anon. Commentary on Plato's Phaedo: 179
APHTHONIUS
Progymnasmata
5–6: 219 n. 4
APOLLODORUS (*FGrH* 244)
frr. 95–9: 204 n. 24
fr. 104: 204 n. 24
fr. 126: 204 n. 24
fr. 135–6: 204 n. 24
fr. 154–207: 204 n. 24
AQUINAS
Contra Averroem: 255 n. 52
ARCHILOCHUS
fragments (ed. West)
1: 97
2: 96
23.17–19: 95
105: 228
128: 96
190: 95
196a: 93
196a.13–15: 93
196a.19: 94
196a.21–4: 94
196a.42–53: 94
ARISTIDES
Orations
33: 234
ARISTIDES QUINTILIANUS
On Music (ed. Winnington-Ingram)
2.9, 68.14–69.8: 38 n. 23
ARISTOPHANES
fragments
PCG iii.2, fr. 233: 178
Frogs
838: 232 n. 27
1034: 226 n. 15
ARISTOTLE
fragments (ed. Rose)
13: 191 n.
70: 14 n. 12

ARISTOTLE (*cont.*)
Categories
16a28–9: 252 n. 41
Generation of Animals
4.10, 777b32: 118 n. 6
On the Heavens
270b14–20: 191 n.
Metaphysics
A.9, 991a20 ff.: 102
A.9, 991a21–2: 142 n. 70
A.9, 991a22: 13
Λ.8, 1074b1–14: 191 n.
Meteorology
1.3, 339b27–30: 191 n.
2.3, 357a24 ff.: 102
Poetics
1, 1447a8: 126 n. 31
1, 1447b18: 14 n. 12
4, 1448b15–16: 14
9, 1451b7: 14
20, 1456b20: 126 n. 31
21–2: 116 n. 1, 126 n. 31
21, 1457b1–3: 12
21, 1457b1–2: 116
21, 1457b3–4: 116
21, 1457b6–24: 117
21, 1457b6 ff.: 7 n.
21, 1457b7 ff.: 13
21, 1457b7: 7, 145
21, 1457b21–2: 144 n. 77
21, 1457b25: 12
21, 1457b31 ff.: 15 n. 15
21, 1457b31: 145
21, 1457b33–4: 126 n. 31
22, 1458a22–3: 125
22, 1458a23–4: 126 n. 31
22, 1458a25: 20
22, 1458a25–6: 4 n.
22, 1458b7: 126 n. 31
22, 1458b21: 118 n. 7
22, 1459a5 ff.: 32 n. 5
22, 1459a5–8: 116, 125
22, 1459a5: 126 n. 30
22, 1459a7–8: 13
22, 1459a8–16: 126 n. 31
Politics
7.10, 1329b25–9: 191 n.
Posterior Analytics
1.22, 83a32–4: 232 n. 25
Rhetoric
2.18, 1392a3: 18
2.20: 8
3.1, 1404a12: 13
3.2–3: 116 n. 1
3.2: 7 n.
3.2, 1404b6 ff.: 13
3.2, 1404b27 ff.: 12
3.2, 1404b34–5: 11
3.2, 1405a5–6: 12
3.2, 1405a8: 13
3.2, 1405a9–10: 13
3.2, 1405a10 ff.: 13
3.2, 1405a11 ff.: 13
3.2, 1405a35–6: 13
3.2, 1405a36–7: 12
3.2, 1405a37 ff.: 20
3.2, 1405b12: 86 n. 2
3.2, 1405b18–19: 13
3.3, 1406b5 ff.: 13
3.3, 1406b8: 13
3.4: 7 n., 8
3.4, 1406b20: 39 n. 25
3.4, 1406b21–2: 18
3.4, 1406b21: 18
3.4, 1406b24–5: 18
3.4, 1407a13–14: 18
3.4, 1407a14 ff.: 16
3.7, 1408a14: 12 n. 11
3.10–11: 7 n., 116 n. 1
3.10, 1410b7 ff.: 32 n. 5
3.10, 1410b14: 14
3.10, 1410b18: 18, 39 n. 25
3.10, 1410b36: 128 n. 38
3.10, 1411a1 ff.: 13
3.11, 1411b24 – 1412a2: 129
3.11, 1411b24 ff.: 13

3.11, 1411b32: 13
3.11, 1412a9: 13
3.11, 1412a10–11: 13
3.11, 1412a11: 14
3.11, 1412a22 ff.: 20
3.11, 1412b32 ff.: 18
3.11, 1413a1: 15 n. 15
3.11, 1413a14–15: 20
3.12, 1413b21 ff.: 15 n. 14
[ARISTOTLE]
Rhetoric to Alexander
23: 12
Topics
6.2, 139b34 f.: 102
6.2, 139b34: 12
ATHENAEUS
Deipnosophistae
9.78, 409f: 187 n. 19
14.63, 653b: 187 n. 20
AUGUSTINE
Christian Doctrine
3.15: 253
City of God
4.31: 210
6.5: 194 n. 4
22.5 ff.: 242
Confessions: 254 n. 45
10.6: 250
11.14: 34 n. 14
12.9: 252 n. 39
12.27: 253
On Free Will
3.10.30: 252
On Genesis read Literally
12.15: 252 n. 38
The Master
10–11: 253 n. 44
On True Religion
16–17: 252 n. 37
The Utility of Belief: 254 n. 45
AULUS GELLIUS
Attic Nights
1.5.2: 45 n. 38
BACCHYLIDES
fragments (ed. Snell)
20b.7: 129–30 n. 41
BION
Lament for Adonis: 203 n.
BOETHIUS
On Interpretation
2.33.24 ff.: 252 n. 41

CALLIMACHUS
Aitia (ed. Pfeiffer)
fr. 1.24: 23 n. 28
Carmina Epigraphica Graeca (ed. Hansen)
1.144.1: 118 n. 6
1.58.2: 118 n. 6
CHAEREMON
fragments (ed. van der Horst)
Test. 9: 204 n. 23
Test. 12: 210
fr. 12.6–9: 210
fr. 15D: 213
CHARISIUS
Art of Grammar (ed. Keil)
i.272: 15 n. 16
CICERO
Academica
1.25: 12
Brutus
6 f.: 36 n. 19
32: 40–1 n. 28
37: 40–1 n. 28
57–60: 20 n. 23
262: 7, 48–9 n. 43
274: 7
300–29: 36
303: 45 n. 38
330: 35, 36–7 n. 20, 42–3 n. 32
On Divination
1.103: 42–3 n. 32
Pro Flacco
23.54: 36–7 n. 20

Letters to Friends
1.9.23: 14
3.11.3: 36–7 n. 20
16.17.1: 11, 17 n. 18
On the Laws
3.3.9: 36–7 n. 20
3.6.14: 40–1 n. 28
Pro Milone
5: 19
Pro Murena
23: 42–3 n. 32
29 f.: 42–3 n. 32
On the Nature of the Gods
1.39–41: 182
1.41: 188, 189
2.13–15: 194 n. 4
2.63: 190
2.70–1: 190
2.92: 24 n. 32
Orator
30: 4 n.
63–4: 39
78: 48–9 n. 43
80–2: 7 n.
80: 25
81: 124 n. 24
92–4: 7 n.
94: 2 n. 4, 20, 183
De Oratore
1.234 f.: 42–3 n. 32, 52 n. 53
1.157: 40–1 n. 28
2.261: 19
2.265–6: 19
3.3: 36–7 n. 20
3.100: 48–9 n. 43
3.152: 21
3.155–66: 7 n.
3.155–64: 16
3.155: 11
3.156: 14, 16
3.157: 18
3.160: 14, 142 n. 69
3.165: 17 nn. 17–18, 39 n. 25
3.166–7: 19
3.166: 2 n. 3
Ad Quirites
11: 36–7 n. 20
Post Reditum in Senatu
4: 36–7 n. 20
[CICERO]
Rhetoric to Herennius
3.22: 49 n. 45
4.45–6: 7 n.
4.45: 16
4.46: 2 n. 3, 20 n. 22
59–61: 7 n.
CLEIDEMUS (*FGrH* 323)
fr. 14: 187 n. 19
CLEMENT
Exhortation to the Greeks
2.26.7: 195 n. 7
Stromateis
1.28.176: 246
COCONDRIUS
On Tropes (ed. Spengel)
iii. 234–5: 19
iii. 324: 228
CORNUTUS
Art of Rhetoric (ed. Graeven)
85, 17.13–16: 2 n. 4, 210 n. 31
Introduction to Greek Theology (ed. Lang)
1: 197
1, 1.4: 198
1, 2.1–2: 198
2, 3.10–11: 202 n. 21
6, 6.11–14: 202 n. 21
6, 6.14–19: 202 n. 21
9: 198 n. 14
15, 18.14–19.9: 198 n. 14, 200
15, 19.17 – 20.5: 198 n. 14
16: 198
16, 20.21–2: 198
16, 20.23: 198
16, 21.1–2: 199

16, 23.6–11: 199
16, 23.11 – 25.2: 199
16, 25.18–22: 200, 201 n. 19, 208
17, 26.7–12: 202
17, 27.19 – 28.2: 198 n. 14
17, 30.1–18: 194–5 n. 6
17, 30.11–13: 200 n.
17, 31.12–17: 197
18 – 19, 33.6–12: 201
20, 35.6–9: 196–7 n. 12
20, 35.9–12: 199 n.
20, 36.1–2: 196–7 n. 12
20, 37.14–17: 199 n.
20, 39.12 – 40.4: 196–7 n. 12, 201 n. 19, 208
21, 40.15–17: 198 n. 14, 201
21, 41.12–15: 202
22: 198 n. 14
22, 42.1–3: 198 n. 14
22, 42.21–3: 198 n. 14
22, 42.21 – 43.2: 201
24: 198 n. 14
25: 198 n. 14
26, 48.15–17: 196 n. 10
28, 52.16–17: 226
28, 54.12–21: 203
28, 55.4 – 56.5: 201 n. 19
28, 56.14–20: 201 n. 19, 208
28, 56.22 – 57.5: 201 n. 19, 205, 208
30, 58.4–6: 197 n. 13
30: 198 n. 14
31: 197
31, 62.23 – 63.7: 200
31, 63.7 – 64.17: 200
34, 72.15 – 73.7: 199 n.
34, 72.20: 199 n.
34, 72.29: 199 n.
35, 76.6–7: 196 n. 10
35, 76.9–16: 195 n. 8

CRATES OF MALLOS
fragments (ed. Broggiato)
fr. 109: 187 n. 20

DEMETRIUS
On Style
78–90: 7 n.
78: 15 n. 16, 16, 17
79: 16
80: 17, 18, 39 n. 26
81: 16
82: 13
85: 15 n. 15
86: 11
89–90: 18
89: 18
99–102: 3 n. 7, 7 n., 209
100–1: 19
101: 183
102: 4 n., 20
142: 16
150–1: 3 n. 7
151: 19
160: 19
172: 19
190: 16
209: 9 n. 4
265: 50 n. 48
272: 16
272–4: 18
282–6: 19
286: 19
DEMOSTHENES
On the Crown
296: 17
Derveni Papyrus
col. ii.6–10: 186
col. v: 186
col. vii: 210
col. xvi.1–11: 184
col. xvii.5: 184
col. xviii.3: 184
col. xx: 186

Derveni Papyrus (*cont.*)
col. xxii: 185, 187 n. 20
col. xxiii.5: 184
DIO CHRYSOSTOM
Orations
12: 234
12.34: 212
18: 225
18.8: 225
52: 234
53.3: 209
DIOGENES LAERTIUS
Lives of the Philosophers
10.6: 233 n.
DIOGENIANUS
Proverbs
2.66: 233 n.
DIONYSIUS OF HALICARNASSUS
On the Ancient Orators
1.2–7: 43
1.2: 46
1.4: 47
1.5: 45
2: 47 n.
On Literary Composition
23.2–4: 48
25: 48–9 n. 43
On the Eloquence of Demosthenes
32: 40–1 n. 28
DIOSCORIDES (ed. Gow and Page)
37.4: 232 n. 23

ENNIUS
Annals
303–4: 20 n. 23
EPICURUS
fragments (ed. Usener)
fr. 163: 233 n.
Epiphanius
Panarion
64: 242 n. 16
EURIPIDES
Bacchae
457–9: 40–1 n. 28
726: 16
Orestes
10: 224, 232
EUSEBIUS
Ecclesiastical History
2.17.20: 212 n. 35
6.2: 250
6.19: 252 n. 42
6.25: 245 n. 24
Preparation for the Gospel
3.9: 252 n. 42
EVAGRIUS
To Anatolius: Texts on Active Life (ed. Kadloubovsky and Palmer)
70, 104–5: 248 n. 28
Instructions to Cenobites and Others (ed. Kadloubovsky and Palmer)
76–8, 116: 248 n. 29

FRONTO
119.10–11: 49 n. 45
153–5: 49 n. 45
156.3–4: 49 n. 45
FULGENTIUS
Super Thebaiden (ed. Helm)
180–1: 151

Greek Anthology
11.363.4: 232 n. 23
16.292–304: 230 n.
16.294: 230 n.
GREGORY OF ELVIRA
Tractatus Origenis (ed. Bulhart)
5.1, 34: 251 n. 35

HERACLITUS OF EPHESUS (22 DK)
B1: 66 n. 36
B52: 119

B73: 66 n. 36
B89: 66 n. 36
B93: 172 n. 31
B123: 214 n. 42
HERACLITUS HOMERICUS [ed. SPB]
Homeric Problems: 8
1–5: 223
1.1: 223
1.2: 224
1.3: 224
1.4: 224
1.5–7: 225
2.1: 225
2.2–5: 225
2.5: 216 n.
3.1: 226
3.2–4.1: 226–7
4.2–4: 227
5.1–6.2 [5.11–9.7]: 228
5.3–9: 19
5.7 [7.3]: 229
5.9 [7.10]: 228
5.13–16: 228–9
6.1 [9.1–3]: 229
6.1 [9.4]: 218
7.3 [10.1]: 218
7.3 [10.12]: 218 n.
9.1 [14.16]: 229
9.9 [15.18]: 219
12.2 [19.8]: 219
16.5 [25.8]: 219
17–20 [25–31]: 219
17 [26.5 ff.]: 227
17.2 [26.5]: 219
18.2 [28.5]: 219
18.7 [28.17]: 219
20.1 [30.10]: 220
20.12–21.1 [31.11–15]: 220
20.6 [30.17]: 220
21.1 [31.15]: 220 n. 8
21.4–6 [32.6–17]: 220
22.7 [33.13]: 217
23.4 [35.5–10]: 226
23.12 [36.8]: 218
24: 209
25.2 [38.9]: 217
25.6–11 [39.1–14]: 220
25.12 [39.15–16]: 221
26–7: 221, 222
27.2–4 [42.9–43.4]: 221
29.4 [44.12]: 218 n.
38: 221
38.5 [55.20]: 221
38.6 [56.2–6]: 221
43–51: 222
43.14 [66.1]: 222
44–48.1: 222
52–8: 221
56.5 [78.6]: 218 n.
60.2 [81.3]: 229
61.1–2 [81.10–17]: 222
63.7 [84.8–11]: 222
69.1–4 [89.9–90.2]: 222
69.7: 233
69.7 [90.2]: 233
69.11 [90.13]: 223
69.15 [90.20–1]: 223
70: 222
71: 222
72: 222
72.15 [95.14]: 218
74 [98.14]: 218
75: 222
75.12 [100.5]: 223
76–9 [100–6]: 230
76.1–7: 230
76.1 [100.8]: 223–4
76.3 [100.14–19]: 225
76.8–79.4: 230–3
76.17 [102.4]: 231 n. 19
78 [104.2 ff.]: 224
78.6 [104.6]: 227
78.7 [104.9]: 232 n. 27
78.7 [104.12]: 232 n. 27
78.7 [104.17]: 233 n.
79.1 [104.15]: 218, 230

HERACLITUS HOMERICUS (*cont.*)
79.2 [104.15]: 227
79.5–13: 233–4
HERMOGENES
On Types (ed. Rabe)
246: 3 n. 7, 209
[HERMOGENES]
On Invention (ed. Rabe)
4.10, 199.4–9: 38 n. 23
HERODOTUS
Histories
1.14.2: 118 n. 6
2.49–50: 202 n. 20
2.91.2: 118 n. 6
2.104: 202 n. 20
4.15.4: 118 n. 6
6.75: 17 n. 17
HESIOD
Theogony
134: 194
HIPPOCRATES
Diseases of Women
1.36: 129–30 n. 41
2.201: 129–30 n. 41
2.138: 129–30 n. 41
Internal Diseases
29: 118 n. 6
Prognosticum
8: 118 n. 6
[HIPPOCRATES]
Acute Diseases [Appendix]
10: 129–30 n. 41
HIPPOLYTUS
Refutation
5.7.23–9: 243–4 n. 19
HOMER
Iliad
1.1: 167
1.47: 219
1.194–200: 219
1.199–200: 226 n. 14
1.399–404: 220
1.528: 226 n. 14
2.8–15: 159
2.35–8: 159, 168
2.272: 117
2.284–90: 166
2.346–7: 234
2.412: 226
2.426: 221
2.478: 231 n. 20
2.484–90: 159
2.484–5: 231
2.484: 167, 231 n. 19
3.2: 38
3.3: 38
3.277–80: 226
4.263: 118 n. 6
4.273 ff.: 9
4.422–6: 9
5.661: 129–30 n. 41
6.102–4: 226 n. 14
6.129: 225
6.146–9: 26
6.506–11: 10
8.199: 226 n. 14
9.44: 118 n. 6
11.218–19: 231
11.218: 231 nn. 19–20
11.458: 129–30 n. 41
11.484: 134 n. 52
11.558–62: 9
12.156–8: 10
12.278–86: 10
12.293: 10
12.299 ff.: 10
13.18: 226 n. 14
13.142: 129–30 n. 41
13.754: 9
15.104: 225
15.263–8: 10
15.542: 13, 129
15.624 ff.: 9
16.298: 10
16.364: 10
16.752–3: 9

17.674–8: 9
17.737: 129–30 n. 41
19.222–3: 228
20.61–5: 181
21.167: 129–30 n. 41
21.195: 184
21.257 ff.: 9 n. 4
21.388: 181
Odyssey
1: 222
1.32: 227
1.185: 117
2.341: 118 n. 6
2.386: 222
4.78: 225
4.426: 118 n. 6
5.314: 129–30 n. 41
6.20: 129–30 n. 41
6.327: 234
8.267–8: 223
8.525: 134 n. 52
9.6–7: 233
9.11: 233
9.373: 129–30 n. 41
11.578: 219
11.598: 13
19.547: 66 n. 36
20.13–15: 9
20.13: 38
20.14–15: 38
20.17: 219
20.90: 66 n. 36
24.299: 118 n. 6
24.308: 118 n. 6
[HOMER]
fragments (ed. Davies)
fr. 20: 15 n. 16
Hymn to Aphrodite (5)
267: 118 n. 6
Hymn to Pan (19)
1: 158
Hymn to Hephaestus (20): 201 n. 18

HORACE
Ars Poetica
10: 23
23: 21
43–5: 23
45–72: 21 n. 24
46–72: 20
46 ff.: 22
46: 23, 26
47–8: 23
48 ff.: 20
48: 23
49: 26
50: 20
51: 23
52: 23
53: 23, 26
55: 22 n.
57: 20
59: 26
60–9: 26
60 ff.: 20
62: 26
70–2: 20
72: 20, 26
97: 21 n. 26
149–50: 27
151: 162 n. 20, 170 n. 25
156 ff.: 22
202 ff.: 22
242: 24
251 ff.: 22
265: 22 n.
306: 22 n.
391 f.: 170 n. 25
440 ff.: 25–6 n. 35
447–8: 21 n. 26, 25–6 n. 35
Epistles
1.2: 168, 175
1.2.1–7: 168
1.2.1–4: 169
2.1: 22
2.1.247: 22 n.

HORACE *Epistles* (*cont.*)
2.2: 20, 21 n. 25, 26
2.2.109–25: 20
2.2.109 ff.: 20, 25
2.2.109: 20, 21
2.2.110: 25
2.2.110–18: 25
2.2.111–19: 21 n. 24
2.2.111–18: 20
2.2.111–14: 24
2.2.111: 25 n. 34
2.2.112: 25 n. 34
2.2.113: 25 n. 34
2.2.114: 24
2.2.115 ff.: 25
2.2.116: 25 n. 34
2.2.117: 20
2.2.118: 20
2.2.119: 20, 25 n. 34
2.2.120–1: 25
2.2.121: 20
2.2.122–3: 25, 25–6 n. 35
2.2.124–5: 26
Odes
1.14: 19, 171, 228

IAMBLICHUS
On the Mysteries (ed. des Places)
1.11, 61: 243–4 n. 19
ISOCRATES
Euagoras (9)
9: 12, 58 n. 13
72: 130–1 n. 44

JOHN CHRYSOSTOM
Homilies on Galatians (ed. Field)
73: 237n.
JOSEPHUS
Jewish Antiquities
1.9: 212 n. 34
1.24: 212 n. 34

JULIAN
Hymn
6, 222cd: 243–4 n. 19

JUVENAL
Satires
7.8: 40–1 n. 28
7.105: 40–1 n. 28
7.173: 40–1 n. 28

LONGINUS, CASSIUS
fragments (ed. Brisson and Patillon)
F10f.: 182 n.
[LONGINUS]
On the Sublime
3.1: 17
9.7: 181, 224
9.8: 226
9.11: 224
9.13: 224, 226
15.5: 17
15.6: 16
31–2: 7 n., 11
31.1: 16
31.2: 17 n. 17
32.1–2: 17
32.3: 17, 39 n. 25
32.7: 4 n.
35.2: 234 n.
37.1: 16
44.1: 218
44.3: 225
LUCIAN
Double Indictment
31: 51 n. 51
The Hall
7: 51 n. 51
The Fisherman
12: 51 n. 51
The Teacher of Rhetoric
6.8: 51 n. 51
6.10: 51 n. 51

6.24: 51 n. 51
LUCRETIUS
On the Nature of Things
2.1004 ff.: 23–4 n. 30
5.1056–90: 128

MACROBIUS
Commentary on the Dream of Scipio (ed. Willis)
1.2.19, 7.23–8.3: 41–2 n. 29
MARTIANUS CAPELLA
Marriage of Mercury and Philology
5.426: 51 n. 52

NUMENIUS
fragments (ed. des Places)
1a: 204 n. 23
30–5: 239 n. 11
55: 41–2 n. 29, 210, 211 n.

OLYMPIODORUS
Commentary on Plato's Gorgias
46.2: 212 n. 35
ORIGEN
Against Celsus
2.9: 242
2.62–5: 242 n. 17
4.15: 241
5.18–23: 242
Commentary on John (ed. Brooke)
2.10: 251 n. 34
13.17, i.264: 241 n. 13
Commentary on Romans
2.13: 241 n. 14
Commentary on Song of Songs (ed. Baehrens)
proem 75.2–9: 245 n. 24
proem 75.17–23: 245 n. 24
proem, 88: 246
proem, 90.4: 247 n. 26
4, 230.23–231.1: 248
Dialogue with Heraclides: 242 n. 15
7: 242 n. 17
First Principles (ed. Koetschau)
1.1.9: 244
1.6.4: 243
1.2: 246
1.2.1: 251 n. 33
1.2.5: 251 n. 33
2.3.5, 120.28: 249 n. 31
2.3.6: 252 n. 39
2.8.5: 250
2.11.7: 247
3.5.6, 277.21: 249 n. 31
3.6.1, 282.6: 249 n. 31
3.6.1, 282.21: 249 n. 31
3.6.2, 283.1: 249 n. 31
3.6.3: 242
3.6.3, 285.3: 249 n. 31
3.6.6, 287.23: 249 n. 31
3.6.8, 289.23–4: 249 n. 31
3.6.9: 242
4.2.1, 307.16: 251 n. 35
4.2.4: 242 n. 15, 243
4.2.6: 243 n. 18, 246
4.2.7, 318.28: 251 n. 35
Homily on the Song of Songs (ed. Baehrens)
1.7, 39.17: 244
To the Martyrs
12: 250
Philokalia (ed. Robinson)
2.3, 72: 241
13: 210, 240
OVID
Amores
1.11.27: 163 n. 22
Metamorphoses
2.837: 163 n. 22
11.585–8: 163
11.588: 163
11.623–9: 163

OVID *Metamorphoses* (*cont.*)
11.625–6: 164
11.647–8: 164
11.658–70: 164
11.666–8: 163 n. 23, 164
Tristia
3.4.40: 163 n. 22
3.7.1: 163 n. 22

P.Graec.Mon. 21: 179
P.Hamburg 128: 7 n., 11 n. 8, 15 n. 14, 23–4 n. 30
P.Heid.G. inv. 28: 179
P.Oxy. II.221
ix.1–2: 184
PERSIUS
Satires
1.103–5: 49 n. 45
PETRONIUS
Satyricon
2: 40–1 n. 28
PHILO
On the Cherubim
48: 210
On the Contemplative Life
78: 212 n. 35
On the Migration of Abraham
93: 212 n. 35
On the Preliminary Studies
73: 3 n. 8
Who is the Heir?
81: 3 n. 8
PHILODEMUS
On Piety
P.Herc. 433, fr. 2.ii: 182
P.Herc. 1088, fr. 1: 182
On Poems 5
col. 28.18–32: 4 n.
On Rhetoric (ed. Sudhaus)
i. 164–81: 7 n.
i. 164: 2 n. 4, 23–4 n. 30
i. 165 [col. 4]: 183 n. 14
i. 170 ff.: 23–4 n. 30
i. 171: 15, 16
i. 173: 17 n. 18
i. 175: 12
i. 180: 14
i. 181: 20 n. 22
i. 181.18 [col. 23]: 183
PINDAR
Isthmian
6: 17
Olympian
2.1–2: 130
13.67: 66 n. 36
Pythian
1.1–2: 131 n. 46
1.75: 119
PLATO
Alcibiades I
129e3–130a2: 239
Apology
22bc: 181
Cratylus
396d4–387a1: 239 n. 10
408a: 157, 198 n. 15
408cd: 158
414a9: 58 n. 11
424e3: 59 n. 14
426e4: 58 n. 11
431c4: 58 n. 10
431c11–12: 59 n. 14
432b: 60 n. 18
432b3: 58 n. 11
432d1–4: 60
439a7–b3: 60 n. 19
Critias
107a7–b4: 67 n. 39
107b: 62, 62 n. 25
107b4–5: 62
107c6–d2: 67 n. 39
107d2: 58 n. 11
107e3: 58 n. 11
116e5: 59 n. 14
Gorgias
517d: 62 n. 25

Hippias Minor
365cd: 181
Ion
533de: 127
Laws
1, 644b9–c2: 61
1, 644c: 62 n. 25
2, 655a4–8: 58
2, 668c7: 59 n. 14
2, 669a7–b8: 59 n. 14
3: 191 n.
4, 720a–c: 62 n. 25
10, 897d ff.: 61
10, 897d8–e2: 61
10, 898b: 67 n. 39
10, 905e6: 58 n. 10
10, 906d8: 58 n. 10
11, 931a1: 59 n. 14
11, 935e5: 59 n. 14
12, 964d8: 58 n. 10
12, 967c8: 58 n. 10
12, 969b: 62 n. 25
Meno
72a: 56
76a6: 56
80c4: 58 n. 10
98b1: 58 n. 10
99cd: 181
Parmenides
130e5–131e7: 238 n. 8
132a1–133a3: 238 n. 7
132d1–133a7: 60 n. 21
137a3: 58 n. 10
147–8: 60 n. 21
Phaedo
76e2: 58 n. 10
87b: 62 n. 25
87b2–e7: 239
92b9: 58 n. 10
92cd: 60 n. 21
95a: 226 n. 15
99e1: 59 n. 15
99e6: 58 n. 10
Phaedrus
229c–230a: 181
235d9: 59 n. 14
237a: 231
237b: 232
239c: 40–1 n. 28
246a: 61 n. 24
246a3–b4: 239
265b6: 58 n. 10
267b: 58 n. 9
267c: 56 n. 4
277d10: 66 n. 36
Philebus
12c–14a: 60 n. 21
39b7: 59 n. 14
49c3: 59 n. 14
61c5: 58 n. 11
Politicus
272c: 191 n.
277a–c: 67 n. 39
277d–279a: 62 n. 26
277d: 65
277d1: 66
277d1–4: 65
277d1–2: 64, 77
277d7: 77
277d9–10: 65
277e–278e: 70, 77 n. 48
277e: 67
277e2–278e12: 68–9 n. 40
277e8: 77 n. 49
278a–c: 70
278ab: 67, 77
278a9–b1: 69
278a9: 76
278b3: 76, 78
278b5–c1: 79
278c: 68–9 n. 40, 77
278c2–7: 68
278c3–e10: 78
278c6: 77
278c8–d6: 69 n. 41
278d2: 77 n. 49

PLATO *Politicus* (*cont.*)
278e: 66, 69, 78
278e9–11: 70
278e10–11: 66 n. 36
278e10: 70
279ab: 78
279a1–6: 73
279a7–b1: 78
279b2: 70
279b4–6: 78
281a: 63
282b: 63
283a: 63
285ab: 63
285d10–286b1: 67
290b7: 66 n. 36
297e8–12: 71
297e9: 58 n. 10
297e12–13: 67 n. 39
305e8: 72
306a ff.: 63
306a3: 64 n. 30
308c: 63
309a: 63
311a1: 64 n. 30
311b7: 64 n. 30
311c2: 64 n. 30
Protagoras
312d3: 59 n. 14
320c–322d: 201 n. 18
331d1–e4: 60 n. 21
347c ff.: 181
Republic
2, 377e1–3: 67 n. 39
2, 378b–e: 181
2, 378d: 3 n. 5, 8
3, 396d4: 58 n. 11
3, 398a: 227
3, 401b2: 59 n. 14
3, 402b5: 59 n. 15
3, 402c6: 59 n. 16
3, 404e1: 58 n. 10
4, 440ab: 59 n. 17
5, 464b2: 58 n. 10
5, 476c8: 66 n. 36
5, 476d3–4: 66 n. 36
6, 487e: 62 n. 25
6, 488a: 67 n. 39
6, 488a2: 58 n. 10
6, 488a5: 58 n. 11
6, 489c4: 58 n. 10
6, 506de: 61
6, 509a: 62 n. 25
6, 509e: 128
6, 509e1: 59 n. 15
6, 510e3: 59 n. 15
7–8, 514a–521c: 60
7, 514a: 62 n. 25
8, 517ab: 62 n. 25
8, 520c6–7: 66 n. 36
8, 531b: 56, 57
8, 531b2–7: 57
8, 533a1–4: 60 n. 19
8, 533b8–c1: 66 n. 36
8, 534cd: 66 n. 36
8, 559e–560e: 59 n. 17
8, 563a6: 58 n. 11
9, 588b–d: 67 n. 39
9, 590c8–591a3: 59 n. 17
10, 617b: 219
Sophist
231a4–b1: 60 n. 21
231a6–8: 60
236a8: 59 n. 14
253b8–e2: 79
Symposium
175e3: 66 n. 36
215a: 56 n. 3
221d1: 58 n. 10
221d4: 58 n. 10
Theaetetus
162e: 60 n. 21
180a: 57
198d: 62 n. 25

198d1: 58 n. 10
Timaeus
29b2–c2: 59 n. 16
37d5–7: 59 n. 16
39e4: 58 n. 11
58b: 55 n. 2
70de: 219
73e: 55 n. 2
92c5–7: 212 n. 36
92c7: 59 n. 16
92d: 250
[PLATO]
Epistles
7: 230
PLINY
Epistles
9.2.3–4: 40–1 n. 28
PLOTINUS
Enneads
6.9.9: 248
PLUTARCH
Against Colotes
1117A: 224 n.
On How to Listen to Poetry: 8
19EF: 2 n. 4, 3 n.5
On Isis and Osiris
367C: 195 n. 7
369C–371C: 204 n. 23
On Monarchy
827C: 234
Parallel Stories
316AB: 169
On Tranquillity
477C: 212
[PLUTARCH]
Life and Poetry of Homer [ed. Kindstrand]: 8
2.19–20: 7 n.
2.19: 15
2.20: 15 n. 16, 16
2.70: 7 n.
2.84–90: 7 n.
2.84: 19
2.92: 210
2.112 [55]: 226
2.122: 227
2.128–9 [60 ff.]: 227
2.150: 233
POLYBIUS SARDIANUS
On Figures (ed. Spengel)
iii. 106.9: 49 n. 44
PORPHYRY
Against the Christians (ed. von Harnack)
fr. 39: 204 n. 23
fragments (ed. Smith)
83F: 252 n. 41
182F.66–70: 214 n. 42
416F: 239
Homeric Questions (ed. Sodano)
2: 25 n. 33
6: 7 n., 9
6, 22.5–23.26: 38
17: 7 n., 9, 38
Homer's Cave of the Nymphs: 8, 239 n. 11
POSIDONIUS
fragments (ed. Edelstein and Kidd)
F35: 207 n. 29
F35.5–7: 207 n. 30
F35.18–24: 207 n. 30
F142–8: 207 n. 28
F146: 199 n.
F169.35–48: 207 n. 29
PROCLUS
Commentary on Plato's Republic (ed. Kroll)
ii. 107.5–7: 214 n. 42
Commentary on Plato's Timaeus (ed. Diehl)
i. 76.1–2: 179
Platonic Theology
1.4: 214 n. 42

PRUDENTIUS
Cathemerinon
9.141–4: 154
Quintilian
Institutes of Oratory
1.2.18: 40–1 n. 28
1.5.5: 122 n. 18
3.6.28: 221 n.
5.11.5: 8
5.12.17–20: 49 n. 45
5.14.34–5: 13
6.3.57–9: 19
6.3.69: 19
8, preface 19–26: 49 n. 45
8.3.38: 23, 38 n. 22
8.3.72–81: 7 n., 9 n. 4
8.3.77 ff.: 19
8.3.81: 19
8.6.1–3: 2 n. 2
8.6.1: 17, 122 n. 18
8.6.4–18: 7 n.
8.6.4: 1, 15, 32 n. 4
8.6.5: 11
8.6.8: 8, 18, 124 n. 27
8.6.11: 16
8.6.13: 16
8.6.14: 2 n. 3, 3 n. 6, 4 n.
8.6.18: 16
8.6.23: 140 n. 63
8.6.44–58: 7 n.
8.6.44: 19, 20 n. 22, 171, 183, 228
8.6.50: 17
8.6.51: 19
8.6.52: 4 n., 20
8.6.67–76: 117 n. 5
9.1.4: 1, 2 n. 2, 171
10.5.17: 40–1 n. 28
11.3.8: 45 n. 38
11.3.27: 40–1 n. 28
11.3.32: 49 n. 45
12.10.47: 48–9 n. 43

SALLUSTIUS
On the Gods and the Universe
3: 211
Scholia on Homer's *Iliad*
ad 6.506–11: 10
ad 11.484: 134 n. 52
ad 11.558–62: 9
ad 12.278–86: 10
ad 12.293: 10
ad 12.299 ff.: 10
ad 13.754: 9
ad 15.263–5: 10
ad 15.624 ff.: 9
ad 16.298: 10
ad 16.364: 10
ad 16.752–3: 9
ad 17.674–7: 9
ad 19.221–4: 229
Scholia on Pindar
ad Isthmian 6: 17
SENECA SENIOR
Controversiae
1, preface 8–10: 49 n. 45
1.22: 49 n. 45
9, preface 4: 40–1 n. 28
Suasoriae
7.12: 49 n. 45
SENECA JUNIOR
On Benefits
3.6.1: 219 n. 5
Epistles
88.21–3: 201 n. 19
90: 192 n., 201 n. 19
90.5: 208
90.7: 208
90.21: 201 n. 19
90.36: 192 n.
114.4 ff.: 48–9 n. 43
SERVIUS
Commentary on Virgil's Aeneid
ad 4.181: 160 n. 18
ad 4.179: 161

SEXTUS EMPIRICUS
Adversos Mathematicos
7.359–60: 213 n. 39
8.10: 214 n. 41
9.60: 194 n. 4
SIMONIDES
fragments (ed. West)
542.3: 129
SOPHOCLES
fragments (ed. Radt)
963: 49 n. 44
Oedipus Tyrannus
178: 134 n. 52
179–81: 133
STATIUS
Silvae
5.2.103–9: 40–1 n. 28
Stoicorum Veterum Fragmenta (ed. von Arnim)
i.264–5: 195 n. 8
i.448: 195 n. 7
i.546: 195 n. 7
i.549: 196 n. 10
ii.108: 213 n. 40
ii.195: 214 n. 41
ii.849: 213 n. 39
ii.908: 3 n. 5
ii.909: 3 n. 5
ii.911: 3 n. 5
ii.911, 252.20–253.18: 199n.
ii.1009: 194 n. 4
ii.1009, 299.10–300.8: 194 n. 4
ii.1009, 300.8–12: 194 n. 4
ii.1009, 300.13–37: 194
ii.1076, 315.17–19: 190n.
ii.1081: 194 n. 5
ii.1086: 194–5 n. 6
STRABO
Geography
1.2.7: 210 n. 31
10.3.23: 200
STRATO (COMICUS)
fragments
PCG vii, fr. 1: 178
SUETONIUS
Augustus
86.2: 48–9 n. 43
TACITUS
Annals
14.53.4: 40–1 n. 28
Dialogus
25–6: 48
26: 37 n. 21
TERTULLIAN
Against the Gentiles
2.1: 194 n. 4
THEAGNES OF RHEGIUM (8 DK)
fr. 2: 3 n. 5
THEOCRITUS
Idylls
15.100–44: 203 n.
THEON
Progymnasmata (ed. Spengel)
ii. 130: 220 n. 6
THEOPHRASTUS
fragments (ed. FSHG)
F689A: 17 n. 18
F689B: 17 n. 18
F689–90: 7 n.
F690: 17
THUCYDIDES
History
2.51–3: 134
3.82: 105
6.55: 118 n. 6
TRYPHO
On Tropes (ed. Spengel)
iii. 8: 49 n. 44
iii. 191–3: 7 n.
iii. 200–1: 7 n.

VALERIUS MAXIMUS
Memorable Doings and Sayings
2.6.7: 219 n. 5
5.3, ext. 3: 219 n. 5
8.3.1: 49 n. 44

8.5.3: 49 n. 45
8.10.2: 45 n. 38
VARRO
Divine Antiquities (ed. Cardauns)
16, 150: 202 n. 20
Latin Language
5.13: 11
5.57–74: 202 n. 20
6.2: 25
6.32: 25
VICTORINUS
Confessions
8.3: 253 n. 43
Commentary on Galatians (ed. Locher)
4.24, 54: 236
VIRGIL
Aeneid
1.1: 132
2.3: 167
4.169–72: 162 n. 21
4.173: 160 n. 15
4.176–83: 160
4.176–7: 160 n. 15
4.184: 160 n. 15
4.185: 160 n. 15
4.188–94: 161
4.188–90: 160 n. 15
4.223: 160 n. 15
4.226: 160 n. 15
4.241: 160 n. 15
4.246: 160 n. 15
4.256: 160 n. 15
4.257: 160 n. 15
6.560–2: 166
6.625–7: 165
12.879–80: 182
12.948–9: 132
Eclogues
6.8: 23 n. 28
XENOPHON
Agesilaus
11.8: 225
Cyropaedia
3.3.58: 225
Symposium
3.6: 3 n. 5

Biblical References

PROVERBS
23.20–1: 243
WISDOM
7.25–6: 251 n. 33
MATTHEW
7.24–5: 249
JOHN
1.1: 255 n. 49
1.1–3: 244
1.14b: 245
1.18: 244, 248 n. 29
9.39: 245
10.35: 245
10.37–8: 245
12.28–33: 245
14.6: 249
14.26: 245
20.31: 245
ROMANS
1.27: 243–4 n. 19
1 CORINTHIANS
3.11: 249
6.17: 242
9.9–10: 247
10.4: 249
10.11: 243 n. 18
15.28: 249
15.52: 248
GALATIANS
4.24: 237 n.
COLOSSIANS
1.15: 250

1 THESSALONIANS
5.23: 242 n. 15
HEBREWS
1.3: 251 n. 33
1 PETER
2.22: 248
3.16: 242 n. 17
2 PETER
2.4–7: 249
1 JOHN
3.3: 244

GENERAL INDEX

Achelous 184
Achilles 219–20, 232
  his shield 222
actio ingrati 219
Adonis 203
adunaton 166
Aeolus 222
Alcibiades 230
allegorical exegesis:
  apologetic 223–34, 243
  Christian 151–2, 190, 215–16, 235–56
  as commentary, not translation 211, 214
  exploits stylistic anomaly 3 n. 8
  Hellenistic 181–3
  is ideological 153, 171–5
  itself allegorical 154–5, 174–5
  Medieval 151–3, 173, 174, 177, 251
  Neoplatonic 3, 8, 180, 190, 204, 210, 211–12, 214–16, 217, 239
  Presocratic 3, 177, 180, 183
  rejected by Antiochene Christians 237
  rejected by Plato 181
  requires knowledge of external context 94
  Socratic 181
  Stoic 182–3, 187, 189–216
  see also Derveni Papyrus; etymology; Heraclitus Homericus
allegory:
  allegorized in messenger scenes 155–65
  for concealment 210–11
  as 'continuous metaphor' 2, 8, 19, 26, 124 n. 26, 171, 183, 236
  in Egyptian philosophy 210–11, 213
  embraces metaphor, metonymy, and synecdoche 236–40
  epic 155–70
  for grandeur 3 n. 7, 19, 209
  humorous 19
  mixed 229
  and mysteries 19, 183–4, 186–7, 205, 212
  non-verbal 198 n. 14
  obscure 4 n. 9, 20
  origin of the term 2, 20 n. 22
  ornamental 3, 8, 171–2, 209
  philosophical 3, 190, 193, 205–16
  piquant 3 n. 7
  and proverb 20
  reflects nature 211–12, 237–8
  reflects relationship of body and soul (and spirit) 212, 239–56
  in the rhetoricians 3–4, 171, 180–1, 209–10, 215–16
  as 'saying one thing and meaning another' 20, 228, 235–6
  terms for 3 n. 5, 8, 20 n. 22, 170 n. 25, 181–4, 210
  and typology 235–7, 240
  unintended 189–90, 193–204, 215–16, 254

alloiosis 249 n. 32
Ambrose 251
analogy 180, 236, 239
  see also metaphor
Anaxagoras 180–1, 221
anthimeria 50 n. 50
antonomasia 171
Aphrodite 194, 198 n. 14, 222–3, 233
Apollo 218–19, 221
Apollodorus of Athens 204 n. 24
archaism 20–5
Archilochus 93–100
Ares 194, 198 n. 14, 201, 221, 222–3, 231 n. 20, 233
Aristarchus 10
Aristippus 233
Aristocles (historian) 169
Aristotle 38 n. 23, 39, 232, 252, 253
  and demonstration 110
  and metaphor (μεταφορά) 7, 11–20, 58 n. 12, 237
    as deviant usage 1 n. 1, 101–2, 114, 118, 145
    as master-trope 15 n. 14, 32, 116–18, 125–6
    in poetry 141–2, 146
    polemical use of 102–3, 108–9
    his term contrasted with modern usage 117–18, 123–4
    the visual immediacy of 128–30
  on mythology 191–2
Artemis 221, 226
Atargatis 202 n. 21
Athena 196–7 n. 12, 199 n., 201, 208–9, 219–20, 221, 222, 226
Atlas 196 n. 10
Atticism 217, 225
  vs. Asianism 32 n. 3, 43–7
Augustine 251–4

Baudelaire, C. 143, 144
Benjamin, W. 153 n. 3, 174–5
Benveniste, E. 84
Black, M. 8 n. 2, 38 n. 22, 52–3, 55 n. 1, 72 n. 44, 74, 76, 84, 85–6, 118, 118–19 n. 8, 119 n. 9, 119–20 n. 13, 144 n. 77
body and soul 212, 239
body, soul, and spirit 240–56
Bohutong 109
Book of Odes 105–6
Briareus 220

Callimachus 180
Calvino, I. 168–9
Cappadocian Fathers 253
catachresis ('necessary metaphor') 11, 12, 15 n. 14, 26, 27, 124 n. 26, 171
Chaeremon of Alexandria 204 n. 23, 210–11, 213
Chrysippus 169, 183, 189, 199 n. 16, 207 n. 28
circumcision 202 n. 20
Cleanthes 194 n. 4, 195 n. 7, 196 n. 10
Clement of Alexandria 195 n. 7, 245–6
Coeus 160, 194, 200 n. 17
coinage, *see* neologism
commentary, ancient 177–9
  see also allegorical exegesis; exegesis; literary criticism
constructivism 75
Confucius 104
Cornutus, Lucius Annaeus 194–5 n. 6, 196–210, 226
Crantor of Soli 169, 179
Crates of Mallos 221
Crius 194

Dante 153 n. 2, 251

Davidson, D. 33 n. 7, 118–19 n. 8, 119–20 n. 13, 122 n. 19, 124 n. 27, 144 n. 77, 172–3
Deio 185
Demeter 185, 188, 194, 203, 205
Derrida, J. 255
Derveni Papyrus 3, 179–80, 183–8, 210
diairesis (division), *see* Plato
Dike 194
Diogenes of Apollonia 187
Dionysus 195, 197 n. 13
Dioscuri 195 n. 7
Donne, J. 99, 122 n. 19, 143

Eco, U. 156
eikon (image, likeness):
  as 'metaphor' 55–8, 128, 212 n. 36
  as 'simile' 8, 19
  use in Platonic inquiry 59–62
  vs. *paradeigma* (model) 70–4, 76, 80–1
Eliot, T. S. 132, 141, 143
Elpis 194
Empedocles 14 n. 12, 102, 117, 131, 222–3, 244 n. 21
Empson, W. 138
enallage 50 n. 50, 124 n. 26
enigma 15 n. 14, 20
Ennius 22
Enyo 198 n. 14, 201
Epicureans 8, 23–4 n. 30
  attack on allegorical exegesis 182–3, 187–8, 189
Epicurus, his debt to Homer 227–8, 232–4
epithet 12, 15 n. 15, 198–9, 202 n. 21, 218, 226
Erinyes, *see* Eumenides
Eros 194, 198 n. 14
ethics, physics, enoptic/theology/theory 240, 245–8, 252
  aligned with metaphor, metonymy, synecdoche 249–50
etymology 180, 239
  in allegorical exegesis 157–8, 196–9, 205 n. 27, 217, 222
Euclid 112
euhemerism 195 n. 7, 204 n. 24
Eumenides 186, 194
Eunomia 194
euphemism 16
Evagrius 248
exegesis 177
  of scripture by scripture 241
  see also allegorical exegesis; commentary; literary criticism

Fama 160–2, 165–7
foreshadowing 9–10
Formalism 120, 125
Friedrich, C. D. 92

Ge 185, 194
gender, in criticism 32, 35–7, 39–51
Gregory of Elvira 251
Giants 208–9, 220
gloss 12
Gnostics 241, 243–4 n. 19
Graces 198 n. 14, 200
grammarians 2 n. 2, 217

Hades 134 n. 52, 203
Hartley, L. P. 142
Hecate 166, 199 n.
Hephaestus 201, 221–3
Hera 185, 194, 220, 221, 225
Heracleon 241 n. 13
Heracles 195 n. 7, 197, 200, 239
Heraclitus Homericus 8, 153 n. 3, 172, 217–34
  his rhetorical background 217–20, 225, 230, 234

Hercules, *see* Heracles
Hermes 157, 194, 198–200, 221
Hestia 185, 226
Homer:
  allegorical exegesis in 3 n.5
  allegory in 153, 158–65, 167–70
  defended by allegorical exegesis 168–9, 181–2, 218–34
  rhapsodic exegesis of 178
Hopkins, G. M. 123, 127 n. 35, 129, 137–8, 143
Horace 8, 20–7, 168–72, 175
Hortensius 35–6
hyperbole 15 n. 14, 117, 124 n. 26
Hyperion 194

image, see *eikon*
Iapetus 194
Iris 157, 163–5
irony 20 n. 22, 236
Isis and Osiris 203

Jakobson, R. 116 n. 1, 120–1, 124, 134–47, 236, 237
James, H. 156
Jiuzhang suanshu 110
John, Gospel of 244–5, 254–5
Juno 162–5, 168
Jupiter 162

Kant, I. 85, 256
Kittay, E. 55 n. 1, 74–5
Kore 203, 205 n. 27

Lactantius 252
Lakoff, G. (and associates) 42 n. 31, 52, 53 n. 57, 55 n. 1, 75 n., 76, 146 n.
Leto 221
Li Chunfeng 111–12 n. 15
literary criticism, ancient 8–11, 12, 25–6 n. 35, 34, 53–4, 172
  see also commentary; exegesis; gender
Liu Hui 110–12
Luther, M. 249 n. 32

Marius Victorinus 235–6, 251
Mercury 160, 162
Merleau-Ponty, M. 83, 86–7, 255
metalepsis 15 n. 14, 171
metaphor:
  absence in Chinese linguistic theory 103–14
  absence in Horace 20–7
  analogical type 13, 15–16, 24, 26
  and analogy 35, 39, 116, 119–20 n. 13, 124–5, 126–7, 130, 239
  ancient classifications of 13–16, 27
  'apologetic' 17, 18 n. 20
  and association 126–7, 130–1
  and aural parallelism 135–9, 140
  and context 23, 37–8, 41–3, 53, 84, 98, 118, 130–1, 144
  dead 11, 24, 26–7, 89, 90, 98, 118, 141 n. 68, 144
  as deviant, vs. the 'proper' use of words 11, 24–5, 58, 84, 101–3, 105, 108–9, 112–13, 116, 121
  elucidating 86, 88, 90, 97, 99, 118–19, 126–8
  fabricated exemplars of 33, 144
  in foreshadowing 9
  incongruous 56–7, 83, 85, 89–90, 99–100
  innovative 85
  interactionist theory 8, 9,

37–8, 118–19, 121, 140, 142, 145
and 'latent field' of experience 86–90, 97–100
and likeness 7, 13–14, 15, 35, 52, 59–60, 116, 124
master–trope 11, 32, 116–18, 125–6, 134
and *mimesis* 14
mixed 17
and model 72
negative 122 n. 19
not exact equivalent of *metaphora* 101, 117–18, 123–4
and obscurity 4 n. 9, 12, 13, 17, 102
in oratory 2–4
and ordinary speech 11, 17 n. 17, 23, 32, 117–18
origin of the term 7
ornamental 1, 4, 7–8, 12–13, 15, 16, 21
a polemical instrument 47, 102–3, 108–9
'perspectival' 74–5
safe 15, 18 n. 20
and simile 17, 18, 37–9
and substitution 7, 107–8, 118, 120–1, 135
suitable 13, 16–17
and technical vocabulary 12, 53, 111–12
and (the metaphor of) 'transfer' 7, 11–12, 24–5, 55 n. 2, 107–8
vs. metonymy 120–1, 124, 134–47, 236
vs. metonymy and synecdoche 236–40, 249–51
and the visual arts 91–2
vivid 9, 13, 16, 17 n. 17, 86, 126, 128–30, 142

see also *eikon*; *paradeigma*; personification; Plato
metonymy 15 n. 14, 39, 53, 117, 120–1, 124, 132–47, 171, 180, 221, 236–40, 249–51
metousia 15 n. 14
metre 22, 98, 137
Metrodorus of Lampsacus 180
mimesis ('imitation'):
in Aristotle 14
in Plato 61 n. 23
model, see *paradeigma*
Morpheus 163–5
Moses 3, 212 n. 34
mysteries 19, 212
Christian 243–5
Egyptian 243
Eleusinian 41, 201 n. 19, 205–6, 230, 243
Orphic 184–7
Phrygian 243
mythological and theological traditions:
of the Brahmans 204 n. 23
Celtic 202
Chaldean 204 n. 23
Egyptian 202–3, 204 n. 23
Greek 102, 187, 191–209, 215, 217
Jewish 204 n. 23
Libyan 202
of the Magi 202, 204 n. 23
Persian 204 n. 23
Phoenician 203
Phrygian 202
Roman 202 n. 21
Scythian 202
Syrian 202 n. 21
Thracian 202

neologism 12, 20–3, 26, 111
Neoptolemus of Parium 21 n. 25

Nietzsche, F. 125, 146 n.

Odysseus 117, 169, 219, 222, 227, 228–9, 231, 232, 233–4, 239
Omar Kayyám 99
oratory 2–4, 10, 13, 32, 35–7, 39–51
Origen 235–6, 240–56

Pan 158, 161
paradeigma in Plato 63–81
  leads merely to opinion 76–9
  and likeness 63–4, 67–9
  and metaphor 70–2, 73–6
  as 'model' 64–5, 101
Paul, St 237, 242, 247
Peirce, C. S. 250, 252
Peripatetics 15, 18, 218
  see also Aristotle
Persaeus 195 n. 7
personification 13, 16, 24, 25, 26, 43 n. 35, 45, 50, 153
  and metonymy 239
  of oratory 32, 35–7, 39–51
  of philosophy 39–41, 50, 51 n. 51
  see also Fama
Philo of Alexandria 3, 190, 245
Plato 39, 48–9 n. 43, 55–81, 101, 181, 183, 207 n. 28, 218, 220, 238–9, 244, 252 n. 39
  debt to Homer 219, 227–8
  a flatterer 227, 230, 232
  his morality attacked 231–2
  terms for 'metaphor' 55–8, 128
  theory of forms 12–13, 102, 142 n. 70, 232, 253
  use of *diairesis* (division) 63 n. 28, 64 n. 31, 79–80
  use of *eikones* ('images', 'metaphors') in inquiry 59–62
  use of *paradeigmata* ('models') in inquiry 63–81
Poenae 194
polemic, Chinese 109
polyonomy 180
Poseidon 198 n. 14, 201, 220, 221, 225, 231 n. 20
Posidonius 192 n., 201 n. 19, 206–8
positivism 75
Pothos 194
Proclus 19 n.
Prometheus 201
proverb 15 n. 14, 20

relativism 75
Renaissance rhetorical theory 32 n. 3, 50 n. 50
rhapsodes 178
Rhea 185, 202 n. 21
rhetorical theory, *see* allegory; Heraclitus Homericus; literary criticism; metaphor; oratory; personification; Renaissance rhetorical theory
rhyme 137–8
Richards, I. A. 35
Ricoeur, P. 1 n., 8 n., 14 n. 13, 33 n. 7, 55 n. 1, 56 n. 6, 58 n. 12, 84, 86, 115, 116 n. 1, 118 n. 7, 119 n. 9, 119–20 n. 13, 121, 124 n. 26–7, 139–47, 237, 238 n. 9

Saussure, F. de 135–6, 141
Seasons 198 n. 14
semantic stretch 11, 112–13
Shakespeare, W. 31, 119, 123, 129, 143
Sibyl 166–7
Sima Qian 109 n.
simile 8–11, 15 n. 14, 18–19, 20,

25–6, 37–9, 45–7, 56, 59, 124, 127, 129, 137, 155, 180
Smith, J. 32 n. 3
Socrates 157–8, 161, 181, 218, 230, 232
solecism 122
Sphinx, allegorical of allegory 213
Stoics:
  and 'intelligibles' 213–14
  on the mythological tradition 192–209, 215
  on primitive man 192–3, 206–9
  use by Heraclitus Homericus 217–18
  see also allegorical exegesis; Chaeremon; Chrysippus; Cornutus
Strawson, P. 84
Surrealist art 92
synecdoche 15 n. 14, 124 n. 26, 140 n. 63, 171, 236, 238–40, 249–50, 253

Thales, debt to Homer 221
Theagnes of Rhegium 3 n. 5
theology, *see* mythological and theological traditions
Theomachy 221, 224
Theophrastus 15 n. 14, 18, 39
Therapeutai 212 n. 35
Thetis 220
threefold hermeneutic, *see* Augustine; Origen
Titans 220
Todorov, T. 153 n. 3, 156
tropes, theory of 4, 11, 15, 24, 116, 124–5
typology 235–7, 240

Uranus 194, 197–8

Valentinus 255 n. 49
Vesta 24–5
Villon, F. 99

Weinrich, H. 35 n. 15, 52
Wittgenstein, L. 147, 254 n. 48, 255

Xenocrates 179
Xenophon 39
Xunzi 104

Yan Tie Lun 109
Yeats, W. B. 123, 127, 129, 140–1, 143

Zeno of Citium 195 n. 8
Zeus 10, 159, 168, 188, 194, 197 n. 13, 198 n. 14, 199 n., 220, 221, 225, 229, 231 n. 20
zhengming 103–5
Zhoubi suanjing 110
Zhuangzi 106–7, 109 n.
Zwingli, U. 249 n. 32